Praise for

Superpower Interrupted

"Michael Schuman takes the reader on an invaluable journey deep into the hinterland of the Chinese psyche, tying Xi Jinping's modern ambitions to the country's centuries-old narratives. From the rise and fall of dynasties to painful interactions with neighboring barbarians and unsavory westerners, Schuman's scholarship vividly describes China's exceptionalism and how it underlines the ruling communist party's objectives to this day."
—Richard McGregor, author of *The Party: The Secret World of China's Communist Rulers* and *Xi Jinping: The Backlash*

"Schuman skillfully narrates more than three thousand years of history through a Chinese lens that places China at the center of the world and Chinese civilization above all others. *Superpower Interrupted* provides crucial insights into Xi Jinping's Chinese Dream of national rejuvenation that seeks to restore China to its rightful place as world leader. *Superpower Interrupted* is essential reading for all those who want a deeper understanding of the historical roots of China's national objectives."
—Bonnie Glaser, Center for Strategic and International Studies

"*Superpower Interrupted* is a concise and elegant survey of China as a dominant power in Eurasia. Michael Schuman provides an illuminating perspective on the Middle Kingdom's rise, fall, and reemergence as a geopolitical superpower and the evolution of its ties with the rest of the world. Those wondering how a rejuvenated China will conduct itself in world affairs will do well to read *Superpower Interrupted* for its deep insights and rich historical knowledge."
—Minxin Pei, Claremont McKenna College, author of *China's Crony Capitalism*

"Timely, eloquent and lively throughout, Michael Schuman has written a book that covers China's long past—and hints at its future."
—Peter Frankopan, Oxford University,
author of *The Silk Roads*

"This is the best book about China I have read in a long, long time. Michael Schuman elegantly walks us through Chinese views of the outside world and reveals why China even today has an antagonistic relationship with the West."
—James McGregor, author of *One Billion Customers: Lessons from the Front Lines of Doing Business in China*

"All too often, foreign commentators talk about China mainly as a foil for their own concerns. Michael Schuman looks at China on its own terms, revealing how their own history has shaped how the Chinese see their place in the world and their future. If you want to understand the 'Chinese Dream,' *Superpower Interrupted* is a great place to begin."
—Patrick Chovanec, School of International and Public Affairs, Columbia University

"As noted historian Jonathan Spence argued some twenty-two years ago, the West has long been guilty of seeing China through the same lens that it sees itself. Michael Schuman provides a fascinating antidote to this bias, examining China's worldview through its own lens. Is history on China's side? Schuman offers some tantalizing hints to the answer of that critical question."
—Stephen Roach, senior fellow Yale University, former chairman Morgan Stanley Asia

"In his extraordinary book, Michael Schuman has provided the West with a much-needed gift—a look at how the long history of China has shaped the China of today. Anyone who wants to really understand China needs to read *Superpower Interrupted*."
—David Rubenstein, co-executive chairman, The Carlyle Group

SUPERPOWER
INTERRUPTED

SUPERPOWER INTERRUPTED

The Chinese History of the World

MICHAEL SCHUMAN

PUBLICAFFAIRS
New York

PublicAffairs
Hachette Book Group
1290 Avenue of the Americas, New York, NY 10104
www.publicaffairsbooks.com
@Public_Affairs

Printed in the United States of America

First Edition: June 2020

Published by PublicAffairs, an imprint of Perseus Books, LLC,
a subsidiary of Hachette Book Group, Inc. The PublicAffairs name and logo is a trademark of the Hachette Book Group.

The Hachette Speakers Bureau provides a wide range of authors for speaking events. To find out more, go to www.hachettespeakersbureau.com or call (866) 376-6591.

The publisher is not responsible for websites (or their content) that are not owned by the publisher.

Print book interior design by Jeff Williams

Library of Congress Cataloging-in-Publication Data

Names: Schuman, Michael, 1968—author.
Title: Superpower interrupted : the Chinese history of the world / Michael Schuman.
Other titles: Chinese history of the world
Description: First edition. | New York : PublicAffairs, 2020. | Includes bibliographical references and index.
Identifiers: LCCN 2019049081 | ISBN 9781541788343 (hardcover) | ISBN 9781541788329 (ebook)
Subjects: LCSH: China—History. | World history.
Classification: LCC DS735 .S4255 2020 | DDC 951—dc23
LC record available at https://lccn.loc.gov/2019049081

ISBNs: 978-1-5417-8834-3 (hardcover), 978-1-5417-8832-9 (ebook)

LSC-C

10 9 8 7 6 5 4 3 2 1

To my father

CONTENTS

CHRONOLOGY OF CHINA'S DYNASTIES

Shang 1554–1045 BC

China's first dynasty confirmed by archeological evidence, the Shang played a critical role in the early development of Chinese civilization, including its famous and highly influential writing system.

Zhou 1045–256 BC

The long-lasting Zhou era laid the basis for Chinese culture, especially its philosophy, literary traditions, and governing ideology. The dynasty is broken by historians into two periods: the Western Zhou, 1045–771 BC, and the Eastern Zhou, 770–256 BC. During the latter period, the power of the Zhou royal court declined and became mainly ceremonial, while the country descended into an extended period of conflict between competing states.

Qin 221–206 BC

Though short-lived, the Qin forged the first unified Chinese empire that became the model for all future dynasties. It also built the original Great Wall of China.

Han 206 BC–220 AD

The Han designed the basic institutions and ideology of the Chinese imperial system, which would survive into the twentieth century. The dynasty also transformed China into a major world power by extending its influence throughout East and Central Asia and forging many of the core principles of Chinese foreign policy. The dynasty is divided into two periods: the Western or Former Han, 206 BC–8 AD, with its capital at Chang'an (modern Xi'an) and the Eastern or Later Han, 25–220 AD, based at Luoyang.

Period of Disunion 220–589

Also known as the Northern and Southern Dynasties period, China had no united central political authority during this long stretch. Instead, numerous rival kingdoms competed for influence. The northern half of the country was ruled by various steppe peoples for the first time. However, even though China was politically divided, its cultural influence spread throughout the region, leading to the formation of a Chinese world in East Asia.

Sui 581–618

Though it had only two emperors, the Sui reunified China and left posterity two major achievements: building the Grand Canal, tying together north and south China more than ever before, and introducing civil service examinations, which became one of the pillars of Chinese society in later dynasties.

Tang 618–907

The Tang ushered in one of the most glorious eras in all of China's history. Culturally, economically, and politically, China reached a level of influence in the world not even the Han could match. Under the Tang, East Asia became a clearly defined cultural zone based upon Chinese civilization. The dynasty was also the most welcoming to foreign influences.

Song 960-1279

Another epoch of tremendous philosophical and artistic brilliance, the Song also witnessed a stage of economic advancement considered something close to an industrial revolution that entrenched China as a major engine of the global economy. Militarily inept, however, the Song failed to defend China from invading steppe armies, first losing control of northern China to the Jurchens in the 1120s and then the entire empire to the Mongols in the 1270s. The dynasty has two periods: the Northern Song, 960–1127, which controlled nearly all of China from its capital of Kaifeng, and the Southern Song, 1127–1279, which ruled over only the south from Hangzhou.

Yuan 1279-1368

Founded by Genghis Khan's grandson Kublai, the Mongol Yuan was the first non-Chinese dynasty to control all of China. Looked upon by Chinese as a period of foreign domination and discrimination, it was also the first time China became integrated into a larger political entity—the pan-Asian Mongol Empire—leading to important cross-cultural exchanges and vibrant trade.

Ming 1368-1644

The Ming reconquered China from the Mongols and claimed to reestablish authentic Chinese rule in China. The two most famous achievements of the Ming were the building of the Great Wall of China as we know it today, and the dispatch of "treasure fleets" led by Admiral Zheng He, one of the most adventurous escapades to promote Chinese global influence in all of China's history.

Qing 1644–1912

China's final imperial dynasty, the Qing was formed by another group of invaders from the north, the Manchus. Voracious conquerors, the Qing expanded the Chinese empire to its greatest geographic extent. But the Qing also fell badly behind the rising West and became prey to European imperialism, leading to the end of the imperial system with the abdication of the last emperor in 1912.

GUIDE TO MAJOR
CHINESE HISTORICAL FIGURES

Ban Gu, Historian. His history of the first two centuries of the Han Dynasty, which he compiled in the first century AD, includes some of the earliest formulations of a foreign policy strategy for China.

Chiang Kai-shek, Politician. He took over the Nationalist Party after Sun Yat-sen's death and tried to unify China, but lost a civil war to Mao Zedong and the Chinese Communists and fled to Taiwan in 1949.

Cixi, Empress Dowager of the Qing Dynasty. Lording over the Qing court in the late nineteenth and early twentieth centuries AD, the conservative policies and misrule of this onetime concubine are often blamed for contributing to the downfall of the dynasty.

Confucius, Philosopher. Born in the mid-sixth century BC, he is considered China's greatest thinker, whose ideas came to shape everything from China's imperial governing system to education to family life.

Daoguang, Emperor of the Qing Dynasty. Reigning from 1821 to 1850 AD, he lost the Opium War with the British in the early 1840s and was forced to agree to the "unequal" Treaty of Nanjing.

Deng Xiaoping, Politician. A luminary of the Chinese Communist Party, he led the economic reform movement in the 1980s that rebuilt Chinese global power, but he also ordered the infamous crackdown on pro-democracy protesters on Beijing's Tiananmen Square in 1989.

Faxian, Buddhist Monk. His travels between China and India around the turn of the fifth century AD left us an early account of pan-Asian trading routes.

Gaozong, Emperor of the Song Dynasty. He rallied Song Dynasty loyalists after its defeat by the Jurchens and became the first emperor of the Southern Song in 1127 AD.

Guangxu, Emperor of the Qing Dynasty. Briefly allied with radical reformers in the late nineteenth century to resurrect the sagging fortunes of the Qing in its conflicts with the West. His plans were dashed by the Empress Dowager Cixi, who sidelined him and took control of the royal court in 1898.

Huizong, Emperor of the Song Dynasty. Ruling from 1100 to 1125 AD, his disastrous policies led to the Song Dynasty's defeat by the invading Jurchens and the loss of north China.

Jia Yi, Statesman. A Confucian scholar of the second century BC, his thought was highly influential in forging imperial Chinese foreign relations.

Kang Youwei, Scholar. He led a radical reform movement in 1898 that aimed to strengthen the Qing Dynasty against European imperialism.

Kangxi, Emperor of the Qing Dynasty. The long reign of this famously open-minded but militaristic Manchu royal—officially from 1662 to 1722 AD—was one of the most glorious in all of Chinese history.

Li Yuan / Emperor Gaozu of the Tang Dynasty. A military officer, he established the Tang Dynasty in the early seventh century AD.

Liang Qichao, Scholar. As an activist, journalist, and thinker, he had tremendous influence over political reformers in China in the early twentieth century.

Lin Zexu, Official. Appointed a special commissioner to deal with European traders in Guangzhou, his belligerent attempts to stop the import of opium inadvertently led to the First Opium War in the early 1840s. He is now considered a nationalist hero for standing up to the West.

Liu Bang / Emperor Gaozu of the Han Dynasty. He led a rebellion against the Qin Dynasty and founded the Han Dynasty in the late third century BC.

Mao Zedong, Politician. He was the Communist leader who founded the People's Republic of China in 1949.

Mencius, Philosopher. Espousing his ideas in the fourth century BC, he is the most influential scholar in the Confucian school (after Confucius himself).

Qianlong, Emperor of the Qing Dynasty. Ruling from 1736 to 1795 AD, this colorful emperor was one of China's most aggressive expansionists. He is also known for writing a famously condescending letter to King George III of England after receiving a British embassy in 1793.

Qin Shi Huangdi, First Emperor of China. Also known as King Ying Zheng, the ruler of the Qin Dynasty created the first unified Chinese empire in 221 BC.

Shang Yang, Philosopher. He espoused a doctrine of authoritarian rule in the fourth century BC that held great sway over government in early China.

Sima Qian, Historian. His epic history, written around the end of the second century BC, is one of the main sources of information about early China as well as the foreign peoples around it.

Sun Yat-sen, Politician. A revolutionary and advocate of democracy in China, he formed the Kuomintang, or Nationalist Party, and became the first president of the Republic of China in the early twentieth century.

Taizong, Emperor of the Tang Dynasty. Ruling from 626 to 649 AD, the second emperor of the Tang Dynasty launched a series of successful military campaigns that greatly expanded the power of the Chinese empire.

Wang Fuzhi, Philosopher. Though he lived and wrote in the seventeenth century AD, his fiercely nationalistic ideas first gained widespread popularity among political reformers in the late 1800s.

Wen, Emperor of the Sui Dynasty. He founded the Sui Dynasty and reunified China in the late sixth century AD after a long period of disunion.

Wen Tianxiang, Statesman. A fierce loyalist to the Song Dynasty, he resisted the Mongol conquest in the late thirteenth century AD and was executed by Kublai Khan.

Wu, King of the Zhou Dynasty. He defeated the Shang Dynasty and established Zhou rule and is considered by Chinese as one of the greatest rulers in China's history.

Wu, Emperor of the Han Dynasty. Ruling from 141 to 87 BC, this sovereign was one of the most important in China's history. He was instrumental in creating the imperial system and, through his foreign adventures, connecting China to the world.

Xi Jinping, Politician. He became general secretary of the Chinese Communist Party in 2012 and president of China in 2013.

Yongle, Emperor of the Ming Dynasty. Ruling from 1402 to 1424 AD, the third emperor of the Ming is most famous for dispatching the great "treasure fleets" of Admiral Zheng He.

Yuan Shikai, Statesman. A senior official and military leader during the late Qing Dynasty, he tried and failed to reestablish the imperial system after its fall in the early twentieth century.

Yue Fei, General. His feisty defiance against the invading Jurchens in the mid-twelfth century AD made him a much-beloved nationalist hero in China.

Zhang Qian, Explorer. His travels in the second century BC connected China to Central Asia and formed the beginnings of the Silk Road.

Zhao Kuangyin / Emperor Taizu of the Song Dynasty. He was a respected general who founded the Song Dynasty in the late tenth century AD.

Zheng He, Admiral. One of China's greatest explorers, he led seven expeditions of the great "treasure fleets" across Southeast Asia and into the Indian Ocean in the early fifteenth century AD.

Zhou, Duke of, Statesman. The duke was instrumental in forging the Zhou Dynasty in the eleventh century BC and in traditional Chinese thought is considered a model for government ministers due to his wisdom and selflessness.

Zhu Yuanzhang / Hongwu, Emperor of the Ming Dynasty. A rebel leader, he chased the Mongol rulers of the Yuan Dynasty out of China and formed the Ming Dynasty in 1368.

SUPERPOWER INTERRUPTED

One

WORLD HISTORY, CHINESE STYLE

The empire, long divided, must unite; long united, must divide.

−*The Romance of the Three Kingdoms,* **a Chinese novel**

There is no such thing as world history, at least not one that holds the same meaning for everyone. Which world history is important to you depends on who you are, where you live and where you come from. It shapes what you believe, how you eat, pray, and marry, the society around you, your view of the world, and your place in that world. The ideas in your head have been put there by the narrative of your world history—the myths, legends, stories, books, and poems that tell of heroes and villains (both real and imagined), critical moments, turning points, defining philosophies, conquests, discoveries, revelations, revolutions, battles won, battles lost, great men, great women—and the not so great.

You share this world history with many other people, but not everyone. The person sitting at the next table at a restaurant, or passing you by in an airport terminal, may have an entirely different batch of beliefs, forged by entirely different books, events, and people from his or her history of the world. The overlap between your world history and someone else's depends, in part, on distance. If you're sitting in New Jersey, for instance, the world history that has formed your views probably means a lot less to another person in Yokohama, or Kolkata, or Addis Ababa than it does to someone in Los Angeles, Toronto, or London.

The history of the world comes in strands, each weaving its own story. These strands occasionally bump into each other. Religions are spread, technology shared, goods exchanged. But to a great extent, for much of history, the strands continued along their own course. Before the age of instant digital communications, jumbo jets, and bullet trains, the strands would cross paths with much less regularity; those that were geographically distant from each other would hardly intersect at all. A philosophical notion, a talented king, a disastrous war that seemed earth-moving to people on one strand may barely register in another. Much of humanity had no clue that a strand of the Americas even existed until Christopher Columbus accidentally tripped over it in 1492.

When you grow up in "the West"—Europe and its offshoots, like the United States—your version of world history usually starts in ancient Greece, with its philosophers, playwrights, and poets. Homer, Aristotle, Socrates, Sophocles, and the gang. And the myths, of Zeus and the gods, Hercules, Perseus. Athens and the roots of democracy. The narrative moves rather effortlessly into Rome. Its law, its republic, Caesar and the empire, Constantine and the spread of Christianity. After that comes the ascent of the Church, Charlemagne and the Holy Roman Empire, the epoch of castles and knights. Next we enter the Age of Discovery, the Reformation, the Renaissance, the Enlightenment, the Industrial Revolution—the building blocks of the worldwide dominance of the West. The formation of nation-states and rights of man. Cervantes, Shakespeare, and Dickens, Rousseau, Adam Smith, and Locke. Newton, Darwin, and Freud. George Washington, Thomas Jefferson, and the birth of the American republic. Along the way, other strands make cameo appearances: Alexander's conquests into Asia; the Crusades and the confrontation with Islam; the invasions of Huns, Mongols, and Ottomans; the slave trade with Africa. But for the most part, events following other strands of history were tangential to this core narrative, even inconsequential. The Maurya, Gupta, and Mughal empires reached great heights in India, the Incas and Aztecs in the

Americas; the Vedas were written, the Buddha preached, the temples at Angkor built; the Polynesian peoples spread themselves across the Pacific—and someone sitting in France wouldn't have noticed, or probably cared much if he did.

The reverse is true for those people living through other strands. We in the West know how Caesar died, that Napoleon met his Waterloo, and Columbus sailed the ocean blue. We learned this stuff in school, or at home, or on television. But much of the rest of the world did not. They learned another history in school from different textbooks; they read their own myths and epic poems; they prayed different prayers to different gods; they emulated different people, studied different philosophers, and talked of different wars. And because of that, they see the world from a different perspective.

Like the Chinese. To them, the narrative above, of Greeks and Romans, Jesus and Luther, the *Iliad* and *Hamlet*, might as well have taken place on another planet. The Chinese have been following their own strand of world history, populated with its own characters, founded on its own literature composed by its own philosophers and poets, with its own great battles, heroic moments, catastrophes, great men and not so great men. And just as we in the West are products of our world history, the Chinese are a creation of theirs.

This book tells the story of that Chinese history of the world. It is not an all-inclusive history of China. You won't find lists of emperors and their comings and goings, or a comprehensive discussion of political or social change, or an in-depth exploration of Chinese culture. You can find that easily elsewhere. What unfolds in the coming pages is the story that has shaped the Chinese view of the world, and more importantly, their perception of their role within that world.

It is a story that few in the West really know. And that's a problem, especially as China grows more powerful on the global stage. We tend to talk about China through the prism of our own world history. Diplomats, academics, politicians, and journalists in Washington or London or Paris muse on how to fit China into our world. But that's not at all how the Chinese see things. They have their own notions about where they fit in the world and what the world should look like based on their history, a very long one at that. Only when we know this Chinese history of the world can we understand China today.

═══

The biggest question of the twenty-first century is, What does China want? China is without question the rising power of the age. What that means for the current global order, crafted and led by the United States since the end of World War II, is the topic of think-tank studies, Congressional hearings, vats of newsprint, and dinner conversations from Washington to Tokyo. What exactly will China do with its new power? Will China become a partner to the West and its allies, or will it wish to change the world, to promote new values, institutions, and patterns of trade and finance? Will it play by our rules, or write new ones?

The answer to these questions is, at its heart, quite simple: China wants what it always had. China was a superpower for almost all of its history, and it wants to be a superpower again.

Of course, the goals of China's political leaders today are not the same as they were in 1000 AD, let alone 1000 BC. Still, there are some startling consistencies in China's attitudes toward the world over the epic course of its history—more than three thousand years of it based on verifiable written records alone. This history has fostered in the Chinese a firm belief in what role they and their country *should* play in the world today, and for that matter, into the distant forever. In their view, the Chinese have a right to be a premier power in the world, and they want to return to their proper position at the apex of the global order.

This perception is, to a degree, based in actual history. China for most of its existence was the biggest, baddest, richest, most advanced civilization in East Asia. The Chinese were writing exquisite poetry before their neighbors were writing anything at all. (And when the Koreans, Japanese, and others started writing, they borrowed the Chinese script.) The Chinese were pioneers in state formation, technological innovation, philosophy, literature, and economic organization. These features of advanced Chinese civilization spread throughout the region, turning East Asia into a cultural zone distinct from the rest of the world, where people from Japan to Vietnam and beyond read Chinese books, copied Chinese legal codes and education methods, followed Chinese diplomatic norms, and, in elite circles, studied the Chinese language. To the Chinese, this Chinese world was the world. Though they knew of, and often respected, other great civilizations well beyond their borders—the Romans, the Persians, the Indians—these other societies were too far off to directly challenge China's primacy on its East Asian turf or, just as importantly, the perception the Chinese held of their primacy.

Over the centuries, challengers did emerge. At times, China was a tremendous military superpower, able to project force deep into inhospitable deserts, steppe, and mountains, matching any exploits the Roman legions ever managed. They were also major innovators of arms and armaments—most famously, gunpowder. But the reality is China was not always militarily dominant, despite its advantages in manpower and wealth. Chinese armies got their butts kicked by Turks, Mongols, and all sorts of other nomadic tribesmen, the Vietnamese, Japanese, Tibetans, British—the list goes on.

Being a superpower, however, requires much more than a good army. Look, today, at the United States. Yes, America is the world's top military power. But that doesn't mean it wins every war; just ask the fine fighting men and women who served in Korea, Vietnam, or Afghanistan. Those defeats or stalemates may have dented American pride and prestige, but they did not significantly undercut America's position as the world's superpower. The sources of American power run wider and deeper than the force of arms. The United States remains the world's largest economy and a leader in critical technologies. The dollar is the currency of choice for trade and finance throughout the world. The gyrations of the Dow Jones Industrial Average, or the decisions taken by the Federal Reserve, determine the movements of global stock markets and currency values. Most important of all, perhaps, is America's unrivaled cultural clout. English is the global lingua franca of business, trade, diplomacy, and education worldwide. Everyone watches Hollywood movies and listens to American pop music. And American ideals—"life, liberty, and the pursuit of happiness," free speech, democratic elections, equality of all—have become the standards for the world, copied by many other nations, and the envy of the unfortunate who live in countries that have not.

For nearly its entire history, China also possessed these other pillars of power, which allowed it to retain its superpower stature through the many ebbs and flows of events. The Chinese economy has been the largest in the world, or close to it, throughout much of human history. It has been the engine of long-distance trading networks going back more than two thousand years. We in the West tend to equate the emergence of a truly global economy with the rise of Europe. But China was the beating heart of a global economic system that existed centuries before the Portuguese, Dutch, and British took control of East-West exchange. And for centuries after the ascent of Europe as well, China maintained its position as the world's premier economy and a driving force of global growth and trade. Recall that when Christopher Columbus sailed into the unknown he was not searching for Mexico, but China.

That was because China played a unique role in the world economy. Not only was it a gargantuan consumer—since it was always among the most populous places on the planet—it was also unrivaled in its capacity to produce stuff the world craved. We marvel today at the scale of Chinese manufacturing as if it is something new; it is really just a return to the norm. China was a manufacturing hub as far back as Roman times. And more importantly, Chinese wares were usually of the highest technology. Many of its customers in foreign lands simply had no idea how Chinese goods were made. Europeans were often not able to reproduce these manufactures for centuries after the Chinese were already churning them out on a mass scale. So desirable were Chinese exports that they were among the world's first truly iconic, global consumer items—the Apple iPhones and Nike sneakers of their age.

Culturally, too, China remained on top. Even when China was broken in pieces or convulsed by political disorder, its neighbors looked to it as a model of law, governing institutions, literary prowess, and artistic styles. Invaders who overran parts, or even all, of China found the culture of the defeated Chinese so irresistible they adopted it. In that sense, the conquered were actually the conquerors. Chinese classical texts and literature formed the foundation of education in Korea until the nineteenth century. For much of history in East Asia, Chinese civilization *was* civilization.

Taken together, Chinese political, economic, and cultural clout was so great that it forged a Chinese world order in East Asia. Its economy sat at the core of a vast trading network; its government set the norms of diplomacy for the entire region; its books, language, philosophy, and art influenced the culture of all other peoples. China made the rules; everyone else followed.

Of equal importance to the tangible power of China was the mythic. The Chinese developed a complex national ideology in which they placed themselves as the lords of "all under Heaven"— the world they knew. Their emperor was not just another ruler, like the kings of other states; he was the Son of Heaven, the divine's representative on earth, and thus had no equals. His power, in theory, faced no boundaries. He was universal. So was Chinese civilization itself. Chinese culture was so superior that it *was* culture. Only those who adopted Chinese ways could be truly civilized (and in some cases, not even then). Sometimes this view of their own superiority was backed up by reality, when the dynasties were strong and other peoples came from all over to bow before the Son of Heaven. At other times, when China was weakened, this worldview leaned more toward the theoretical. But it endured, through the many twists, turns, triumphs, and devastations of China's imperial history. And it acted as a sort of glue, holding together a Chinese view of the world through the vicissitudes of the Chinese history of the world. Ideas can sometimes have more power than facts.

Then came an interruption, as in the title of this book. A sudden, crushing onslaught against all aspects of Chinese power erupted when the Chinese history of the world crashed into another strand of world history—the Western one. Chinese armies suffered ignominious defeats before the guns of the Western powers. But that alone did not interrupt China the superpower. The Chinese had endured military debacles with unfortunate frequency throughout their history. The interruption happened because China's confrontation with the West knocked away all the pillars of its power. Its economic might—gone. Its technological advantage—gone. Its cultural clout—gone. Its long-cherished governing system— useless. The Chinese world crumbled as the West remade East Asia. Even the Chinese ideological conviction in their cultural superiority came under assault as they began to doubt the value of their own traditions. China, the superpower, was no more.

This period, when China was demoted from its superpower status, however, was a mere blip on the long Chinese time line, a few pages in historical volumes that fill a library shelf. It occurred only in the mid-1800s—by Chinese standards, practically yesterday. Ever since, Chinese leaders have sought to restore China's power, to fix the broken narrative of the Chinese history of the world, and to set it back on the track it had always followed. The Chinese have managed this before—they have routinely rebuilt the pillars of their power. They are striving to do that again, now, in the twenty-first century. Will they succeed? In a truly globalized world, where one person can influence another on the far side of the globe with the tap of a smartphone screen, the answer will determine the course of everybody's strand of world history.

=====

Empires come and empires go. The Greek, Roman, Byzantine, Spanish, British, Ottoman, Abbasid, Persian, Mongol, Mughal, and so on are all gone. Their vestiges remain in borders, law, architecture, and language, but as political entities, they have vanished. In China, you might think the same has happened. China no longer has dynasties and emperors; the old royal palace in Beijing, the Forbidden City, is now a tourist attraction.

But China is different from the other empires. To a great degree, it still exists. China, as a nation-state, is a version of previous, independent Chinese political entities that formed in the same general geographic location. The Chinese political system, at its core, has proven remarkably resilient. The age of imperial dynasties in China lasted an amazing 2,100 years. We in the West tend to see Chinese history as a series of dynasties, one after the next, as if they were tenants in the Forbidden City. When one dynastic lease ran out, another royal couple moved in. The names of the assorted imperia may change, from Tang to Song to Ming, but they are more or less interchangeable. That's not exactly how things happened. At some periods, often long ones, China was broken into competing states or ruled by invading foreigners. Though the diverse dynasties shared similarities—they were all top-down monarchies—they were far from identical. Each had its own special characteristics, adapted to its age; later incarnations built upon the institutions and ideologies created by their predecessors.

Yet the most incredible aspect of China's political history is how often the empire was reassembled. China could easily have gone the way of Europe—where a region with a common cultural and historical background eventually splintered into competing countries with their own languages, governments, and goals. But in China, the pieces were always put back together again. The idea of one "China," forged before the time of Christ, held firm. If China wasn't unified, its political elite, again and again and again, wished it to be. The revered, fourteenth-century Chinese novel *The Romance of the Three Kingdoms* opens with this sentence: "The empire, long divided, must unite; long united, must divide."[1]

The China of today might seem to abrogate that maxim. The last emperor was chased from his throne in 1912. The government in Beijing considers itself Communist, its core ideology based on Marxism-Leninism (an import from another strand of world history). Modern China is not an empire, or a dynasty, but a nation-state, formed along Western lines. It is a member of the community of nations as conceived by European norms of international relations.

Yet the Chinese realm of the twenty-first century bears much more resemblance to its imperial predecessors than meets the eye. The structure of government today is not all that removed from that of the dynasties, first forged two millennia ago: a centralized state, with power emanating from the capital, that controlled the country through a sprawling bureaucracy. The provinces, then as now, often had a fair degree of informal autonomy, leaving top officials in the capital, then as now, routinely frustrated by their far-flung and independent-minded functionaries. One Chinese proverb—"Heaven is high and the emperor is far away."—is as true today as it ever was.

Ultimately, though, the Chinese imperial order was an autocracy. There were no formal constraints on the authority of the emperor. His behavior and decisions were kept in check only by moral injunction, court precedent, and sometimes strong-willed councilors. But technically, the emperor's word was law. Kangxi, emperor of the Qing Dynasty, wrote that "giving life to people, and killing people—those are the powers that the emperor has."[2] And he was by no means exaggerating.

Today, no one person in China commands the power over life and death. The People's Republic, formed in 1949, has a constitution, a legislative process, and a judicial system. That division of authority exists on paper, however. In practice, Kangxi's characterization still rings true. Top leaders can do as they please, and party cadres, court justices, and civil servants will do as they are so ordered. Those who challenge the state are treated roughly. If anything, the Chinese political system in the twenty-first century is bordering on the totalitarian. The current president, Xi Jinping, had term limits on his office removed from the country's constitution in 2018, meaning that if he so chooses, he can reign for life like an emperor. And the often paranoid imperial mandarins would have loved to have gotten their hands on the modern technology Xi now has at his fingertips to monitor the Chinese people's phone calls, text messages, emails, movements, shopping habits, and financial transactions.

And the current regime is becoming more like the dynasties in ways that directly influence its view of the world and actions on the global stage. The Chinese Communist Party was born a century ago as a reaction to China's confrontation with the Western powers. Its founders, like many other intellectuals at the time, believed that traditional Chinese statecraft and the institutions formed from it were ill suited to the modern world. If China did not discard its ancient ways, the Chinese people were doomed to colonial slavery under the boot of the more muscular European states. For much of its existence, the Communist Party was committed to eradicating all aspects of traditional China—its religions, philosophies, family values, education, economic system, and so on and so on. Communism's mission, after all, is to destroy an existing, corrupt society and replace it with a utopia free of exploitation. "From each according to his ability, to each according to his needs," as the mantra goes. Modern China, with its Wild West capitalism, Tesla-crammed parking lots, and luxurious shopping malls, resembles nothing of the sort. So the leadership is busily resurrecting the traditional culture it spent so much effort trying to uproot. President Xi personally promotes the old ethical codes, literature, and governing ideology of imperial times. Increasingly, the Communist regime is morphing into a new kind of dynasty.

To many of us in the West, this turn toward the totalitarian is distressing. There has been a longing for greater democratic rights in China, dating back about a century and a quarter, that has continually gone unrealized. Authoritarianism, however, is more in line with the Chinese history of the world. Unlike those of us in the West, the Chinese cannot look back fondly on ancient republics. The political ideal throughout the millennia-long course of Chinese political development has been authoritarian monarchy. That's not to say that Chinese deserve or want to live under oppressive regimes. But it does mean that Chinese leaders would have to look to the European or American models to create a representative government along Western lines, rather than to their own past.

That is true more broadly, too. What we in the West consider normal, even crucial, to a modern society is relatively new to the Chinese. The concept of humanity's inalienable rights, the equality of states in international diplomacy, constitutional government, independent courts, gender parity—these are all fresh concepts to China and are not part of its long history. (To be fair, they are pretty recent in the West as well.) We tend to forget when looking at the world that other peoples do not share our political, social, and economic development and therefore may not share our ideals and priorities. That statement is not meant to justify the repression under which the Chinese people now suffer. It is just meant to note that the Chinese history of the world has produced different outcomes than the history of the West. And as China rises on the world stage, it is bringing with it the baggage it has carried along its long historical journey—both the honorable and the dishonorable.

=

History is what you make of it. Though we can often all agree on basic facts—a war started in year X, or Mr. Y won an election—interpreting events and what they mean is an ever-morphing, often contentious process. How we characterize a historical figure or explain a chain of events is determined by the age in which we live, how we are educated, and what strand of world history has shaped our worldview. I learned this lesson during my freshman year in college at the University of Pennsylvania in Philadelphia. After attending a rather standard public high school in suburban New Jersey, I had decided upon arriving on campus to register for classes on subjects about which I knew little or nothing. That landed me in a course on the modern history of India, taught by an endearing, energetic, and somewhat enigmatic professor, David Ludden. The class focused mainly on the nationalist period—Gandhi, Nehru, and the quest for independence. Ludden assigned three books on the period, written by scholars of diverse backgrounds at different times. The stories they told diverged so thoroughly that it was as if the three books were not about the same subject. That was Ludden's point: history cannot be separated from the human mind and its current surroundings.

It is especially so over the course of the three thousand years this book covers. The way scholars today write about Chinese history is not necessarily the same as what was penned a century ago, or five centuries ago, or at the time of the events themselves. The farther back we go, the more confusing matters become. The understanding of Chinese antiquity is altered every time an archeologist has a fortunate turn of a shovel. The problem is especially acute at the moment since the current regime has a special fascination with the rewriting of history to serve its own ideological purposes.

What to do? There are no easy answers. What I have tried, to the best extent possible, is to examine what Chinese officials, historians, poets, and other scholars said about the events through which they lived, or at least use sources as close to the contemporary as available. In this way, we get a Chinese view in something like real time. Even this, though, is only a partial solution. Chinese historians, for instance, have a tendency to color circumstances with an ideological brush. Rather than allowing the proceedings to shape their analysis, they squeeze them into preconceived notions of how the world should work. For example, Chinese philosophy taught that virtue determines the ups and downs of history. That means dynasties always had to fall because bad people were running them; dynasties rose because good people were founding them. What really happened, obviously, was far more complex.

I've taken certain liberties in this history as well. One of the great complications of writing about the history of China and the

Chinese is that, for most of the time, there was no such thing as "China" or the "Chinese," at least not in the modern conception of those terms. There were only dynasties, or people of a shared civilization. For the sake of sanity, I still simply refer to "China" and the "Chinese" throughout the book. The entire notion that the Chinese worldview today is a product, at least in part, of what happened two thousand years ago may irk some, as will other interpretations of the story I'm about to tell. Obviously, no society, no matter how proud of itself, persists unchanged over countless centuries. The Chinese of today are, needless to say, not the Chinese of one hundred years ago, let alone one thousand years ago.

Yet in my research I was surprised to discover how many core ideas and beliefs have endured through all the political and social transformations China has experienced. All of us are, to a certain extent, the creatures of our own histories of the world. We in the West still judge right and wrong by the millennia-old Ten Commandments, or the fables of Aesop. Our thinking about society is influenced by the musings of Plato, the theories of St. Augustine, or the principles enshrined in the Magna Carta, formulated eight centuries ago. Why should the Chinese be any different?

There is then only one place to start. In the beginning . . .

Two

BORN SUPER

I have heard of men using the doctrines of our great land to change barbarians, but I have never yet heard of any being changed by barbarians.

–Mencius, philosopher

The earth was square, molded from the primordial vapor that was the origin of all things by the opposing forces of light and dark. Empress Nuwa kneaded yellow clay into the first human beings. She labored ceaselessly, crafting more and more black-haired people, until her toil became too burdensome even for a goddess. So she dragged a cord through the mud to produce yet more men and women. Even then her work was not complete. Disaster struck the world when the poles holding up the sky collapsed. Fires and floods ravaged the earth. Ravenous beasts devoured the people. Nuwa cut the legs off a sea turtle to support the crumbling pillars and piled the ashes of burnt reeds to stem the raging waters. The world was safe, and the black-haired people flourished.

Then the heroes arrived to help the men and women. Ju Ling, the Divine Colossus, split the mountain into two with his hand, allowing the Yellow River to flow, and leaving the imprint of his fingers and palm on the cliffs. Suiren, the Fire Driller—not quite god, not yet man, who could traverse the cosmos—came upon a tree that spewed clouds and fog. A bird that looked like an owl pecked at the tree, and flame shot out of it. The Fire Driller understood the importance of this discovery and, taking a twig from the magical tree, taught mankind to make fire. Shennong, the Farmer God, formed a plow from wood and taught the black-haired people how to cultivate crops. He collected herbs to cure the sick, tasting all of the plants to separate the palatable from the toxic—at great personal sacrifice. He once poisoned himself seventy times in a single day.

Or so the old myths tell us. The true origins of China's civilization are shrouded in the usual mist and mystery common to deep antiquity everywhere. All we know about the earliest settlers of what later became China is what we can piece together—literally—from the shards of pottery, fragments of stone tools, and the ruins of buildings they left behind for posterity. They tell us that thousands of years ago, these first villagers created a vibrant, complex, technically advanced society long, long before just about anyone else on the planet.

There was, of course, no "China" so far back in time, nor could the people who lived there have considered themselves "Chinese." That came much, much later. Early society in China was composed of a myriad of diverse, regional cultures liberally splattered along the Yellow and Yangzi Rivers and their assorted tributaries. Settled farming communities had emerged by 6500 BC on the north-central China plain. These were hardscrabble places, where people sheltered in semi-subterranean square dwellings, tended their fields with stone hoes and sickles, made simple but distinctive three-legged pottery jars, and ate millet. Further south, in the warmer, wetter valleys of the Yangzi River, early urbanites preferred rice—in fact, the early Chinese were almost certainly the first people to cultivate the crop. These settlements did not share the same cultural practices. We know that by tracking their pottery. Some painted their clay wares with red stripes or decorated them with comb or cord patterns; others molded giant cauldrons and enlivened their ceramics with images of pigs, shrimp, and fish. Life was not all mundane tilling and cooking, though. They played bird-bone flutes and egg-shaped wind instruments and adorned themselves in jade jewelry—open windows to the beginnings of China's rich artistic tradition.

Over the next four thousand years or so—time frames are hardly precise—these settlements inched toward something like a civilization. Villages became towns; towns became bigger and more permanent; their populations swelled. So thin, so fine were potters' clay creations that archeologists compare them to eggshells. Then these early Chinese figured out how to smelt, hammer, and cast copper, a major advancement—stronger metal tools produced heftier harvests, and greater affluence. One of the world's oldest solar observatories, dating to the mid-third millennium BC, was devised in what is today's Shanxi province. Rows of scribbles on pottery, some shaped like animals (a snake, a bird, and a buffalo) could be an early form of writing. Religious ceremonies became more elaborate, shamans more influential. The spiritual in northeastern China more than five thousand years ago could pray for wealth or health before the many female figurines in an especially ornate sacrificial temple, including a life-sized goddess with painted lips and piercing jade eyes. Rich were divided from poor, both within cities and between them. Larger towns turned into regional business hubs, surrounded by smaller, less prosperous villages. These budding metropolises were often protected by packed-earth defensive walls, an indication the Chinese had begun killing each other. Walls, too, enclosed posh districts in city centers, playgrounds for the rich and famous. Within these gated compounds lived the chiefs in large houses with courtyards for ceremonies and offices for administration.

Were these nascent kingdoms? The beginnings of regional governments? Scholarly debate rages. But when true states did arise, around 2000 BC, they did so only on the Chinese northern plain—in today's Henan and Shanxi provinces. It is a puzzle. Diverse cultures still dotted the river valleys, yet it was in that one region that these varied societies coalesced into what became Chinese civilization. This development had consequences that would rumble down the millennia. Ever after, north-central China, the domain of the Yellow River, would be the heartland, the font of Chinese culture. The *zhongguo*, or Middle Kingdom or Central States, the core of the Chinese world, glimmering like the sun on the grand river that flowed through it. The Chinese emotional attachment to that patch of land, sometimes taken to the hysterical, would become one of the defining themes of their history of the world.

The first China state is known as Erlitou. Based near the modern city of Luoyang in Henan province, this monarchy, backed by a strong government and military, was easily the political, economic, and cultural powerhouse of its age, likely lording over smaller towns and villages. The capital—far larger than anything built before it—may have been home to thirty thousand residents. A rectangular, walled compound, studded with wooden pavilions and covered hallways amid stately courtyards, could have been China's first traditional royal palace—not all that different in its basic form from the intimidating Forbidden City in Beijing. Surrounding the palace was a road system for wagons. Archeologists even uncovered the ruts worn by their wheels. Workshops churned out bronzes, jades, turquoise jewelry, and other luxuries. The influence of Erlitou spread far and wide. We know that, again, by following the pottery shards: Erlitou's distinctive styles of gray-colored ceramics could be found in towns across Shanxi and Henan. Did political control extend with the clay cups and vases? No one can say for sure. But we do know that there was nothing like Erlitou anywhere else in China—possibly in all of East Asia.

=

Who were these early Chinese kings? We don't know. They didn't tell us. But later historians may have. The old written records talk of China's first dynasty, the Xia. The story has long been dismissed as a myth. But there are tantalizing clues that the Erlitou state is the Xia Dynasty. Nothing conclusive, of course—archeologists will have to do more digging before we can be absolutely certain. The rough time frame—around 1900 to 1600 BC—and general location fit neatly, though. And even if mere legend, the founding of the Xia is one of the defining tales of Chinese civilization.

The story will sound surprisingly familiar to any Bible reader: A great flood inundated the realm, so severe it consumed mountains. The black-haired people were forced from their homes and fields to live in caves above the cascading waters, harassed by voracious beasts, birds, and dragons. The man who saved the day was Yu the Great. Described by one ancient historian as "quick, earnest, and diligent, not deviating from virtue, kind, and lovable,"[1] Yu threw himself into his daunting task with inexhaustible energy. He dug canals and channeled the waters so that they drained into rivers that led to the sea, and used a soil with the power to regenerate itself to protect and rebuild the land. For ten years Yu did not rest. Three times he passed by the door of his own home but would not spare even a moment to visit his family.

Yu ended the great flood and rescued China. The people returned to their fields and homes, and the vicious dragons and animals were chased away. The achievement convinced the emperor, another mythical figure named Shun, that Yu could be trusted with the throne. Yu, as is considered decorous, protested that the job should go to someone more worthy, but Shun would have none of that. "Go and attend to your duties," Shun directed.[2]

That he did, with unparalleled flair. He surveyed the land, banked up marshes, and improved the roads, and farmers flourished. Governing with virtue, he justly distributed the resources of the realm to aid the poorest provinces, thus ensuring widespread prosperity.

Yu's family, however, broke with political precedent. His two esteemed predecessors—Emperors Yao and Shun—had designated their successors based on merit, not blood. Yu tried the same, naming a loyal minister as his chosen heir, but after the great savior died on an inspection tour of his kingdom, his subjects switched their allegiance to Yu's capable and honorable son, Qi. Thus began the first Chinese hereditary dynasty, the Xia, or so China's ancient historians recorded.

Yu the Great can be considered the founder of China, as Moses was to the Israelites—the visionary who led his people through trials to the promised land. His dynasty would come to hold such importance to the Chinese that they would often refer to themselves as the people of Xia. Fact or fiction, Yu's story was already embedded in Chinese memory three thousand years ago. The Yu legend is recounted in some detail in an inscription on a bronze can dating all the way back to around 900 BC. "Heaven commanded Yu to spread out the soil, and to cross the mountains and dredge the

streams," it reads. "Thus he cut off the trees to open land for plan-
tation, taxed the subjugated people, and oversaw virtues."[3]

Yu was also held up by future historians and political thinkers
in China as a model ruler—honest, benevolent, selfless, and just.
He defines how the Chinese came to see good government. In the
West, world history is traced back to Greece, Rome, and their early
republics—the roots of modern democracy, what we believe is the
ideal form of governance. In the Chinese history of the world, perfect government was defined by Yu. China's desired state had at
its apex not an elected assembly of the people but an enlightened
sage-king on a throne, to guide the people with virtue and wisdom.
This notion of proper government would be elaborated upon and
expanded over the coming centuries into a complex political ideology that would remain entrenched in Chinese world history, for a
long, long, long time.

=====

Good men earn thrones; bad men lose them. That's the lesson of
Chinese history, or at least how the Chinese write their history. It
was inevitable, then, that when a dishonorable descendant took
Xia's helm, the dynasty was doomed. Emperor Jie, in the words of
one ancient historian, "was oppressive, and his rule dissipated."[4]
The moment was ripe for a new hero, and the man who seized the
opportunity was named Tang, probably the ruler of a rival kingdom to the Xia. Tang was as humane as Jie was not. One day, we're
told, he was out and about and ran into some rustic fellow who
was hanging nets in every direction, vowing to catch every bird he
could. That didn't seem like fair play to the upright Tang, who took
down most of these nets to give the birds a flying chance.

No less distressed by the malignant Jie, Tang sent a trusted envoy
to the Xia cities to learn more about the state of the dynasty. When
he returned from his three-year spying mission and reported that
the Xia ruler was widely despised, Tang resolved there and then to
act. In a rousing speech to rally the people, Tang charged that the
Xia's Jie "exhausts the strength of his people, and exercises oppression in the cities." Brushing aside their fears and doubts, Tang
presented his mission as divinely sanctioned. "It is not I, the little
child, who dare to undertake a rebellious enterprise; but for the

many crimes of the sovereign of Xia, Heaven has given the charge to destroy him," Tang said.[5]

That he did, with ease. When Tang marched at the head of his army, carrying a halberd, the Xia's soldiers refused to defend their hated king, whom Tang banished from the empire. The victorious Tang returned to his home city of Bo and was proclaimed the ruler of the realm—the new Shang Dynasty. Apparently overwhelmed with the weight of responsibility placed upon his shoulders, Tang composed a heartfelt message to his subjects. "I am fearful and trembling, as if I were in danger of falling into a deep abyss," he wrote.[6]

These tales could all be fables, too. They sure sound like it. And the Shang Dynasty was thought to be mythical as well. There was no corroborating evidence dug up anywhere in north China that confirmed the Shang ever existed.

That was until the early twentieth century, when sleuthing archeologists tracked the source of animal bones with scribbles on them, originally discovered being ground up as a malaria treatment in a Beijing pharmacy, to a site in northern Henan province called Anyang. There they uncovered a massive city and, more importantly still, a treasure trove of cattle bones and tortoise shells. These were oracle bones—tens of thousands of them—used in divination ceremonies by the very Shang rulers who were not supposed to have existed. The Shang were real!

We know that because they told us. Unlike the still-doubted Xia, the Shang learned to write. And better yet, they wrote in Chinese characters—not exactly the ones used today, but clearly their predecessors. The invention of Chinese script was one of the most pivotal contributions to the Chinese history of the world. Chinese characters would eventually travel throughout East Asia, and with them Chinese literature, philosophy, and learning. Simply, Chinese script was the transmitter of Chinese culture, the Internet of ancient days. The characters were indispensable to the creation of a Chinese world, binding other peoples to China and separating East Asia as a distinct cultural zone from the rest of the world. The writing first appeared around 1200 BC, but it was already quite complex, so it might have been in use for some time earlier, scratched onto perishable material that has not survived. That makes the Shang's characters the basis of the world's oldest writing system, now in use for more than three thousand years.

Back to those old bones: they were, it turned out, something like government documents. It was common in Shang culture to seek guidance from the spirits on critical matters of state. Should we attack the enemy? Will a royal birth be a good one? (In other words, a boy.)[7] The advice from beyond came in the form of cracks that appeared on bones and shells when seared with a heated brand or poker, which were then translated by divination experts. The question thus asked, the identity of the enquirer, the date, and the result were often engraved onto the cracked bone, and then—thankfully, for us today—saved as a formal record. Scholars were able to match the names of Shang rulers etched onto the bones with those mentioned in later historical texts. Voilà! Myth became history.

Still, the oracle bones only provide the bare bones of Shang history. Sometime in the mid-sixteenth century BC, Erlitou collapsed and the Shang rose, with the dynasty's founding dated at 1554 BC. Anyang was probably the last of several capital cities. It was a gargantuan urban sprawl for its age: perched majestically on the Huan River, the royal compound had fifty-three large buildings, one possibly as long as a football field. The economic might and technical skill of the Shang loomed just as large. A bone factory is estimated to have churned out four million tools in the 150 years it operated. A 1,900-pound cauldron, the largest bronze ever made, must have required one thousand artisans working in unison to cast. The Shang elite amassed so much wealth that a royal consort named Lady Hao was entombed with enough stuff for multiple eternities: 468 bronze vessels and weapons and 755 jade items.

How powerful the Shang were remains an open question, however. The domain under their direct control may not have been particularly large—perhaps just sections of Henan and Shanxi provinces. What was critical about the Shang, though, was its cultural clout. Tracking pottery styles and bronze technology, archeologists have shown Shang influence spread across the region—to the area of Hebei in the north, down toward the Yangzi River in the south, off to Shandong in the east, and in the west into Shaanxi (which is a different province from Shanxi). The great diversity of cultures that had existed in earlier times was being replaced by a more homogenous one across the northern plain, with the Shang as the source. A "Chinese" civilization was being forged, centuries before the rise of Greece and Rome.

=====

The Shang were also not alone. Other centers of power emerged over the roughly five centuries it flourished in north China. As Shang influence waned toward the eleventh century BC, its royal house was toppled by a rival kingdom called Zhou, located on the western fringe of the Shang heartland, in what is today Shaanxi province. The stories left to us in later written histories sound all too familiar. Like the Xia, the Shang were brought to an inglorious end through immoral leadership, this time by a king named Xin who reveled in debauchery and depravity—boozing, womanizing, roasting his enemies over bonfires, and doing other things good Chinese rulers are not supposed to do. As one historian lamented, King Xin "made a pond of wine, hung the trees with meat, made men and women chase each other about quite naked, and had drinking bouts the whole night long."[8] To pay for all his gluttony, he heavily taxed the masses and filled his treasuries with money, grain, and livestock. As resentment boiled over, King Xin refused to heed warnings from his ministers, and even his son, that he would lose his crown if he did not mend his wayward ways.

Clearly, the Shang's days were numbered; it was just a matter of who would perform the coup de grâce. That man was King Wu, ruler of Zhou. His father, King Wen, had already started the assault on the Shang, and his forces may have gotten within striking distance of its capital. But the campaign was cut short when he suddenly passed away. The job fell to King Wu. At a gathering of allied nobles and officials, King Wu listed the crimes of the Shang ruler and, much like the founder of that dynasty centuries earlier, proclaimed that he had divine permission to rid China of this evil tyrant. "The iniquity of Shang is full," he told the assembled dignitaries. "Heaven gives command to destroy it. If I did not obey Heaven, my iniquity would be as great."[9]

Four years after his father's death, King Wu brought his allied forces—a huge host of forty-five thousand soldiers—to a place called Muye. There, at dawn, he rode to the front of his army wielding a golden battle axe and exhorted his men to "be like tigers and pan-thers, like bears."[10] The scene that unfolded is immortalized in one of China's most revered poems.

> *The wilderness of Mu spread out extensive;*
> *Bright shone the chariots of sandal;*
> *The teams of bays, black-maned and white-bellied,*
>   *galloped along.*[11]

A battle royal it was not. The vast army of Shang, "collected like a forest" in the words of the poet, had no will to fight. At the first charge of King Wu's men, the Shang soldiers rebelled and turned their swords onto their own leaders. His army in tatters, the Shang tyrant King Xin fled into a tower he used as a treasury, dressed himself in luxuriant robes and jewels, and set himself on fire. Finding the charred corpse after entering the defeated capital, King Wu dismounted from his horse, lopped off King Xin's head with his golden axe, and hung it on a white banner. The people of the city wisely submitted to their conqueror. Another new dynasty was born, called the Zhou. It was 1045 BC.

==

King Wu is one of the most important figures in Chinese history, a sage-king ranking right up there with Yu the Great. The Zhou Dynasty he forged lasted for an amazing eight centuries, a record unmatched by any other royal house in China's long history (and possibly anywhere else). At the time, though, the Zhou's success did not appear so certain. King Wu had won a resounding victory, but still he was troubled. One night, not long after the battle at Muye, his brother visited him and asked why the king couldn't sleep. King Wu responded that he was consumed with the chal-lenges ahead. The Shang had left him a realm in decay and dis-order. Insects infested the fields that should have been producing grain; deer grazed on lands that should have been feeding live-stock. The corrupt officials of the Shang had to be replaced by the righteous. That was the only way to rule. "I shall exalt my works until my good deeds are clear to all," he said.[12]

King Wu led a reformation of government. He sent away his battle-hardened horses to faraway fields as a signal to the people that war was at an end. Opening the state's granaries, he ensured the masses had enough to eat. Within the royal court, he restored the proper frugality and rituals. These were all deeds to make Chinese philosophers swoon. King Wu's methods became hallmarks of sagely leadership: elevating civil over military rule, providing for the well-being of society's most vulnerable, and keeping the royal purse strings tight. "He showed the reality of his truthfulness, and proved clearly his righteousness," one ancient history records. "He honored virtue, and rewarded merit. Then he had only to let his robes fall down, and fold his hands, and the kingdom was orderly ruled."[13]

Yet the Zhou were almost snuffed out as quickly as they rose. King Wu died a mere two years after beheading the Shang, and Wu's son, King Cheng, was too young to assume the complicated affairs of state. So a regency was formed, with the child-heir and two of King Wu's brothers governing the new kingdom together. One of those brothers was the Duke of Zhou, another towering figure of Chinese history, credited with tremendous contributions to statesmanship. It was the Duke's expert management and clarity of purpose that probably saved the Zhou from early extinction.

Trouble began when disgruntled princes who had been excluded from the ruling triumvirate conspired with a scion of the Shang royal clan and rebelled against the duke and the heir. This left them in a tough spot. Do they go to war to assert royal authority? To answer that question, King Cheng sought the wisdom of the divine. The verdict, via a cracked tortoise shell, was auspicious: he would win the war. Still, some of King Cheng's advisors warned him against taking military action, but he insisted on defending his authority. He would put his trust in the word of Heaven, revealed by the cracks on the shell. "Heaven's mandate is not to be presumed upon," he pronounced.[14]

This was a very early expression of a core tenet of Chinese political thought: the "Mandate of Heaven." It was the all-powerful yet intangible force called Heaven that conferred upon a man the right to rule. That right, that "mandate," was conditional: if a ruler was immoral, cruel, or inept, the mandate could just as easily be withdrawn and bestowed upon someone more worthy. Heaven only selected the most virtuous to rule. The greatest legacy of the early Zhou rulers was their promotion of this idea, to claim the Zhou court had the moral right to rule and divine sanction for its actions. It was a stroke of political genius.

This concept of the Mandate of Heaven became the defining justification for imperial rule through much of Chinese history. Chinese dynasties would assert they possessed the Mandate of Heaven to legitimize their rise to power. What's more, the concept sat at the heart of a greater worldview—a universal order, ordained by Heaven, that encompassed the entire world and all the peoples in it. The emperor, in this philosophical construction, was no run-of-the-mill ruler—if he possessed the Mandate of Heaven, that made him the Son of Heaven, the representative of the divine on earth. With that special status, the authority of the Son of Heaven had no boundaries—he had the right to govern "all under Heaven," the entire world the Chinese knew, or at least the civilized parts of it. Thus the Chinese ruler possessed a universal quality. And if the Son of Heaven held such boundless sovereignty and was anointed by the grandest of deities, then how, exactly, could other rulers be his equal? Impossible! This political philosophy, as it developed, shaped Chinese relations with the rest of the world for thousands of years.

Armed with their heavenly mandate, King Cheng and the Duke of Zhou marched against the rebels. It took three years, but not only did the Zhou smash their clan rivals, they in the process significantly expanded the territory under their control. The newly constituted Zhou Dynasty now ruled farther in every direction than any previous north China state—deep into Shandong and Hebei, and possibly south almost to the Huai River.

To govern their new empire, the Zhou court revolutionized state administration in China, creating executive officials and secretariats with scribes and civil servants. In other words, the Zhou may have invented Chinese bureaucracy (for good and bad). But the new regime was hardly a centralized state—such an innovation would wait a further eight hundred years. The Duke of Zhou stabilized the Zhou through a sort of feudal confederacy. He divvied up the conquered lands into fiefs and handed them out to loyal royals and trusted allies, who governed them with a great degree of independence in the name of the Zhou house. That may have seemed wise and efficient from an administrative standpoint. Managing such an expanse from the capital in an age when roads were few and transport glacial was a challenge, to say the least. Later Chinese scholars would regard this form of government as the ideal. But it would prove a disaster for the cohesion of the Zhou Dynasty.

What really endeared the Duke of Zhou to future emperors, ministers, and scholars is something he didn't do. He commanded such respect that he could probably have grasped the throne for himself, but chose not to. When the young King Cheng came of age, the Duke of Zhou dissolved his regency and remained no more than a devoted advisor. Ever since, Chinese philosophers have held him up as the model of integrity in government. A millennium later, when another dying emperor wished another regent to show the same decency to a young heir, he gave the man a painting of the Duke of Zhou.

=

The ancient Chinese had developed an advanced society, with a complex political system, productive economy, and vibrant cultural life. But they were hardly unique. Other peoples around the world were crafting early but brilliant civilizations, which in some respects surpassed the one rising on the Yellow River. The Chinese were actually late to the state-building game; by the time Erlitou rose, Hammurabi was already proclaiming his famous code in Babylon. The pyramids at Giza were some 1,500 years old by the time of the Duke of Zhou. And the great Harappan civilization of the Indus River valley, with its oddly standardized urban planning and undeciphered script, had already come and gone. But the residents of China, comfortably ensconced on the far eastern end of Asia, had no way of knowing any of that. The distances were too great, and the available technology too feeble to bridge them. Though the Chinese might have had some scant contact with Central and South Asia during the Zhou period, they remained pretty thoroughly isolated from other major civilizations until the late second century BC. A long way off at this point in our story. Closer to home in these early centuries, the Chinese did not confront any other society with the same degree of political and economic organization or level of literacy. Beyond its own borders were no more than tribes, many pastoral and not yet engaged in agriculture, and, as far as we know, mostly illiterate. So as far as the people of the Zhou could tell, their civilization was superior to any other. They were the super elite, their kingdom a superpower. Ignorance is bliss, after all.

Still, we shouldn't sniff at the achievements of the ancient Chinese, either. The long Zhou period witnessed an incredible flourishing of artistic and literary expression and innovation—one of the most influential in all human history. What happened under the Zhou was nothing short of the forging of classical Chinese civilization. The writings and ideas that flowed from this period of intellectual ferment and flowering would form the foundation of Chinese culture through the centuries, and down to the present day. The Zhou civilization, based on certain texts and philosophical tenets, then spread to other parts of what became China, as well as much of East Asia, creating a Chinese cultural domain that stretched from Japan across the continent into Southeast Asia. Simply, the West has its Athens, East Asia its Zhou.

Many of the works composed during the Zhou age became classics, the literature at the very foundation of society. One of these texts, the *Classic of Poetry*, is probably the oldest collection of verse in the world. Some of the odes may have been composed around 1000 BC. The *Book of Changes*, a work on divination, has traditionally been credited to the Duke of Zhou and King Wu's father. But even if that is apocryphal, which is probably the case, scholars believe parts of it were written in the first centuries of Zhou rule. Entries in a compendium of historical records, called the *Classic of History*, are possibly even older, and may date from the first decades of the Zhou. *Zuo's Commentary on the Spring and Autumn Annals*, completed in the fourth century BC, offers a wealth of information on the events of the later Zhou centuries and is possibly the first historical narrative produced anywhere in the world. The outpouring of all of this literature shows how important reading and writing had become to Zhou society. Literacy was essential to anyone claiming membership in the Zhou elite.

More important than the texts themselves were the ideas within them. The latter period of the Zhou Dynasty was the age of the greatest Chinese philosophers, who gave birth to a distinctly Chinese body of thought. While Socrates taught in Athens, the Buddha achieved enlightenment in northern India, and the Hebrew prophets were infusing their monotheism with a new universality, a group of Chinese thinkers were espousing doctrines that would have just as much influence over global civilization, if not more.

The most influential of these philosophers was Confucius. Born in 551 BC in eastern China and raised in poverty by a single mother, this scholar and statesman came to be called the "Supreme Sage," whose school of thought became the defining ideology of China's imperial dynasties. The texts known as the "Confucian classics"—since he has traditionally been credited (probably incorrectly) with writing, editing, or embellishing them—formed the basis of education in China (and parts of East Asia) until the twentieth century. His ideas came to shape relations between father and son, husband

Confucius, China's most important philosopher. His doctrine became the core ideology of the imperial dynasties.

Private Collection / Peter Newark Pictures / Bridgeman Images

and wife, and ruler and subject; the principles of good government; the position of women in society; attitudes toward authority; and the role of the individual. Confucius taught the Chinese how to gauge right from wrong and how to see the world around them. For centuries, the government was managed by scholars infused with his teachings. It is difficult to separate Confucius's doctrine from Chinese civilization itself. Anywhere you went in China—from the emperor's audience chamber to the farmer's bedchamber—you'd find Confucius at work.

Confucius the man could never have predicted his future fame. Though he strove tirelessly to convince the dukes and princes of his day to adopt his theories on good government—based on virtue and benevolence instead of coercion—he had little success. In his old age, he retired to teaching, and he died in 479 BC surrounded by only a handful of loyal disciples. Yet his ideas survived, passed down from teacher to student through the centuries and preserved in the *Analects*, a collection of his famously pithy sayings compiled by his followers sometime after his death. More than two millennia later, this collection remains the most important single text in Chinese history, and one of the most influential philosophical works ever produced anywhere.

Confucius's doctrine was centered on the *dao*, or "the Way," of the sages. If people acted with propriety and moral uprightness, the world would enjoy harmony, peace, and prosperity. This was especially true of the ruler, who had a special responsibility to behave virtuously—leading by example, his good deeds would have an infectious effect by encouraging similarly moral behavior among the masses. For a model, Confucius looked back to an even earlier age in Chinese history, to sages like Yu the Great and the Duke of Zhou, who set the standard for righteous leadership. Yet everyone has his or her proper role to play to ensure society is in order. Cultivating oneself to be more virtuous and honorable should be a lifelong task. But Confucius's idea of self-improvement wasn't meditating under a Bodhi tree, Buddha-style. He was very much a man of the world, and he wanted to change that world. Only through a commitment to incessant learning could a man foster his goodness and become a gentleman (a tradition that drives the Chinese mania for education to this day). The learned then had a responsibility to

serve the people; only the most virtuous should command authority. Here we find the radical nature of Confucian thought. Though
later condemned as an arch-conservative, during his own age—of
nobles and commoners—Confucius was a champion of merit over
birthright, who believed men should be judged by their morality
and wisdom, not by wealth, clan, or status. It was a notion that
eventually became embedded in the imperial system of education
and government.

Confucius, though, must share the philosophical spotlight with
other thinkers of equivalent brilliance. The foundation of another
consequential Chinese doctrine—Daoism—also dates to the Zhou
era. Though Daoism has some common traits with Confucianism—
such as a focus on this world rather than the next—it differs sharply
in others, most of all in its view of the world of man. While the
Confucians are fixated on social norms and rituals, the Daoists believe the constructs of human society inhibit the natural force of the
dao, in their view the intangible "Way" of the universe. The goal of
the sage is to empty himself of the discriminations and distractions
created by humankind and clear out the artifices of everyday life,
in order to accord oneself with the Way. The best-known Daoist
text, the *Daodejing*, was compiled no later than the fourth century
BC, and is credited to Laozi, which just translates to "Old Master." Legend has it he wrote the whole thing in two seconds. If he
existed—and historians doubt it—he might have been a near contemporary of Confucius. (One ancient scribe claims the two titans
actually met, with an elder Laozi giving the younger Confucius a
good tongue lashing.) Daoists have had tremendous influence over
art, literature, medicine, and religious practice in China. Taken together, Confucianism, Daoism, and other strands of Chinese philosophy form a corpus every bit as important to global civilization
as the works of the Greek philosophers or the South Asian Vedas.

What coalesced in central China during the Zhou period was
a distinctly "Chinese" culture of shared rituals, social practices,
foundational texts, political and mythic heroes, moral values, and
philosophical principles that defined what being "Chinese" actually
meant. The Chinese began to think of themselves as Chinese, with
a common "Chineseness," a bond that set them apart from others.
The concept of "China" was being born.

This "culture of ours," as the Chinese came to call it, proved to be the glue that bound China's society together as it dissolved politically. Beginning in the eighth century and lasting for five hundred years, the Zhou court steadily lost real power and eventually ruled in name only. The nobles managed their regional realms—the decentralized system implemented by the Duke of Zhou—and officially remained loyal to the Zhou kings, but in practice, they acted more and more as independent rulers governing separate states. And these principalities—at one point, dozens of them—began incessantly squabbling with each other over territory and treasure. The battles were bloody. Over the centuries, cultural practices deviated between these different states. (In one, the state of Yan, "in exchanges of guests, they had their wives attend them overnight," an ancient scribe enticingly recorded.)[15] Yet through it all, a sense of commonality remained—the shared values, traditions, and social norms—that made civilized people civilized. The zhongguo, the heartland, may have decomposed into competing polities, but the idea of a "Chinese" central cultural zone did not.

=

When the Chinese looked at the other peoples living around them, they weren't all that impressed by what they found. These foreigners did strange things, dressed in odd clothing, and spoke incomprehensible tongues. They didn't follow the correct rules of polite society or abide by the established niceties of diplomatic etiquette. They just weren't like us at all, and clearly our ways were far better—far more "civilized." Since Chinese civilization *defined* civilization, only those who were part of it were civilized. Everyone else, almost by definition, wasn't. They were no more than barbarians, and that's exactly how the ancient Chinese described them.

The early Chinese perceived the world as a series of concentric zones (at first five, then nine). At the center was the seat of the emperor and the territory under his direct control. That also represented the beating heart of Chinese culture. With each band that stretched out from this core, the more barbarous the people living there became. One ancient text called the most remote area the "Wild Domain."[16] This unsavory locale was home to those most ignorant of Chinese civilization, and therefore, the most savage.

Obviously, this was a simplistic and idealized construct, but it had a strong influence on Chinese relations with the outside world.

Since these "others" were not literate, everything we know about them we've learned from the Chinese. And that isn't much. Chinese scribes at this period showed scant interest in the customs, politics, or lifestyles of their neighbors. After all, what could these "barbarians" possibly have to offer? The Chinese often didn't distinguish very carefully between the different types of "barbarians." They were usually referred to by generic labels: the Di in the west, the Rong in the north, the Man in the south, and the Yi in the east.

In the eyes of the Chinese, these barbarians were no better than animals, with no order in their societies, no proper relations between people. It was chaos out there! "Their people live like elks and deer, birds and beasts," scholars wrote of the surrounding tribes in the third century BC. Everything they did was the opposite of what was acceptable among the Chinese. "The young give orders to the old, the old are afraid of the adults, the strong are considered the worthy and the haughty and violent are revered. Day and night they abuse each other having no time to rest, exterminating thereby their kind."[17]

What made these barbarians so abhorrent was that they didn't follow the same rituals, cherish the same virtues, or have the same civilized tastes as the Chinese. "Ears that do not hear the harmony of the five sounds are deaf," a Zhou dignitary is quoted as saying of one group of Di tribesmen in the seventh century BC. "Eyes that do not distinguish the displays of the five colors are blind; hearts that are not patterned after the basics of virtue and propriety are obstinate; mouths that do not pronounce loyal and trustworthy words are raucous. The Di pattern all these, their four perversities are complete."[18]

Deaf and blind to China's civilization, the barbarian tribes lacked the patience, tolerance, and moderation of the Chinese. One Zhou king, sickened by the crude behavior of tribute-bearing ambassadors, described them with derision. "Rong and Di enter hastily and despise order, they are greedy and unwilling to yield, their blood and breath is unmanageable, just like that of birds and beasts. When they arrive to submit tribute, they cannot wait for fragrance and fine taste; therefore we make them sit outside the gate and send the translator to give them" the meat of a sacrificed animal.[19]

Confronted with these outsiders as they migrated closer to and even into the zhongguo, the residents of the Zhou world began to demarcate themselves from these other groups. They were the Huaxia—the "hua" representing a mountain centrally located in the Zhou domain, and the "xia" a reference to the mythical Xia Dynasty. This is a sign of how the people of Zhou culture started to see themselves as possessing a common identity, distinct from other peoples. Simply, the Chinese began defining who they were by comparing themselves to others.

Faced with barbarous outsiders, the Chinese had to stand together, whatever their political divisions. It was just a matter of "us" and "them." The great civilization of China had to be protected. In 661 BC, a canny minister in the state of Qi named Guan Zhong employed just such rhetoric to convince his ruler to come to the aid of another Chinese state that had been invaded by Di tribesmen. The Di "are wolves and jackals who cannot be satiated," he said. The Chinese "are kin who cannot be abandoned."[20]

Yet the ancient Chinese didn't believe the barbarians were hopelessly irredeemable. The common thinking at the time was more enlightened than it might appear—all people were more or less the same, and inherently good in their inner nature. Just because they were unrefined didn't make them inherently bad folk. One commentary from the third century BC made clear that the barbarian tribes "differ in all: in their clothing, caps and belts; in their palaces, living houses and places of dwellings; in their boats, chariots and utensils; in their sounds, colors, and tastes. Yet their desires are the same."[21]

The barbarians would cease to be barbarians, then, if they became more like the Chinese. Being Chinese, from this viewpoint, was a matter of culture, not genetics. Anyone could become "Chinese" by adopting "Chinese" learning, moral values, and rituals. Once exposed to Chinese life, the barbarians would doubtlessly perceive its merits and quickly adopt it. No less a figure than Confucius believed it so. In one passage in the Analects, Confucius remarked that he'd like to live among the "Nine Barbarian Tribes" of the east. A listener, apparently startled, asked, "But could you put up with their uncouth ways?" No problem, Confucius responded. "Once a gentleman settles amongst them, what uncouthness will there be?"[22] Chinese culture thus was transformative: it could convert the barbaric into the civilized.

However, the reverse—barbarians teaching the Chinese—was unthinkable. There was only one culture worth anything, and that was China's. Mencius, the most revered Confucian philosopher after the original sage himself, who probably lived in the fourth century BC, summed it up neatly: "I have heard of men using the doctrines of our great land to change barbarians, but I have never yet heard of any being changed by barbarians."[23]

This isn't to say the Chinese never borrowed from others. They did. But adopting foreign influences was controversial—because they weren't Chinese. How could anything devised outside of the civilized world be of any value? That very question caused trouble for the king of the state of Zhao in 307 BC. He had taken up barbarian dress—probably trousers—as part of his plan to introduce cavalry into his armed forces (another innovation imported from foreign, nomadic tribes). The court was appalled with this breach of decorum. His younger brother pleaded with him to change his mind. "I heard: Central States [the zhongguo] are the place where cleverness and wisdom dwell," he told the king. "Here sages and worthies are teaching, and benevolence and propriety are implemented." The barbarians should be copying Chinese practices, not the other way around. "It is the place to be visited by those from afar, and this way is what the Man and the Yi must implement." Accepting foreign practices, even something as seemingly innocuous as a pair of pants, was akin to turning against his own people. "Now the king discards this and adopts the clothing of the distant regions, changes old teachings, modifies old ways, goes against the people's heart, turns his back to the knowledgeable, abandons the Central States."

The king responded that tradition and sagely principles were all well and good, but even the Chinese should learn from outsiders if it benefited them. "Different localities require change in the use; different undertakings require modification of rites," he said.[24] It was a debate that would rage down through the centuries.

Relations between the states of the Zhou and their barbarian neighbors were often frigid. Battles, raids, and invasions, launched by one side or the other, were all too frequent and stretched all the way back to the Shang Dynasty. Historical texts and bronze inscriptions have left to posterity an alarming record of recurring communal violence. The Zhou's King Cheng "chastised" a tribe called the Huai-Yi that lived in what is today Anhui province, and then inflicted the same on the eastern Yi. King Kang in 981 BC appointed a military supervisor named Yu, who, two years later, scored a great victory over a people called the Guifang, who probably lived in northern Shaanxi and Shanxi provinces. And so on and so on.

As the hold of the Zhou royals over their dukes and barons deteriorated, relations between the Chinese and the barbarians became more complex and began to play a bigger role in the history of China. The Di, Rong, and other frontier peoples got embroiled in the endless scheming of the rival Chinese states. One minute, the barbarians could be enemies, the next allies, in a confusing and shifting swirl of partnerships and betrayals. An especially ornery group of foreigners, called the Xianyun, even played a part in destroying the political power of the Zhou Dynasty. By the early eighth century BC, these barbarians had been threatening the Zhou capital, near modern-day Xi'an, for some time, but the royal forces had been able to hold them at bay. As would prove true again and again through China's long history, however, weakness at the center gave outsiders the opportunity they needed to wreak havoc, and invariably, that weakness was caused by a ruler with more vanity than virtue, in this case, King You. The story goes that King You became infatuated with a consort, divorced his wife, and replaced the original heir with the son of his new favorite. Bad move. The discarded queen just happened to be the daughter of the ruler of a state called Shen. Bent on revenge, the lord of Shen forged an alliance with the Xianyun and encouraged them to attack the Zhou again. The foolish King You sealed his fate by repeatedly calling out his allies to defend the capital for no reason except to extract a rare smile from his otherwise ill-tempered consort. So when the Xianyun did attack, in 771 BC, the king, like the boy who cried wolf, found no one rode to his rescue. The Zhou capital was destroyed and the hapless King You killed.

The real story is probably much less entertaining—King You seems to have lost out in a factional struggle for power. But it is true that the Xianyun were allies of the king's opponents, and after his defeat, the Zhou court had to reconstitute itself under his son at a new capital in the east, at Luoyang. This is the start of what's called the Eastern Zhou Dynasty, to distinguish it from the earlier, and more impressive, Western Zhou period. Officially, the Zhou limped on for another five centuries. But the court never recovered its former glory.

Though the barbarian peoples got drawn into the interminable contests between the warring Chinese states, they were not treated as equals. A sort of code of chivalry was honored between the Chinese states in their battles; for the barbarians, however, any trickery or atrocity was fair game. Barbarians were, after all, like beasts, and could only understand the stick. "It is virtue by which the people of the Middle Kingdom are cherished; it is by severity that the wild tribes around are awed," one ancient commentary recommended.[25] Sometimes the Rong, Di, and assorted others were the victims of aggressive Chinese rulers greedy for land and resources, as the states pushed their boundaries farther north toward inner Asia. All the while the barbarian tribes were getting absorbed into China—in other words, adopting the cultural practices of the Zhou world. A perfect example of this process is the state of Zhongshan, which reached its apogee during the fourth century BC. Though modeled on the other Chinese states, it was founded by Di tribesmen, and as archeological finds attest, its elite had been highly influenced by the thought of Confucius—more so, at the time, than the authentic "Chinese" societies around them. Confucius's confidence in the irresistibility of Chinese civilization was not misplaced. In fact, by the end of the third century BC, the Rong, Di, Yi, and Man evaporate from Chinese historical records. They had become indistinguishable from the "real" Zhou Chinese.

But as that Chinese world continued to expand, the Chinese butted into other civilizations that weren't so easily assimilated or conquered. That would change the Chinese history of the world forever.

Three

SUPERPOWER, CREATED

To command the barbarians is the power vested in the Emperor on the top, and to present tribute to the Son of Heaven is a ritual to be performed by the vassals at the bottom.

–Jia Yi, Han Dynasty statesman

The wars raged across China for five centuries. The states that emerged from the political decay of the Zhou Dynasty set upon each other like hungry wolves, the big devouring the small, the bigger consuming the big. In the eighth century BC, there were some seventy of these mini-kingdoms; by the fifth century, about two dozen, and by the third, only seven. Their battles became bloodier as the states grew larger. At first, their soldiers could be counted in the thousands; wars then were gentlemanly outings, often waged on chariots. In the later conflicts, with the advent of conscripted peasant infantry, the numbers swelled to hundreds of thousands. The dead left bleeding on battlefields across the zhongguo in these colossal contests were often greater than entire legions had been when the wars began. Occasionally, there would be a respite, a sort of balancing of powers or attempts at a negotiated peace. But they could not last. The quest for supremacy was unrelenting.

As is the case in any war, it was the ordinary people who suffered most dearly. Those who escaped death in battle would find their homes and families ravaged. This was a time of bloodletting almost unmatched in Chinese history. "The multitudes of our people, husbands and wives, men and women, had no houses left in which to save one another," a Chinese statesman lamented after one devastating defeat, recorded in a historical narrative of the time. "They have been destroyed with an utter overthrow, with no one to appeal to. If the fathers and elder brothers have not perished, the sons and younger brothers have done so. All were full of sorrow and distress, and there was none to protect them."[1]

The intensity of the warfare is almost impossible to comprehend. From 535 BC to 286 BC, there were a staggering 358 wars among these states.[2] The incessant battles defined the entire age, so much so that the final 250-year stretch, starting around 475 BC, is simply called the Warring States period. And then, finally, it all ended. Not with a crescendo of tragedy befitting such an epic drama, but in anticlimax. One of China's greatest historians described the finale almost in passing. "Qin ordered General Wang Pen to march south from Yan and attack Qi," he wrote of the concluding campaign. "He seized King Jian of Qi. With this Qin succeeded in bringing all of the states under its rule."[3]

That changed China forever. In 221 BC, the state of Qin overran its only surviving rival, the state of Qi, forging China into a unified empire for the first time. The unification of China was probably the single most important event in the Chinese history of the world. The idea of one China, with one emperor atop it, remained entrenched as the standard, the irresistible goal of every future rebel chief, ambitious warlord, and wannabe dynast. For our story, the Qin victory was the moment when China elevated itself from a superior civilization to a true superpower.

At the helm of this ancient juggernaut was King Ying Zheng, better known as Qin Shi Huangdi, or simply "the First Emperor." Despite his undeniably globe-altering influence on history, the First Emperor often merits little attention in the Western narrative. Those few who know of him outside of China are familiar because of the army of terra-cotta warriors he had sculpted for his tomb, now resurrected by archeologists for the viewing pleasure of tourists

秦始皇

Qin Shi Huangdi, the First Emperor, as depicted in an eighteenth-century portrait. His Qin Dynasty unified China in 221 BC and forged the model for all future dynasties.

British Library, London, UK / © British Library Board. All Rights Reserved / Bridgeman Images

near the modern metropolis of Xi'an. But the First Emperor is the Alexander the Great and Julius Caesar of the Chinese history of the world. Like those definitive figures of the West, he was an empire builder, military genius, visionary politician, and cultural icon. In fact, his impact may be even greater than his Western counterparts'. The empires of Greece and Rome have long since vanished; the First Emperor's handiwork is very much still with us.

For the Chinese, though, the First Emperor is among the most controversial figures in their history. While other rulers of antiquity—like Yu the Great or the Zhou's King Wu—are universally considered sages, the Qin emperor is not. On the one hand, the Chinese have recognized his indomitable will, relentless energy, and undeniable achievements; but on the other, they have recoiled at his heartless brutality, unbounded ambition, and terrifying tyranny. The images Chinese scholars have left us of the man betray this ambivalence, at once respectful of his valor while deploring his viciousness. "Brandishing his long whip, he drove the world before him," one statesman wrote a short time after the First Emperor's death. "He reached the pinnacle of power and ordered all in the Six Directions, whipping the rest of the world into submission."[4] Nine centuries later, a poet enshrined that sentiment in verse:

> The king of Qin swept through every direction,
>   his tiger gaze so courageous!
> Brandishing his sword, he parted the floating clouds,
>   and the feudal lords all came westward.[5]

The First Emperor is both a model of the imperial sovereign—he practically created the position—and a warning against the abuse of its power. To some, he is almost an antihero, a pivotal figure of Chinese history, yet one to offend the properly virtuous spirit, a study in how man should not act. To others, even the most liberal-minded, the boldness of his vision, his determination to forge a new China, was admirable, even if his methods were not. Hu Shi, an influential reformer of the early twentieth century, who was part of a movement to revolutionize the Chinese state and society, approved of the Qin's willingness to break with tradition and start anew. "Political dictatorship is surely frightening," he wrote, "but the dictatorship of adoring the past is even more frightening."[6]

The controversy surrounding the First Emperor began with his very birth, in 259 BC—that is, if you believe the salacious rumors. He was dogged by the taint of illegitimacy; palace whisperers had it that his true father was not the ruler of Qin but rather one of his senior ministers, who had illicitly impregnated a favorite royal concubine. Such impropriety was no surprise to the scribes of antiquity. To many of them, Qin was not a card-carrying member of the zhongguo, but an interloper, or a "guest" as one writer politely put it. (Others were less kind, referring to Qin as a "state of tigers and wolves.") Located in the far west, in what is today Shaanxi province, Qin was a society at the crossroads of civility and barbarism, heavily influenced by Chinese civilization but not entirely part of it.

Perhaps that's why the Qin were at the forefront of political change in ancient China. The groundwork for the Qin unification was laid more than a century before the rise of the First Emperor, when his predecessors reengineered the relationship between state and society in ways that earned them a military edge over their rivals. The political experiments strengthened the position of the government to a degree unseen up to that point in Chinese history, allowing the Qin leadership to marshal men and material in the war effort on an unparalleled scale. By the time 221 BC approached, the Qin had become a superstate—a well-oiled steamroller combining military might, economic power, and administrative efficiency.

The credit goes to a wily statesman of the fourth century BC named Shang Yang. Though often overlooked compared to better-known thinkers of that age, Shang Yang's political theorizing was the inspiration for many policies and practices of the imperial Chinese government. Some would say unfortunately so, since he is the philosophical godfather of Chinese authoritarianism. His school of thought, known as Legalism, arm-wrestled with Confucianism for influence in early Chinese statecraft, and its ideas lurked in the background of ruling ideology through China's many dynasties.

Shang Yang was born into the royal family of the small state of Wei, in today's Henan province, but aware that opportunity knocked more loudly elsewhere, he left home in search of official posts in more substantive states, hoping to advise the high and mighty. In 359 BC, he won the ear of Qin's ruler, Lord Xiao, after intellectually pummeling the court's more conservative advisors in policy debates, which earned him the title of chief minister. It was then that the ambitious Shang Yang got to put his theories into practice.

The goal of his program was to maximize state power. In his view—encapsulated in a text called *The Book of Lord Shang*, attributed to him but of uncertain authorship—the polite niceties of Confucian political philosophy—that people can be motivated by virtue—was a recipe for national failure. The masses are inherently selfish and corrupt; they must be contained and manipulated if a ruler is to succeed. "In the past, those who were able to regulate All-under-Heaven first had to regulate their own people; those who were able to overcome the enemy had first to overcome their own people," Shang Yang believed. "The root of overcoming the people is controlling the people as the metalworker controls metal and the potter clay."[7] To do that, governments had to devise clear laws and apply them impartially to everybody—no matter what wealth, status, or political connections they might possess. Those laws must be enforced with strict punishments and lavish rewards, but more the former, including mutilations and executions. The harsher the penalties, the less likely anyone would break the law, leading ultimately to a society of complete peace and order. People's freedoms in such a system would have to be greatly proscribed. "Do not allow the people to shift locations on their own initiative," Shang Yang warned.[8] His most radical suggestion was to remake society based on merit—or at least his definition of it. The entire population would be separated into ranks that determined how much land they owned, how many slaves they could have, their social stature—in other words, their place in the new Qin order. A person's rank was not based on birth or riches, but on their contributions to the state—and for Shang Yang, that meant military prowess. The better one performed on the battlefield—counted in enemy heads severed—the higher one's rank at home. That, Shang Yang believed, would motivate the otherwise useless masses to fight with gusto. "The people's desire for riches and nobility stops only when their coffin is sealed," he said. "And (entering) the gates of riches and nobility must be through military (service). Therefore, when they hear about war, the people congratulate each other."[9] With that, he said, "the bravos and the worthies from All-under-Heaven will follow him (the ruler) just as water flows downward."[10] Simply, Shang Yang's state was built for war.

When implemented in Qin, Shang Yang's reforms touched just about every aspect of life. They effectively decimated the nobility—a sea change in a society where pedigree had been primary—and welded each citizen's destiny to state policy. To enforce his brutal penal code, the Qin government registered every household and organized them into groups that would suffer penalties collectively if any one member violated the law. Those who failed to report crimes were chopped in half. Fathers and sons were forced to separate into independent abodes—the more families, the more taxpayers and conscripts for the army.

The reforms—perhaps distasteful to a liberal-minded reader—worked wonders. From a marginal player in the bloody contest for hegemony, the Qin became a force to be reckoned with. Shang

Yang personally led an army that smashed a rival state, turning it into a subordinate vassal in 340 BC. Yet his supreme power and unpopular reforms also proved his undoing. When his patron, Lord Xiao, died, Shang Yang was falsely accused of plotting a rebellion by the new ruler. In an attempt to flee, or so the story goes, Shang Yang tried to hide out at an inn, but the proprietor refused to accept him as a guest without proper identification—a regulation the statesman himself had imposed. In one of those luscious twists of history, the great oppressor was knocked flat by his own iron fist. He was tied to chariots and ripped to pieces in 338 BC.

The Qin, though, excelled without him. One of its more prominent victims was the last king of Zhou. By the third century BC, the powerless Zhou had become reliant on the goodwill of their erstwhile vassals. One of these royal nonentities, King Nan, made the mistake of allying with one of Qin's enemies. That proved unwise. In 256 BC, he surrendered himself and his titular throne to the Qin, who six years later executed him on suspicion of scheming a comeback. After eight centuries, the once glorious Zhou had come to an inglorious end.

By the time the future First Emperor, King Ying Zheng, ascended the Qin throne, in 246 BC, his state was poised for a final victory. All that was needed was one big burst of military aggression to polish off the skeletal remains of the other six Warring States. King Zheng picked them off in quick succession starting in 230 BC—Han, Zhao, Wei, Chu, Yan, and finally Qi. "Thanks to the help of the ancestral spirits, these six kings have all acknowledged their guilt and the world is in profound order," King Zheng proclaimed.[11] Figuring he had outdone the mere kings of the past, he required a more imposing title than they held as well—Huangdi. The title combined the word *huang*, which means "mythical ruler," with *di*, of "God." We translate it into the more convenient "emperor." King Zheng transformed into Qin Shi Huangdi—"the First Emperor." China would never be the same.

⸺

The First Emperor did more than merely consolidate China; he *created* China. Before the Qin conquest, China had never been a single political entity under a single government. Previous rulers had governed through a feudal-like system that broke up political authority between the king and local leaders. The Zhou had some central bureaucracy, but the allies running their individual states had a fair bit of autonomy. And for the five centuries before the Qin ascension, different competing states had been at each other's throats. There was no common language or writing system, no uniform laws or administration. Though bound together by "this culture of ours" into a like-minded community, there was no shared identity of being "Chinese." The First Emperor altered the direction of Chinese history toward enhanced centralization, integration, and standardization across the Chinese world.

The Qin had their work cut out for them. Since China had never before been China, the varied areas under Qin control—built to fight one another, not cooperate—had to be forged into one domain. The centralizing reforms that had been implemented in Qin, starting with Shang Yang, were now introduced on an empire-wide scale. A totalitarian state expanded into a totalitarian empire.

The fancy new title taken by the Qin ruler was the first step. By adopting Qin Shi Huangdi, the First Emperor elevated himself into a semidivine figure and the ultimate authority at the top of the known world. Needless to say, such a lofty figure could not share center stage with anyone. Out went the traditional fiefdoms and the barons who controlled them. The First Emperor had learned that the Duke of Zhou's system of localized rule spawned rival centers of power that could threaten the control of the emperor and the cohesion of the empire. When some advisors suggested instating such a Zhou system shortly after Qin's final victory, the First Emperor rejected it out of hand. "To reestablish princedoms means to sow weapons," he said. "Will it not be difficult then to demand peace and tranquility?"[12]

Instead, the empire was divided into provinces staffed by civil servants, who were managed by the central monarchy. A national professional bureaucracy demanded conformity. The Qin introduced a new calendar and set standards for all sorts of weights and measures—often in obsessive detail. (Even the axles of carts had to be of uniform width.) Most importantly, the Qin created a standard script of simplified characters, designed to be written more quickly, to help the new bureaucracy keep records and compile reports. In, too, came the Qin's practice of registering every citizen for taxation, forced labor, and military service. Backing up that system were the Qin's draconian regulations and punishments, now imposed on the entire population. Shang Yang would have been well satisfied.

A dynamic new empire needed the physical bonds to tie it together, too. The First Emperor engaged in road building on a massive scale, laying a network believed to be comparable to, and perhaps even longer than, the better-known Roman system.[13] The main thoroughfares radiated out of the capital, Xianyang (near today's Xi'an), leaving little doubt who resided at the center of the Chinese universe. The new roads, the standardized weights, and a new coinage all facilitated economic development, much of it in typical Qin style, controlled by the state. The Qin may not have wanted a free society, but they did desire a prosperous one.

Other projects were designed more to promote magnificence than money. Always thinking ahead, and obsessed with his own mortality, King Zheng might have started the construction of an opulent mausoleum for himself upon claiming the Qin throne in 246 BC (which would have made him an exceedingly dreary thirteen-year-old). Perfectly designed for an Indiana Jones movie, the inner chamber was booby-trapped with crossbows that automatically fired at uninvited intruders. The interior was a miniature of his empire, with replicas of his palaces and the Yellow and Yangzi Rivers (flowing with mercury instead of water). Arrayed outside were the terracotta warriors; the army that led him to empire would do the same in the afterworld. The old records claim seven hundred thousand people labored on the tomb's construction over several decades.

The most spectacular of all Qin undertakings, however, was the first Great Wall of China. The Qin wall is not the one tourists visit north of Beijing today, which is the handiwork of the later Ming Dynasty (see chapter 7). The First Emperor's barrier, mostly pounded earth, has long since eroded. Though the Qin's was probably a patchwork amalgamation of existing defensive walls built by the Warring States, it is still a tremendous achievement in such an antiquated age. Three hundred thousand people worked under such harsh conditions on the remote frontier. It is probably safe to say the Great Wall was built upon the sacrificed peasants the First Emperor bastinadoed into serving his new empire.

The reason why the Qin went through so much trouble building a wall is a critical part of our story. As the Chinese of the central plain pushed northward, they began encountering new barbarians, whom the Chinese referred to as "*hu*." Once again, Chinese scribes made little distinction between different types of *hu*. They were all bunched together into a batch of steppe nomads, of an especially militant and unsavory disposition. The Chinese may have first run into them in the mid-fifth century BC, and the *hu* turned into a bigger nuisance than the Rong, Di, and the like ever were. They raided the settled communities of the frontier, then galloped off and melted into the wilderness.

The First Emperor, fed up with looting nomads, ordered the Great Wall built to keep these ornery barbarians out of his empire. According to an old history, he succeeded, driving the *hu* deeper into the steppe, "so that the barbarians no longer ventured to come south to pasture their horses and their men dared not take up their bows to vent their hatred."[14]

But that success proved fleeting. The wall, no matter how grand a feat of ancient engineering, was insufficient to ward off the nomads. A confrontation was brewing that would be a major turning point in the Chinese history of the world.

=

The First Emperor would not live to see it. Having already prepared his elaborate final resting place, he was intent on never resting in it. He searched ceaselessly for some magical elixir or remedy to give him everlasting life. It is ironic, then, that he died in 210 BC while chasing a wild rumor of a time-reversing potion along China's east coast. His sudden demise—could he have been poisoned?—sparked a political crisis, which, badly handled, quickly unraveled the Qin Dynasty.

Worried about rebellions if the news of the First Emperor's death became widely known, two senior ministers, Li Si, a Shang Yang disciple, and Zhao Gao, a palace eunuch, kept it secret as they hurried back to Xianyang. To maintain the ruse on the long journey, attendants routinely brought meals to the imperial carriage and carts of salted fish were drawn up alongside it to mask the stench of rotting emperor. Li Si and Zhao Gao hatched another conspiracy that smelled even worse. Secretly destroying a note left by the dying emperor that named his first son his heir, the two ministers instead plotted to make his more feeble-minded second son, who was traveling with them, the successor—the better to control the government themselves. The conspirators fabricated a letter they said was composed by the emperor, in which he accused his elder son and rightful heir of incompetence and impropriety, and demanded he take his own life. When this letter reached the elder son, he wept, and did as he thought his father had commanded.

It was all part of a power grab by Zhao Gao. With the heir out of the way, Zhao Gao installed the dim-witted younger son as the Second Emperor upon their return to Xianyang. The corpse of the first was finally interred in the fancy tomb, along with a bevy of excess concubines and some of the artisans who constructed it—and knew too many of its secrets. As one historian grimly noted, "All the workers and craftsmen who had buried the treasure were shut in, and there were none who came out again."[15]

That was just the start of a grotesque bloodletting. The devious Zhao Gao turned on his partner in crime, Li Si, and had him detained on trumped up charges of plotting a revolt, flogged until he made a false confession, and executed. Next he tricked the Second Emperor into committing suicide. While the Qin court was devouring itself, uprisings broke out across the empire. In 206 BC, rebel forces overran Xianyang. The Qin Dynasty was over. It lasted only fifteen years.

=====

Were the Qin really so horrible? We can't say for certain. The penal codes were real enough—a bamboo-strip book of the harsh Qin regulations was discovered in an ancient tomb. But what of the Qin's most nefarious deeds? The old histories tell of a state intent on spreading terror to ensure its dominance—massacring prisoners of war, burying scholars alive, and burning cherished ancient texts to stifle opposition and criticism. Yet much of the Qin's history was written by its enemies after the dynasty was already gone. The main source is Sima Qian, one of the world's greatest historians. Greece had its Herodotus; ancient China, Sima Qian. The scribe, who did most of his writing around 100 BC, left posterity a monumental narrative of early China, stretching all the way back to the early mythical emperors and marching forward to his own day. His intellectual rigor propelled him to examine many issues and events firsthand—making him, at times, more journalist than white-tower academic. Like all good historians, he was also a master bard, with an eye for the arousing detail, dramatic flourish, and dark irony. There is also no historian in any age who sacrificed more for his craft. Because he defended a disgraced general at court, Sima Qian fell afoul of the emperor, who condemned him to death or castration. He was expected in such a circumstance to take his own life—the preferred course at the time, since it preserved one's honor—but that meant leaving his grand project unfinished. The alternative was to pay a stiff fine, which would usually appease even the angriest of emperors by easing his purse, but Sima Qian, a mere scholar, could not afford it. So he decided to accept the worst and most disgraceful course and be castrated. It was a humiliation in Chinese society, but one that at least allowed him to complete his history. "If it may be handed down to men who will appreciate it and penetrate to the villages and great cities, then, though I should suffer a thousand mutilations, what regret would I have?" he wrote.[16]

He should have none. His work still penetrates the cities and villages 2,100 years later. But is he accurate? Modern scholars have their doubts. By the time Sima Qian was writing about the Qin, about a century after the dynasty's demise, the First Emperor and his gang had been vilified for decades. The seemingly invincible Qin had crumbled in only a handful of years. Something had gone horribly wrong. There were obviously lessons here for future Chinese rulers about how to govern and build an enduring government. But what? The scholars buried themselves in their classical philosophy and studied the wise ways of the sages, and found the answer: The Qin were too cruel to stand. The path to good government was not paved with punishments, but built upon benevolence. The sagely ruler was a virtuous one, who won the hearts of the masses. Only tyrants required severity. True monarchs had no need for despotic laws; the common people followed him willingly. Forever after, the story of the Qin became a parable of the perils of absolute power. The emperor needed more than a whip to rule China.

This reasoning had a profound influence on the next dynasty, the Han, and, for that matter, every dynasty thereafter. While the Qin created a unified Chinese empire, it was the Han that forged the true imperial system. Building on the ruined foundations of the Qin, the Han began crafting many of the institutions and principles that typified Chinese dynastic rule, which survived for 2,100 years. The Han would last four hundred of those years, and become a model dynasty for its many successors to follow.

At the time, such longevity was far from assured. The Han Dynasty was officially founded by Liu Bang, a onetime minor Qin official turned rebel kingpin, in 206 BC. Four years of civil war followed, with Liu defeating his main rival for national power in 202 BC. Even then, the "China" Liu Bang inherited had been soldered together by the First Emperor for only a handful of years before it fell apart again. The new emperor, known as Gaozu, hardly had a grip on his entire domain; adhering to Zhou rather than Qin practice, Liu Bang had awarded his allies in the civil war semi-independent kingdoms under the Han umbrella (which he instantly set about undermining). Something was needed to glue this mess of an empire together.

Emperor Gaozu was not the right man for that job. Far more comfortable carousing with his former campsite companions than playing the part of a dignified sovereign, his transition from rebel to royal did not go smoothly. His ministers tried to nudge him in that direction by dusting off old court ceremonies from the Zhou era and tutoring him on the ways of the ancient sage-kings. Gaozu was not always receptive. On one occasion, when a counselor pontificated on the classical texts of the Zhou, the emperor protested, "All I possess I have won on horseback!" The advisor had a ready response: "Your Majesty may have won it on horseback, but can you rule it on horseback?"[17]

Wise advice indeed. But it was Gaozu's successors who took it to heart. What formed under the Han—slowly, over decades, even centuries—was a comprehensive system of governing, rooted in classical philosophy and erected upon a solid (if not always efficient) administrative structure; taken all together, it became the bedrock of imperial China, expanded and elaborated upon by later dynasties all the way up to the twentieth century.

The genius of this system was how well it disguised the emperor's whip. The Han very much wished to retain the state power the Qin had imposed on the empire, and though the strictures of the Qin were relaxed somewhat, the new dynasty was not fundamentally more benign. The Han court just did a much better job of acting like it was. Influenced by classical scholars, the Han couched imperial power in Confucian pleasantries—an ideology that stressed the emperor's benevolence and righteous rule. The Han also revived the old Zhou concept of the Son of Heaven who possessed the Mandate of Heaven. Once again, the emperors claimed the divinely sanctioned right to rule, based on their unrivaled virtue. As Confucian scholars gained a tighter grip on the machinery of state over the long course of the Han Dynasty, this governing principle became ever more entrenched.

The Han did not survive on quaint philosophy alone. Behind the doctrinal veneer stood a state machinery of amazing scope and complexity. By the end of the first century BC, the Han bureaucracy had some 130,000 civil servants. Add in military officers, and the Han state employed about ten times more officials than the government of the Roman Empire around the same time.[18] While Rome preferred to rule many localities indirectly, the Han court instead penetrated deep into Chinese society to a degree simply astonishing for the age.

=

This imperial system did not appear out of thin air. Intellectually, Chinese elite society was already ripe for such a strong regime and the ideology to justify it. For centuries, Chinese thinkers had been thinking about peace and war, good and bad government, and the role of the state in society, laying the groundwork for the imperial system by immersing the educated in shared principles about proper rule and rulers. The philosophers did not all agree, of course. The likes of Shang Yang wished the state to dominate over society; the Confucians almost believed in the absence of state power—since the ordinary people will willingly follow a virtuous ruler, the state requires no onerous laws to control them. But there were commonalities as well, which generally pointed in the same direction: a unified state with a strong emperor.

Much of China's early political philosophy was a product of the late Zhou period of constant war, death, and destruction. Living through such horrors, the ancient philosophers were obsessed with ending them. What would restore peace, order, and sagely rule? They reached the logical conclusion that political division led to devastation; only if the zhongguo was under one government could it find tranquility. Otherwise, competing regimes would just keep slugging it out. As Mencius, the Confucian philosopher, summed it up, "Stability is in unity."[19]

And of course, one government can only have one ruler, a single source of authority. Confucius himself believed that. "There are not two suns in the sky, nor two sovereigns over the people," he is quoted as saying.[20] This sovereign, too, was given extraspecial status as a savior, the difference between civilization and barbarism. "There is no turmoil greater than the absence of the Son of Heaven," scribes brushed in the third century BC. "Without the Son of Heaven, the strong overcome the weak, the many lord it over the few, they incessantly use arms to harm each other."[21] Even more than that, the emperor was a moral exemplar, whose virtue radiates and transforms. "The Son of Heaven is the most respectable in terms of his power and position and has no rivals under Heaven," wrote Xunzi, one of China's greatest political philosophers, who flourished in the mid-third century BC. "His morality is pure, his knowledge and kindness are extremely clear. . . . The one who unites with him is good, the one who differs from him is bad."[22]

China's emperor thus took on a universal quality. He was not merely the leader of the Chinese, but of the entire known world. The First Emperor had already seized on this principle to portray himself as a world monarch. "Wherever human traces reach, there is none who did not declare himself subject," he bragged in an inscription.[23] The First Emperor declared he was a "sage, knowledgeable, benevolent, and righteous," who "radiates and glorifies his teachings and instructions, so that his precepts and principles reach all around."[24] Han Dynasty–era thinkers added further to this notion. "The King is the Son of Heaven," explained Jia Yi, a statesman in the early decades of the Han Dynasty. "Wherever boats or carts may go; wherever the footprints of human beings may reach, even if it be Man, Mo, Rong, or Di (foreign territory), what is there that is not the seat of the Son of Heaven?"[25]

During the Han Dynasty, the emperor became the focal point of all political authority. In Confucian philosophy, the power of the ruler was constrained by moral precept and the Way of the sages. But that was in theory. In practice, the emperor's word was law, his power contained by no formal limitations. The making of policy became increasingly concentrated in the hands of the emperor and his coterie of advisors within the court. On top of that, Han scholars even managed to infuse the emperorship with cosmological significance. Dong Zhongshu, the most important Confucian thinker of the early Han, envisioned the emperor as part of a triumvirate with Heaven and Earth, the critical connection between the divine and humankind. Only the Son of Heaven ensured the harmonious workings of the universe. What a heavy responsibility. The formation of an imperial empire, then, was a mechanism through which all humanity could achieve moral redemption. The Son of Heaven's virtue, coursing through the veins of the government down to the common people, would transform all in his vast realm.

This ideology that surrounded the emperor had a direct and lasting impact on the Chinese history of the world. If the Chinese emperor was a universal sovereign, and a representative of Heaven on Earth, his power could not possibly end at the empire's frontiers. It had to extend beyond, to "all under Heaven." The implications for China's relations with the outside world were huge—as the Han Dynasty's neighbors were about to discover.

═══

The new Han Dynasty had barely established itself before it stumbled into its first foreign policy fiasco. The northern nomads, whom the Chinese called the Xiongnu, had taken advantage of the disorder in China after the fall of Qin to reclaim the land in the great bend of the Yellow River—known as the Ordos—that had been taken from them by the First Emperor. In 200 BC, Gaozu brazenly tried to take it back, personally marching at the head of a Han army into the borderlands in the middle of winter, only to find himself surrounded by Xiongnu horsemen in northern Shanxi province. After a week under siege, the Xiongnu opened the trap and allowed Gaozu to withdraw, with what little was left of his frost-bitten army (and his pride).

The humiliating defeat presented the Han with imperial China's first major border security crisis. There would be many, many, many more to come. The long northern frontier of the Chinese empire would prove a never-ending source of trouble for one dynasty after the next. The dynamics along the border were custom made for conflict. The steppe north of China would be home to a series of nomadic peoples who found themselves in the same predicament: able to scratch out a meager living from their wandering herds of sheep, yaks, and horses, the nomads had a much better chance of survival with access to the grain, tools, and other helpful items produced by agrarian China. Often they could fulfill their needs through trade, but their recurring desperation compelled them to raid and plunder the settled Chinese communities along the frontier. That created a repetitive cycle of violence and reprisals. When the tribes were bickering with each other, which was usually the case, the Chinese could get the upper hand. But when the nomads managed to coalesce into a coordinated political entity under a dynamic chief, they could forge themselves into a formidable power, able to stand toe-to-toe with the emperors and, due to their mobility and military prowess, sometimes claim the strategic advantage.

That's exactly what occurred in the years before the rise of the Han. Probably in response to the northern incursion of the Qin, the assorted Xiongnu tribes united behind a charismatic chieftain, known as the *chanyu*, to forge a steppe empire of considerable strength, at its largest sweeping from what is now far west China through Mongolia and into Manchuria near the Korean peninsula. From little more than a nuisance as dispersed tribes, the Xiongnu had become a serious threat to the Han, as Gaozu had clearly proven, one that the newly constituted dynasty could not defeat on the battlefield.

Somehow, the barbarians had to be contained; otherwise their hooves would be stomping all over the zhongguo. Continued Xiongnu raids south focused the Han minds. So, the Han court decided discretion was the better part of valor. The emperor chose to bribe his persecutors.[26]

In 198 BC, the Han Dynasty and the Xiongnu confederacy signed their first treaty. From the Han perspective, it was a distasteful agreement that, in effect, turned the Son of Heaven into a vassal of the barbarian chanyu. The Han agreed to deliver an annual payment to the Xiongnu of food and Chinese luxuries like silk; in return the Xiongnu pledged not to raid. A Han princess— Gaozu's eldest daughter—was thrown into the deal and shipped to the steppe to be the bride of the chanyu. The treaty also recognized the two empires as diplomatic equals, ushering in a bipolar order in East Asia.

The Chinese called the strategy *heqin*, or "peace through kinship relations." Basically, they purchased the end of a conflict they couldn't win. It was the first of many "unequal treaties" the Chinese were forced into by uncouth but militarily superior foreigners at a moment of weakness in the Middle Kingdom.

Generally, however, the strategy worked. For about a half century, the two powers avoided a major confrontation. And the cost was minimal. The treasure sent north each year was a pittance for the Han, but a windfall for the poor shepherds of the steppe. Proponents of the heqin strategy also took the view that it would soften the Xiongnu by making them dependent on Chinese luxuries and, through the marriage of the Han princess, turn the chanyu into a relative of the Han emperor, and a subordinate one at that.

That thinking was based on a dim view of their northern neighbors, as simpletons who were easily bamboozled and manipulated. The brilliance of Chinese civilization was lost on these incorrigibles, so the only way to tame them was with money. "People like the Xiongnu cannot be converted through humanity and justice, but can only be appeased with huge profit," Dong Zhongshu, the Confucian scholar, recommended. "The policy should be to corrupt them with wealth."[27] Statesman Jia Yi suggested an approach called "three standards and five baits." The "standards" were to deal with barbarians in good faith, pretend to enjoy their strange appearance, and take interest in their stranger habits; the "baits" were to clothe the barbarians in silks and feed them delicious food; entertain them with music, dancing, and women; give them mansions with slaves; and shower them with attention. In sum, spoil them rotten to win their compliance.[28]

Yet the strategy still rankled. As the condescension of Dong Zhongshu and Jia Yi exposes, the Xiongnu presented a military challenge to the Han Dynasty, but not a civilizational one. The Han empire might lose to them in battle, but not in literacy or cultural advancement. Barbarians were, after all, barbarians. That made the peace arrangement intolerable. It was bad enough that the superior Chinese were forced to pay tribute to a bunch of steppe herdsmen. It was worse that by treaty, the glorious Son of Heaven was reduced to the "brother" of the felt-covered Xiongnu chief. The temerity of the Xiongnu knew no bounds. The chanyu once even had the gall to ask the widowed empress of the Han founder for her hand in marriage! "We are both bored, and are both bereft of what could console us," he wrote in a letter to the empress. She gently turned him down, careful not to insult. "My hair and teeth have dropped out and my stride has lost firmness," she admitted in her reply. "You ought not sully yourself. I, who stand at the head of an impoverished domain, am not to blame (for refusing) and should be pardoned."[29]

Oh the indignities! The spectacle of a Chinese empress pleading for her country was bad enough. But the whole heqin arrangement was an affront. If the Chinese emperor was truly the Son of Heaven, then the entire relationship with the Xiongnu was a bastardization of proper world order. "The situation of the empire may be described as like that of a person hanging upside down," wrote scholar-statesman Jia Yi, in a memorial to the emperor. "The Son of Heaven is the head of the empire. Why? Because he should remain on the top. The barbarians are the feet of the empire. Why? Because they should be placed at the bottom. Now, the Xiongnu are arrogant and insolent on the one hand, and invade and plunder us on the other hand, which must be considered as an expression of extreme disrespect toward us. . . . To command the barbarians is the power vested in the Emperor on the top, and to present tribute to the Son of Heaven is a ritual to be performed by the vassals at the bottom. Hanging upside down like this is something beyond comprehension."[30] This argument, cited repeatedly down the centuries, became a core principle of Chinese foreign policy—the Son of Heaven was above all, and had to be treated that way.

Opposition to the heqin program grew as the Chinese came to see it more as appeasement than pragmatism. Critics made the case that the treaties were not only demeaning, but did not actually bring peace to the frontier, either. The raids into Han territory continued, as the chanyu could not compel the assorted local chiefs of the confederation to abide by his promises. Despite those incessant infractions, the Xiongnu demanded larger and larger payments to maintain the peace. It was extortion! Some Chinese officials began to feel like chumps, sacrificing a fortune to tribesmen who failed to honor their side of the bargain.

The Han finally lost patience during the monumental five-decade reign of Emperor Wu, which began in 141 BC. He was without question the most powerful of all the Han royals, who built the China of his day into something that looked a lot more like the country we know today, mainly through tireless military expansion and diplomatic roughhousing. Yet many leading figures of his day were not so appreciative, decrying his imperious nature, foreign adventurism, grandiose spending, and burdensome demands. He became the model for the emperor-autocrat, obsessed with his own aggrandizement. One Chinese historian lamented that the next sovereign "inherited the evils of extravagance and indulgence remaining from Emperor Wu and his military expeditions," while the country "was depopulated and exhausted."[31]

It is undeniable, though, that the imperial China Emperor Wu bequeathed to history was much different than the one he inherited. At home, he founded a national academy for training government officials and designated the classical texts associated with the Confucians as the official curriculum. Those texts would remain the basis of education and government until the twentieth century. These efforts to recruit professional bureaucrats also planted the seeds for what would later become the famous civil service examination system, one of the pillars of imperial China. Abroad, Emperor Wu's policies opened China to the rest of the world far more than ever before. Along the way, he created the basis of a system of foreign affairs that would govern China's relations with other peoples for the entire imperial period. Simply, it was during Emperor Wu's reign that China began defining its role in the world.

騎都尉　休屠像

Emperor Wu of the Han Dynasty, with an official of Xiongnu ancestry, as shown in a second-century AD shrine in Shandong province. One of the greatest emperors, he helped shape the imperial system of government and connected China to the world beyond.

Pictures from History / Bridgeman Images

It all started with the Xiongnu. Emperor Wu was just the sort of belligerent egomaniac to find the humiliations of the heqin treaties unbearable. Rejecting appeasement, he decided to settle matters with the sword instead of silk, tipping off one of antiquity's great superpower showdowns, the Far Eastern version of the Roman-Parthian slugfest, but on an even more colossal scale in terms of geographic scope and forces engaged. The Han opened hostilities in 133 BC with a sneaky attempt to lure the chanyu into a trap; it failed, but in response, the peace treaty was torn up and a wider war began. In 127 BC, the Han scored their first major victory, pushing the nomads out of the area south of the Yellow River that Emperor Gaozu had failed to reclaim seven decades earlier. The Han reoccupied the old Great Wall of the Qin's First Emperor. From there, the 120s were a back-and-forth punching match, with one punishing encounter after the other, leaving both sides bloodied. By the end of that decade, the weight of Han manpower and material resources began to tell, and the Xiongnu were forced northward, deeper into what is now the Mongolian steppe.

That wasn't enough for Emperor Wu. Nothing short of crushing the confederacy and permanently eradicating the threat it posed to his empire would satisfy him. In 119 BC, Han generals launched their most ambitious assault yet against the steppe warriors. Two armies marched north, each with 150,000 cavalry and infantry. One of the prongs smashed into the chanyu's forces near modern-day Ulaanbaatar, the capital city of Mongolia. Using a well-timed sandstorm to break an impasse, the Han commander outflanked the Xiongnu; the chanyu fled, abandoning both his army and a key headquarters site.

Imagine, for a second, the massive logistical undertaking this campaign required: Those three hundred thousand men had to be moved nine hundred miles, through the imposing Gobi Desert, with enough provisions for both men and the animals carrying them and their equipment. Another one hundred thousand men were probably recruited just to ensure the army had enough food, fodder, and weapons to engage the enemy. All of that material had to be hauled by cart and pack animal through incredibly inhospitable territory for long distances. The sheer size of the fighting force is also staggering. Alexander conquered western Asia with only about a tenth of the Han legion, while the largest assemblage of Roman forces, at Actium in 31 BC, reached a quarter of a million.[32] This was a feat only superpowers can pull off. It's the ancient equivalent of mounting the D-Day invasion.

The clashes persisted for decades, but repeated defeats, some smart Han diplomatic maneuvering and, most of all, widening dissension among the Xiongnu tribes sapped the strength of the steppe empire. By the end of Emperor Wu's fifty-four-year reign, with his death in 87 BC, the Xiongnu were a continual nuisance but no longer a mortal danger to China. In 54 BC, one major Xiongnu chieftain, like a punch-drunk boxer, threw in the towel and accepted Han suzerainty. The northern border was secure. For the moment.

=====

The impact of the Xiongnu outlasted the war. The experience with the Xiongnu transformed how the Chinese perceived themselves and the world around them, more so than their earlier contacts with any other outsiders. By comparing themselves to the Xiongnu, the Chinese became more "Chinese"—the differences between themselves and others sharpened, and the people of the zhongguo came to view themselves more distinctly as a community that shared a common culture and resided in a homeland, while the foreigners became more foreign. In other words, the northern nomads helped create the idea of China.

As we explored in chapter 2, the boundaries between barbarism and civilization in Chinese eyes were porous. Foreigners might do strange things and behave badly, but they were still just people and could be redeemed by adopting the superior ways of the Chinese. That thinking—that anyone could be Chinese—didn't completely fade until the modern era. But with the coming of the Xiongnu, Chinese views of outsiders hardened, too. Perhaps not everybody could, should, or would become Chinese. Maybe some barbarians were just barbarians, and incapable of being anything but barbarians.

Chinese thinkers began to portray themselves as polar opposites to the northern nomads. The Xiongnu were like running beasts, always on the move. The Chinese lived in settled cities and communities. The Xiongnu ate meat and dressed in furs. The Chinese dined on the grains they cultivated, and wore silk. These were two separate worlds. How could the Xiongnu ever adopt Chinese ways? No longer were the surrounding barbarians inherently good, either; their corruption could not be so easily cleansed by the cultivating light of Chinese culture. The Xiongnu were just plain *different*— barbarians through and through, and always would be. Historian Sima Qian, though sincerely curious about the daily life, politics, and language of the Xiongnu, also reveals how the nomads had altered Chinese attitudes toward foreigners. "The people are accustomed to attacking and raiding," he wrote of the Xiongnu. "This is their Heaven-endowed nature."[33] Those last few words—"Heaven-endowed nature"—say it all. The Xiongnu were not only a bad bunch, they were bad to the bone. Heaven itself had made them that way.

The Chinese were reassessing their earlier view that the only real difference between themselves and others was in habits. The Xiongnu were, by their very nature, incapable of becoming civilized. By Sima Qian's reckoning, these Xiongnu did a lot of nasty stuff Chinese would never do. They didn't fight honorably, but ran away. They failed to respect their elders, a mortal sin in Chinese society. "Only profit attracts them; they know nothing of ritual and righteousness," he wrote. "From the rulers on down, they all eat the meat of the herd-animals and use their skins and hides for clothing, covering themselves in felt and fur. Those who are hardiest eat the fattest and choicest (pieces); the aged eat the remnants. They value hardiness and vigor and depreciate age and weakness. When the father dies, (the son) takes his step-mother as his own wife, and when their brothers die, they take their (brothers') wives as their own."[34]

The Han scribe set about rewriting the history of Chinese relations with outsiders, too. No longer was the story one of shifting alliances, shared cultural attributes, and amorphous borders. Under Sima Qian's brush, there was always a clear separation between the Chinese and barbarian worlds, going all the way back to the days of the ancient sage-kings. And the two worlds were in perpetual conflict. The Xiongnu were the direct descendants of all those Di, Rong, and Yi who had invaded again and again and again. Sima Qian created an "us versus them" world, and the idea stuck. Later historians would borrow his division and enshrine it as the basic narrative of Chinese relations with the surrounding barbarians.

Sima Qian was apparently not alone in these sentiments. He made sure to excerpt a memorial to the emperor from an influential palace official, Zhufu Yan, written around 130 BC: "Ours is not the only generation that has found the Xiongnu difficult to control," he wrote. "They make it their business to practice robbery, raiding and invading; this is so because of their Heaven-endowed nature. . . . [Ancient Chinese rulers] regarded them as birds and beasts, for they do not belong to the category of mankind."[35]

Still, Sima Qian was likely considered a "barbarophile" by some of his contemporaries.[36] His views were not nearly as hostile to the northern nomads as other writers of the age. Another Chinese historian, Ban Gu—who was at work on his history of the Han Dynasty, the *Hanshu*, about a century and a half later—had even nastier things to say about the Xiongnu. The barbarians "are greedy and profit-seeking," he wrote. "Their human exterior conceals the nature of a beast. They dress and dine differently, and have disparate customs and language from the Middle Kingdom."

Ban Gu took his analysis one step further into the first, coherent attempt at a theory of Chinese foreign relations. He proffered that there was an "inner" world, enlightened by Chinese civilization, composed of the Chinese dynasty and those societies immersed in its culture, and an "outer" world of the unsalvageable barbarians. These two worlds were meant to be separated by the geographic barriers Heaven erected between them. The Chinese, tilling their farmlands, and the nomads, wandering the steppe, each demanded a different way of life. The Xiongnu "live in cold, remote, wild areas in the north, grazing as the grass takes them, making a livelihood with bow and arrow," he wrote. "Separation by valleys and obstruction by deserts are Heaven's way to divide the inner and outer worlds."

Here, then, could be found an important lesson for the emperors: relations with the barbarians must differ from those with more civilized peoples. If the Xiongnu and others like them wished to pay homage to the Son of Heaven, then fine, but otherwise, dealing with them could only be a source of trouble. "A sane king treats them as animals, neither forming alliance with them nor waging wars against them," he wrote. "Alliance costs gifts and results in deceit; war exhausts the troops and invites invasion. . . . Therefore reject instead of accept them, and estrange them instead of being intimate. Political and moral principles do not apply to their people; . . . Punish and defend against them when they come; prepare and guard against them when they go. If they admire the righteousness and pay tribute, treat them pursuant to the rituals, befriend them unceasingly, thus making them in the wrong [when conflicts occur]. Such is a sane king's common way to control barbarians."[37]

The Xiongnu led the Chinese to believe in a distinction between China and the rest of the world. The physical wall separating China from the northern steppe was matched by an intellectual wall the Chinese erected between their society and others. Who would and would not be invited into the Chinese world changed from century to century, based on the ebb and flow of China's power and confidence. Like a perpetually swinging pendulum, Chinese attitudes toward foreigners would alternate between great openness and paranoid xenophobia. Needless to say, Chinese civilization would always be superior, but the idea of "China" had its boundaries, too. The Chinese were Chinese; others were not, and never would be.

=

The contest with the Xiongnu not only altered Chinese minds, it also expanded their horizons. The war led China to look farther afield than ever before, and put the Middle Kingdom in contact with new peoples, states, and cultures. No longer would China be isolated from other civilizations; the Chinese had an awakening to a larger world, beyond their own. And they had to figure out what their place within it should be. The ideas they formed all the way back in the Han Dynasty led to the formation of a system of foreign affairs that would endure for the next two thousand years.

By the time of Emperor Wu, the Chinese had a sense that there was a lot about the globe they didn't know. Zou Yan, a philosopher of the late Warring States period, believed that the world was divided into nine continents, each of which had nine regions. These continents were separated by vast oceans. Zou Yan placed China within the Red Region of the Spiritual Continent. So by his reckoning, China was only one of the eighty-one divisions of the world. Still, China's knowledge of these eighty other regions was likely sparse. Much of the rest of the world was separated by deserts, mountains, oceans, and mystery.

The fog lifted during the age of Emperor Wu. In 138 BC, his court decided to seek out a people called the Yuezhi and forge an alliance with them against the Xiongnu. The Yuezhi, the emperor had learned from Xiongnu defectors, had no more love for the northern nomads than the Chinese. The Xiongnu had evicted them from their homeland in what is now Gansu province in western China, the skull of their slain king turned into a drinking vessel for the victors. The Yuezhi fled somewhere deep in the unknown lands to the west. If the Han could find these people and convince them to join the fight against the Xiongnu, the Chinese could squeeze the nomads in a pincer and gain an advantage in the coming conflict.

Zhang Qian, a palace courtier, volunteered for the mission. He was characterized by one writer of the period as "a man of great strength, determination, and generosity." Zhang "trusted others and in turn was liked by the barbarians."[38] His journey was destined to be a perilous one. Not only did he have no idea where the Yuezhi might have gone, Zhang would have to chart a trail through an unfamiliar region hostile in terrain, climate, and people—the route would take him through Xiongnu-controlled territory. But like all great explorers, Zhang was unfazed by the dangers. He set out with an escort of one hundred men.

Zhang didn't return for twelve years. When he finally stumbled into Chang'an, the Han capital (near modern Xi'an), only one other member of his original posse was with him. The journey he recounted to Han officials—probably quite surprised to see him—was certainly dramatic. Soon after departing the Han empire, he was captured by the Xiongnu and spent the next decade as their prisoner. He had become so settled that he took a Xiongnu wife. But he never forgot his imperial assignment, and as the Xiongnu became accustomed to his presence, they let down their guard, and Zhang was eventually able to escape and continue his search for the Yuezhi.

He eventually located them, in the area of modern Afghanistan. But the Yuezhi had no stomach for another encounter with the Xiongnu, and refused Zhang's proposed alliance. (In one of those great "what ifs" of history, the Chinese pathfinder had just missed the Greek kings of the area, leftover from the conquests of Alexander the Great in the fourth century BC. The Yuezhi had recently expelled them and taken over the region for themselves.) Though he failed in his chief purpose, Zhang's odyssey turned out to be one of the most important feats of exploration in the ancient world. The information he gathered about an entirely new—and surprisingly advanced—society in Central Asia had a profound impact on

China. Before he limped home, the Chinese had been comfortable in their ignorance, perceiving themselves as a superior civilization, surrounded by barbarians who were either adopting more cultured Chinese ways or, like the Xiongnu, were simply beyond the pale. But Zhang Qian gave notice that the Chinese weren't the only civilization out there. China wasn't alone.

In his search for the Yuezhi, Zhang discovered other peoples who lived in cities, cultivated farms, and had cultures all their own. He learned of "Shendu," or India, where "the inhabitants ride elephants when they go into battle"; and Mesopotamia, home to "great birds which lay eggs as large as pots" and "people [who] are very skillful at performing tricks that amuse the eye." Even more startling, in "Anxi," or the Parthian empire in Iran, "the people keep records by writing horizontally on strips of leather"— and not in Chinese characters, either. Who could have imagined! In the vibrant marketplaces in Afghanistan, the locals shopped for goods traded from all around the region.[39] From the viewpoint of these societies in Central Asia, the Chinese weren't in the center of anything.

At the Han court, Zhang's findings were a revelation. The emperor learned of "all great states rich in unusual products whose people cultivated the land and made their living in much the same way as the Chinese," one contemporary writer recorded. The ever-expansive Emperor Wu took more than academic interest in this new world. "If it were only possible to win over these states by peaceful means, the emperor thought, he could then extend his domain 10,000 *li*, attract to his court men of strange customs who would come translating and retranslating their languages, and his might would become known to all the lands within the four seas."[40] (A *li* is a Chinese unit for measuring distance. In modern usage one li is equivalent to about 500 meters, which means the 10,000 li mentioned here is about 5,000 kilometers, or 3,100 miles.)

An opportunity to pursue this policy emerged in 121 BC. A Xiongnu chief and his army of forty thousand surrendered to the Han, turning over a strategic piece of real estate on the western frontier to Chinese control. That cracked open the door to Central Asia by clearing a safe passageway between the Han domains and the lands to its west, which the Chinese referred to simply as the

"Western Regions." In a memorial to the throne, Zhang eagerly advocated for a forward policy, as we'd call it today. He proposed using some Han gold to lure a people called the Wusun, who resided in what is today northwestern China, into an alliance. "If we could get them to obey us, it would be like cutting off the right arm of the Xiongnu," Zhang prognosticated. After that, "the other countries to the west could all be persuaded to come to court and acknowledge themselves our foreign vassals."[41]

His ego sufficiently stroked, Emperor Wu was sold on the strategy. In 115 BC, Zhang was on the dusty tracks west again, this time with a larger escort, and heaps of gold and silk to present as gifts from the Han emperor to the rulers of Central Asia. He likely reached what is today northern Xinjiang province, where he found the Wusun. However, they, like the Yuezhi, were unconvinced of the value of a Han partnership. In fact, the Wusun leadership initially treated Zhang with great disrespect. "Zhang Qian was greatly outraged," one text recounts, "and, knowing that the barbarians were greedy, said, 'The Son of Heaven has sent me with these gifts, but if you do not prostrate yourself to receive them, I shall have to take them back!'"[42] Still, Zhang's second mission bore fruit. He had dispatched envoys throughout inner Asia, and they returned to Chang'an accompanied by delegations from various Central Asian kingdoms, to the great delight of Emperor Wu.

But the Chinese were far from satisfied with their newfound friends. The rulers of inner Asia were not sufficiently deferential to the great Son of Heaven. "The states to the west all relied on their remote situation and retained an air of arrogance and calm; they could not be won over by a sense of suitable conduct nor managed by the establishment of ties," Sima Qian's records recount. The fact was that they didn't respect Han power. While the western peoples were happy to trade for silk and other Chinese luxuries, this was an area under the sway of the Xiongnu. Thus when a Xiongnu ambassador rode through the region, he was feted with food and fresh horses; their Han counterparts had to purchase everything they needed. As Sima Qian bluntly put it, the Central Asian states "were more afraid of the Xiongnu than of the Han envoys."[43]

That, of course, would not do. Obviously, these faraway kingdoms had not yet realized that the Son of Heaven stood above all others. Relations between the Han and other states could only exist on the basis of Chinese superiority. The problem demanded more decisive—and aggressive—action. Emperor Wu decided a little "shock and awe" was necessary, and he dispatched an army out west in 108 BC to conquer the states in what is today northern Xinjiang province. These kingdoms were independent but under the thumb of the Xiongnu. The Han forces first conquered a state called Loulan, then lurched northward to the area around the modern oasis outpost of Turpan, and defeated two more there. The Xiongnu, fully aware of the danger of getting cut off from the area's rich urban centers, fought back, and the region became a key battleground between the Xiongnu and Han for decades. But the Han campaigns extended the Chinese empire farther to the west than it had ever reached before.

The Han victories further widened and secured a highway deeper into Central Asia, and an opportunity arose to capitalize on it a few years later. Emperor Wu had become enamored with the excellent horses of Central Asia—he called them "heavenly horses"—and he heard from his emissaries to the region that Ferghana (in today's Uzbekistan) had especially fine specimens. So he sent envoys to the main state there, which the Chinese records call Dayuan, with a thousand pieces of gold and a golden horse to offer to its king, in exchange for horses. The Dayuan ruler had no interest in the arrangement and turned the Chinese down flat. Amid the dispute, the Dayuan had the Han envoys killed.

How intolerable! These should-be vassals had to be put in their place! In 104 BC, Emperor Wu launched the most daring of his many military escapades. He sent a large force west with orders to teach the treacherous Dayuan about the true nature of imperial power. The commander's first attempt failed; his beleaguered force withered along the long route and came straggling back to Han territory. Some advisors at court urged Emperor Wu to call the expedition off and focus on the Xiongnu. But Wu wanted to send a message: don't trifle with the Han Dynasty. The general was ordered back with a bigger and better-provisioned army to try again two years later. After defeating a Dayuan army, the Han invaders besieged its capital city for forty days, cutting off its supply of water. Noblemen, fearing the worst, assassinated their own king and surrendered his severed head to the Han. After that, Emperor Wu surely secured a steady supply of "heavenly horses."

We have to appreciate how incredible an achievement the Dayuan campaign was for its day. The Han were able to project military power over an amazing distance at an age when transport moved not much more quickly than a fast-paced walk, and through inhospitable regions with nothing even close to modern infrastructure. Tens of thousands of Han troops first traversed the arid deserts of western China, then the life-threatening passes through the Tianshan mountains, before enduring a further march into Central Asia—an astounding 1,500 miles from the Han's western frontier (as the crow flies).

The victory in Ferghana elevated China into a major force deep in Asia's interior. After the defeat of Dayuan, "all of the states of the Western Regions were shocked and frightened," one Han-era history boasts. "Most states sent envoys to present tribute to the Han."[44] In 60 BC the Han established an office called the Protector General of the Western Regions, whose occupant was to keep the assorted states of Central Asia in line. To solidify its hold on the area, the Han government formed colonies of about five hundred soldier-farmers each, scattered across what is now far west China. These outposts proved especially useful in protecting and provisioning the now regular embassies the Han court sent west into Central Asia, some of them long caravans of a hundred people. The Han believed the Son of Heaven was a universal monarch; they were striving to match ideology with reality.

=

Even that, however, wasn't enough to satiate Emperor Wu. No point on the compass was left undisturbed by Han foot soldiers. In the southeast, an independent state known as the Southern Yue dominated the area that is now Guangdong and Guangxi provinces and northern Vietnam. The First Emperor of the Qin had tried to conquer the region, at one point sending an army supposedly five hundred thousand strong, but when the Qin tottered, a local military leader named Zhao Tuo took advantage to carve out his own kingdom in 204 BC. The Han Dynasty then sent a prominent official to Southern Yue to convince Zhao Tuo to submit to the empire.

He did, but as it turned out, only superficially. Zhao Tuo maintained a remarkable degree of independence from his domineering northern neighbor—even, at one point, claiming the title "emperor" like his Han counterpart. Relations between the two governments alternated between sweet and sour over much of the second century BC. One moment, the Han sent armies to support Southern Yue against an aggressive rival; another moment, the Han were sending armies to overrun Southern Yue itself. The turning point came in 113 BC, when the empress in Southern Yue, who just happened to be from the Chinese heartland, sent a memorial to the Han court in the name of her young son, recently installed on the throne, offering to submit to the empire's administrative control. That sparked a coup by Southern Yue's powerful prime minister, who was determined to keep the state independent. He assassinated both the empress and the youngster-king, and placed the unfortunate royal's stepbrother on the throne. When the Han sent a force of two thousand men to keep the peace in Southern Yue, the prime minister attacked and slaughtered them.

That would have been a risky move under any circumstances, but with the short-fused Emperor Wu lording over Chang'an, it was a death sentence. The emperor sent an army of one hundred thousand to conquer Southern Yue in 111 BC. They burned the capital city, the prime minister and king fled, and the Southern Yue kingdom vanished forever.

After that victory, Emperor Wu turned his gaze to the region next door in what is today Yunnan province. The Han had eyed the region for some time. More than two decades earlier, a Han magistrate visited the Southern Yue court, where he was served a certain type of berry sauce that, it turned out, was shipped in by river through Yunnan from the Sichuan area to the northwest. That piqued the magistrate's interest. If berry sauce could travel that way, so could troops. Better to secure the Yunnan region than have a problem later. He suggested to his superiors that the Chinese place guard posts along the river route to control it.

It was Emperor Wu, of course, who acted. The king of the main power in the region, the state of Dian, apparently feeling secure in his remote jungle bastion, rebuffed Han bullying and insisted on remaining independent. Not for long, however. In 109 BC, a Han army sent to Dian quickly changed the king's mind. "The whole affair of Han relations with the southwestern barbarians came about because someone saw some . . . berry sauce," Sima Qian noted sardonically.[45]

At about the same time, Emperor Wu was further justifying his name—which means "Martial Emperor"—in the east as well. In 109 BC, the Han launched a two-pronged invasion of the Korean peninsula—one by land, one by sea—on the pretext that it had become a shelter for Chinese deserters. One year later, the Han forces had coerced local rulers to surrender, and four administrative districts were set up to govern the northern part of the peninsula. Han officials controlled at least as far south as present-day Pyongyang, where they formed a Chinese colony.

=

By the time of Emperor Wu's death, in 87 BC, the Han had become a colossal empire. Stretching from the Korean peninsula in the east, to the desert oasis of Xinjiang in the west, to northern Vietnam in the south, Emperor Wu's creation enveloped far, far more territory than the Chinese had ever controlled before.

But even the mighty Chinese empire could digest only so much, and the voracious Emperor Wu had overloaded the government's plate. The court discovered that holding on to all of its compass-bending conquests was as hard as conquering them in the first place. In Korea, the Chinese started losing their grip almost immediately. By 82 BC, two of the administrative units there were abolished. Then came local competition. The native Koguryo Dynasty formed during the first half of the first century AD around the Yalu River, and in 106 AD, it pushed the Chinese off the peninsula. It became clear that Korea was never going to be part of China. Meanwhile, in the Western Regions, the court's approach to the vast expanse ebbed and flowed with the emperors' appetites for foreign exploits, and the size of their wallets—the cost of maintaining the Han presence was enormous. One moment, the Han again had armies campaigning and conquering through the Western Regions; the next, the court pulled back from the area almost entirely. Clearly, there was only so much of "all under Heaven" the emperors could swallow.

The real-life burdens of being the Son of Heaven clashed with his ideological responsibilities. Though thanks to explorer Zhang Qian, the Chinese had become well aware that they shared the world with other great civilizations, their sense of exceptionalism had not wavered (and would prove amazingly resilient). Chinese intellectuals held firm to the belief that their culture was superior, and their emperor was a world sovereign who could never rub elbows with those ordinary kings and chiefs. If the Son of Heaven was just another ruler among many, then the entire philosophical legitimization of imperial rule was shaky. Yet even the rich Chinese empire did not possess the money or manpower to literally lift the Son of Heaven above all. My oh my, what a mess.

If the Son of Heaven could not command "all under Heaven" with troops and administrators, then he'd have to lord over it symbolically. Foreign leaders were expected to come in person—or send admirable representatives—bearing tribute to the Han emperor to acknowledge his superior status. The tribute they brought to Chang'an was a cornucopia of exotica—jade, wine, precious stones, rare animals, and, of course, horses; such gifts were local specialties in the varied states of Central Asia, but choice rarities in the Chinese capital. Foreign states that showed the proper deference were considered dependent vassals by the Chinese court. Their affairs were monitored and sometimes Chinese officials were appointed to positions within these foreign governments. Rulers and officers of vassal states were usually confirmed as rightful authorities by the emperor and awarded Chinese titles—a process known as "investiture"—which often came with certain duties. By around the time of Christ, the Han had bestowed 376 titles on rulers of Central Asian states alone. Sometimes rulers sent their sons to the Chinese court as a sort of insurance policy for good behavior. (In 94 AD, for instance, fifty states in the Western Regions shipped such princely hostages to the Chinese capital.) "Overawed by military strength and attracted by wealth, none did not present strange local products as tribute and his beloved sons as hostages," boasted one historian describing the later Han period. "They bared their heads and kneeled down toward the east to pay homage to the Son of Heaven."[46]

For the Han court, the more embassies that came, and the greater the distance they traveled, the more virtuous the emperor became, and the more glorious his reign. In Confucian thinking, winning the voluntary loyalty and obedience of foreign peoples showed the greatness of the Son of Heaven more than any military victories. The Confucians were, generally speaking, pacifist in their outlook. True sage-kings have no need to conquer others with violence; to earn the loyalty of foreign princes, they required nothing more than benevolence. "If remoter people are not submissive, all the influences of civil culture and virtue are to be cultivated to attract them to be so; and when they have been so attracted, they must be made contented and tranquil," Confucius advised in the *Analects*.[47] "When one by force subdues men, they do not submit to him in heart," the Confucian thinker Mencius added. "When one subdues men by virtue, in their hearts' core they are pleased, and sincerely submit."[48]

Being a vassal of China was, in many respects, more a matter of style than substance. Foreign rulers who recognized Chinese suzerainty were generally left to their own affairs, to govern their realms with minimal Chinese interference, if any at all. (However, as we'll see later, sometimes the emperors could be overbearing overlords.) Yet the process wasn't a meaningless stage show, or a ritual pleasantry to boost imperial ego. It sometimes allowed the Chinese dynasties to wield real power over their vassals. The titles and royal seals conferred upon subordinate rulers offered them a form of legitimacy, which gave the threat of withdrawing those honors sharp teeth. The Han and future dynasties were sometimes able to influence who ruled or emerged from local political squabbles. (On occasion, the Chinese even sent military aid to rescue a beleaguered vassal.)

It might seem odd, even bewildering, that independent rulers would choose to subordinate themselves to another when they were not forced to do so. Yet they came, a steady stream of ambassadors kneeling to the Son of Heaven. Even during Han times, some endured lengthy journeys at tremendous personal risk—crisscrossing blistering deserts and ice-encrusted mountains, from places almost certainly out of the range of Han armies or the acquisitive gaze of the emperors. What motivated them, for the most part, was not fear, but rather tangible self-interest. In return for tribute, the Han court dispensed lavish gifts as a sign of favor and a display of the emperor's noble generosity. Gold, silk, and other luxuries were handed over in copious quantities—financial support that a local potentate could use to bolster his own position at home. It was only proper, of course, for the magnanimous Son of Heaven to give more than he received; the exchange of gifts created something of a courtly trade deficit. Add in the private commerce that embassies were allowed to conduct with Chinese merchants while in the empire, and tribute missions could be lucrative outings. Basically, tributary states chose access to China over diplomatic equality. The profits earned, the prestige gained, made a little symbolic groveling well worth it.

For the Han, receiving the allegiance of so many other rulers elevated the Chinese empire to supreme status in East Asia. But it also proved fantastically expensive for the Han court. On top of the ample gifts given, the emperor found himself doling out financial assistance to his vassals. The bills became so onerous that on occasion the Han court suspended the incoming missions simply to save cash. If the Son of Heaven wished his glory to spread across the world, he'd have to pay for it. "Envoys from the Western Regions will follow one another making endless demands for aid," one court official lamented in 119 AD. "To meet them is beyond our means, but to reject them will surely cause alienation."[49]

For that and other reasons, not all comers were treated the same way. Some foreign states were so remote from the Han that expecting them to fulfill the duties of full-fledged vassals was too burdensome. The Han did not wish to be bound to the responsibilities (and bills) imposed by such a relationship, either. For instance, sending punitive expeditions to discipline a wayward but far-off tributary was impractical and purse-emptying. What to do? The Han decided to keep a "loose rein" on such outliers—neither binding them to the court as tributaries, nor severing the relationship entirely. If a foreign chief managed to make his way to the Chinese court, he'd be entertained lavishly. But other than that, relations would remain cordial, but somewhat distant.

This process of tribute and ceremony was a core aspect of a distinctly Chinese foreign policy. Of course, the international affairs of imperial China were not consistent over its 2,100-year history; nor were all peoples treated identically at all times. Still, embedded within this Chinese-style statecraft were principles that shaped the Chinese view of their place in the world. Chinese foreign affairs were based on unequal relationships with other states. Only if foreigners accepted and acknowledged the superiority of China could they engage in peaceful diplomacy with the empire. The Chinese thus saw the world as a hierarchy, with themselves firmly at its apex. In real life, however, China's relations with other peoples were not necessarily so "unequal"—the so-called vassals could hold considerable leverage—but at least in official terms, the emperors considered all as subordinates. Those relations operated entirely on Chinese terms and on Chinese rules. Those rulers who would not abide by the norms imposed by the Chinese were excluded, and thus denied the wealth and grandeur of China. What the Han had started to forge was a Chinese world system, with China at the center and operating as the Chinese saw fit.

=

As Chinese contacts with the west intensified, they learned about a place they called Ta-qin, or Great Qin. It was the Roman Empire. In most cases, Chinese writers did not describe other countries favorably—they were home to barbarians, after all. But the Chinese were suitably impressed by what they heard of Rome—maybe because they thought the Romans resembled themselves. "It contains over four hundred cities, and of dependent states there are several times ten," one fifth-century AD text about the later Han period described. "They cut the hair of their heads, wear embroidered clothing, and drive in small carriages covered with white canopies; when going in or out they beat drums, and hoist flags, banners, and pennants. . . . The inhabitants of that country are tall and well-proportioned, somewhat like the Chinese. . . . The country contains much gold, silver, and rare precious stones, . . . They are honest in their transactions, and there are no double prices."[50]

Obviously, these were a civilized bunch worth getting to know. In 97 AD, a Han general sent an emissary named Gan Ying to make contact with the Romans. He got as far as the Persian Gulf, intending to board a ship to the Great Qin, until Persian sailors warned him the journey could take as long as two years. "There is something in the sea which is apt to make man homesick, and several have thus lost their lives," they told the (apparently credulous) envoy. That was sufficient to scare him off.[51] Those crafty Persians clearly had a motive to keep the two great empires apart. Rome's "kings always desired to send embassies to China, but the Persians wished to carry on trade with them in Han silks, and it is for this reason that they were cut off from communication," a Chinese writer contended.[52]

Finally, in 166 AD, an embassy from Rome found its way to China, probably by sea. The representatives of Emperor Marcus Aurelius Antoninus turned up on the Vietnam coast, bearing gifts of ivory, rhinoceros horns, and tortoise shell. "From that time dates the direct intercourse with this country," one Chinese historian declared.[53]

Well, maybe. Even this ancient source casts doubt on whether this historic meeting between East and West actually happened. There is also some speculation that even if it did, the Roman emissaries were not ambassadors dispatched formally on an official mission, but traders from somewhere in the Roman domains who floated their way east. In fact, Han China may not even have known of Rome itself. Most likely, what the Chinese called Great Qin was just the eastern section of the Roman Empire, in the Middle East. The intermingling of the world histories of China and the West would have to wait.

Four

SUPERPOWER, SECURED

That Western houri with features like a flower—
She stands by the wine-warmer, and laughs with the breath of
spring, . . .
Dances in a dress of gauze!
"Will you be going somewhere, milord, now, before you are drunk?"

—poem by Li Bo

The unthinkable happened. In 311 AD, those Xiongnu, the arch-nemesis of Emperor Wu, massed at the gates of the city of Luoyang. The barbarians' cavalry had already caught the main Chinese army southeast of the city, ill prepared and poorly led, and massacred it to a man. That left Luoyang itself sparsely defended. The Xiongnu smashed through one of the gates quickly, but then its brave residents stiffened and fought as hard as they could against the barbarian onslaught. For two weeks, the desperate battles clogged the streets. But the outcome was inevitable. The Xiongnu overran the entire city and plundered its palaces and treasure-filled ancestral graves—a distressing affront in Chinese culture that so honors the deceased. The number of dead soared to the tens of thousands.

Then the Xiongnu burned Luoyang to the ground, and made off with their loot.

The destruction of Luoyang was a catastrophe beyond description, much like the Goths' sacking of Rome, but probably even worse. At the time, Luoyang was one of the world's great metropolises, home to six hundred thousand people, ranking second only to Rome. And, like its European competitor, its charms were innumerable and an inspiration to poets. Ban Gu, known for his verse as well as history, enshrined the wonders of the city in a famous first-century poem praising the city's sacrificial temple, linking Heaven and Earth, and "the royal academy surrounded by waters, a symbol of the spreading richness of virtue."[1]

The sickening loss of riches and residents had no-less-indigestible symbolism. Luoyang was at the heart of the heartland. The old Shang capital, with its hoard of oracle bones, was nearby. Luoyang was capital of the Zhou for five centuries and of the Han for two (after the court moved from Chang'an). Now the hated Xiongnu, those beasts in human form, had destroyed it, their stinking animals and mutton despoiling the promised land, the zhongguo. Where was Emperor Wu when you really needed him?

By the time of Luoyang's fall, however, the mighty Han were long gone. The venerable dynasty, its vitality dissipated in rebellions and palace intrigues, came to an end in 220 AD with the abdication of its final emperor. The problem for China was that there was no replacement ready to step in. The empire disintegrated into competing contenders, one consuming another. Dynasties shifted shapes and names in a barely decipherable smorgasbord of part-time kingdoms—Wei, Qi, Wu, Chen, Liang, even a Zhou tossed in for good measure, to note just a few. The era is somewhat euphemistically called the Period of Disunion, and it lasted a bloodcurdling 369 years.

The occupant of Luoyang at the time of the Xiongnu sack was the Jin Dynasty, which had managed to unify China in 280 AD, only to see the achievement crumble twenty years later in a scramble for power among competing princes. The civil war left China in tatters. "Many suffered from hunger," one old history recorded. "The rivers were filled with floating corpses; bleached bones covered the fields."[2] The bloodbath weakened the Jin and its ability to fend off the barbarians when they came carousing. The Xiongnu had been nursing grievances against the Jin for some time—one of the tribe's elite griped that the Chinese court "uses us as if we were slaves"[3]—and, taking advantage of the chaos, rose up in 304 and swept into central China. The Jin would survive the disaster at Luoyang, even though their emperor was captured and later executed by the Xiongnu. The dynasty reconstituted itself south of the Yangzi River in the town of Jiankang (modern Nanjing). Many remnants of the northern literati, with their Confucian texts and ancient rituals, reassembled to carry on the old court traditions. The city turned into a vibrant cultural and commercial center with some one million residents.

But to some, that was poor compensation. The Xiongnu were not the only barbarian interlopers to intrude on the beloved zhongguo; all sorts of steppe peoples infiltrated north China and erected a series of barbarian kingdoms with Chinese-sounding names. The heartland was lost to uncivilized horsemen and their smelly herds of sheep. Oh what a horror!

For the émigré northerners, sweating it out below the Yangzi, the south was a backward frontier, still inhabited by strange locals who were not "Chinese" in their background, language, or habits—other types of barbarians, perhaps not as threatening as the Xiongnu, but barbarians nonetheless. For many, the dream of returning to the north never faded; it was like a thorn in the paw, or a love unreciprocated. In a memorial to the Jin emperor in 362, a statesman and military commander named Huan Wen pleaded with the Jiankang court to reestablish the capital in Luoyang. In a military campaign north, he had managed to recapture the ruins of the storied city. "Ever since the powerful barbarians unleashed violence, China proper has fallen into chaos, (the people) have become desperate and dispossessed," he wrote. To him, the court had been forced out of the real China, to survive ignominiously in what was no better than a foreign land. If the Jin did not take advantage of this opportunity to move north once again, "we will forever root ourselves in the southern corner and abandon the divine provinces [of the north]. Even children . . . will cover their mouths and sigh."[4]

Many children must have sighed. The Jin's hold on Luoyang soon slipped, and the emperors settled in to their sweaty southern somnolence. Two more centuries would have to pass before north and south were unified once again under a Chinese dynasty. In the meantime, foreign rule became a fact of life in the central heartland. The time when Emperor Wu's armies were marching across the continent, and the Son of Heaven stood above, felt a distant fantasy indeed.

How far China had fallen.

=

Actually, not as far as it seemed. We can see why in the story of a Xiongnu chieftain named Liu Yuan.

It was Liu who rose up against the Jin, and whose son destroyed Luoyang. But Liu wasn't like the Xiongnu that Emperor Wu battled four centuries earlier. He and his tribe lived inside the empire, around modern-day Taiyuan, where they had been resettled by the Chinese government in the third century. Liu had spent time as an attendant in the court at Luoyang and received an education in the Confucian classics. As part of his strategy to conquer northern China, he claimed descent from the old Han emperors—his distant ancestor, after all, wed that royal Chinese princess, gifted to the Xiongnu chief—proclaimed himself "King of Han," and formed the Han Zhao Dynasty.

Liu never became "Chinese." He was unquestionably loyal to his Xiongnu brethren. But the pull of Chinese culture remained irresistible. The empire may have been in pieces, the heartland trod by barbarian hooves, government in disarray, but China remained East Asia's most brilliant culture. Like all great powers, China's clout rested on far more than the shoulders of soldiers or statesmen. China had a more powerful and much more enduring foundation for its superpower status: its civilization. Even during the "Period of Disunion," the prestige and appeal of Chinese philosophy, language, literature, governing institutions, and other aspects of its society rose above its political and military weaknesses, and continued to spread far and wide. By the end of that war-torn age, the basis of a Chinese order had taken shape in East Asia, even though there was no Emperor Wu around to enforce it. Modern political scientists call it "soft power," and no one in the region had more of it than the Chinese.

The advancement of Chinese civilization was taking place both inside and outside China's borders. The "China" of the time was not a culturally uniform place. (We can argue it still isn't!) The empire forged by the Qin and Han was still not "Chinese" in the sense we would understand today. Despite the centripetal practices introduced by those ruling houses—the deluge of bureaucrats, the standardized script, the miles and miles of roads—China was still a somewhat artificial amalgamation of different regions, peoples, and customs. If anything, imperial policy had inadvertently promoted such diversity, and not just through conquest. The Chinese concept of universal empire might have suffered a bloody nose in its slugfest with the Xiongnu, but the idea remained very much alive. Much like the contemporary Roman Empire—where you didn't have to be a Roman to be Roman—the Chinese of the Middle Kingdom maintained the belief that anyone could participate in their world if they only embraced their culture. During the Later Han period, the government actively encouraged assorted barbarians to settle within the empire and along its borders in an effort to quiet their often unruly tribal neighbors. Large numbers of a people known as the Qiang—precursors of the Tibetans—as well as diverse bands of tribesmen from the northern steppe moved into or near Chinese territory. The Han state treated them much like their Chinese subjects, hoping to turn them into taxpaying, soldiering members of the empire. Han generals were more than happy to employ these outsiders, known for their martial prowess and equestrian skills, often against more ornery nomadic tribes. (Thus the old Chinese saying: "Use barbarians to fight barbarians.") With the breakdown of centralized authority, and the invasions of Liu Yuan and other non-Chinese, China proper became even more diverse, ethnically and culturally.

Over time, however, the advanced culture of the zhongguo became more national. Like Liu Yuan, other northern barbarians adopted aspects of Chinese culture as they became more exposed to it and set up ruling regimes in north China. In the northeast, for instance, another tribe known as the Murong rose to prominence, in part by copying Chinese-style government. The result was something of a Chinese-barbarian fusion. The onetime nomads recruited Chinese administrators to manage agricultural production and military advisors to add Chinese infantry to the usual mounted forces of the steppe. In 308, Murong Hui, the chieftain and founder of the nascent state, declared himself "great chanyu," borrowing from the Xiongnu, but his successors in 337 formed the new state of Yan, resurrecting the name of one of the old Warring States, and in 353 declared themselves emperors.

These ruling houses of former steppe wanderers forged a hybrid Chinese-barbarian culture, too. One such member of the barbarian elite was buried in a lacquer coffin decorated with scenes from classic Chinese tales of dutiful sons—a staple theme of folk stories—all dressed in steppe nomad attire. The cultural mingling went in the other direction, too. The Chinese thinkers of old may have believed that the barbarians had little to offer the superior Chinese, but the infusion of foreign people and ideas into the zhongguo made the Chinese more receptive. Some of that was simply bowing to reality. Since steppe tribesmen and their descendants controlled the reins of power in north China for almost three hundred years, it was logical for the Chinese to start learning their tongues and customs to curry favor and appointments with the new rulers.

The most important of all foreign influences in China during this period was Buddhism. The teachings of the Buddha had traveled over the Central Asian trade routes from its Indian homeland into China probably in the later years of the Han Dynasty, and spread rapidly during the Period of Disunion. The import would become so influential in China that at times in the mid-first millennium it challenged homegrown Confucianism for primacy within royal courts. To some Chinese, the appeal of a foreign religion cast doubt on the assumed superiority of their own civilization. Maybe—just maybe—not all barbarians were truly barbarians. Knowledgeable foreigners were even afforded tremendous respect, especially those learned in Buddhist teachings. A Chinese eulogist for a deceased Central Asian Buddhist monk in the fourth century, for instance, made the very modern assessment that people of worth could come from anywhere. "The outstanding people of a generation may be born among the barbarians, while there are also those of exceptional talents among us here," he commented. "Therefore we know that eminence and greatness are granted by Heaven. How could this depend on being Chinese or 'barbarian'?"[5] The remarks are even more incredible since the deceased monk apparently didn't even speak Chinese! Yet the eulogist was echoing public opinion. If a foreign teaching like Buddhism could be so wonderful, then perhaps foreign nations could be as well. India, the birthplace of the Buddha, rose in stature in Chinese eyes. Chinese monks who made the dangerous journey to India were treated as heroes, such as Faxian, who returned to China carrying a library of sacred texts in the early fifth century.

Buddhism, though, was something of an anomaly. For the most part, Chinese culture proved an unstoppable force. Representative of this cultural effusion was what happened in China's south. There, the people of the zhongguo encountered locals they called Yue, a term used generically (like Rong or Di) to refer to the varied peoples who lived below the Yangzi River in what is now China's provinces of Guangdong, Fujian, Zhejiang, and Guangxi. These folks originally had more in common culturally with Southeast Asia than the Chinese heartland. The languages they spoke were probably closer to Vietnamese and Thai than Chinese. The states that formed in the area, though they got dragged into the incessant warfare of the later Zhou period, were never considered truly part of the Middle Kingdom. The Yue were yet another distant "other" with strange uncivilized ways—who "tattooed their bodies, cut their hair short, and cleared out weeds and brambles to set up small fiefs," in one description.[6] In other words, they were barbarians not that much more worthy than the nomads of the north.

Still, the Yue took on Chinese characteristics, too. That process accelerated once the region became firmly incorporated into the empire under Emperor Wu. Immigrants, officials, and soldiers flowed from north to south, bringing with them Chinese language, texts, and social practices. As the imperial bureaucracy spread its tentacles, it acted as a cultural transmission system. When the north got overrun by barbarians during the Period of Disunion, the terrified fled for safe havens below the Yangzi, mixing northerners and southerners together more than ever before. At first, the émigrés treated the Yue as barbarians, exploiting them as forced laborers and military conscripts, and expropriating their agricultural land. But there was intermingling as well, through intermarriage and business ties. By the end of the Period of Disunion, the southeast had apparently undergone a cultural transformation. Describing one major city in the area in the late sixth century, an imperial history noted that "shops were lined up in its market just like in the two (northern) capitals, and the people were a mixture from all directions, so that their customs were all rather similar."[7]

The transformative power of Chinese civilization couldn't be contained by China's usual borders, either. The ideal that China had a right to ascendancy over "all under Heaven" was based not so much on Chinese political or military power as it was on the strength of Chinese culture. The political elite still believed that the Son of Heaven should stand above all other rulers. Or, in the case of the Period of Disunion, "Sons of Heaven," since there was a multiplying of emperors and kings. So entrenched was this thinking that even the fractured mini-dynasties adopted the principles of imperial foreign affairs into their governing ideologies. In 472, the ruler of the Northern Wei, a kingdom founded by a partially Sinicized but non-Chinese steppe tribe in north China, informed the king of a Korean monarchy that "we look down upon the Four Seas as Lord, and govern all living things."[8]

Other peoples of East Asia accepted that China remained at the heart of East Asia.[9] Regional leaders still respected the varied Sons of Heaven as they had the unified Han. The Koguryo kingdom in Korea dispatched a remarkable eighty-six tribute missions to the Northern Wei. In many cases, local rulers sought titles from the Chinese monarchs as well. As early as the third century, a Japanese princess lobbied for Chinese recognition as a boon to her quest for political authority among the contentious tribes of Japan's islands. Then in the fifth century, thirteen missions arrived in China from the Yamato court of Japan seeking political support. The nascent states of Korea eagerly pursued the same. In 386, the ruler of the newly emerging kingdom of Paekche in southern Korea was invested as "deputy king" by the Eastern Jin, another of those alphabet soup monarchies of the Period of Disunion. Gaining Chinese approval bolstered the stature of these budding monarchs both at home and within the region—even if the Son of Heaven granting it was just one of many.

In fact, the new states of East Asia—especially in Korea and Japan—were to a great degree formed in China's image. After all,

China, even in disarray, was still the wealthiest and most literate and politically advanced society anywhere in view. That made China the sole model available to guide would-be sovereigns elsewhere in the region looking to form their own stable kingdoms. These states became Sinicized—independent of China, but very much like China.

The Korean peninsula had been influenced by China from an early stage because of Emperor Wu's conquest of the northern half. Chinese immigrants had moved in, hauling with them Chinese literature, language, and ceremonial practices. "The rural people eat and drink off of bamboo platters," records one Han Dynasty–era history, but "in the cities they are inclined to imitate officials and merchants from the inner (more Chinese) commanderies, and often use cups and utensils to eat."[10] The rise of Koguryo ensured Korean independence from China's empires, but didn't dissuade the Korean dynasty from copying them. Infusing Chinese methods of state-building into its government enhanced Koguryo's strength. Its court, for instance, introduced a Chinese-style law code and founded an imperial academy along the lines of Emperor Wu's in the late fourth century. Similar borrowing was taking place in the south of the peninsula, where the Chinese never extended their direct rule. In the southeast, the budding state of Silla started absorbing Chinese customs and institutions in the late fifth century—a penal and administrative code, posthumous titles for kings along Chinese lines, rites for mourning, and styles of court dress. In 545, the Silla ordered the compilation of a Chinese-style court history.

Binding these states together even more tightly was the Chinese writing system. For much of China's early history, its foreign neighbors were simply not writing at all, leaving Chinese texts as the sole source of information about them. It took a remarkably long time for many of these barbarians to catch up. But when they eventually did, they chose to write in Chinese characters. The earliest known written work that is undoubtedly Korean is in Chinese characters—an inscription on a stele found near the Yalu River that dates to 414 AD. That's a full 1,600 years after the Shang were scribbling on burnt bones and shells. The Japanese probably started writing roughly around the same time (likely with the aid of Korean scribes). The earliest writing yet discovered in Japan, also in

Chinese characters, is an inscription on a sword that dates from no earlier than the fifth century.

The choice to borrow Chinese characters may seem obvious—there was no other alternative writing system in sight. But it wasn't. The script was easy enough to adopt when writing in the Chinese language—which is what these societies first did. But later, when they tried jotting in their own languages, it proved quite awkward. Japanese, Korean, and Vietnamese derive from entirely different language groups than Chinese, and their oral pronunciation and grammar are distinct. But scholars in these three societies engaged in great efforts to make the characters fit the demands of their own tongues—the linguistic version of squeezing round pegs into square holes—and they persisted in using them long after these countries devised their own local alphabets.

Chinese script is what makes East Asia a region of the world, separated off from every other. It also firmly entrenched China at the cultural core of that Asian world. Unlike an alphabet, the letters of which can be reorganized in any way the sounds of a language require, Chinese characters represent words—and therefore, they inherently convey the ideas behind those words. Chinese characters bring with them the cultural lingo of Chinese civilization. As they spread throughout East Asia, so too did societal concepts—Chinese concepts—that created a common cultural foundation that bridged languages, ethnicity, and borders. There are certain characters that are used to convey the same meaning across Chinese, Japanese, Korean, and Vietnamese, even though they are pronounced differently in each. With the characters, then, came a tremendous amount of vocabulary borrowed from the Chinese and meshed into local languages. Most tellingly, one of those common terms is for "civilization," a character that is literally translated as "transformation caused by writing."

Chinese written script brought with it the Chinese language itself, which became the official mode of diplomatic and elite discourse across the East Asia region. The Chinese had little reason, of course, to concern themselves with unintelligible foreign tongues, so if those vassal kingdoms, barbarian tribes on the fringes of the empire, or anyone else wished to communicate with the Chinese rulers, they'd just have to do it in Chinese. In practice, this meant a large corpus of early documentation in Japan and Korea—the writings that form the main sources for their early histories—are not in their own languages, but in classical Chinese. And as scholars and court officials learned Chinese, they also began reading Chinese classical texts, which often became the basis of local education. The literate elite across East Asia was therefore steeped in the same history, philosophy, and cultural references read in the same books.

What began to emerge by the close of the Period of Disunion in the late sixth century was not only a more culturally cohesive China, but the framework of a region-wide Chinese world order. An East Asia, distinct from the rest of the world, was forming, with China firmly at its core.

=

The man who finally reunified China was the Duke of Sui. He was a senior court official at one of the barbarian kingdoms of the north, known as the Northern Zhou, in the late sixth century, and he typifies the sort of cultural and ethnic mixing and mingling that marked the Period of Disunion. The duke was not entirely Chinese, but rather was from an aristocratic part-Chinese, part-nomad family. In his politics, though, he was very Chinese. He aimed to re-create the institutions, grandeur, and broad geographic scale of the Han Dynasty, then defunct for more than 350 years.

The duke got his chance when an especially hapless Zhou emperor died in 580. He finagled his way into the job of regent for the child-heir, then a year later accepted the throne himself after, of course, the usual professions of inadequacy. The Mandate of Heaven, of course, pursues the man, not the other way around. Now emperor of the new Sui Dynasty, and known to history as Emperor Wen, he set about reunifying China, like all good Sons of Heaven are supposed to do.

The royal family he supplanted gave him a healthy head start, having already taken control over the entire north and Sichuan in the southwest. What remained to be conquered was the current southern dynasty, the Chen, based at Jiankang, just beneath the Yangzi. Emperor Wen left nothing to chance. In 588, he organized a million men into eight armies, lined them up along the river, and launched a coordinated assault on the Chen. For good measure, he tossed into the battle a flotilla of vessels, some a formidable five decks high and probably the largest ships on water anywhere in the world at the time. The Chen didn't stand a chance, and China was finally one again in 589.

Emperor Wen may have wished to re-create the Han, but instead, his empire much more closely resembled the Qin. Like the Qin, the Sui also forged institutions that would become standard features of imperial rule, most notably the civil service examination system. The Sui started the process of regularizing exams to recruit government officials in an effort to promote bureaucrats who were more talented—and more loyal to the central government. Candidates could attain different degrees, one of which, the *jinshi*, would come to signify the highest accolade of academic excellence. Under later dynasties, the system would become even more extensive and standardized, and blossomed into the primary route to state employment. By opening the exams to anyone (or, more accurately, any man), the exams offered an avenue of social mobility for poor families unmatched in Europe until modern times.

Also like the Qin, the Sui were known for their engineering genius. The First Emperor built the original Great Wall; the Sui, the equally impressive and undoubtedly more productive Grand Canal. Emperor Wen and his son and successor, Emperor Yang, oversaw the construction of a series of canals and conduits that stretched 1,200 miles, linking the port town of Hangzhou below the Yangzi with the urban centers of the northern plain. The project, one of the age's greatest feats of human ingenuity, did more than any other to knit together the never-quite-integrated north and south—the cultural heartland of the zhongguo with the commercially critical southern rice paddies and coastal ports. In that respect, the Sui were truly among China's greatest unifiers.

But also like the Qin, the Sui were short-lived, surviving a mere two emperors and thirty-seven years. And their brevity had many of the same causes. Emperor Wen, like the First Emperor, might have had grand vision and relentless energy, but he also possessed a penchant for cruelty, only too quick to send enemies and critics to their deaths. His son Yang was even worse, if you believe the old histories—which could be colored to fit the Confucian theme that last emperors must be bad emperors. Emperor Yang was accused of

murder, fooling around with his father's concubines—a serious offense in Chinese eyes—and other tyrannical horrors. What cannot
be denied, though, is how the ambitious Sui strained the empire to
the breaking point, with millions pulled from their farms to dig its
canals or fight in its never-ending wars, the most demoralizing of
which was the failed attempts to crush Koguryo. In 618, Yang was
assassinated by the son of a Sui general. The Sui Dynasty, like the
Qin, disintegrated under the weight of its own sins. A host of Son
of Heaven hopefuls rose in its place. The Sui reunification looked
like a false dawn, another brief respite to the Period of Disunion.

Instead, it marked the beginning of one of China's most golden
of ages.

＝

Li Yuan bided his time, commanding a frontier garrison in Taiyuan
in north-central China, as the Sui fell apart around him. Much like
the Sui royal family, to which he was related by marriage, Li was of
mixed Chinese-nomad heritage, a man of the borderlands. And like
the Sui, he had grand ambitions for himself, and China. In 617, Li
made his move, marching on the Sui capital, Chang'an, overcoming
half-hearted resistance, and installing a new emperor, one of Yang's
sons. But it was clear that the Sui had lost the Mandate of Heaven,
and a year later, Li did what the founders of new dynasties do: he
submitted to the will of Heaven, voiced by the calls of the people,
and took over the job of emperor for himself. He was the duke of
Tang, and his new empire was the Tang Dynasty. He was given the
name of Emperor Gaozu, like the progenitor of the Han Dynasty
eight centuries earlier.

The Tang has no equal in China's incredibly long history. It represented the pinnacle of Chinese cultural, political, and military influence. The Han Dynasty was great; other, powerful emperors would
come. But the Tang, at its height, was the empire's empire, a land of
tremendous wealth, artistic excellence, and military majesty recognized at the time throughout much of the world. At no other period
was China more engaged with the world, more open, more cosmopolitan. The Tang gave "all under Heaven" an entirely new meaning.

But that was to come. First, Li the upstart had to press his claim
to the Mandate and piece his empire together. He was far from the

only dignitary with imperial designs as the Sui dissolved, and much of his reign—from 618 to 626—was spent stitching China back together, by force. China was pacified by 628, though not entirely unified. Magnates who had gained authority in local areas during the chaos accepted Tang suzerainty, but nominally.

The bigger threat, however, came once again from the north. Just as the Han founder was quickly confronted by steppe aggressors, so too was the Tang progenitor. The nemesis of the Han days, the Xiongnu, had vanished from the scene, dispersed or absorbed; the new northern villains were the Turks. Ironically, Li Yuan was compelled to become a vassal of the *qaghan* (or khan) of the Eastern Turks during his initial quest for imperium. Fearful of a Turk attack in his rear as he marched on Chang'an, and needing all the help he could muster, Li in 617 made an offer to the Turks—lend support, or just stand by, and the rewards would be generous. He informed the qaghan that he had assembled an army to restore order to China and sought friendship with the Turks. "If (you send soldiers to) follow me, and if they do not harm common people, such spoils from my expeditions as prisoners of war, women, jade, and silks will all belong to you." Otherwise, if "[you] instead allow friendship and communication (between us) you will still receive treasures without fighting a single battle."[11]

The Turks, though, wanted more: Li's submission. At first, Li rejected the demand. But the realities of his situation soon forced him to change his mind. His soldiers badly required horses for the campaign—a necessity the Turks possessed in untold quantities. Li took a title granted him by the Turks, and in return, they supported him with two thousand horses for his advance on Chang'an.

However, the Turks and the Tang weren't friendly for long. The qaghan was all too happy to aid Li Yuan and other Chinese imperial pretenders as part of a wider strategy to keep China divided, and thus too weak to challenge Turkish power on the steppe or refuse demands for tribute. But when it became clear that the plan backfired, and their onetime supplicant Li Yuan was rebuilding the Chinese empire, they changed tactics, first switching their support to anti-Tang rebels, then raiding into central China to destabilize the new regime. Li Yuan's son and successor, Emperor Taizong, found a Turk army on the outskirts of Chang'an only a short time

唐太宗 李世民

Emperor Taizong of the Tang Dynasty ushered in a golden age of Chinese power, wealth, and global influence.

Pictures from History / Bridgeman Images

after claiming the throne in 626. He bravely rode out in person with a mere six attendants to parlay with the qaghan of the Eastern Turks, known as Xieli. "I shall . . . show my disdain toward them by going to the front alone wearing no armor," he assured one royal advisor worried about the emperor's safety.[12] The real purpose of his mission, however, was not defiance. He likely paid off the qaghan to save the capital, not all that different than what the Han founder, Gaozu, had done to hold off the Xiongnu at the start of that dynasty.

Taizong, though, was not the type to swallow his pride. Exhibiting an odd combination of tolerance, sagacity, determination, and ruthlessness—he deposed his father and killed two brothers to claim the throne—he became an ardent expansionist with a passion for conquest and a desire to match, if not even exceed, the far-flung boundaries reached by the Han Dynasty. As a result, Taizong is considered the towering figure of the Tang, who rebuilt Chinese political and military power in East Asia and ruled over one of its most enlightened and prosperous periods.

His powerlessness before the Turks, therefore, badly rankled. His father "became a vassal to Xieli for the sake of the common people," he commented. "How could I not feel bitter about this? How could I not resolve to subdue the Turks? Before achieving this goal, I could neither sit peacefully nor have an appetite for food."[13] Much as Emperor Wu had done to the Xiongnu seven hundred years earlier, Taizong switched from conciliation to confrontation as soon as his new dynasty strengthened. He chose his moment wisely. The winter of 627–628 on the windswept steppe was especially cold, decimating the nomads' all-important herbs, and Xieli's authority was undercut by defections and dissension (deftly encouraged by a crafty Taizong). In the autumn of 629, Taizong launched his offensive, taking Xieli completely by surprise while he camped at a town called Dingxiang. The nomad chieftain was forced to flee for his life and sue for peace. A cease-fire was arranged while talks got under way. But Taizong's generals planned a secret attack anyway, catching the Turks off guard again in the spring of 630 and slaughtering ten thousand of them. Xieli managed an escape, but the battle effectively destroyed the Eastern Turks as a political and military force. Most of the lesser chiefs submitted to Taizong, leaving the Tang in uncontested mastery over the Turks. Taizong was an unusually lenient victor. "Those of their chieftains and leaders who came to submit were all appointed to be generals, generals of the palace gentlemen, and other officers," recorded one Tang history. "More than one hundred of them were arrayed at court as officials above the fifth rank, and as a result several thousand families of Turks came to dwell in Chang'an."[14] How magnanimous was the Son of Heaven! Taizong also accepted the title "Heavenly Qaghan" and justified it by reasserting the universal nature of the Chinese sovereign. Taizong had broken down completely the distinction between what was Chinese and barbarian. "Since antiquity, everyone has honored the Chinese and looked down on barbarians. I alone love them as one. Therefore their tribes follow me like a father or mother."[15]

Taizong then turned his attention further west. In his quest to match the Han, he coveted the old Western Regions—modern

Xinjiang—that Emperor Wu had invaded in his war with the Xiongnu, but which the Chinese had long since abandoned. By the time of the Tang, the area was dominated by another, muscular nomadic confederation called the Western Turks. Again, Taizong's timing was fortunate. Like their eastern compatriots, the Western Turks were embroiled in internal political disputes and tribal conflicts, allowing some oasis-states to break away from Turk control and offer their loyalty to the Tang. Taizong sped matters along in 640 by destroying the somewhat Sinicized Central Asian state of Gaochang, which was located in the area of modern-day Turpan. Gaochang had dared to partner with the Turks, attack a Tang ally, and harass foreign embassies heading for China. (Gaochang's overconfident king should have heeded a little rhyme passing among his subjects that warned of just such a disaster: "The troops of Gaochang are like frost and snow, and those of the Tang, like the sun and the moon. When the sun and the moon shine on frost and snow, they soon melt.")[16] Tang armies took hold of all the major oasis towns, as far west as the famed market hub of Kashgar (near the modern border with Pakistan). Then, in 648, one major Western Turk leader, Ashina Helu, submitted to the Tang, expanding Chang'an's influence north of the Tianshan mountains. Taizong passed away in 649, thinking he had recreated Han dominance of the Western Regions.

However, the Tang had to expend more effort, and blood, to firm its grip. Three years after his submission, Ashina Helu defected, shifted further west to the valley of the Ili River (which flows in northwest China and southern Kazakhstan), defeated local Turkish tribes there, and declared himself a new qaghan. The new emperor, Taizong's son Gaozong, was determined to squash the threat; in 657, he ordered a fresh campaign into Central Asia and dispatched two armies after Ashina Helu. Copying his father's tactics, Gaozong also sowed divisions among the Turk chieftains. In a decisive battle along the Irtysh River (the course of which runs from northwest China into Siberia), the outnumbered Tang forces killed or captured tens of thousands of Turks when Ashina Helu sent his cavalry hurtling toward Chinese soldiers who were well-prepared with long spears. The qaghan fled west, with the Tang on his heels, pressing the pursuit through heavy snow. "This is the best chance for us to render an outstanding service to the court," the Tang commander told his cold and weary horsemen to steel their endurance.[17] Ashina Helu got as far as a town near today's Tashkent (in Uzbekistan), where local officials arrested him and handed him over to the Tang. That was the end of the Western Turks. Tang influence was extended across Central Asia and Afghanistan, all the way to the Persian border—the farthest west Chinese imperial power would ever stretch. The Tang restored China as a political and military superpower.

In fact, the Tang emperors could even boast they had outdone the indomitable Emperor Wu. Chinese troops stomped all the way to India. Harsha, the emperor of a large realm in northern India in the early seventh century, had sent embassies to Chang'an, and Taizong thought it only proper to return the favor. In 643, the court sent a military officer named Wang Xuance with a delegation to Harsha, and that went so well that five years later, Wang was sent back, with an even more impressive coterie. In his absence, however, Harsha had died, his empire was falling apart, and the traditionalists who had gained control were wary of Chinese meddling. Wang and his party were robbed and detained, and he fled for his life to Tibet.

The Tibetans and the Tang were usually at odds, but Wang was fortunate to arrive during a brief detente. Infuriated by his ill treatment in India, Wang demanded the Tibetan ruler lend him troops to avenge the affront—no one, but no one treats an emissary of the great Tang so rudely! The Tibetans agreed, and Wang marched back to India, over the Himalayas, with a joint Sino-Tibetan army. He restored the honor of the Chinese empire by defeating the Indian forces, capturing the man who usurped Harsha's throne, and hauling him back to Chang'an. In remembrance of the exploit, a statue of the rogue Indian leader was erected at Taizong's tomb.

The Tang also surpassed Emperor Wu in the northeast, on the Korean peninsula. Initially, the Tang court tried to keep the peace with the fierce Koguryo state. In 624, Li Yuan, the Tang founder, sent a Daoist priest to the Koguryo court, where Daoism was gaining popularity, as a goodwill gesture (and to spread some of that invaluable Chinese "soft power"). But Chang'an's friendly stance didn't last long. Taizong and his advisors still considered Koguryo a strategic threat and an impediment to re-creating the geographic scale of the Han Dynasty. A coup against the Koguryo king in 642 offered both a pretext and an opportunity; three years later, when

Taizong launched a two-pronged attack on Koguryo, he claimed to be punishing an illegitimate and unpopular usurper, while at the same time hoping to exploit the political discord in Korea in the same way he had with the Turks. In a highly unusual decision, Taizong joined the main army in person, so critical did he consider the destruction of Koguryo.

Even the emperor's personal presence, however, was not enough to salvage the campaign. After some initial successes, Taizong's army got bogged down in front of the mountain fortress town of Anshi (now Yingchengzi in China's Liaoning province). Though Taizong decimated a large Koguryo force sent to relieve the city, he couldn't overcome the stout defenders bottled up inside Anshi, who parried every Tang attempt to breach its defenses. When the Tang army constructed a man-made hill overlooking the city walls, Koguryo soldiers burst from a gate to overrun the structure, entrenched themselves, and fought off repeated Chinese efforts to retake it. With the weather worsening, supplies running low, and a second army, sent to the peninsula by sea, stalled outside of Pyongyang, the Koguryo capital, Taizong was left little choice but to abandon the campaign. As he retreated from the unconquered walls of Anshi, an impressed Taizong left the town's unrelenting commander one hundred bolts of silk as a sign of his respect.

The task of subduing Koguryo fell to the equally acquisitive Gaozong. The Korean kingdom of Silla, in the peninsula's southeast, had been agitating for Tang intervention on its behalf for some time, against Koguryo and Paekche, located in the southwest, both of which had been chomping at its borders. Silla envoys were skilled at stressing their deference to Tang superiority, as well as the threat Koguryo and Paekche posed to the survival of such a loyal vassal state. Without aid from the Tang, "our hope of scaling big mountains and crossing vast seas to offer tributes to China will be forever dashed," one Silla royal pled during an embassy to Chang'an.[18] The strategic importance of Silla was not lost on the Tang court. With Silla's cooperation, Koguryo would be forced to fight a two-front war, north and south—one that even its stubborn leadership could not win.

The first victim of this Tang-Silla alliance was the more vulnerable Paekche. In 660, the Tang threw 120,000 soldiers and 1,900 warships across the Yellow Sea at Paekche, while a Silla army invaded from the south. Squeezed between these jaws, the Paekche capital fell quickly. (Not even a naval armada sent by Japan, a close friend of Paekche, could save the Korean kingdom. The fleet was encircled and burned by Chinese warships.) After overcoming some stiff resistance from Paekche rebels, Tang and Silla were poised to turn their attention to the real prize, Koguryo.

The Tang were able to take advantage of a rare moment of weakness in otherwise unflappable Koguryo. In 666, the Koguryo strongman died, his sons bickered over the succession, and one of them called upon the Tang for support. Gaozong didn't let this opportunity slip. In 667, he sent an army against Koguryo, which smashed through opposition on its way to Pyongyang. There, a Koguryo general, convinced resistance was useless, betrayed the court and opened the city gates to the Tang army. After nearly seven decades, the Chinese finally destroyed defiant Koguryo.

At the end of the war in Korea, much of the peninsula was in Tang hands, with the former Koguryo occupied by two hundred thousand Chinese troops. Meanwhile, in Silla, the Tang had installed a royal prince they believed to be compliant to Chinese wishes. Emperor Wu would have been proud, and probably a bit jealous.

==

The unparalleled success of the Tang Dynasty got the empire's scholar elite thinking again about the civilization's role in the world. Why did the Sui fail, and the Tang rise? What was the secret behind the glorious Tang victories that elevated the Son of Heaven to his proper place in the world? Their answer was *de*, or "virtue." Sure, China was a superior civilization in terms of wealth, knowledge, and political organization. But that wasn't sufficient to build a great power. A society required something more, something beyond the material—the money, the weapons, the manpower. That *je ne sais quoi*. It had to also possess superior virtue, and that virtue was the true source of its power. As we've seen, the historian Ban Gu made the separation between an "inner" and "outer" world—one basked in the warmth of Chinese greatness, the other left in the dark of ignorance. Now that distinction was blurred. Just as Taizong reveled in being both emperor and qaghan, the virtue of China knew no barriers, of culture or geography. Everyone could be drawn to China by its virtue. As one scholar of the age simply put it, "With virtue, they came; without the Way, they went away."[19]

This concept of foreign relations had immense appeal for the elite of China. The Confucian philosophy that formed the basis of their education stressed the importance of benevolence in government. Good rule was virtuous rule—that's what the old sage-kings of antiquity taught. So it just seemed a natural next step to equate dynastic success in the world with dynastic virtue.

The proof was in the Tang pudding. Historians examined where the Sui went wrong, and determined it was because it relied entirely on its brawn alone and lacked *de*. That means the Sui were not superior to the barbarian hordes who denied Chinese civilization. "Counting on one's prosperity and strength within and longing for extensive land without, incurring enmity with pride and waging wars based on anger—it is unheard of that this would not lead to one's demise," commented the authors of the official Sui history, compiled in the seventh century. "Therefore, one needs to permanently keep in mind the lesson from the barbarians!"[20]

However, the Tang Dynasty was so triumphant, on the battlefield and off, because it was virtuous. *De* separated the Tang from the mass of foreign barbarians, and elevated the dynasty above them. The government "should only be anxious if it did not have virtue," one history of the dynasty explained.[21] The superiority of China, then, was not based merely on power, but power paired with benevolence. This is how the Chinese perceived their role in the world. As a force for the good of humanity, as a source of civility and civilization.

═══

Even virtue could carry the Tang only so far. Just as the dynasty reached its grandest, its emperors, much like their Han predecessors, discovered the limits of Chinese power. The burden of the Tang's voracious appetites became heavier as its borders stretched and a new batch of enemies arose to pressure them. Tang society was exhausted by the relentless marches for the glory of empire. Li Bo, one of the greatest poets in Chinese history, captured the grim and weary mood in a verse possibly composed in 751:

The King's armies have grown gray and old
Fighting ten thousand leagues away from home . . .
The beacons are always alight, fighting and marching never stop.
Men die in the field, slashing sword to sword;
The horses of the conquered neigh piteously to Heaven.
Crows and hawks peck for human guts,
Carry them in their beaks and hang them on the branches of
*   withered trees.*[22]

The experience solidified another idea in dynastic political philosophy, one that also harks back to Ban Gu and his assessment of the imperialist Emperor Wu: foreign adventurism may sound exciting, but by its nature, it was also dangerous. As an eleventh-century Chinese historian put it, the Tang wished to "swallow the peoples of the four directions."[23] He didn't mean that as a compliment.

Barely had the conquests hit the Tang stomach before getting spit up. In Korea, Tang control proved short-lived. The fiercely independent populace of Koguryo refused to submit, with loyalists staging constant revolts against Tang authority. They were aided, surprisingly enough, by Silla, Tang's erstwhile ally. The Sillan rulers were happy to have had Tang assistance to destroy their peninsular rivals; they were less enamored by the Tang decision to stay. Relations between the allies collapsed, with the two coming to blows in 675, with the Koreans generally coming out on top. At stake was mastery over Korea. But desperately in need of troops elsewhere, even the aggressive Emperor Gaozong lost the will to fight another Korean war. In 676, he pulled out, leaving Silla to unify the peninsula under one government for the first time. China, ironically, thus played a critical role in the formation of a single Korea.

The story was similarly depressing on other fronts. From the 660s, the Tibetans, aspiring to an empire of their own, threatened Tang possessions in the Western Regions. The battles between them lasted for a century and a half and stretched over a vast area, from the Pamir mountain range, centered in what is today Tajikistan, to Sichuan in China's southwest, with the Tang often getting the worst of it. The Tang also got clobbered in an invasion of the Nanzhao kingdom, based in today's Yunnan, losing tens of thousands of soldiers in the failed assault on the jungle bastion. In the northeast, the Tang border came under pressure from yet another steppe threat, the Khitan.

Meanwhile, in Central Asia, the Tang also found themselves blocked by an entirely new power in the region. Tang commanders got embroiled in a power struggle between local potentates. One of them was backed by the Abbasid Muslim caliphate, based in Baghdad. The squabble between their clients dragged the Tang and Abbasid into a conflict of their own. Their armies met somewhere near the Talas River, located in modern Kyrgyzstan, in 751. This was a true superpower confrontation, with the two great empires of medieval Asia face-to-face in the heart of the continent. The Tang, like the Han, were projecting their might a tremendous distance. For two days, the two fought to a standstill, but on the third, the troops of a Turkish tribe allied to the Tang suddenly turned traitor and switched sides. That led to a collapse of the Tang army, with soldiers and even the commanding general fleeing for their lives. The army "was crushingly defeated, the bulk of soldiers killed with only a few thousand survivors," one Chinese historian later recorded.[24]

It was not this defeat that undercut Tang power, however, but an internal rebellion. In 755, a Tang general (of Turkish Sogdian descent), An Lushan, rose up against the emperor and marched on Chang'an. He and his rebel successors nearly brought down the dynasty. An's treachery, likely a result of palace intrigues, is one of the most tragic events in China's long history. Though the rebellion was eventually quelled in 763, the depleted Tang never fully recovered. Less than a year later, a Tibetan army was able to temporarily occupy Chang'an itself, sending the Son of Heaven fleeing. The Tibetans overran much of the Western Regions, and the Tang eventually gave up all claims to the area. (The Chinese would not return for a millennium.) Nanzhou, meanwhile, nibbled away at the southwest. The Tang would score an occasional victory, and notch a gain here and there, but its military preeminence was fundamentally broken.

Yet as was the case during the Period of Disunion, Tang military setbacks did not dispel Chinese imperial power in East Asia. If anything, the lure of Chinese civilization was stronger than ever under the Tang. Its riches—both material and cultural—were irresistible. Silla may have rejected Tang hegemony in Korea, but not the

Tang. Though relations between the two were frosty in the years immediately following China's expulsion from the peninsula, they quickly mended fences. Silla sent sixty-five embassies to the Tang court between 686 and 886, on average one every three years. Sillan communities formed in Tang cities, and Sillan students studied in Chinese academies, with some even passing its tough civil service exams. In 682, the Korean kingdom created its own imperial university along Chinese lines to teach the Confucian classics, while in 788 it established an examination system similar to the Tang's. Silla's kings "served the Middle Kingdom with the utmost sincerity," one Korean text, probably from the thirteenth century, proudly recorded. "Embassies scaling (the mountains) and navigating (the seas) to pay court were without interruption. They constantly sent their children to serve in the [Chinese] court's Imperial Bodyguard and enter the academy to learn (the Chinese classics) by recitation whereby they might inherit the example of the Sages, change the local customs of their vast wasteland, and become a country of *li* [rites] and *yi* [justice]."[25] Even the founder of the succeeding Koryo Dynasty, known for its more independent stance toward China, accepted the superiority of Chinese culture. "We, in the east, have long admired the Tang style," he told his heirs in 943. "Our literary matters, *li*, and music all follow their institutions. It is just that in various regions and different lands the people's names are each different, and they need not lightly be made uniform."[26]

The Korean experience was typical. The spread of Chinese civilization now became supercharged under a dynasty reaching new heights of political and cultural clout and actively promoting it. To the industrious Tang emperors, everyone not only *could* become Chinese, as the old philosophers thought, but *should* become Chinese. In 631, the Tang constructed 1,200 dorm rooms for foreign students from Korea, Japan, and elsewhere to make it easier for them to come to China and study. In 732 when envoys from Tibet asked for Chinese classical books, a debate ensued within the court over whether they should be granted, with advocates arguing these works would teach the barbaric Tibetans "honesty and integrity" and thus turn them into a civilized people.[27]

Even the Japanese were eager disciples of Chinese ways. The royals of Japan were often uncomfortable with the notion of Chinese hegemony. The Japanese rulers never sent tribute to the Chinese emperor after 838, and had pretensions of being his equal. But the way in which the Japanese royals chose to display that independent spirit was certainly very Chinese. In 600, the Empress Suiko, the first woman to rule Japan, sent an envoy to the Sui court bearing a letter in which she used a form of the title "Son of Heaven," a first for a Japanese sovereign. The next mission she sent, seven years later, brought an even more provocative message. "The Son of Heaven in the land where the sun rises addresses a letter to the Son of Heaven in the land where the sun sets."[28] Perhaps she meant no insult—the sun had become an important feature of the imperial cult in Japan—but clearly the empress was setting herself on the same pedestal as the universal Chinese emperor. Reading it a certain way, she was even suggesting she was superior, since the sun was rising over her country, while setting over China. Still, in an unusual act of grace by the hardboiled Sui, the court sent its own envoy to the empress in return. If imitation is the sincerest form of flattery, then the Chinese sovereign should have felt pretty flattered.

It is telling that the Japanese court chose to bolster its power within a Chinese framework. Imperial Japan modeled itself quite closely on the Chinese version. It was the Tang's aggressiveness in the seventh century that convinced the royal court to create a more centralized political system. The basis of that new, stronger state was a series of political reforms probably drawn up in the late seventh and early eighth centuries aimed at creating a Chinese-style monarchy, with legal codes, a military, and systems of taxation and landholding all borrowed from the Tang. Japanese sovereigns were also enamored by Confucian ideals of good government, at least in their official proclamations. The "Seventeen Article Constitution," a code of moral precepts for rulers dated, or so it is believed, to 604, included the very Confucian notion that adhering to proper rites would morally transform society and render government almost unnecessary. "The Ministers and officials of the state should make proper behavior their first principle," it read, "for if the superiors do not behave properly, the inferiors are disorderly; if inferiors behave improperly, offenses will naturally result. Therefore, when lord and vassal behave with propriety, the distinctions of rank are not confused: when the people behave properly the Government will be in good order."[29] A perfect government is one in which "superiors shepherded inferiors with humanity, and inferiors uphold superiors with the utmost sincerity," according to Japanese statesman Miyoshi Kiyotsura in 914.[30] Such lofty Chinese ideals were not for the elite alone. In 757, Empress Koken, imitating an earlier Tang decree, ordered every Japanese household to keep and study the *Classic of Filial Piety*, a Han Dynasty–era text that features Confucius pontificating on one of his favorite virtues. Even the name the Japanese began using for their own country was made in China. The word—Nihon—was chosen in the seventh century for the meaning of its Chinese character—"origins of the Sun."

Chinese influence over its neighbors went well beyond the political, into art, literature, education, and lifestyles. Japan inherited temple architecture from China as it passed through Korea. The Yamato court designed its capital city like those of China's imperial dynasties. *The Tale of Genji*, written in the early eleventh century, is considered a Japanese masterpiece and is probably the world's first novel, unusually for the time written in the Japanese language, not classical Chinese. But it has elements in common with elite Chinese literature nonetheless. The author, Murasaki Shikibu, quoted Chinese texts in 185 places.[31]

With the spread of Confucian texts and ideals, the societies of East Asia also became more Chinese, with greater separation of the genders, hierarchy in social relations, and an emphasis on the central role of the family. Even Buddhism, originally an import from India, became part of this Chinese cultural order. As Buddhism in India faded, and Islam replaced it in Central Asia, China became the center of the religion in East Asia, where monks from Japan and Korea traveled for study.

As Chinese influence declined in the west, it increased in the east. A shared set of "Asian" values was forming across the region, based on Chinese practice. East Asia, as a region with its own social, economic, and political systems, was becoming more and more distinct, with China at its core. By the late first millennium, East Asia was a Chinese world, with governing institutions, philosophical beliefs, literary and artistic styles, written language, and, increasingly, diplomatic norms and educational practices all based on China's model. Here we find what truly made China a superpower:

its ability to influence the societies around it by the force of its civilization, rather than its arms. Many countries can create a strong army; only the most powerful can create a world.

=

Even though the flow of culture tended to be from China to the outside world—just as it should have been, of course—the Middle Kingdom was at times surprisingly absorbent of foreign ways as well. And at no point was that more true than under the confident and glittering Tang Dynasty. The Tang elite had a craving for the produce, people, and philosophies of faraway places that was rarely matched during any other period. Emperor Taizong envisioned his empire as universal, and it truly encompassed all the known world. Foreigners were placed into positions of power and influence more readily by the Tang emperors than by any other Chinese sovereigns. Forty-three non-Chinese served as grand councilors during the Tang. The general who commanded the Tang armies at the Battle of Talas was Korean. Foreigners were regular participants in everyday life, too. Some 1.7 million of them became Tang subjects in the dynasty's first century alone. Tang cities were crammed with barbarian merchants, shopkeepers, moneylenders, monks, dancers, students, and, needless to say, prostitutes. Taverns on the eastern fringe of Chang'an were well-known havens for these exotic beauties, and many a young Chinese man was captivated by their intoxicating mix of soft, green eyes and stronger wine. Poet Li Bo captured this mesmerizing experience in verse:

> That Western houri with features like a flower—
> She stands by the wine-warmer, and laughs with the breath
>   of spring, . . .
> Dances in a dress of gauze!
> "Will you be going somewhere, milord, now, before you
>   are drunk?"[32]

The Tang court itself was a hotbed of foreign peoples, foreign culture, and foreign styles. As had been the case since the days of Emperor Wu, the greater the distance foreign emissaries traversed to bow to the Chinese sovereign, the greater the prestige of the

The Tang Dynasty court attracted visitors from throughout Asia. This mural from a seventh-century AD Tang royal tomb near Xi'an depicts two ambassadors from Korea on the right, and in the center a westerner, probably from Central Asia.

Pictures from History / Bridgeman Images

court. In that sense, the Tang royals reveled in their virtue. Embassies arrived from such far-flung locales as Java (now an island in Indonesia), Persia, and Arabia. More than fifty tribute missions were exchanged by the Tang court and Indian princes between the dynasty's founding and 750. Visiting missions had to follow strict rules of protocol and ceremony. Every official ambassador had to carry half of a bronze fish, awarded to his country when relations with the Tang were formalized. If the half fish, engraved with the number of the month on which the mission was scheduled to arrive in Chang'an, matched the other half held by the Tang court, the ambassador was welcomed as a formal representative of the foreign state. The Tang were then generous hosts, housing the foreign guests in special ambassadorial hostels and offering free meals during their stay.

Such generosity was not merely polite hospitality, but a display of Tang power. All of the palace's dealings with foreign envoys were crafted to impress, bedazzle, and awe. Ambassadors invited to a special reception held on the first day of winter passed through twelve ranks of guards on their way to the audience hall—archers, lancers, and swordsmen, all in distinctive uniforms. Envoys on more ordinary occasions still encountered five troops of royal guards, with staves and swords and attired in scarlet. The ambassador presented official tribute—a cornucopia of rarities from his homeland—and performed the expected prostrations to the throne; the emperor would bestow honorary titles onto him and his sovereign, and extend expensive gifts in return. (Not personally, of course, but through a court official. The Son of Heaven's dignity could be sullied by communication with a barbarian.)

Not all visitors to the court were of such lofty status. The Turkish kingdoms and Tibet delivered young girls to serve as concubines for the Son of Heaven. Foreign musicians, dancers, wise men, dwarves, and assorted other human oddities were frequent court guests as well. In 724, the maritime kingdom of Srivijaya (based in what is now Indonesia's island of Sumatra) sent the emperor a rare black slave girl (possibly from Africa, possibly from Southeast Asia) and two pygmies. One long-serving Tang emperor was a fan of a racy dance called the Western Whirling Girls, during which Sogdian women from Central Asia in crimson robes and deerskin boots spun on top of rolling balls.

Foreign residents could be found throughout the empire. The international trading hubs in China were packed with foreign traders from around the world. During the Tang, a large portion of the two hundred thousand residents of the southern outpost of Panyu (now Guangzhou) were Persian, Indian, Arab, Javanese, or Malay, all clustered in a foreign quarter south of the main Chinese town set aside by imperial decree. The port of Quanzhou had a community of Tamil traders from southern India. They kindly left archeologists two hundred statues of Hindu gods there. In Yangzhou, a fabulously wealthy city at the juncture of the Yangzi River and Grand Canal, several thousand Arab and Persian merchants had shops in the first half of the eighth century.

With foreigners came foreign ideas, cultural practices, and doctrines. The first Christian church to open its doors in China did so in Chang'an during the Tang. Its founder, a man named Aluohan, was dispatched by a patriarch in the Middle East in 638 to carry the word to the Far East. So many Persians lived in Luoyang that it had three Zoroastrian fire temples. Those foreign faiths joined the wildly popular but imported Buddhism, which by now had innumerable temples and monasteries throughout China, many of them bursting with wealth.

The Chinese of this period were not merely tolerant of such foreign ideas—they relished them. Foreign dress, music, art, food, and literature were all the rage, from the imperial court down to the regular urban household. Chinese women in the cities adopted a "curtain" hat, with a shoulder-length veil and a hood, an offshoot of a type worn by wandering nomads to keep the sun off their heads. They were considered so risqué in polite Confucian society—the unwashed stranger might catch a glimpse of the wellborn feminine face that ought to be discreetly concealed—that an edict of 671 attempted to ban it (to no avail). Also popular with the Tang trendy were Persian-style blouses with fitted sleeves and bodices, pleated skirts, and "un-Chinese" makeup. The son of the great Emperor Taizong was enamored by nomadic customs; he set up an entire Turkish tent camp on the palace grounds, dressed his attendants as Turkish slaves, spoke Turkish instead of Chinese, and dined on boiled mutton he sliced with a sword.

The spirit of the Tang times may be best captured in an essay composed by a scholar named Chen An. After an Arab was recommended to the court for an official position, critics complained that such an honor should have been given to a Chinese. Chen An disagreed, and said so eloquently. Being Chinese had more to do with a person's virtue than background or ethnicity. "Someone who was born in the central lands (China) but whose behavior does violence to the *li* [rites] and *yi* [justice], is Chinese in appearance but barbarian in his mind," he contended. "Someone who was born in barbarian regions, but whose behavior conforms to the *li* and *yi*, is barbarian in appearance but Chinese in his mind."[33]

Anyone could be a part of this grand Chinese world. All that was necessary was to believe in certain shared values, in the virtues of a superior civilization. Could the brilliance of China shine any brighter?

Five

BARBARIANS AT THE WALL

My ambition as a warrior
Is to satisfy my hunger with the flesh of the barbarians.

–poem by Yue Fei, Song Dynasty general

A tale from the Tang Dynasty tells of a man named Lu Yong who loved to eat food made of flour, but the more he consumed, the skinnier he became. One day a group of "westerners"—Central Asians, probably Persians—showed up at his door with enough wine and victuals for a feast. They told Yong that they had long lived among barbarians, but had "crossed oceans and scaled mountains" to seek the transformative splendor of China's civilization. Yong, a student at the Imperial Academy, was a real, live classical scholar! They wanted to be friends.

Yong modestly invited them in, and they ate and enjoyed themselves. Ten days later, the westerners were back, this time with gold and silk. They talked Yong into accepting the gifts, but even the trusting Yong became suspicious of their true intentions. Other students found out what was going on, and warned Yong that "those westerners love profit more than their own lives. They wouldn't think twice of murdering each other over something as trifling as salt and rice; . . . You should hide out in the wild, to avoid another visit."[1] Now frightened, Yong hurried for the countryside and barred himself inside of a house.

In the end, those westerners did have ulterior motives, but not nefarious ones. They extracted a parasitic creature from Yong's stomach that was the source of his weight problem—it devoured flour even more voraciously than he did, gobbling up whatever Yong swallowed. Then they invited Yong on an exotic adventure at the seashore that left him fabulously wealthy.

But there was that assumption: That the westerners were up to no good. That they had some unsavory motivations. That they couldn't be trusted. They'd do anything for money, a sign of suspect morality in Confucian ethics. The Tang Chinese may have believed this tale to be true, and even if they didn't, it reflects how they thought about foreigners in their midst.

The Tang may have salivated at Central Asian beauties or borrowed trendy nomad fashion. They may have appreciated the foreigner who mastered their philosophical texts, or the talent of dancers on rolling balls. The dignitaries bringing official tribute were, of course, always welcome. It was all so fresh and exotic! But there was a condescension about it. Foreigners were curiosities. Entertainment. They weren't quite as upright or honorable—or civilized—as the *real* Chinese. After all, barbarians will be barbarians.

For some, the intrusion of outsiders and their inferior culture had already gone too far. In 819, a Tang scholar, official and noted poet, Han Yu, wrote a memorial to the emperor that stands out for its sheer intemperance. A devoted Confucian, he bristled at the popularity of Buddhism, which, he believed, misled the common people and betrayed the true moral traditions of Chinese civilization, enshrined in Confucianism. What prompted his irate memorial was a decision by Tang Emperor Xianzong not only to welcome a relic of the Buddha—a bone from the great man's body—but also personally view the grand procession carrying it from a palace tower. Such a display of respect for a barbaric doctrine would only encourage the uneducated masses to worship the Buddha even more reverently. The sage-kings of Chinese antiquity would never have done something so improper! Han Yu felt it his Confucian duty to convince the emperor of his poor judgment. You can hear his blood boiling as you read the memorial.

"Buddhism is no more than a cult of the barbarian peoples," he told the emperor. "Buddha was a man of the barbarians who did not speak the language of China and wore clothes of a different fashion. His sayings did not concern the ways of our ancient kings. . . . How then, when he has long been dead, could his rotten bones, the foul and unlucky remains of his body, be rightly admitted to the palace? . . . Now without reason Your Majesty has caused this loathsome thing to be brought in and would personally go to view it. . . . Your servant is deeply shamed and begs that this bone be given to the proper authorities to be cast into fire and water."[2]

The Son of Heaven didn't take kindly to Han Yu's self-righteous lecture and banished him to a post in the far south of the country, then seen as a form of internal exile.

The intolerant spirit of the memorial, however, lived on. In 845, a later Tang emperor issued an edict banning Buddhism, Zoroastrianism, and Christianity. His cash-starved eye was on the statues and ceremonial vessels in their houses of worship, which he wanted to melt down into badly needed currency. The government confiscated most of the property held by Buddhist monasteries in Luoyang and Chang'an. The next emperor lifted the ban on Buddhism in 847, and the religion survived. The others did not. The fire temples and churches closed.

As the Tang empire weakened in its later period, and its confidence was shaken by military defeats, shrinking borders, and internal divisions, its fascination for things foreign contracted as well. Foreigners, once so warmly received, became targets of discrimination. A Turkish people called the Uighurs had allied with the Tang during the rebellion of An Lushan, and their hard-charging cavalry helped save the dynasty. That didn't stop the court from issuing an edict in 779 that mandated Uighurs living in Chang'an had to wear their native dress and banned them from taking Chinese wives or concubines. So much for imperial gratitude. Similarly, in 836, the governor of Guangzhou, China's primary port city, was horrified to find Chinese and foreigners living together, so he forcibly segregated the communities. He banned foreigners from marrying locals and even prohibited the sale of land and homes to non-Chinese. The governor could not accept the idea of Chinese and foreigners treating each other as equals. The barbarians had to know who was superior, and in charge.

=====

Barbarians came to loom much, much larger in China's history of the world as the Tang tottered. In fact, China's confrontation with barbarians would define its course for five hundred years. Much like the conflict with the Xiongnu during the Han Dynasty, the experience would change the Chinese and their attitude toward themselves and the world around them.

In the official imperial records, the Tang Dynasty came to an end in 907, when its last emperor, Ai, was forced to abdicate to a general who then declared his own dynasty, the Later Liang. But by that point, the great Tang had been in decline for 150 years. To end the An Lushan rebellion in the mid-700s, the Tang court allowed the rebel generals to retain much of their authority in China's northeast as provincial governors. Bad move. Within a couple decades, they began taking the title of "king" and breaking away from Tang control as effectively independent, competing states (similar to what happened during the Zhou Dynasty period). Tang's death throes started in the 870s when an unemployed scholar-turned-bandit-leader Huang Chao launched another major rebellion in Tang's eastern provinces. After a three-thousand-mile march that saw him ravage much of southeast China, Huang Chao captured Chang'an in 881 and his unruly troops destroyed it. What had been the world's greatest city would never rise again.

The empire disintegrated, as it had after the fall of Han, with small or short-lived kingdoms all slashing at each other. The era is known as the "Five Dynasties and Ten Kingdoms" period, which tells you all you need to know about the political stability of the period. As in other times when the empire was not united, this one was filled with the requisite devastation and death brought about by incessant betrayals and battles. The eleventh-century scholar Ouyang Xiu, who wrote the authoritative history of this period, lamented that this was a time without Confucian honor. "For the

Five Dynasties era, I can identify only three men of total integrity," he wrote.[3]

At least this interregnum between empires was mercifully short, by the lengthy standards of Chinese history—only about a century. In 960 a new dynasty rose, the Song. Its founder, a respected general named Zhao Kuangyin, kicked out the boy-emperor of what was then the ruling dynasty in northern China, the Later Zhou, and usurped the throne for himself. Over the next thirty years, Zhao—known to history as Emperor Taizu—and his brother-successor, Emperor Taizong, reconquered the core of the Tang empire. Miraculously, the deed was done with a minimum of bloodshed compared to past unifications. The brothers also managed another amazing feat—creating a governing system far more centralized and far less susceptible to the sort of political fragmentation that whittled away at the Han and Tang. To rid themselves of potential rivals, the Song royals bought off and retired many of their military leaders to assert the new court's authority, earning themselves eternal plaudits from Confucian scholars, who always favored civilian control over the country and army. They also expanded and regularized the civil service examination system and raised it to become the main route to government employment. In the process, they fostered a trained bureaucracy entirely loyal to the Song court. These Confucian-educated bureaucrats became the backbone of the Song administration.

The Song ushered in yet another of those exuberant periods of artistic and literary expression in Chinese history, picking up where the great Tang left off. Of all its many cultural achievements, none surpassed the vibrant philosophical exploration of the Song era, arguably the most important for China since the days of Confucius himself. Song scholars and statesmen produced an entire new library of philosophical works, mainly in a school of thought known as Neo-Confucianism, in which they mixed a fresh spirituality and universalism into the often overly grounded Confucian doctrine. This refurbished creed would dominate the scholarship of the rest of the imperial age and come to have tremendous influence over China's East Asian neighbors.

There was, however, a "but" to all this. The "but" was that the Song rulers were never able to complete the reunification of the empire, or more accurately, the empire as the Chinese at the time defined it. Parcels once controlled by the great Han and Tang were outside of the Song's borders, ruled by barbarians. A legitimate Chinese dynasty that possessed the Mandate of Heaven should rule what was properly Chinese. Without control over these former imperial territories, the Song suffered a blot on its right to rule China.

The problem, as always, was in the north. Amid the disarray following the Tang collapse, the Khitans had built themselves a powerful state encompassing Manchuria, Mongolia, and parts of northeastern China. The Khitans called their new empire the very Chinese-sounding Liao Dynasty. Their territory included parts of today's Shanxi and Hebei provinces that had been under Tang control and were home to a large Chinese population. Present-day Beijing was in this zone, and the Liao named the city its southern capital. This contested area was called the Sixteen Prefectures, which included a vital area known as Yan.

The Song considered this barbarian infiltration into Chinese lands intolerable. Without the Sixteen Prefectures, the Song could not claim to have truly made the Chinese empire whole. The Song founder and first emperor knew that all too well. In 975, after Song armies had consolidated control of most of the south, his courtiers suggested he take the new title of "unifier." The emperor rejected it. Since Yan had not been recovered, "how is it not an exaggeration to refer to (what I have done) as 'unification'?"[4] The Song tried to compensate by making the valid case that the core of China was in Song hands. A stele erected in 974 proclaimed that the dynasty had "recovered the distant limits of the Traces of Yu"—referring to lands once under the sway of the sage-king of deep antiquity, Yu the Great.[5] But the incompleteness of the Song created a mania within the political elite to recapture these lost prefectures, one that would endure until the end of the dynasty. "I cherish this region of Yan, which once was within our frontiers, but has fallen into the hands of the stinking caitiffs," Taizong, the second Song emperor, declared in a 986 edict. "Families there harbor great indignation . . . ; By means of our imperial campaign, they will cleanse themselves of a generation of shame."[6]

Those campaigns—two of them—launched by Taizong failed. The first ended with Taizong personally fleeing the field of battle badly wounded in a donkey cart, and the second defeat came at the hands of a woman, no less—the Empress Dowager of Liao ruling in the name of her young son. It was hard to tell which was more embarrassing.

Ten years later, in 1004, the empress was back, this time thrusting a Khitan army into the heart of the Song empire and nearly reaching the Chinese capital, the city of Kaifeng. The expected barbarian rampage, however, never happened. The two sides instead brokered a peace settlement. The Song agreed to pay the Khitan Liao an annual treasure of two hundred thousand bolts of silk and one hundred thousand ounces of silver—an unimaginable windfall to the barbarians, but pocket change compared to either the cost of continued war or the total revenues of the rich Chinese empire. Yet it stung nonetheless. Unreciprocated, the payments, though labeled "military expenses" by the Song, were in fact tribute by another name. The treaty maintained a fiction of Chinese superiority—the two states were described as brothers, with the Khitan being the "younger." But there was no way of hiding that the treaty symbolized Song weakness before a militarily stronger foe. The Son of Heaven was forced to accept the idea of another ruler with the title of emperor in northern China.

In that sense, the accommodation with the Khitan smelled suspiciously like the one made by the early Han emperors with the Xiongnu. But there was a key difference. The Liao were no tribal confederation wandering the Mongolian steppe like the Xiongnu. It was a formal state, parked on Chinese soil. A boundary was formally drawn up between the two, stretching nearly four hundred miles from modern Tianjin on the eastern coastline to Datong in the north. What that meant is that the Liao was not just another barbarian kingdom loitering in China's north. It was a valid contender for power in China, and arguably, for the Mandate itself.

To make matters even worse, if that were even possible, the Khitans weren't the only barbarians trespassing on Song credibility. To the northwest, another bunch known as the Tanguts, a people likely related to the Tibetans, had forged their own state encroaching on traditional Chinese territory, which was called the Xi Xia Dynasty. And the Tanguts also had imperial aspirations. By the mid-eleventh century, the Tangut state had expanded into a mini-empire, encompassing parts of western China and territory once controlled by the Tang. This success gave the Xi Xia king, Weiming Yuanhao, the confidence to challenge the Song and take the title of emperor in 1038. The Song emperor, Renzong, couldn't stomach the affront. War was inevitable, and it came in 1039.

Neither empire was militarily capable of cowing the other, and after five years of fruitless conflict, the two sides got down to negotiating a settlement. For the Song, it turned out a bit better than their agreement with the Khitan. The Tangut Xi Xia accepted nominal Chinese suzerainty, but in return, the Song permitted its leader to retain the title "emperor" and other marks of imperial status—implicitly raising him to a level of equality with the Son of Heaven. And the Song also had to pay up to the Tangut as they did the Khitan, with annual gifts of tea, silk, and silver—again, tribute in all but name.

Now there were three emperors in north China. Yet for the most part, the peace held, especially with the Khitan Liao. A steady stream of embassies trudged back and forth across the border each year. Many of these officials came to see the peace with Liao less as a necessary evil and more of a practical method of preserving the dynasty and its wealth. Even more, the Liao, just like other barbarians, were imbibing the intoxicating spirits of Chinese civilization—so much so that the political class of the Khitan began to share Chinese ideals and cultural norms. In 1088, Song statesman and scholar Su Shi was surprised, but pleasantly, when a Khitan ambassador tried prodding him into yet another banquet toast by citing two lines of Su's poetry. "I myself have observed their assembled officials; there are many Chinese literati among them," he later commented.[7]

But not everyone agreed. As with the Han Dynasty's tribute-for-peace agreements with the Xiongnu, other court dignitaries still harbored hopes of recovering Yan and the lost Sixteen Prefectures. One scholar-official submitted unofficial battle plans to the court in 1050, which featured the use of newfangled lances and chariots of his own design. The obsession with the loss of the Sixteen Prefectures, combined with the apparently permanent encampment of barbarians on prime China real estate, altered the Chinese history of the world. The Chinese had long defined themselves in relation to outsiders—and most of all, the northern barbarians—going all the way back to the Rong, Di, and Xiongnu. And during the Song, they did so again. The Song scholar-officials, more than ever steeped in common ideas about history, culture, and philosophy with the standardizing influence of the now entrenched and expanded civil service exams, began talking about the Chinese as a "nation," defined both by a shared culture and ancestral roots.[8] They called themselves the "Han people," a term used to this day to describe the majority Chinese ethnic group. It was originally used by the steppe tribes to refer to their settled Chinese neighbors, and it got absorbed into the political lexicon of the Song educated elite. These "Han people" lived in a specified land, of historically and culturally determined territory that was rightfully Chinese. The northern border again became the Great Wall—now more in theory than fact. Not only was the Qin-built wall snugly inside Khitan territory, it had also become mere ruins, left to crumble by the more open-minded Tang. But the wall's symbolic power remained, as the dividing line between the civilized Han people of China and barbarism. As one Song poet wrote in the eleventh century,

The azure sea traverses the Western Regions,
The Great Wall rises up in the north; . . .
I long for when these separated us from the "wilderness zone."[9]

These Chinese Han people residing in a Chinese land transcended the changes of dynasties and the intrusions of steppe invaders. There was something greater, grander about the community of Chinese, not connected to any one government or age or section of the country. And since these Han people had a common culture and history, they were meant to be ruled by a truly Chinese Son of Heaven. Song literati pined away for the "people left behind," those good Han folk trapped under barbarian rule in the north—and, to the more hawkish, abandoned by the court to a cruel fate. The Han people under Khitan rule, commented diplomat Fu Bi in 1044, "are of the mind to submit (to Song), and frequently resent the fact that the Middle Kingdom is not able to rule them; they are always filled with frustration, and appear to weep bitterly."[10]

This view was a reversal of earlier Chinese thought. For much of China's history, philosophers imagined that being Chinese was a matter of being civilized. A barbarian could be just as Chinese as anyone born in the zhongguo if he was educated in the classics, followed the proper rites, and embraced Chinese moral tenets. Now Chinese saw themselves as Chinese because of their historical roots and ethnic background, no matter what their habits and lifestyles might be. "The village elders of those prefectures are our people who have been left behind," one Song scholar wrote about the Chinese in barbarian-controlled territory in the eleventh century. "Though they drink milk and drape themselves in felt [like steppe nomads], they still think longingly of the land of *Hua*," a reference to China proper.[11]

All of this new thinking about what made China China created an obsession among the Song literati to reunite what they considered all the Han people and Han territory. Without the Sixteen Prefectures, China was incomplete, the Han people divided. Many in the political elite were biding their time, waiting, wishing for an opportunity to reclaim the Chinese territory in the Khitan Liao empire.

And then it arrived, or so they thought, in the form of another barbarian horde from the remote north, known as the Jurchens. Probably originating in eastern Siberia, by the time of the Song, they had made their home in far northeast Manchuria near the modern border between Russia and China. At first, they were nominally subordinate to the Khitan, but they generally maintained their independence and kept to themselves. That was until the early twelfth century, when the Jurchen chieftain, an energetic and ruthless man named Aguda, capitalized on growing resentment toward the Liao, raised an army, and stampeded into the Khitan empire. Aguda proclaimed himself emperor of a new dynasty, the Jin.

An aggressive coterie of top advisors to the Song emperor, Huizong, pressed for an alliance with the Jin that would carve up the Khitan Liao empire between them and restore the coveted Sixteen Prefectures to Chinese control. "China's old territory has long been in the hands of the barbarians," one senior councilor, Wang Fu, reminded the emperor in 1119. "Today heaven gives signs that Your

Majesty will achieve great things. If we do not take advantage of the opportunity, I fear we will regret it."[12]

Many senior officials perceived more peril than promise in the prospect of an alliance. But Huizong was won over to the idea, marginalized the peaceniks, and began negotiations with the Jin. Envoys shuttled between the Song and Jin courts to hash out a deal. In the eventual framework, Aguda agreed to hand over the region of Yan to the Song, on the condition that the Chinese dynasty help defeat the Khitan by launching an attack on the city of Yanjing (now Beijing).

The arrangement was doomed from the start. In 1122, a eunuch-general and leading war hawk, Tong Guan, set off to conquer Yanjing with one hundred thousand troops. He pursued a confused policy—at one moment trying to stoke a rebellion against the city's Khitan rulers, at another negotiating with them. When he finally ordered an assault, it failed when a key general retreated without authority. Undeterred, Huizong doubled the size of the invading army and tried again. This campaign started out with greater promise, claiming territory south of Yanjing without even a fight. The attack on Yanjing itself began with a ruse. Song soldiers were dressed as civilians and sent to a market outside the city, from where they infiltrated inside the walls and took control of its gates. The Khitan ruler, now a widowed empress, counterattacked with fresh troops from inside her palace and regained the upper hand. The Song forces fled the city and the Chinese again retreated in disarray.

In the end, the Song's inept campaigns exposed to the rising Jin just how weak the Chinese dynasty's armed forces really were. That proved lethal. Clearly, the Jurchens had no need for the Song alliance. While Huizong's generals were bumbling at the walls of Yanjing, the Jurchens continued to steamroll through the Khitan Liao empire, scoring victory after victory, including at Yanjing, which surrendered to the steppe army without a fight. Aguda kept changing the terms of the alliance, making greater and greater demands for silk and money. The Jurchens, however, did turn over the area of Yanjing to the Song, as they originally promised. An ebullient Emperor Huizong heralded the return as the "fulfillment of our ancestors' long-standing ambitions" in an edict he composed with his own hand.[13] But the achievement was fleeting. Rather than rescuing those poor "people left behind" and matching the greatness of the Tang, the Song's obsession with reunifying China only left the empire ripe for disaster.

==

In 1125, the Jurchens invaded the Song empire. Among the first parts of China to fall was Yanjing. From there, the Jin onslaught sped toward Kaifeng. With the barbarians literally at the gates, some of Huizong's advisors came to believe the only hope was for the unpopular emperor to abdicate in favor of his son, to help rally support for the dynasty. "If Your Majesty is able to make this decision [to abdicate], then the central plains will be Chinese for the next several centuries," one official told him. "If you are not able to take this step, then the central plains for the next several centuries will be barbarian."[14] The fate of the Han people and the zhongguo was in Huizong's hands. After thinking over the matter for a short time, Huizong consented, and turned the empire over to his son, Qinzong. So reluctant was the new emperor to take on his weighty Mandate with the barbarians' breath on the back of his neck that Huizong had to order eunuchs to forcibly carry Qinzong and sit him on the imperial throne.

Could a reign start any less auspiciously? The Song court managed to buy off the Jurchens with a big payout of silver and silk and the cessation of some territory, saving the capital. But some more prescient officials believed the settlement was a mistake. The Jurchens, now fully aware of both the Song's spectacular wealth and its suspect defenses, would be back for more. A final reckoning with the Jin was unavoidable.

And so it was. By the end of 1126, the Jurchens were back at Kaifeng's gates. They assaulted the city and claimed the outer walls. Qinzong ascended to the top of a palace gateway to encourage the people to resist. But thousands of soldiers and civilians fled the capital. Once again, Qinzong tried negotiating a bribe. This time, the Jurchen demands for gold and silver were too massive for even the rich Song empire. Song bureaucrats scoured the city's private homes for jewelry and other valuables to ship to the Jurchen camp. Nothing satisfied the invaders, not even the emperor himself. In early January 1127, Qinzong departed Kaifeng for the Jurchen camp. He promised the loyal citizens lining the road that he would return to the capital the next day. But the Jurchens locked Qinzong alone in a small room without food or blankets to protect him from the cold.

With the emperor held captive, the Jurchens' demands for loot became more relentless. Unable to raise the cash, the Song tried to settle the ransom with women: 11,600 in all were handed over to the Jin—from royal princesses, palace consorts, and girls from noble families to entertainers and courtesans—to be parceled out among the Jurchen officers and men. The already married Princess Fujin, Huizong's daughter, was delivered tied up. The wealth of imperial China—the palace's priceless art collection, ceremonial robes and vessels, the jewels and pearls—all got heaped onto carts and hauled north, along with much of Kaifeng's human talent—its craftsmen, engineers, and artists. Perhaps fifteen thousand people—Qinzong included—were compelled to march north to the Jin capital. Some didn't survive the journey.

Before they departed, though, the Jin generals inflicted the most stinging humiliation of them all. Emperor Qinzong was brought before the Jin generals and troops and "ordered to kneel to hear the edict demoting him to commoner," one account reads. The Jin leader then told two officials "to take off the younger ruler's hat and robe." Qinzong was then forced to issue an order that a new ruler from a different family be elevated to the throne in Kaifeng.[15]

=

Some Song loyalists, however, refused to concede. Serving barbarian invaders had always been controversial among China's proud scholar-officials, and many of them refused to work for their Jurchen overlords. "I was born to be an official of the Great Song," an imperial envoy, Dou Jian, declared. "How could I bear to hand the clan of the Great Song over to enemies?"[16] He then strangled himself.

Others rallied around a young scion of the imperial family. By chance, Prince Gou had been dispatched to parlay with the Jurchen generals, but was blocked on his way by a mob of angry Song loyalists opposed to another embarrassing capitulation. As the Jin army marched on the capital, he was unable to return to Kaifeng and thus avoided Qinzong's destiny. He evaded capture, fled south, and restored the Song Dynasty as Emperor Gaozong. Chased by Jurchen forces, Gaozong at one point escaped their grasp only by boarding a ship and sailing off the coast. In 1138, the Song set up what many expected to be a temporary capital below the Yangzi at Hangzhou (near Shanghai). It ended up being permanent. Gaozong was the first emperor of a new stage of the (now truncated) empire, known as Southern Song. Though the dynasty survived, the Son of Heaven had been chased from the heartland by barbarians. What would Emperor Wu think? Yes, peace was restored, but the Song never accepted the loss of north China. Many Song officials held fast to the dream of reconstituting the empire.

The man who came to symbolize this undying, patriotic spirit was a popular general named Yue Fei. One of the Song's most successful military leaders, he was also an outspoken proponent of continued resistance to the Jin. Born to a poor peasant family, Yue Fei rallied to the call to arms to defend the Song from the Jurchen invaders, and when that defense deteriorated, he joined a rebuilding Song army south of the Yangzi. Possessed of unrivaled courage, physical strength, and a resolute commitment to the Chinese cause, he revived the sagging morale of Song troops. In the years following 1134, Yue Fei won a series of military engagements with the Jurchens, reclaiming much of the territory lost in the 1120s. His advance brought him within striking distance of the old capital of Kaifeng itself. These battles were grisly meat grinders. Yue Fei sent troops with axes to hack at the legs of the Jin's heavily armed cavalry. But the spirits of his troops remained stratospheric, and as he triumphantly marched northward, more Chinese joined his merry forces. A return to the north seemed on the verge of becoming reality.

Emperor Gaozong himself was lavish in his praise for Yue Fei. "With someone like you supporting the country, I don't need to say any more," he wrote to the general in a personal letter. In another, the emperor noted how Yue Fei was tirelessly at work, even while suffering from a bad cold. "Who could know that you even ignore yourself for the sake of the nation? . . . I praised you and frequently sighed in admiration."[17]

General Yue Fei fought for the Song Dynasty against Jurchen invaders in the mid-twelfth century AD and is a paragon of loyalty and a nationalist hero to this day.

Pictures from History / Bridgeman Images

Yet these letters masked a more sinister design. The emperor and his court were wooing Yue Fei in an attempt to gain better control over the military; Yue Fei and other top brass operated in the field almost like independent warlords. But more dangerous to Yue Fei, he and the emperor diverged on the matter of the war. Yue Fei remained as determined as ever to rid "all under Heaven" of the barbarian menace. But from the standpoint of the imperial court in Hangzhou—the only one that really mattered—the situation was more precarious. Yue Fei's success in the field was an exception in a campaign that was not making as much progress. It had become clear, to both Jurchen and Song, that neither possessed the capability to subdue the other. Coexistence seemed the only viable strategy, and a peace camp gained clout at the Song court.

Rather than a hero, Yue Fei looked like a problem. The court issued firm orders for him to withdraw and relinquish the northern territory he had bought so dearly with Song blood. He complied, but grudgingly. "The achievements of ten years have been dashed in a single day,"[18] he lamented. He poured his unfulfilled hopes and patriotic zeal into verse:

> My ambition as a warrior
> Is to satisfy my hunger with the flesh of the barbarians.
> Then, while enjoying a rest,
> Slake my thirst with the blood of the tribesmen.
> Give me the chance to try again
> To recover our mountains and rivers
> Then report to the emperor.[19]

It was not to be. Rather than rousing the emperor's spirit, Yue Fei's stubborn belligerence impeded a settlement with the Jin. Other pro-war advocates were silenced with bribes. But something more drastic was necessary to remove the incorruptible Yue Fei. The obstinate general was summoned to Hangzhou and stripped of his military power. Defiant as always, however, the peace party decided Yue Fei had to go. In 1141, he was jailed on trumped-up charges of insubordination, tortured to force a confession (which he never made), found guilty anyway, and killed in prison.

Yue Fei was not forgotten, however. His legend only grew over time, until he became the archetype of a certain Chinese hero—the brave soul who sacrificed himself to defend the Han people from the barbarians, a paragon of patriotism and loyalty to the state. His story was told and retold (and generously embellished) in numerous poems, plays, and novels, and in temples erected to honor him. He was even anointed a Daoist deity. Zhao Mengfu, a late Song poet, wrote of his sorrow upon seeing the great general's tomb:

> . . . Lords and ministers
> In their Southern exile
> Drank and danced

Indifferent to the fate of their country . . .
The hero [Yue Fei] is dead:
Sighing won't bring him back.
And the country collapsed.
Enough: this is the wrong place to sing this song.
Just seeing the West Lake (in Hangzhou)
Draws out my tears.[20]

With the general out of the way, the two empires inked a treaty in 1142 that set the Huai River, just north of the Yangzi, as their formal border. This document, though, discarded the euphemisms that had previously preserved the fiction of Song superiority. The treaty obliged the Song to send ample tribute to the Jurchens, with no pretense of it being anything else, and accept being called an "insignificant state." Rather than the usual familial language used to describe the relationship between rival rulers, this treaty referred to Gaozong not as "brother" or "nephew," but simply "Servant Gou," using the emperor's personal name—a demeaning slight. There was no question as to which empire was supreme. The Song Dynasty was a Jurchen vassal, and that was that.

That was more than some diehard patriots could take. Yes, peace had come, but the price was too steep. The storied zhongguo, the land where its superior civilization was born, the home of Yu the Great and the Duke of Zhou, where the great Han and Tang lorded over "all under Heaven," was lost. How could the emperor still the army and cede the north to the foreign foe? Lu You, one of the Song era's most revered poets, captured his disappointment and anger in verse:

Our generals fight no more but idly guard the border.
Vermillion gates still and silent; inside they sing and dance;
stabled horses fatten and die, bows come unstrung.
From garrison towers the beat of kettles hurries the sinking moon;
lads who joined the troops at twenty, white-haired now.
In the sound of the flutes who will read the brave man's heart? . . .
But when have traitorous barbarians lived to see their heirs?
Our captive people, forbearing death, pine for release,
even tonight how many places stained with their tears?[21]

The scholarly elite of the Song, trapped in their sweltering southern exile, dreamed endless dreams of a return north. Lu You fantasized of achieving that task personally, as did many other Song literati.

> *The mountainous city of Xianyang*
> *Is site of the old capital of the Qin and Han dynasties.*
> *The imperial qi [energy] dissipates in the evening mist;*
> *The palace halls are overgrown with spring weeds.*
> *How might I, in the tow of the imperial army,*
> *Sweep clean (this region) and welcome back the emperor's*
>   *carriage?*[22]

Such sentiment was not limited to the wistful poet. Many Song elite, including some of the emperors' top officials, remained unreconciled to the loss of the north. The land of their forefathers was now overrun by felt-clad, mutton-chomping steppe barbarians. An outrage! Contemplating a map detailing the extent of previous dynasties in the late twelfth century, scholar-official Huang Shang felt his blood boiling. "Myriad miles of contiguous territory are in rebel (i.e., Jurchen) hands," he noted. "How can one not shed tears and sigh deeply because of this? This surely fills one with indignation!"[23]

To these Song loyalists, what had been lost was not merely territory, but civilization itself. The steppe people were corrupting hallowed ground. Another twelfth-century poet, Cao Xun, described it thus:

> *A rainbow in the Heavens disappeared in the daylight,*
> *As the Central Plains became a territory of sheep and dogs. . . .*
> *And the court officials hid out in one corner of the world. . . .*
> *The people who fled (long for home like) birds piping for*
>   *their nests.*
> *Whenever I think of home, the Huai River stands in my way,*
> *But my heart drifts far away alongside the soaring clouds.*[24]

The damage done by the loss of the north went beyond mere military embarrassment. It raised uncomfortable and unavoidable questions about China's role in the world. The Chinese empire was, after all, still richer, better organized, and—do we even need to say it—culturally superior, not merely compared to the steppe barbarians, but to any other society in view. And yet these northern tribesmen chased the universal Son of Heaven from the historic zhongguo. The Chinese world was not supposed to work this way.

And it grated, like a pea under a princess. The Song was as vibrant and wealthy as any of China's previous dynasties. Great poets were still composing great verse; philosophers still philosophized great thoughts; technology continued to advance; the world's merchants flocked to its marketplaces. But the idea of China was being challenged—the virtues of its civilization and the supremacy of its stature. Could the Song claim to have the Mandate of Heaven if the dynasty was confined to the south?

Some Song devotees tried to dance around this problem by making the case that the Song had done more to reunify China than any other claimant to the Mandate of Heaven since the collapse of Tang. But others had their doubts. A dynasty that truly held the Mandate of Heaven must surely unify "all under Heaven." The Song had miserably failed, and that represented a mark on its very legitimacy. Confucian philosopher Chen Liang addressed this very issue in an 1178 memorial to the court. "Your obedient servant ventures to suggest," he wrote, "that only China—the standard energy of Heaven and Earth—is that which the heavenly mandate to rule endows, where the hearts of the people gather, where the ritual of civilization cluster, and that which kings and emperors have inherited for a hundred generations. Is it at all conceivable that such a country could be violated by the perverse energy of the barbarians? Unfortunately, it has now been so violated; violated to the degree that we have taken China and civilization and lodged them in this remote, peripheral place."[25]

Making matters even worse, the Jurchen Jin could easily make a claim to the Mandate, too. Even before conquering northern China, the Jurchens had started adopting characteristics of a Chinese-style dynasty, like many steppe peoples had in the past. And upon occupying the north, they suddenly found themselves a distinct minority—a few million at best—surrounded by perhaps twenty million Chinese. To govern, the Jurchens had little choice but to build a government along Chinese lines. Its emperors wore

Chinese robes, listened to court music during court ceremonies, and were given Chinese reign names. The Jin reestablished the civil service examination system, adopted the Chinese court's rules for audiences, and used the Chinese calendar. New government buildings in the capital were designed with Chinese architectural styles. The Jurchens honored Confucius, built Confucian temples and schools for the study of the Confucian classics, and constructed ancestral temples like their Chinese predecessors. The Jurchen rulers were educated in the Chinese classics themselves.

The Jurchens did not want to be completely Chinese. The Jin tried imposing a law forbidding marriage between Jurchens and Chinese, to prevent the minority steppe people from being absorbed into the Chinese mass (but it was routinely flouted). However, Chinese culture was hard to resist. One of the Jin emperors, Shizong, feared Jurchen culture was being corrupted by Chinese ways. But he also commissioned Jurchen-language translations of Confucian texts, and was such a fan of the old Duke of Zhou that he took that ancient age of sage-kings as a model for his own rule.

So while the Song shook in revulsion at the barbarian conquest of north China, the real question was, Who had really defeated whom? Like steppe invaders going back into deep antiquity, the Jurchens were being conquered by Chinese civilization. The Song emperors might have lost on the battlefield, but the Chinese, in a sense, were winning the war. The Chinese could rest assured that though the Jurchens were a political and military threat, they did not present a challenge to the superiority of Chinese civilization.

Yet for some in the Song, the fact that the Jurchens took on the trappings of the Chinese meant little. One firebrand Song loyalist made that all too clear in a discussion of a previous invasion of steppe people that invoked the long-ago comparisons to foreigners as beasts, and reflected his views on the Jin in north China: "For barbarians to perform the functions of the Central State, this is not a blessing from the barbarians, but is actually a calamity brought on by them. It is as if an ox or a horse were one morning suddenly to understand the language of men while still wearing a hairy tail and standing atop four hoofs. Even a young child no more than three feet in height would on seeing such a sight, do no more than exclaim 'ox-horse demon!' He would dare not call such a thing a 'human.'"[26]

No matter how hard they tried, barbarians would be barbarians, and the Song didn't seriously question their right to rule China, despite the dynasty's military setbacks. The Song court at Hangzhou never gave up its dream of returning to the north. In 1206, the war party tried yet again. The feeble-minded and easily manipulated emperor, Ningzong, fell under the sway of a courtier with dictatorial sensibilities, Han Tuozhou. Able to sideline most of the professional scholar-officials with the unwitting support of the sovereign, Han grasped so much power that by 1200 he was effectively running the empire himself, and he engineered a new conflict with the Jin. As part of a pro-war propaganda blitz, he resurrected the memory of the heroic Yue Fei and re-interred his body in a prominent tomb in a Hangzhou temple.

Han's skills were better suited to the palace than the battlefield. The Song offensive was poorly coordinated and conceived, and though it managed some early success, the Chinese army quickly got pushed back by a well-organized Jin counterattack. Soon it was the Song, not the Jin, fighting for its life. The fiasco spelled the end of Han Tuozhou. He was stopped by palace guards on his way to his usual morning audience with the emperor, dragged outside the walls, and beaten to death. The order likely came from the empress herself.

Meanwhile, at the front, stalemate ensued yet again, and a peace agreement was reached in 1208—one unusual condition of which was the delivery to the Jin court of the head of the hated Han. It was duly lacquered and shipped in a box.

Another failure! Over the decades of frustration, the Song poets returned to their brushes to express a growing sense of fatalism, of mourning. Could the north be permanently lost? Would the Han people ever be liberated from the hooves of the barbarians' horses? Would the stink of sheep ever be washed away? Perhaps not.

> *I think of the arrows that hung at my waist and my sword in*
> *its scabbard,*
> *Now moth-eaten or covered with dust.*
> *What did they accomplish? How fast the time has gone.*
> *My heart is still passionate but my years are numbered. . . .*
> *Yet I have heard that the old who were left behind in the*
> *central plains*

Constantly look toward the south
Hoping to see the decorated imperial chariots,
Arriving at this place makes this traveler's feelings well up
And his tears fall like rain.[27]

=

Far to the north, the steppe was stirring once again. The latest swarm to emerge from the distant grasslands would be the most famous and momentous of them all—the Mongols, under Genghis Khan. In 1210, one hundred thousand mounted archers flooded south with that dazzling speed only the most skilled equestrians can attain. The Jin put up a fierce resistance, but even their fearsome cavalry couldn't hold back the Mongolian tide. By 1233, they had bottled up the Jin court in the city of Caizhou (in today's Henan province). The Song, having failed to learn from history, conspired with the Mongols to dismember the despised Jin and sent an army to join in the siege. In early 1234, the combined force stormed the city, the last Jurchen leader was killed in hand-to-hand fighting, and the Jin Dynasty came to an end.

This moment truly deserved celebration. For more than a century, the Jurchens had threatened the Song and gorged on its wealth. Now, finally, they were wiped from the Chinese map. The more hawkish at the Song court wanted even more. To them, the Jin collapse was a once-in-a-lifetime opportunity to reclaim the heartland and finally reunify China before the Mongols solidified their control over the northern plains. An expeditionary force was aimed at Kaifeng and Luoyang.

This proved a serious blunder. Though the Song force managed to get to Kaifeng by mid-1234, troops sent to take Luoyang were ambushed and decimated by the Mongols, who soon had the entire Song army in disorderly flight back south. The fiasco had more than military consequences. It soured the Song's relations with the Mongols. Not a good idea. Distracted by other conquests, the Great Khan might have left the Song alone, at least for a while, but after Hangzhou's ill-conceived grab for Kaifeng, the Mongols unleashed their military machine on the Chinese dynasty. In 1235, three Mongol armies plunged into Sichuan and kicked the Chinese out of the lands they had claimed after the Jin demise. The next year, the Mongols were back, this time practically eradicating Song forces in Sichuan and killing tens of thousands. Only the death of the Mongol commander compelled them to withdraw. Elsewhere, though, the Song defenses held. The Mongols tried again in 1237 and 1238, but Song resistance stiffened, and the conflict reached yet another Chinese-barbarian, eye-to-eye standoff.

The two empires, though, never sealed an accommodation like the Song had with the Khitan Liao and the Jurchen Jin. Aside from a short-lived nonaggression pact reached after another failed Mongol invasion in the late 1250s, the Song expended little effort to attain the sort of stable peace that had kept the previous nomad dynasties at bay. Emboldened by their army's success in holding off the Mongol incursions, the Southern Song court maintained a hostile stance against their new northern neighbor. On the other side of the Yangzi, the Mongols, too, had scant interest in a permanent settlement. The purpose of their empire was conquest, and though their efforts to destroy the Song faced delays and setbacks, the commitment to doing so remained unchanged.

The job fell to the illustrious Kublai Khan. One of Genghis's grandsons, Kublai was given control of the Mongols' domain in north China after his brother became Great Khan in 1251. At the time the Mongols still perceived their empire as global, with one chief leader and successor to Genghis overseeing the entire, continent-wide creation. After his brother's death, Kublai succeeded to that lofty position in 1260, but his election was disputed, and the civil war that resulted opened a rift between Genghis's descendants that never fully healed. Kublai maintained his title of Great Khan and nominal suzerainty over the other chunks of the Mongol realm. But in reality, the different branches of Genghis's family ruled over their own parcels of empire more or less free of the Great Khan Kublai's interference.

That sealed the Song's fate. Kublai became more reliant on his position in China than before, and that meant he needed to bolster his legitimacy as a Chinese emperor. In 1271, he proclaimed a new dynasty, and he chose a dynastic name never used before—the Yuan. No copying of Chinese antiquity here. The Mongols were signaling that a new era in China had begun. The problem was, with the Song still alive and kicking in Hangzhou, claiming the

Mandate of Heaven was effectively impossible. For Kublai's reign over China to thrive, the Song had to die.

The final push began in 1268. The Mongols had grown accustomed to quick, overwhelming victories, but not this time. The Song staged a bitter, bloody fight to the death. Kublai immediately ran into two strongholds protecting the central Yangzi. The Mongols floated five thousand boats on the river to prevent the Song from reinforcing or supplying the two key fortresses. Still, the stubborn Song commanders stopped Kublai cold for five years. A breakthrough was achieved only after Kublai imported Muslim specialists in siege warfare to build a catapult able to hurl stones large enough to breach the fortress walls. The first to fall, Fancheng, was overrun in 1273. All of its inhabitants, possibly ten thousand people, were massacred, and their bodies stacked up along the river as a dire warning to the still-standing second fortress at Xiangyang. Sufficiently shaken, the commander there defected to the Mongols and the city surrendered.

After a two-year hiatus, Kublai's army of two hundred thousand crossed the Yangzi, with most of the troops heading down the river toward the Song capital at Hangzhou. The Song's Empress Dowager, then acting as regent for a boy-emperor, made a desperate call to the people to defend their three-hundred-year-old dynasty; two hundred thousand loyal subjects rallied to the throne. In a last-ditch effort to save the Song, the empress and her court emptied what was left in their treasury to throw one last, major army at the Mongols. Dispatched in early 1275, the force of one hundred thousand soldiers and thousands of ships met Kublai's host near the metropolis of Yangzhou, and it was a disaster for the Song. Two thousand vessels were lost; many simply surrendered to the invaders. After that, no organized force stood between the Mongols and Hangzhou.

Even then, though, the Chinese fought tenaciously, however they could. Spontaneous anti-Mongol uprisings dogged Kublai's armies behind the front lines, and the Mongol generals turned to terror, butchering ten thousand men, women, and children in the town of Changzhou, which had stubbornly resisted, as a stark warning to others unwilling to submit. Such brutality convinced the Song court at the turn of 1276 to spirit two young scions of the Song royal family, aged four and three, out of Hangzhou, to set up an alternative court to ensure the fire of resistance kept burning even if the capital was lost.

At this point, that calamity was inevitable. Abandoned by some of her top lieutenants, the empress surrendered the city. In February 1276, the boy-emperor acknowledged the divine right to rule had passed into barbarian hands. "Now, the Mandate of Heaven has been restored, Your servant chooses to depart from it."[28] The Mongols occupied Hangzhou in March, while the young emperor and much of the rest of his court were escorted to the Mongol capital in the north. Exiled to Tibet, he entered a Buddhist monastery, then committed suicide in 1323.

The Song weren't finished just yet. Three more years would pass before the Mongols were able to occupy the whole country. Song loyalists lost and reclaimed the port city of Guangzhou from the Mongols five times. Yet it was hopeless. Mongol troops resorted to their usual massacres to quell resistance, and they relentlessly chased the baby royals and their courtiers, eventually off the mainland entirely, to the island of Yashan off China's southeast coast. There the last loyal remnants of the Song made their final stand in 1279. One of the Mongols' senior commanders sent a note to the Song court recommending surrender. Zhang Shijie, a loyal minister, responded: "I would rather die than betray my country."[29] The ensuing naval contest was fierce, but ultimately futile. After a full day's fighting, only a handful of Song vessels remained willing or able to continue the fight. On the deck of one of these battered ships, a minister took into his arms the final Song sovereign, the child-emperor Dibing, wearing his imperial robes, and plunged into the sea.

=

Watching from the deck of the Mongol flagship was Wen Tianxiang. The Song senior councilor turned war prisoner was brought on board by a Mongol commander to witness the final destruction of his beloved dynasty. By then, Wen had earned a well-deserved reputation as one of the Song's most resolute and implacable defenders. Three years earlier, in 1276, with enemy forces already on the north side of Hangzhou, the empress dispatched Wen to negotiate terms with Bayan, the Mongol general. The belligerent Wen was the wrong man for the job.

"Do you have good will towards my country or are you set on extinguishing the Song?" he asked Bayan.

"My Emperor is very clear; we are set to extinguish the Song," the general bluntly answered.

"In that case please immediately pull your troops back. . . . If you insist on wiping the Song off the map, the people in the south and the Song army will fight you to the bitter end, and you will reap a bitter fruit."[30]

Angered by Wen's testiness, Bayan detained him and sent him north. But Wen managed to escape and make his way back into Song territory, where he raised an army in Jiangxi and fought the Mongol advance. By early 1279, however, Wen found himself cornered in the mountains of southeast Guangdong, and the Mongols managed to capture him in a surprise raid.

After the fateful naval battle at Yashan, Wen was moved to Kublai's capital at Dadu (modern Beijing). Kublai was unsure how to handle the Song hero. Fearful of Wen becoming a martyr to rally further Chinese resistance, his officials first treated Wen well and tried enlisting him into the Yuan government. When Wen rebuffed these offers, they eventually chained him into a prison cell that was often flooded with water. In 1283, Kublai decided to try to co-opt Wen one last time. Invited into an audience at the palace, Kublai Khan personally offered Wen the job of his chief minister. Again, Wen refused. "Only by dying now would I feel comfortable in the company of the patriots and heroes who died before me." Determined to win over Wen, Kublai then asked him to become the military affairs commissioner. "All I want now is to die," Wen responded.[31]

Realizing Wen would never submit, Kublai accommodated him. Wen was brought to a public execution ground where thousands had gathered to witness the final moments of the great patriot. Wen asked the crowd which direction was south, then bowed reverently several times in that direction. His last words were, "I have completed my service."[32]

Wen was far from alone in choosing death over cooperation. Many palace officials, elite intelligentsia, bureaucrats, and others who could not tolerate life under Mongol rule committed suicide after the fall of Song. Often, they strangled or starved themselves to death. It was their final act of defiance to the barbarians. Their stories were handed down to future generations—the official, court-written history of the Song Dynasty is stuffed with their biographies—and they became symbols of loyalty, not just to the Song emperors, but to the very concept of Chinese dynastic rule.

The feeling was somewhat mutual. Kublai Khan had no choice but to rely on large numbers of Chinese officials to fill the Yuan's vast bureaucracy, but he never fully trusted them, especially those hailing from the south, which had so feverously opposed him. He was also concerned that his Mongol compatriots would become too assimilated into the far more numerous masses of Chinese with their comfortable lifestyles and tasty food. The Yuan went so far as to ban marriages between Mongols and Chinese (with little success).

More effective was a hierarchical, four-tier system Kublai introduced that controlled access to government positions based on ethnic background. The Mongols were of course at the top. Next came the "green-eyed" people—which meant mainly Central Asians, many of them Muslims. The Han Chinese were placed below the foreigners, with northerners in the third tier and those recalcitrant southerners at the very bottom. Never before had a regime in China made ethnicity the key factor in determining who governed the state. As a result, many of the most influential positions in the Yuan administration were held by foreigners. Even those Chinese who served the Yuan state weren't completely trusted by their Mongol overlords. The Mongols appointed censors to travel incognito around the realm to report back to the court on what the Chinese officials were up to.

To implement such a system, Kublai had to suspend the beloved civil service exams that would have favored Chinese candidates steeped in the necessary classical education. (Many of the Mongols, including Kublai himself, never learned the Chinese language.) That allowed the Yuan to appoint government officials based on recommendation alone. Even after the exams were reinstated by one of Kublai's successors in 1313, they were not the sole route to state service, and they were altered to discriminate against Chinese students. Mongols and other foreigners got easier exams, while their better-educated Chinese competitors were restricted by a quota.

The Chinese had become second-class citizens (or actually, third- and fourth-class) in their own homeland. Meanwhile, foreigners flooded into government in China in numbers never witnessed before. Mongols, Persians, Central Asians, Tibetans, and others filled Kublai's court. (The famous Venetian Marco Polo served the Yuan for about three years.) Muslims were especially prominent in managing the state's finances. One of Kublai's most trusted advisors was a Tibetan Buddhist monk, the Phags-pa Lama, who also tutored the royal children. The barbarians hadn't just scaled the walls, they made themselves at home in the living room.

Needless to say, such measures brewed resentment among the Chinese elite. Scholar-officials had dominated the bureaucracy for centuries—under the Song, more than ever before. Now they found themselves sidelined in their own country. Some, of course, served the Yuan willingly and reached relatively senior positions. Many more who remained in government got stuck in lowly, poorly paid clerical jobs with little opportunity for advancement.

For others, though, the Mongols were simply beyond the pale, and they continued to resist. What was truly offensive about the Mongols was not that they were northern mutton-eaters—the Chinese political elite had long experience with such uncouth intruders. It was the Mongols' disregard for principles of Chinese rulership that really irked the literati. The fact that the Mongols were exceptional warriors meant little to scholar-statesmen who favored the pen over the sword. By denigrating the position of the educated civilian scholar, the Mongols trampled on China's Confucian heritage. That was an indignity many Chinese elite could simply not tolerate.

They protested in a Confucian way—not with violence, or street marches, or rebellion, but withdrawal. Though Confucius believed the educated had a duty to engage in public service, he also realized that that responsibility could conflict with something even more important: virtue. A proper gentleman should not serve a ruler who is not benevolent. "When right principles of government prevail in the kingdom, he will show himself; when they are prostrated, he will keep concealed," Confucius had said.[33] Many Confucian-trained officials chose to follow their master and refused any connection with the Yuan government, instead finding work as doctors, artists, or private teachers. Typical of this breed was scholar and poet Liu Yin, who repeatedly turned down offers of attractive positions in the Yuan to teach and write. In a poem, he suggested why:

> Those who uphold the dao (i.e., ethics) frequently are led to
> follow a solitary course.
> This practice has existed since Zhou and Qin times.
> The solitary course of the recluse moreover merits approval;
> What kind of person would weakly submit to defiling himself? . . .
> In a degenerate final age,
> Is it not meaningless to possess Confucian rank and office?[34]

Some took their resistance to more extreme levels. Xie Fangde, a Song official who was frequently critical of its policies and sickened by its recurring incompetence, still remained loyal to the dynasty for the rest of his life. In 1278, he retired to his home province to become a teacher. Xie went so far as to refuse to use the Yuan calendar, and he continued to refer to the final Song emperor as if he was still on the throne. He rejected every one of numerous offers of government posts from the Yuan, and reproached those Chinese who accepted them. The Yuan court, however, was insistent, and when Xie was brought to Beijing in another attempt to press him to serve, he starved himself to death. Another famous loyalist, Zheng Sixiao, a renowned Chinese painter, passed his first civil service exam, but the Song fell before he acceded to any office. He refused to sit or lie facing the north, indicating he wasn't a subject of the new rulers, whom he derided as beasts and trespassers. As he wrote,

> In the past, in the age of the former emperor, . . .
> The bright light of learning and refinement flooded the world,
> And superior and heroic men stood before their ruler.
> But since the barbarian soldiers invaded,
> With sudden shock, Han rule was toppled.
> To this day the proper ways of men are in chaos.
> To lonely mountain valleys have fled all the worthies of the
> former age.[35]

Zheng also infused resistance into his famed paintings using symbols—for instance, depicting flowers without roots. A similar spirit was displayed by Gong Kai. A minor official in the Song government, he would not serve the Yuan barbarians and fell into extreme poverty. To support his family, he sold paintings or exchanged them for food. At the time, paintings of horses were extremely popular with the steppe invaders. To protest their rule, Gong Kai instead depicted an emaciated steed—an avatar for the withered conditions of China under the Mongols.

Those who succumbed to the desire for status and collaborated with the Mongols suffered for it. One such figure was Zhao Mengfu. His was a betrayal twice over: he was not only a former Song official but also a descendant of the dynasty's royal family. Many of his friends stopped speaking to him, and some in his own clan would no longer recognize him as a member and wrote criticisms of him. Zhao himself was queasy about his decision, as he expressed in verse, composed after examining a painting of an official who resigned from his post when the past dynasty he had served fell:

> *Each person lives his life in this world according to his own times;*
> *Whether to come forth and serve, or to retire in withdrawal, is not*
> *   a fortuitous decision. . . .*
> *How readily he gave up his official position,*
> *And bore poverty, dozing contentedly by his north window.*
> *Rolling up this painting, I sigh repeatedly;*
> *How long since the world has known the likes of this Worthy?*[36]

=

If Kublai Khan had any hope of governing China, somehow he had to prove to the skeptical Chinese that he, a barbarian, had earned the Mandate of Heaven. So he realized he had no choice but to become more Chinese. There was no way the Han people would accept a steppe barbarian as their emperor unless he acted something like his Tang and Song predecessors. That is why, despite his misgivings about Mongol absorption, Kublai ended up adopting and even promoting many aspects of Chinese traditional government, culture, and art.

Kublai, for instance, maintained most of the Chinese governing institutions bequeathed to him by previous dynasties, and he had to play the role of the Chinese emperor by participating in the court rituals of his Chinese predecessors. One of the criticisms hurled at him by his political opponents within the Mongol empire was that he had "gone native" and thus was unfit to rule over his own people. As was the case with the Jurchens, the question was, Who had really conquered whom? The Mongols couldn't escape the pull of Chinese civilization.

Kublai's main justification for Yuan rule was the undeniable fact that he had unified "all under Heaven," something that had gone unaccomplished since the end of the Tang, almost four centuries earlier. Following the practice of preceding dynasties, Kublai ordered official histories written for the Song and Jin, in the process meshing his own regime in the long narrative of Chinese imperial history. The Yuan khan-emperors also introduced new practices that succeeding dynasties accepted as standard. Kublai requested his scholars produce a national gazetteer—a compendium of geographic, administrative, and cultural information from across the realm. The first edition appeared in 1291. Future dynasties would publish their own versions. Though they came to favor Tibetan Buddhism, the Mongol rulers of the Yuan ended up heavily supporting Confucianism as well, and in ways that rippled through all of East Asia. When the Yuan restarted the civil service exams, the court mandated that the new Song-era Neo-Confucian interpretations be the core curriculum—a major change in education policy that stuck for the remainder of the imperial period, and helped spread Confucian teachings to other states in the region.

Kublai went so far to polish his Chinese credentials that he relocated the Mongol capital. In 1267, he ordered a new city to be built at Dadu—modern Beijing—and the seat of Mongol government transferred there from Karakorum, farther north in Mongolia. There he constructed palaces and other buildings largely along Chinese architectural lines. Except for a fifty-year hiatus, the city has remained the capital of China to the present day. Despite his preference for non-Chinese officials, the structure of the state itself stayed very much the same. He preserved the standard system of ministries, and on a local level, not much changed at all. In one significant alteration, the Yuan broke the country up into a dozen provinces, which served as the basis for China's administration down to modern times.

=

Ultimately, though, the Mongols failed at ruling China. The Yuan Dynasty survived less than a century, barely a few pages in China's voluminous history. Chaotic and often bloody scrums over the imperial succession—between 1307 and 1333, ten khans sat on the Yuan throne, one of them twice—contributed to an undisciplined, corrupt, and ineffective government. The Mongols' endless wars and grandiose building schemes created big bills that the Yuan paid by raising taxes. Some 150,000 Chinese were dragged into labor brigades to repair Yellow River dikes in the mid-1300s; they got compensated in worthless Yuan script. Unpopular from the start as a barbarian intrusion, the Yuan's missteps primed the country for rebellion. The last Yuan ruler was chased from Beijing by rebels led by Zhu Yuanzhang in 1368. The Mongol court fled back to their Mongolian homeland; Zhu founded the Ming Dynasty.

The Chinese look back at the Mongol period as a time of oppression under a foreign regime that cared little for their country or well-being. Some Chinese scholars refused to acknowledge that the Yuan was a legitimate dynasty. Barbarians like the Mongols could never hold the Mandate of Heaven since they did not share the civilized culture of the Chinese, and could never attain the virtue necessary to rule during their short bursts of control over China. "It is on these grounds that the former kings treated barbarians as though they were animals and did not put them in the same category as the people of China," wrote scholar Fang Xiaoru in a famous essay on the matter. "The upright men and great Confucians of former times knew that barbarians were unacceptable as leaders." The Yuan khans were therefore incapable of being considered the true emperors of China. "During the century of Yuan rule, everyone became barbarized" and the Chinese "were acclimated to these things." As a result, "everyone would have been shocked and amazed to hear them (Mongol rulers) repudiated on the grounds of barbarism." That, he went on, "is not an outlook that is in accord with the Way."[37]

But there is no denying that the Mongols left their permanent mark on China. In fact, they forever changed the Chinese history of the world, arguably more than any other batch of invading barbarians. For the first time, China became part of a bigger world. Sure, the armies of Han and Tang had marched all the way to Central Asia, and Chinese civilization still dominated in the countries of East Asia. But with the Mongol conquests, China became integrated into the Mongol Empire, and thus into the rest of the world in entirely new ways. When the Mongols were still unified, the Chinese were latched into a common administration for the entire empire. But even after the descendants of Genghis Khan broke up the empire into semi-independent domains, the links between them remained strong. Mongol rule merged China more tightly than ever into the world around it.

The Mongols actively encouraged such interaction between their diverse conquests, stretching from East Asia to Eastern Europe. They constructed roads, policed them with troops to keep them safe, and lined them with postal stations to speed communications and caravanserais (the ancient equivalent of modern truck stops) to provide havens for travelers. Over these new thoroughfares—the Internet of the thirteenth century—surged people and products, ideas and ideologies, food and fashion, art and armies, science and scripture.

China, as one of the world's most advanced civilizations, was both a change agent and forever changed by this medieval world wide web. Even under the Mongol thumb, Chinese culture held such power and appeal that it still heavily influenced global civilization, only now its ideas, art, and technology traveled even more smoothly along the cross-continental linkages knit by the vast Mongol conquests. Relations between the Yuan in China and the Mongol Ilkhanate, which was centered on Iran, were especially close, sparking an avid mixing and mingling of the great Chinese and Persian cultures to an extent never witnessed previously, leading to advancements in varied arts and sciences.

Persians and others from the Mongols' Middle Eastern domains helped translate Iranian medical texts into Chinese and built Persian-style hospitals in China. Meanwhile, Chinese doctors and their traditional herbal concoctions were popular at the Ilkhanate court. Back in China, Chinese medicine benefited from an influx of new ingredients as previously unknown foods drifted their way from Eurasia. The Chinese and Persians also shared information on astronomy at a Mongol-built observatory. Rashid al-Din, the great Persian scholar-statesman of the time, appears to have had access to Chinese historical records for his groundbreaking and monumental world history, *The Compendium of Chronicles*.

Islamic art flourished during the Mongol period, to a great degree because of cross-cultural influences seeping in from China and elsewhere. The development of one of the Islamic world's most cherished and distinctive artistic traditions—the miniature painting—was a creation of incoming Chinese styles floating through the Mongol Empire and intermingling with local practices. The Mongols imported Chinese scholar-officials to help them manage their Persian domain, and these bureaucrats were also often experienced artists, who enjoyed painting pictures for each other. The Persians took note of their technique and added it to their own repertoire, giving birth to a syncretic form of painting. Commonly used Chinese depictions of dragons, clouds, and plants influenced designs on Middle Eastern textiles and pottery. Islamic painters adopted the Chinese method of presenting framed human figures amid rocks and other natural features. From west Asia, Chinese artistic styles hopscotched through the Black Sea to Italy, where they influenced art there, too.

The more mundane filtered back and forth between China and the Middle East as well. A form of wheat was introduced to China during the Mongol period that was better suited to making noodles and dumpling wrappers, forever embellishing the Chinese diet. It also appears the production of cotton fabric arrived in China from the Middle East, promoted by the Mongols, who favored it for army uniforms.

Perhaps the most consequential legacy of the Mongol Empire is that its bandit-free highways and trade-friendly policies helped initiate direct contact between the West and China. It appears that a sufficient number of traders from Europe made their way to the Far East to encourage one Florentine businessman, Francesco Balducci Pegolotti, in the mid-fourteenth century to pen a merchants' handbook, the *Pratica della mercatura* (*Practice of Marketing*), with specific directions for reaching Beijing. The most famous of these

Western travelers was a young Venetian trader named Marco Polo. What he saw and learned in Yuan China, and shared in one of history's most important books, *The Description of the World*, shaped European views of China for centuries to come, and inadvertently contributed to events that would abruptly redirect the Chinese history of the world.

Six

MADE IN CHINA

Rumble rumble of carts to haul the priceless cargo;
heaps, hordes to dazzle the market—men race with the news.
In singing-girl towers to play at dice, a million on one throw;
by flag-flown pavilions calling for wine, ten thousand a cask . . .

–poem by Lu You

For Marco Polo, imperial China in the thirteenth century was a vision of the future. China was a bustle of commerce, both local and international, and a fountain of inventive genius. And it was rich. Really, really rich. Polo traveled through Mongol-run China like a starstruck tourist, agog at its palatial architecture, teeming cities, and—he was a merchant, after all—well-stocked marketplaces. Europeans like Polo had simply never seen anything like it back home. By comparison, Europe was still a backwater, a region whose time had yet to come. His account of his twenty-four-year journey to China and back—made between 1271 and 1295—sounded so fantastic to dumbstruck readers in the Europe of his day that they dubbed him *Il Milione*, the Man of a Million Tales.

Tall tales were a Chinese specialty. Everywhere Polo went, he gushed about the overflowing stacks of silk, gold, grain, and other ample "provisions," the merchant ships crowding riversides, the richly decorated palaces and mansions. In Chengdu, a metropolis in Sichuan in the southwest, he discovered on the Min River "so many ships—such a great multitude—that no men's hearts or eyes that have not seen it for themselves could believe it. So great is the multitude and great abundance of great merchandise that merchants carry up and down this river that no man in the world who has not seen it could believe it." Polo recounted that he traveled ten days in the area of Beijing, "the whole time finding many beautiful cities, many beautiful castles of great trade and great crafts, beautiful fields, beautiful vineyards, and civilized people." But such were so common that Polo then declared that "there's nothing special to mention; therefore, we won't tell you anything about it."[1]

What he found in the lands that had been the Southern Song left him practically speechless. "It's impossible to relate the great wealth in this kingdom," he admitted. "There was no kingdom in the whole world worth half as much as this one, for the king had so much at his disposal that it was a marvelous thing."[2] Arriving at the Yangzi, Polo said that "more ships, with more expensive things of greater value sail on this river than on all the rivers of the Christians, or on all their seas."[3] More impressive than even that was the Grand Canal. "Very great quantities of grain and rice are collected and carried by water" to the capital, he explained with obvious awe. "Do not think that this is by sea, but by river and through lakes." The government "had a very large, wide, and deep moat made from one river to the other and from one lake to the other. Great ships sail it going in this way."[4]

The Song cities he described as wonderlands of palaces, temples, gardens, stately homes, busy markets, and architectural marvels. In the city of Suzhou, he found "a good 6,000 stone bridges that one or two galleys could well pass under."[5] Hangzhou, the former Southern Song capital, "is without a doubt the best and the noblest city in the world," he exclaimed. "There are so many and such rich merchants there doing so much business that no man could say the truth of it, for it was beyond measure." Around the city's famous lake, "there are many beautiful palaces and many beautiful houses belonging to nobles and great men, so wondrously made that they could not be better or more richly devised or done."[6] The palace of the former Song emperor was especially spectacular. "This palace has 20 halls, all of the same size; and they are so large that 10,000 men could easily eat at table; and all are very nobly painted and worked in gold."[7]

On the coast, Polo was amazed by China's foreign trade. In the port city of Quanzhou, Polo said, ships from India arrived with pearls, precious stones, and other luxurious merchandise that was then shipped onward into the rest of the empire. "For each shipload of pepper going to Alexandria or other places to be carried to Christian lands, a hundred come to this port" of Quanzhou.[8]

The image that Polo painted of "Cathay," of a fairy-tale land of gold and silk, became the standard perception of China in the West for centuries to come. And though Polo (or perhaps the man who wrote his story) was certainly fond of hyperbole, on the economy of China he stayed close to the mark. Today in the West, China is described as an "emerging" economy, catching up with the richer, more advanced United States and Europe. But that situation is an aberration. China was either the largest or second-largest economy in the world continuously from 1 AD to the nineteenth century. (Its main rival was India.)[9] China was a manufacturing powerhouse, a high-tech exporter, an innovation hub, and an engine of the global economy long before Marco Polo embarked on his famous journey. In the Chinese history of the world, its economy never had to "rise" on the world stage. China was comfortably on top, watching everyone else scrambling to catch up. For most of recorded history, China was an economic superpower.

===

Marco Polo is the most famous trader to have braved the dangers of the trek to China in the days before daily airline flights and supersized container ships. But by the time he began his journey, China had been firmly at the center of global trade for more than a millennium. Countless other merchants had already trod the path to the Middle Kingdom, on camels and horses, lugging their wares in carts across desert wastes and mountain heights, or sailing the tumultuous tropical seas in squeaking, wooden sailing ships, their hulls packed with spices. For Europe, Polo was a pioneer, a novelty; for much of the rest of the world, he was following trading routes that had been well-worn since Roman times.

We tend to equate the formation of an integrated world economy with the rise of Europe. When the Portuguese felt their way around the Cape of Good Hope and into the Indian Ocean in the late fifteenth century, the cross-continental trading networks that bound the West with the Far East were forged. But that is a very Euro-centric view of economic evolution. In the Chinese history of the world, a global trading system existed for centuries before the Portuguese washed up on the shores of India. And unlike Western Europe, which played a bit role in this early world order, China was its beating heart, pumping lifeblood into the entire global economy. China was both a voracious consumer of stuff from the rest of the world—from jade to pepper to Buddhist relics—and a production center capable of making luxury goods on a mammoth scale no other economy could match. Yes, China was a manufacturing force two thousand years before today's iPhones were even in man's imagination. China also held a unique geographic position in global networks of exchange—a terminus of a series of interconnected sea and land trading routes that linked its gargantuan economy to other rich civilizations in South Asia, Central Asia, the Middle East, and the Mediterranean.

The origins of China's dominant position in this pre-Western world system go all the way back to the Han Dynasty's Emperor Wu, and his war with the Xiongnu. When his determined explorer, Zhang Qian, made his way to Afghanistan in the second century BC and marveled at the myriad goods stacked in market stalls there, the most surprising items he discovered were from home. Chinese-made bamboo canes and cloth had arrived in inner Asia before the Chinese themselves. The wares had somehow trickled through India from China's southwest. Zhang took note. There was already demand for Chinese products outside of China, and the Chinese didn't even know it.

When Zhang returned to the Han capital, he convinced the court of Emperor Wu to send him off on another mission, this one to locate that mysterious trade route to India. He never found it. Blocked by tangled jungle and hostile tribes in the wilds of what is today Yunnan province, Zhang and his party were forced to turn back. But his exploits did help create an even more important trade route: the Silk Road.

When Emperor Wu sent his armies west in the wake of Zhang's discoveries, he kicked down the remaining barriers to trade between China and Central Asia. And from there, to the Roman Empire. In the century before Christ, trading networks were being knit that spanned the Eurasian landmass, connecting the great civilizations of China, India, Persia, and Rome.

The Silk Road was not a single highway stretching between East and West. It was a series of paths, tracks, and passes winding their way through the deserts, mountains, and steppe at the center of Asia. Few individuals managed the entire journey. By the time a parcel of goods wound its way to its final destination, it had probably passed between numerous hands, markets, horse carts, and river barges.

The amount of trade that took place was relatively small at this early stage—there's only so much a camel can carry—but the influence of the Silk Road went far beyond the material. Its biggest impact was from the exchange of ideas between the world's civilizations. Buddhism would come to China from India over these caravan tracks. So did Islam and Christianity, and the many sorts of people who practiced these foreign doctrines. Critical Chinese technology that shaped the rest of the world shuffled west. The Silk Road was an early thoroughfare of globalization, with China at the forefront.

==

What is most amazing about these ancient exchanges is that they happened at all. The Silk Road was a dangerous one, each stage another test of endurance, guts, and survival skills. There were the natural hazards—the storms, the swollen rivers, the waterless wastelands, the precipitous peaks—and also the man-made. Rarely were the caravans safe from bandits, sticky-fingered bureaucrats, or marauding armies. Trade was literally a matter of life and death.

Departing from China, the route took travelers west through what is now Gansu province to remote Dunhuang. Once the intrepid passed through this dusty outpost, they were walking into an unfamiliar world of strange foreign peoples, tongues, and cultures. Caravans had to navigate around the fearsome Taklamakan Desert, an ocean of towering sand dunes. The route connected a series of oasis towns where the parched and hungry could find water and provisions—either to the northwest through culturally diverse Turpan, or southwest to wealthy Khotan (modern Hotan). The two prongs met at the ancient market town of Kashgar (today near the Chinese border with Pakistan). The perils of this desert trek were captured in a memoir by a Chinese Buddhist monk named Faxian, who survived the journey around the turn of the fifth century AD. His motive wasn't money, but mantra. He undertook the long trip to India in search of Buddhist scripture to enhance the knowledge of the increasingly popular faith in his home country. The horrors that awaited him as he departed Dunhuang for the western desert could paralyze the stoutest of hearts. "There are many evil demons and hot winds," Faxian recalled. Travelers "who encounter them perish all to a man. There is not a bird to be seen in the air above, nor an animal on the ground below. Though you look all round most earnestly to find where you can cross, you know not where to make your choice, the only mark and indication being the dry bones of the dead (left upon the sand)."[10]

Things didn't get much easier. From Kashgar, the travelers confronted some of the world's highest mountains—the Pamirs. Here, the Tianshan, Kunlun, Karakoram, Hindu Kush, and Himalaya ranges smash into each other, creating a spine-tingling tangle of icy cliffs and death-defying passes. Some envoys from northern India, on their missions to China, had to climb over the Kunlun and Karakoram ranges, where they required an armed escort to protect them from bandits. The cliff ledges narrowed to a terrifying eighteen inches wide, and at some points the travelers had to be roped together for safety.

The movers and shakers of the ancient Silk Road were the Sogdians, a people based in Samarkand (now in Uzbekistan). They were the merchants extraordinaire of their time, with the expertise in financing, stocking, and managing caravans, knowledge of the region's markets and pricing, and sheer bravery to grease the exchange between China, India, Central Asia, and Persia. Their language was the lingua franca of early Silk Road trade. They were joined, however, by a myriad of peoples from across Eurasia. Old documents stashed in a cave in Dunhuang reveal a polyglot trading community, with papers written in Sanskrit (from India), Sogdian, Tibetan, Uighur, and Khotanese. One sheet even has Hebrew on it. The fussy bureaucrats of Chinese dynasties often kept a careful eye on the comings and goings of these merchant barbarians. During the Han Dynasty, any foreigners traveling into China on the Silk Road had to have a pass denoting their route inside the empire, the goods they carried, and even personal details—sort of a photo ID before the era of photos. One such pass from the third century AD describes a thirty-year-old visitor as having "medium build, black hair, big eyes, with moustache and beard."[11]

These tenuous overland tracks were not the sole links connecting China and the world. Sea routes for trade were established at an early date, too, probably by the first century AD between China and India. By the time of Faxian, the maritime traffic had become quite regular. Faxian chose to sail back home along these ocean lanes, probably because it was faster and cheaper than the tedious overland trek. The journey, though, proved no less harrowing. The ship, a merchantman carrying about two hundred people, encountered a storm on its way from Sri Lanka to Southeast Asia. "The merchants were greatly alarmed, feeling their risk of instant death," the narrative recounts. "Afraid that the vessel would fill, they took their bulky goods and threw them into the water." Faxian, however, clung to his precious Buddhist texts and icons that he had risked so much to acquire and refused to dump them into the sea.

Mariners at this early date were not yet using compasses to navigate in the open ocean (although the Chinese had already invented it—more on that below), and when the sun and stars were obscured by clouds, they simply lost all sense of direction and distance. "The great ocean spreads out, a boundless expanse," Faxian's memoirs recount. "If the weather were dark and rainy, (the ship) went as she was carried by the wind, without any definite course. . . . The merchants were full of terror, not knowing where they were going. . . . If she had come on any hidden rock, there would have been no way of escape."[12] The ship managed to patch a leak in the hull and make it safely to Sumatra (an island in Indonesia today), where Faxian changed vessels for the final leg of his trip, to the Chinese port city of Guangzhou. This boat, too, ran into serious trouble. Again plagued by clouds, the ship got carried off course. "The provisions and water were nearly exhausted. They used the saltwater of the sea for cooking, and carefully divided the (fresh) water, each man getting two pints. Soon the whole was nearly gone." Faxian eventually landed in China—but in the Shandong peninsula in China's east on the Yellow Sea, a full one thousand miles from the ship's original destination.

Over time, though, maritime travel across the Indian Ocean became more consistent, reliable, and efficient, and hence more important. By the eighth century, these sea routes had overtaken the old overland Silk Road as the primary avenue of trade between China and the rest of the world. Part of the reason was that ship construction improved, making them both safer and capable of hauling larger and heavier amounts of cargo. By the 700s, vessels called Kunlun ships with one thousand men were plying the sea-lanes to and from China. They were apparently constructed by sewing wooden planks together with cord made from the bark of coconut trees. By the eleventh century, the Chinese were building even more imposing craft, hammered together with iron nails, which made them sturdier on the rolling waves. Chinese mariners had by that time also figured out how to navigate on the open ocean with a compass, freeing them from the sun, moon, stars, and coastlines.

With such technological advancements, maritime trade became more complex. Rather than risking the entire voyage from the Red Sea or Persian Gulf all the way to southern China, ships often kept to shorter, regular routes and dropped off their cargoes at convenient locations, such as southern India and western Indonesia, where the merchandise got reloaded onto other vessels for the next leg of the journey. Much like the old Silk Road, maritime trade was an interlocked series of regional shipping networks, which passed goods from China to South Asia, the Middle East, and ultimately the Mediterranean world.

China was absolutely critical to these far-flung trading operations, and therefore economic progress in much of the world. The Chinese imported tremendous quantities of spices, aromatics, frankincense, horses, tropical wood, camphor, ivory, cinnabar, rosewater, pearls, gems, coral, and cotton fabric, from India, Southeast Asia, and Persia. This globe-spanning economic system was well in place by the 1300s, but the roots of it go back much further, perhaps six centuries earlier, to the days of the Tang.

By the time of Marco Polo's cross-continental adventure, not only was this seaborne trade flourishing, but the Silk Road through Central Asia was enjoying a renaissance, too. The Mongols' empire encapsulated more or less the entire trading area from Persia and the Black Sea, across the inner Asian steppe, and down to the semitropical ports of southeast China. These regions were melted into something of a proto-free-trade zone, in which the Mongol rulers reduced the costs and uncertainty of doing business down the length of the Silk Road. The Yuan emperors also cut taxes on merchants, built roads, allowed travelers to shelter at state postal stations, and offered low-interest loans to trade organizations. Polo took note of how the security provided by the Mongols encouraged commerce. "They maintained such great justice in their kingdom that no one did any bad deeds; at night, shops remained open and nothing was taken, for you could go about at night as if it were day."[13] And the roads themselves "are paved so that one can travel there very cleanly, both by horse and on foot."[14] The khans had trees planted along the roadways "so that everyone could see the road and not get lost for you will find these trees on out-of-the-way roads—a great comfort to merchants and sellers."[15]

By the thirteenth century, China was a crucial and unique connection point for global trade—tying together the overland roadways through Central Asia with the maritime lanes weaving their way from the Red Sea to the south China coast. With new technology and safer travel, larger quantities of goods were being shipped between East and West. Long before the rise of the West, an interconnected economic system stretching across the known world, and driven to a great degree by China, was well established. The Europeans were not the creators of the global economy. They were latecomers.

====

What compelled merchants to brave evil desert spirits, typhoons, and icy cliff ledges to get to China? The Chinese had a lot of money to buy their wares. But more than that, China made stuff that the world desired and no one else could make.

We associate China today with low-grade, bottom-shelf merchandise, copycat counterfeits, or other things that fall apart. Many products stamped "Made in China" are merely assembled there—stitched, screwed, hammered, or glued by the countless hands available among the world's largest population. The design, technology, and many of the parts—the real source of value—were invented elsewhere. But for much of human history, China was known for its exquisitely engineered, top quality luxury items, often produced with technology and expertise unknown or unmatched anywhere else.

The most famous of these high-tech specialties was silk. The Silk Road is called the Silk Road because that shimmering fabric was among the most desirable items traded along it. The Chinese were the first to develop the technology to produce silk, and in antiquity, it was most likely the largest manufacturer of the coveted textile. Much of the rest of the world simply had no clue how it was made. Writing in the first century AD, Pliny the Elder, the renowned Roman naturalist and philosopher, got it all wrong. The Chinese are "so famous for the wool that is found in their forests," he said of silk in his *Natural History*. "After steeping it in water, they comb off a white down that adheres to the leaves," which was then spun into thread.[16]

Silk was actually produced from the stringy material silkworms use to form their cocoons. Somehow the Chinese figured out, a long, long time ago, that the thread can be unwound and woven into a light but durable fabric. We don't know exactly how this technology was developed, or who invented it. If you believe an old myth, credit belongs to a legendary empress, named Leizu, who was the principal wife of an equally legendary emperor. While enjoying a pot of tea in a garden under a mulberry tree, a silkworm cocoon dropped into the steaming brew. Lifting out the melting cocoon, she discovered she could draw out a long glimmering thread from it. The hot water, it turned out, loosened the sticky stuff the worms used to bind their cocoons together, allowing the strands of silk to unravel. The quick-witted empress realized that these threads could be the raw material for a beautiful fabric. She began cultivating silkworms in a cluster of mulberry trees—the leaves of which are the critters' preferred diet. Tradition also has it that she invented the first silk loom. The Chinese silk industry was born.

There is no evidence that this story is true. But Empress Leizu became a focus of cult worship as the first sericulturist, both at the royal court and within humble villages, probably starting during the Han Dynasty and continuing, in varying degrees of seriousness, until the twentieth century. Sacrifices and ceremonies honoring the silkworm and sericulture were common even earlier, however. As early as the Shang Dynasty, specialists in divination offered sacrifices to silkworm spirits. Zhou Dynasty empresses participated in a ceremony each spring, at which they collected mulberry leaves to encourage a bumper crop of silkworms. Such reverence for silk and the silkworm at the highest levels of Chinese society is just one indication of how important the textile was in early China.

Archeologists don't know for certain when China began making silk, but it was no later than 2850 BC, the rough date of silk fragments discovered in a bamboo basket in eastern China. There are hints that silk dates back much earlier. If you believe that silkworms carved into ivory is a sign of their cultivation, silk may have already been produced by 4000 BC. Recently, a team of Chinese scientists contended they found evidence of silk in a tomb dating all the way back to 6500 BC.

What we do know is that sericulture was already well established in the Shang Dynasty. Mentions of it can be found scrawled on those oracle bones. And by the time of the Han Dynasty, China was producing silk in such quantities that it was used as a type of currency. Soldiers manning the garrisons out on the empire's remote frontiers were often paid in bolts of silk rather than scarce and inconvenient coins, which they could then barter for the necessities of life with local merchants. As early as the Han Dynasty period, households were even allowed to pay their taxes in silk.

While silk was an expensive luxury item available only to the richest few in most of the world, and would remain that way for centuries to come, the fabric was very much an everyday cloth in China. Sericulture was so widespread by the early first millennium that it was common knowledge to the average family. Farmers' wives would weave silk cloth at home. A verse in one of China's oldest and most revered collections of poetry, the *Classics of Poetry*, captures how silk weaving was a part of the rhythm of life at a very early date:

> *In the silkworm month they strip the mulberry branches*
> > *of their leaves,*
> *And take their axes and hatchets,*
> *To lop off those that are distant and high;*
> *Only stripping the young trees of their leaves . . . ;*
> *In the eighth month, they begin their spinning;*
> *They make dark fabrics and yellow.*
> *Our red manufacture is very brilliant,*
> *It is for the lower robes of our young princes.*[17]

The degree of expertise in silk weaving was high in ancient times as well. Han Dynasty silks came in an eye-watering variety of colors and types—prized "ice white" fabrics, damasks with raised patterns, cloth with zigzags, curls, depictions of animals and faces, horsemen, even Chinese characters. Greatly coveted as

Silk was one Chinese invention that became core to global trade. This scroll from the Song Dynasty period shows the spinning and weaving of silk.

Pictures from History / Bridgeman Images

a sign of social status, silk found its way out of China long before the opening of the Silk Road. Silk has been discovered in Siberia dating back to the fifth century BC. The Han court handed out silk to the Xiongnu in large quantities as part of its peace settlement starting from the early second century BC. And silk was a standard gift given to foreign potentates and tribute missions by the emperors. This fabric found its way into markets across Central Asia and further west, often providing the rulers there a tidy source of profit. Leaders of states in Central Asia sometimes chose to become vassals simply to get their hands on these silken mother lodes. What the Chinese called "tribute," their neighbors sometimes thought of as "trade." Chinese silk was highly prized across Asia. In India, aristocratic families wore it as a sign of their wealth before the start of the Common Era. The sister of King Harsha, the eighth-century ruler who sent delegations to the Tang, wore Chinese silk for her wedding.

Silk also made its way to the Roman Empire. How much, however, is a matter of debate. If you listen to Roman writers, enough for the more self-righteous to gripe about it. To Seneca, writing in the first century AD, silk represented how love of luxury was destroying the moral fiber of Roman society. "I see there raiments of silk—if that can be called raiment, which provides nothing that could possibly afford protection for the body, or indeed modesty, so that, when a woman wears it, she can scarcely, with a clear conscience, swear that she is not naked," he ranted. "These are imported at vast expense from nations unknown even to trade, in order that our married women may not be able to show more of their persons, even to their paramours, in a bedroom than they do on the street."[18] Pliny shared the outrage. "So manifold is the labor, and so distant are the regions which are thus ransacked to supply a dress through which our ladies may in public display their charms."[19] The only thing more distasteful was men exhibiting such impropriety. According to Tacitus, the Senate deemed "that men should not disgrace themselves with silken clothing from the East."[20] They even tried, unsuccessfully, to ban the wearing of silk.

To Pliny, the damage done to Rome by such imported unnecessities went beyond the moral. In a complaint that rings familiar today, he argued that trade with China was dissipating Rome's economic vitality. Rome's pleasure-seeking rich were wasting fortunes on perfumes and other exotica, paying exorbitant prices marked up by profiteering middlemen. "At the very lowest computation, India, the Seres [China], and the Arabian Peninsula, withdraw from our empire one hundred millions of sesterces every year—so dearly do we pay for our luxury and our women."[21] That's a staggering sum—the equivalent of more than 10 percent of the empire's annual budget or half of its yearly mint output.[22]

Some modern scholars believe Pliny and his compatriots were greatly exaggerating.[23] Archeologists have found no silk in Rome itself that they can without doubt confirm as Chinese. The closest place they've unearthed clearly identified Chinese silk is from Palmyra (in what is now Syria) dating from the first to third centuries AD. Still, it's not easy to know, since it isn't exactly clear where else the silk Pliny complained about would have been made. By the Han Dynasty period, other societies had started weaving their own silk. On the Greek island of Cos, they used an inferior process that produced silks of lesser quality than China's. There is new evidence that silk production began on the Indian subcontinent earlier than originally believed.

Yet it is widely believed that the method developed by the Chinese—of cultivating silkworms, boiling the cocoons, and unwinding the silk in long, single strands—was proprietary technology in antiquity, akin to a secret software code or microchip design of today. Tall tales abound about how this technical know-how got smuggled out of China. One features a lonely Chinese princess sent off to a marriage in a foreign land, who hid silkworms in her hair to ensure a steady supply of her beloved fabric in her new, less civilized home. Another recounts an act of espionage by Christian monks who concealed silkworm eggs in their robes to unveil the unknown marvels of silk to the West.

The reality is probably less romantic. The Chinese state did not do a particularly good job of keeping silk's secrets secret. Sericulture seeped out of China slowly, but surely. Chinese immigrants probably brought it to Korea as early as the second century BC; from there, it made its way to Japan, where silk was being produced by the third century AD. The remains of a mulberry orchard dating from that same century have been found near Khotan, now in far western China but then a wealthy Silk Road trading hub. The technology didn't make it to the West, however, until the mid-sixth century, when Emperor Justinian introduced the silkworm to Byzantine Constantinople. China, though, managed to outmuscle the competition. Long after the knowledge of sericulture became widespread, Chinese silks remained highly prized. It remained the top Chinese export until the Song Dynasty period, and even after that, it was a significant item of trade throughout the imperial period.

==

Silk was not the only Chinese specialty to travel over the Silk Road. Another product invented in China had a much greater impact on the progress of global civilization: paper.

The distinction of inventing paper is traditionally awarded to a palace eunuch named Cai Lun. He began serving in the Han Dynasty court sometime around 75 AD and was later promoted and placed in charge of the royal workshops manufacturing instruments and weapons. According to one old text, Cai devised how to make paper from a concoction of mulberry tree bark, pieces of hemp, fishing nets, and rags. Presenting the idea to the emperor in 105 AD, he received lavish praise. "From that time," the text recounts, "paper has been in use everywhere and is universally called 'the paper of Marquis Cai.'"[24]

Though the story itself may be true, Cai probably receives too much credit. There is evidence of papermaking in China from several hundred years earlier. Probably the oldest scrap was dug up in a tomb near Xi'an that dates to the reign of Emperor Wu, at the latest—some two centuries before Cai. But fragments of some sort of paper-like material have been discovered from two to three centuries even earlier than that. They might have been made by pounding rags in water. Textual evidence exists, too, including a tale from 12 BC that describes a murder committed by a poison wrapped in paper. Cai's contribution may have been improving the process of manufacturing and the quality of paper by adding in tree bark.

The use of paper spread quickly after Cai's innovations. The first slip of paper uncovered with writing on it was found in a watchtower and dates from around 110 AD. Early on, though, paper was used more commonly for wrapping, clothing, and home furnishings;

it wasn't until the third century AD that paper began to replace wood and bamboo strips as China's primary writing material.

The technology of paper and papermaking drifted west even more incrementally than sericulture. Paper has been found in what were then Silk Road oasis towns, now located in western China from the third century AD, and it was probably already being locally produced in the Turpan area in northern Xinjiang by the fifth century AD. By the middle of the eighth century, paper had wound its way into the Middle East. One frequently repeated story claims that Muslims learned the techniques of papermaking after they captured some Chinese with the necessary skills in the famous Battle of Talas in 751. But that's probably apocryphal. It was the Muslims, though, who very likely brought paper into Europe, through Islamic Spain, in the tenth century, but it wasn't manufactured there until the twelfth century—a full one thousand years after Cai Lun.

While the Chinese had rapidly embraced paper, the Europeans did not. Some influential Europeans even opposed it. The flimsy sheets seemed unworthy of the written word compared to hardy and more familiar parchment. On a pilgrimage in the twelfth century to the tomb of Saint James in Santiago de Compostela in northern Spain, Peter the Venerable, the abbot of the monastery at Cluny in France, saw Jewish artisans printing paper copies of the Talmud, a compendium of rabbinic commentaries. Peter didn't approve. The paper was made "from old rags or from some other more vile material." Three centuries after Peter, a German Benedictine monk named Johannes Trithemius warned professional scribes against the frailty of paper: "The word written on parchment will last a thousand years," he wrote. "The printed word is on paper. How long will it last? The most you can expect a book of paper to survive is two hundred years. Yet, there are many who think they can entrust their works to paper. Posterity will judge."[25]

The Chinese, on the other hand, adopted paper for what may seem an even more sensitive purpose: as money. One of the other great innovations from China is the concept of paper currency. The idea was originally hatched around 1000 AD in the southwestern commercial hub of Chengdu. Merchants and artisans there had grown weary of lugging around strings of iron coins, then the main currency circulating in the area. A string usually held around 1,100 coins. Try fitting that into your pocket. The larger the transaction, the heftier the load. Local businessmen began issuing their own form of bills of credit to allow money to change hands without the need for all those coins. In 1005, Chengdu officials stepped in to regulate the practice by standardizing the form of the note.

The notion went national after the Song Dynasty government took over the issuing of paper currency in 1023. The idea greatly appealed to Song officials, since it solved a financial problem it had with its neighbors. They feared that the coins circulating in China, especially of copper, would get exported to the barbarian states threatening the Song from the north, thereby strengthening China's enemies while simultaneously weakening the domestic economy. By switching to a controlled paper currency, such an outflow could be mitigated. The government formed a Bureau for Exchange Bills in Chengdu and introduced a formal bill on a printed slip of paper that permitted its bearer to receive the amount of cash specified on it at designated state offices. At first, one bill was equivalent to one string of coins, but later, different bills with diverse values were issued. The government controlled the entire process of producing the paper cash, from the raw materials used to manufacture the paper to the bills' distribution. Silk and other fibers were mixed into the pulp, and hard-to-replicate patterns and serial numbers were printed on the bills to stymie fraud. The penalty for counterfeiting was printed right on the bill as a rather stiff warning: "By imperial decree: Criminals who counterfeit paper money are to be punished by beheading."[26]

The paper currency system was amazingly modern in its conception and operation. The Song court decided not to back the bills entirely with reserves of cash but, much like modern central banks, believed their value would be ensured by confidence in the economy and the state. That would maximize the economic benefits of the paper money system. It just made trade and exchange so much easier, which facilitated economic growth and business activity. "Money, one of those magic things created by man, is useful to its creator only when it is in constant circulation; it loses the meaning of its existence when it is taken away from the market and locked up in an iron chest," noted one Chinese scholar at the time.[27]

Marco Polo was captivated by China's paper money. The Europeans had nothing like it, and his memoir reads as if even he had trouble convincing himself such a system was possible. "Several times a year merchants come—several together—with pearls, precious stones, gold, silver, and other things (that is, cloth of gold and silk) and the merchants present all these things to the great lord [the Yuan emperor]," he recalled in amazement. In payment for these valuables, court officials offer the merchants no more than paper notes. "The merchants take it most willingly, and use it for all the things they buy throughout the lands." Even more incredible, "all the people and populated regions under his rule willingly take these notes in payment, because with them they'll go and make all their payments (for) merchandise. . . . You can buy everything with them."[28]

There is a good reason why we call fine tableware "china" in the West—because for centuries, the very best came from China, and the product forever became associated with its East Asian roots. Of course, ceramics, unlike silk or paper, was a widely practiced art in most societies around the world, and from a very early date. But the Chinese started very, very early, and proved especially adept at making it.

Though the first pottery kiln—a sort of oven to bake and therefore strengthen clay—was probably invented in the Middle East, the Chinese weren't far behind. Those ingenious tinkerers of the Yellow River valley devised a kiln sometime in the mid-fifth millennium BC. The Chinese also learned how to fire pottery at very high temperatures at a much earlier stage than elsewhere, a technique that produced a harder type of ceramic. That gave the Chinese pottery industry a clear advantage in international markets. No one could produce plates, vases, and other clay-based wares at better quality and on such an industrial scale. By the Tang Dynasty period, China was exporting fine ceramics in incredibly large quantities, much of it shipped from the southeast coast to entrepôts in Southeast Asia and onto ports in the Persian Gulf. One Arab vessel, on its way from the Chinese trading hub of Yangzhou in the Yangzi River delta to the Persian port of Siraf in 835, carried a staggering seventy thousand ceramic bowls, dishes, cups, and other tableware.

Imagine the technical genius and organizational prowess required to supply such tremendous quantities of a high-tech product in an age before trailer trucks, electricity, even steam. Highly effective "dragon" kilns, constructed with a series of chambers up the slope of a hill, could fire up to twenty-five thousand pieces at one go, all while maintaining an exceptional high standard. Merchants in major trading ports like Yangzhou had also become adept at catering to the tastes of foreign buyers. The tableware headed to Siraf featured Arabic calligraphy and depictions of birds and plants specifically designed to appeal to their Islamic audience. The marketing worked. Tang-era ceramics were sold around the world, from Japan to Indonesia to Egypt. Chinese ceramics became so popular among the wealthy elite of the Abbasid Caliphate, based in Baghdad, that they altered the Islamic dinner table, replacing the metal plates traditionally used for serving and eating, even in the royal palace itself.

China's global dominance was cemented with the invention of porcelain, probably in the seventh century. Chinese potters had been tirelessly experimenting with ways to make pure white ceramics, and the first artisans to figure it out were likely in Jiangxi province in the south where the necessary materials were especially abundant.* What distinguished porcelain from preceding pottery is its higher degree of hardness, whiteness, and translucence. Those finer qualities turned porcelain into China's premier export during the eleventh century, replacing silk. And the most popular, must-have-it-on-my-table type was known as "blue and white," for its distinctive mix of that clean whiteness with patterns of cobalt blue. (The color and idea were borrowed by the Chinese from the Islamic world in the fourteenth century during the great cultural exchanges of the Mongol period. They called it "Muhammadan Blue.")

The elite of Europe already had Chinese porcelain in their homes by the early 1300s; Europe's rich and famous couldn't get enough of it. Emperor Charles V had plates made with his monogram on them—perhaps the earliest porcelain custom-made for a European customer—while his son, Philip II, supposedly collected three thousand pieces. That royal attention tipped off a porcelain craze. In

---

* Experts may differ on when porcelain was invented in China depending on how they define what porcelain is. Some argue that the innovation of true porcelain took place later, perhaps in the tenth century.

the sixteenth century, a competition erupted across Europe among noble families for the best collections. Anybody who was anybody just *had* to serve on blue and white during parties and banquets; polite society would accept nothing less. Beakers, dishes, soup tureens, coffee pots, and cream jugs were all popular in aristocratic dining rooms. It was common for the well-to-do to order entire dinner sets of sixty to seventy pieces. Some showed off their especially exquisite acquisitions in display cases, or even specially designed galleries. In the 1680s, Portuguese royals built a "porcelain room" at their Lisbon palace with a pyramidal ceiling to house 260 fine specimens. King Frederick I of Prussia installed a mirrored cabinet for four hundred porcelain items—just a part of his holdings—at his Charlottenburg palace in Berlin.

Chinese kilns churned out more and more, riding the tidal wave of global demand. Much of the porcelain shipped to Europe was made at the town of Jingdezhen in Jiangxi province, which specialized in that highly prized blue and white style. During the Song Dynasty period, the city had three hundred kilns employing twelve thousand skilled artisans and probably a similar number of unskilled laborers. By the early seventeenth century, ambitious Dutch traders began importing Chinese porcelain into Europe directly from Asia. Between 1602 and 1657, the Dutch East India Company, a state-sanctioned trading firm, shipped three million pieces of Chinese porcelain to Europe. Increasingly, these items were made-to-order, based on designs created by Dutch agents and handed to Chinese potters for manufacture (not that much different than the way iPhones are made today). To speed up the process and bring prices down, the Dutch ordered basic porcelain from Chinese kilns and had it painted for European tastes in Guangzhou before shipping it home. Eventually each style was given a number, making ordering in Europe easy. Just waltz over to your local shop, list out your model numbers, and kilns half a world away would make whatever you desired.

At first, porcelain was a mysterious wonder to the Europeans, who had no idea how it was made. That didn't stop them from trying. The immense popularity of Chinese porcelain inevitably invited imitators. Producers in the Middle East, Italy, and the Netherlands devised a way of copying the look of Chinese porcelain using cheaper materials and less advanced technology to spew out cut-rate, lower-quality knock-offs of the real Chinese deal. The European middle class, who aspired to the refinement of the nobility but couldn't afford it, flocked to the discounted copies. In a twist of history, China was the victim of counterfeiters.

Eventually, the Europeans cracked the porcelain code. The man behind the quest was Augustus the Strong, king of Poland. Mere collecting wasn't sufficient for the prestige-craving nobleman. He funded research into this miraculous tableware and, in 1710, opened the first porcelain factory in Europe, in Meissen near Dresden. It took at least eight centuries for European potters to finally catch up to the Chinese.

Yet the proprietors of this new porcelain workshop quickly learned that they could not compete. The Chinese were so efficient that they could produce porcelain of exceptional quality, ship it all the way around the world, and still undercut the prices of the Dresden kiln. That limited the market for European porcelain makers until the nineteenth century. The long experience of the Chinese potters in design and production, and their advanced techniques and technology, gave their products an edge in quality, appearance, and reputation that simply could not be beaten.

===

Porcelain shaped global trade and was the first truly international consumer product. But it was not the Chinese creation that had the greatest impact on human civilization. "Printing, gunpowder and the compass," remarked Sir Francis Bacon, the English philosopher and statesman, in the early seventeenth century. These three, "though a small number, and not remote in invention, have changed the face of things, and the condition of the world; the first in literature, the second in war, the third in navigation; and hence have flowed infinite mutations in the state of things . . . so that no empire, sect, or star, seems to have had a stronger influence, and, as it were, ascendant over human affairs than those mechanical works."[29]

And all three were originally invented in China.

Here we find yet another source of China's superpower stature—its amazing ability to create and invent, in a wide range of sciences and technologies, from astronomy to chemistry to nuts-and-bolts manufacturing. The Europeans could not compete with China in technology for much of recorded history. A whole host of gadgets and machines, both grand and small, emerged from the scholars, technicians, craftsmen, and scientists of the Chinese empire: lacquer (thirteenth century BC); the wheelbarrow (first century BC); the umbrella (fourth century AD); matches (sixth century AD); and brandy (seventh century AD), to name just a handful.

Few, though, had a greater impact on the world than Bacon's trifecta. The history-altering consequences of the compass, for one, cannot be understated. The compass made possible the trading links and seafaring discoveries that shaped the modern world.

The origins of the magnetic compass go back so far in Chinese history that scholars have not been able to date them. There is evidence from an old text from the fourth century BC that the Chinese were already using a compass to find their way on land. This was before the age of the needle, so they instead employed a magnetic lodestone. Scholars, though, think it is almost certain that the compass was invented much earlier than even that. Originally, compasses were not primarily used for navigation, but for geomancy—the art of placing and arranging buildings and other structures auspiciously, by aligning them with the unseen but powerful forces of the earth. When Chinese sailors first figured out the compass could also be handy when guiding ships on the open ocean is not known, though it could have been as early as the mid-ninth century. By the Song Dynasty period, the compass became standard aboard Chinese vessels. "The ship's pilots are acquainted with the configuration of the coasts; at night they steer by the stars, and in the day time by the sun. In dark weather they look at the south-pointing needle," the governor of Guangzhou wrote in 1117.[30] After that, there is speculation among scholars that the compass might have migrated west from China to the Middle East and then into Europe.

Gunpowder was an equally world-changing, but arguably less beneficial, contribution. Some scholars believe the Chinese developed gunpowder as early as the ninth century. But perhaps it is better to say stumbled upon it. The great irony is that the Chinese invented one of humanity's most deadly preparations while trying to save lives. Gunpowder was likely the result of determined alchemists looking (vainly) for an elixir for eternal life, who began experimenting with mixtures of saltpeter and sulfur. That turned out to be playing with fire, literally. One text called *Classified Essentials of the Mysterious Dao of the True Origins of Things*, believed to have been composed in the mid-ninth century, warns the curious alchemist to avoid one such mixture—of saltpeter, sulfur, and honey (which probably played the role of carbon). "Smoke (and flames) result, so that their hands and faces have been burnt, and even the whole house (where they were working) burned down," the author recounted.[31] The first published formula for gunpowder dates from 1040. The author, a scholar named Zeng Gongliang, provided three different versions for the military-minded, one for a sort of exploding bomb to be hurled by catapult; another for a burning bomb to set wooden structures ablaze; and a third to make a poison-smoke bomb. Gunpowder may have been used for the first time by the Chinese in an actual battle in 919, in an especially horrific weapon that spewed ignited fuel onto enemy soldiers.

The invention of moveable-type printing is almost always associated with Johannes Gutenberg. However, the famed German was late to the game. Printing already had a long and storied history in China by the time he set up his press in the mid-fifteenth century.

There is a lot of academic speculation as to why China beat Europe to the printing punch. Among the many possibilities proffered is that the long-standing Chinese practice of applying inscribed seals to authenticate documents could easily have progressed into stamping larger amounts of text. The exam-based education system could also have spurred printing, since it increased the demand for books for study. The world's first printed book is often identified as a seven-sheet paper scroll with a Chinese version of a Buddhist sutra, which is dated 868 AD. It is most likely, however, that others that have not survived preceded it. Chinese printers began carving woodblocks to produce books and other materials starting from around 700 AD.

Moveable type was introduced in the middle of the eleventh century—a hefty four hundred years before Gutenberg. Not much is known about the supposed Chinese inventor, Bi Sheng, beyond a description of his technique in a text composed by a contemporary scholar. "He took sticky clay and cut in it characters as thin as the edge of a coin," the writer recounts. "He baked them in the fire to make them hard. He had previously prepared an iron plate and he had covered his plate with a mixture of pine resin, wax, and paper ashes. When he wished to print, he took an iron frame and set it on the iron plate. In this he placed the types, set close together. When the frame was full, the whole made one solid block of type. He then placed it near the fire to warm it. When the paste (on the plate) was slightly melted, he took a smooth board and pressed it over the surface, so that the block of type became as even as a whetstone. If one were to print only two or three copies, this method would be neither simple nor easy. But for printing hundreds or thousands of copies, it was marvelously quick."[32]

Just as Gutenberg's invention sparked a revolution in education, literacy, and knowledge in Europe, so too did advancements in printing in China—but at a much earlier date. Books plunged in price and increased in availability, further encouraging a society long intrigued by literature and learning to gorge on the printed word. Or as one Chinese commentator in the early eleventh century put it, "Printed editions of these works are abundant, and officials and commoners alike have them in their homes."[33] That was an exaggeration—the average Chinese farmer was not likely to have a sizeable personal library—but the arrival of printing in China did spread scholarship on a wider scale than anything Europe could imagine at the time.

The Chinese generally had an edge in technical skill over Europe for much of its history. For instance, China was the first country to produce cast iron, probably way back in the fourth century BC—a metal that didn't become widely available in Europe until the late fourteenth century. And though Chinese metallurgists did not invent steel, they did figure out how to make it from cast iron at an early date—the second century BC. This early adoption of advanced metals spurred improvements in a range of necessary implements—ploughs, hoes, and other farming tools, as well as knives, pots, and axes—that boosted economic production and people's livelihoods. It should come as no surprise, then, that China developed sizeable industrial enterprises in ancient times. After Emperor Wu of the Han Dynasty formed a government monopoly on iron production in 119 BC, the state produced it in large workshops. During this period, the Chinese phased out the use of the bloomery furnaces for iron smelting—which Europeans were using in the twelfth century—and replaced them with more effective blast furnaces. Increasingly, products from weapons to silk were being fabricated in large, industrial complexes, often located in major cities. In the Song capital of Kaifeng, the government's armories and workshops alone employed thirteen thousand ironworkers making everything from swords to nails. In fact, China during the Song period experienced a near-industrial revolution. During the eleventh century, technical advances in the iron industry sparked a boom in output much like the one England would experience in the early stage of the Industrial Revolution centuries later. By the late eleventh century, Chinese smelters were cranking out as much as 150,000 tons of iron annually, roughly the same amount all of Europe produced at the beginning of the eighteenth century.[34] Chinese iron production is estimated to have surged twelvefold between 850 and 1050. In the textile sector, the Song Chinese developed a frame that allowed two workers to operate multiple reels to wind silk thread, allowing them to produce as much per day as later steam-powered European machinery. By the thirteenth century, villagers used waterpower to run spinning wheels to twist fibers into textile-ready yarn on a significant scale.

====

China's unmatched technical wizardry, industrial might, agricultural abundance, and global reach made the empire exceedingly rich. This was a land of lavish palaces, luxuriant fields, and crammed marketplaces. And that was true long, long, long, long before Marco Polo's eyes practically popped from his head in dizzying bewilderment at China's wealth. The Han Dynasty, more than a millennium earlier, could already boast twenty major cities with populations between thirty thousand and one hundred thousand people. The first Han capital, Chang'an, may have been home to as many as six hundred thousand. Not only the empire's administrative heart, the city also hosted seven markets—one, situated in the city's east, was larger than the biggest shopping mall in the United States.[35] Towering over the city was the Weiyang palace, built by the first Han emperor atop the Dragon Head Hills, with dramatic terraces carved up the slopes. (This was appropriately symbolic, since the Han founder had adopted a myth that his father was a dragon.) Emperor Wu, as you'd expect, added to Chang'an's grandeur, building three new palaces, a center for ceremonial sacrifices, and, most famously, the Shanglin hunting park, into which he stuffed a giant palace with a maze of corridors, an artificial lake with a statue of a whale at its center, and exotic animals he had been given as gifts from foreign lands, including elephants, camels, and rhinoceroses. One poet in the second century BC could barely contain his awe:

> Gazing about the expanse of the park
> At the abundance and variety of its creatures,
> One's eyes are dazzled and enraptured
> By the boundless horizons,
> The borderless vistas . . .
> Here the country palaces and imperial retreats
> Cover the hills and span the valleys,
> Verandas surrounding their four sides;
> With storied chambers and winding porticos,
> Painted rafters and jade-studded corbels,
> Interlacing paths for the royal palanquin,
> And arcaded walks stretching such distances
> That their length cannot be traversed in a single day.[36]

Under the Tang Dynasty, a (rebuilt) and even more glorious Chang'an was likely the largest city in the world, with one million residents. Inside its walled neighborhoods were palaces, office complexes, mansions, temples, and academies. An entire "pleasure quarter," tucked conveniently next to the emperor's enclosure, bustled with bars and entertainers (many of them foreign, and therefore exotic). In some houses there lived government-registered courtesans, skilled in music and verse, who served high-ranking officials and rich merchants (and thus were the ancestors of Japanese geisha). For those with shallower purses, the quarter had less-refined wine houses and prostitutes. Vibrant marketplaces housed butchers, apothecaries, fishmongers, goldsmiths, and tailors. Visiting merchants were able to store their goods in large warehouses, place their money in bank-like institutions, and find shelter in numerous inns, some with as many as twenty rooms. The Western Market, the terminus of the Silk Road, was a medieval international hypermarket, where Persian traders and Uighur moneylenders jostled with Chinese shoppers from across the empire amid stalls stacked with the produce of the world: Siberian furs, Japanese knives, Indonesian cloves, Indian pepper, and frankincense from the Middle East.

The Tang court collected a vast number of foreign rarities, often given to the emperor as official tribute—rhinoceroses from the Southeast Asia kingdom of Champa (one type considered "Heaven-communicating"); mongooses; ostriches; multicolored, talking parrots; precious gems; golden suits of armor; leopard skins; and sofas, jugs, and just about anything you can think of encrusted with jewels, ivory, or silver. Occasionally, the emperor—who, by Confucian ethics, was to amass righteousness, not riches—would experience a pang of sobriety and refuse to accept an especially expensive gift. The Tang founder, for instance, returned a large pearl, sent as tribute from the Western Turks. "What we give weight to is a true-red heart," an attached note from the court explained. "We have no use for the pearl."[37]

Usually, such prizes were readily accepted. During the Tang period, the palaces and mansions of the royal family and other aristocrats were decorated with the most luxurious furnishings. The sweet scents of tropical woods wafted from living quarters. A Tang pharmacologist noted that even though sanderswood did not grow in central China, "men have it there everywhere."[38] Armrests, game boards, and boxes for ceremonial offerings were just some of the fine items crafted from the special wood. Such utilitarian wares as chopsticks, combs, and hairpins were made of precious ivory. Rattan furniture was hauled in from Southeast Asia. The elite became so accustomed to such foreign delights that when they ran short— as in the 760s, when a rebellion in the southeast disrupted shipments from the trading ports on the coast—dismay set in quickly. "About the luminous pearls of the South Seas, it has long been quiet," lamented the poet Du Fu, adding that "recently the provision of a live rhino, or even of kingfisher feathers, has been rare."[39]

Other cities in Tang China rivaled the wealth of Chang'an. The Southern Market at Luoyang, considered the dynasty's second capital, had three thousand shops and four hundred inns within its walls. Chengdu, in Sichuan in the southwest, had become famously rich due to its highly desired tea, fine paper, and, most of all, quality silk. The center of cloth weaving south of the main town was known as Damask City. One Tang poet described it in glowing terms:

> In Damask City, in the silkworm markets,
> Hairpins of pearl and emerald fill the street.
> A hundred thousand rouged faces, jade cicadas and gold peacocks
> In priceless coiffed hair, earrings of tinkling flower bouquets
> And embroidered gowns.[40]

Ports, and the towns around them, were buzzing commercial hubs, crammed with merchants and stacked high with the produce of China and the world. Guangzhou on the southeast coast was one of the main connection points between China and the global economy, and grew fat as a result. In the nearby estuary of the Pearl River could be found "the argosies of the Brahmans, the Persians and the Malays, their number beyond reckoning, all laden with aromatics, drugs, and rare and precious things, their cargoes heaped like hills," according to a Buddhist monk, Jianzhen, who visited in 748. The trade enriched those Chinese businessmen willing to sacrifice the comforts of more tame regions—Guangzhou then was considered a frontier outpost, no less remote than a Silk Road oasis. But the rewards were often worth the troubles. Jianzhen told of the local governor, "who carries six yaktails, with an army for each yaktail, and who in his majesty and dignity is not to be distinguished from the Son of Heaven."[41] (The emperor would probably have disagreed.)

The tremendous wealth wasn't limited to the biggest cities. Signs of prosperity were everywhere in the empire. Fan Chengda, a government official, described the stately homes, lofty mansions, and busy marketplaces of the countryside as he traveled by river from Chengdu to Suzhou (not far from modern Shanghai) in 1177. He found that two villages he passed through in the early days of the journey "are flourishing and prosperous, like a thriving town." Everything was a model of Chinese industriousness. "Village women grouped together and observed us on the road. All of them were knitting hemp as they walked, and there was not one among them with idle hands."[42] Later in the trip, he stopped at one Yangzi River town (now modern Wuhan) that was even more impressive. "Along the course of the river are several tens of thousands of homes," he wrote. "The marketplaces and villages here are very prosperous. The rows of shops are as thick as the teeth on a comb. The tower railings of the wine shops are especially grand and beautiful. . . . There is nothing that is not sold. Moreover, the quantity does not matter, for in one day everything is gone, so prosperous and vigorous is the trading here."[43]

The amount of wealth was so alluring that it even made one educated gentleman—Song-era poet Lu You—question (at least lyrically) the standard Confucian preference for scholarship over salesmanship.

> *The great ship, tall-towered, far off no bigger than a bean; . . .*
> *Matted sails: clouds that hang beyond the embankment;*
> *lines and hawsers: their thunder echoes from high town walls,*
> *Rumble rumble of carts to haul the priceless cargo;*
> *heaps, hordes to dazzle the market—men race with the news.*
> *In singing-girl towers to play at dice, a million on one throw;*
> *by flag-flown pavilions calling for wine, ten thousand a cask;*
> *the Mayor? the Governor? we don't even know their names. . . .*
> *Now I know that merchants are the happiest of men.*[44]

Seven

PAX SINICA

They loyally came to allegiance and then, looking to Heaven, they bowed and all said: "How fortunate we are that the civilizing influences of the Chinese sages should reach us."

–inscription by the Yongle emperor, Ming Dynasty

When Zheng He's treasure fleet glided into the rich port of Aden, at the mouth of the Red Sea, in the early fifteenth century, the local king came running. He "led his major and minor chiefs to the seashore, and welcomed the imperial edict and the bestowal of gifts," one of the Chinese seafarers recorded. Zheng He, a Muslim eunuch and royal favorite, had been dispatched by the Ming emperor, and the locals in Aden knew what that meant. He and his officials had to be treated with the courtesy and pomp befitting representatives from Asia's superpower. Chinese envoys were brought to the palace, where the king "rendered a ceremonial salutation with great reverence and humility." He then issued an order that only "precious things" could be traded to the visiting Chinese. Nothing but the best would do for the glorious Son of Heaven! In flowed rare gems, pearls, coral, amber, and rosewater—just the sort of exotic dainties coveted by the Ming elite. Aden's ruler, "filled with gratitude for the imperial kindness," presented the Chinese ambassadors with two gold belts inlaid with jewels, a gold hat covered in pearls and gems, and other pricey items, as well as a memorial written on gold leaf, as tribute for the Ming emperor.[1]

The king's generosity was a fine display of the warm hospitality of the East. But he may also have felt he had little choice but to entertain Zheng He lavishly. After all, the Chinese eunuch-admiral arrived at his shores with an awe-inspiring display of Chinese naval might. The vast armada presented a breathtaking expanse of masts and flags—an ocean of plank and sail atop the sea. The fleet anchored off Aden had dozens of ships, perhaps as many as 250, the biggest of which were the imposing "treasure ships," gargantuan junks that may have been the largest wooden vessels ever to ply the seas. Stacked on the decks were thousands of soldiers, brandishing swords and other weapons. The world had never seen anything quite like it before.

The admiral, though, had not come to conquer, but to make an announcement: The Chinese were supreme once again. Centuries of barbarian rule were over. A new and true Chinese dynasty was ascendant in the Middle Kingdom. The Chinese wanted the world to know it.

The reason why the new Ming Dynasty expended a fortune in money and energy on Zheng He's ambitious maritime expeditions—seven of them, between 1405 and 1433—was to cow the potentates throughout the known, civilized world into acknowledging the hegemony of the Son of Heaven. The mission took Zheng He all the way across the Indian Ocean to the east coast of Africa, and just about everywhere in between. Sufficiently impressed (or unnerved) by the unparalleled demonstration of Chinese power, the rulers Zheng He visited usually cooperated. Embassies from Southeast Asia, southern India, the Persian Gulf and Arabia, and what is today Kenya and Somalia streamed into China to pay their respects before the Ming emperor; occasionally, the kings undertook the journey personally to show their reverence. On one of Zheng He's voyages, he returned visiting envoys from eighteen states to their home countries. These tribute embassies brought the Son of Heaven gold, gems, exquisite fabrics, and a menagerie of exotic animals, including zebras, rhinoceroses, and giraffes, which the

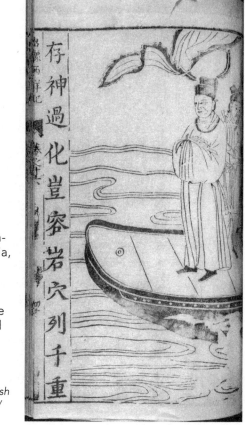

Admiral Zheng He led the expeditions of massive "treasure fleets" to Southeast Asia, India, the Middle East, and Africa in the early fifteenth century to expand Chinese influence across Asia and the Indian Ocean. He is pictured here in an illustration from a Chinese book published around 1600.

British Library, London, UK / © British Library Board. All Rights Reserved / Bridgeman Images

Chinese court mistook for a mythic creature that only appeared at rare, especially auspicious moments. Amid the complex ceremonies of the royal court, visiting dignitaries were expected to perform the "kowtow," an especially obsequious prostration in which they fell to their knees and placed their foreheads to the floor, as a mark of their deference to the Chinese emperor. Yes, the world was humbled before the greatness of China. "The barbarians from beyond the seas, even those who are truly distant, . . . all have come to court bearing precious objects and presents," Zheng He told us in a 1431 inscription. "The Emperor has delighted in their loyalty and sincerity."[2]

Zheng He's treasure fleets were arguably the most ostentatious display of China's superpower status in the Chinese history of the world. For the Ming emperors, the arrival of tribute-bearing barbarians from lands on the edge of the world was proof positive of their virtue. Surely Chinese imperial influence had achieved heights never reached before! The attention-craving emperor who championed Zheng He's excursions, Yongle, needed all the positive reinforcement he could get. Though one of the sons of the Ming Dynasty's founder, his father had passed him over to name a grandson his heir, and Yongle claimed the throne after a three-year civil war. That stain on his record left Yongle feeling a touch insecure, which could explain his outsized efforts to proclaim the power of China—and, by association, himself. While the other great expansionists of the Chinese history of the world—such as Emperor Wu or Taizong, the Tang emperor—were motivated by unyielding confidence, Yongle might have been moved by a lack of it. One supposed reason he launched Zheng He's fleets was to find his deposed predecessor, who was killed in a fire but who Yongle continued to worry was hiding out somewhere in the world, plotting a return.

The treasure fleets were just one of Yongle's power-proclaiming undertakings. He also built a fabulous new capital at Beijing. Hundreds of thousands of laborers worked on the construction. At its heart was the imperial palace known as the Forbidden City. This complex of marble-encrusted courtyards, towering, ornately carved pavilions—with a staggering nine thousand rooms—became home to the royal family in 1421, and remained the center of Chinese political authority until the end of the dynastic period six centuries later.

Zheng He's fleets were no less a marvel of engineering and organizational prowess. The largest "treasure ships" were likely four hundred feet long, possibly more, and they were made seaworthy by ingenious design features unknown at the time in the West, including a retractable rudder, special internal bulwarks, and a layout of masts that could better catch the ocean breezes. The Europeans, in fact, probably never produced a wooden ship of such scale. Four centuries after Zheng He, British Admiral Horatio Nelson won the Battle of Trafalgar on a warship, the *Victory*, that was half the length of a Ming treasure junk. The *Santa Maria*, which ferried Christopher Columbus across the Atlantic to the New World in 1492, was only about one-sixth the length.

Because of the scope of Zheng He's voyages, the eunuch is often called the Chinese Columbus. The comparison, though, is off the mark. The motivations of the two famous seafarers were quite distinct. Columbus sailed in search of the riches of the Far East, and into the unknown. Zheng He was for the most part navigating on long-established thoroughfares of maritime trade. In fact, Chinese mariners already dominated the sea-lanes between India and China by the time of Zheng He's missions. The Morocco-born world traveler Ibn Battuta arrived at the Indian port of Calicut in the fourteenth century to find thirteen Chinese ships in the harbor. "On the Sea of China travelling is done on Chinese ships only," he recounted. "The large ships have anything from 12 down to three sails. . . . A ship carries a complement of a thousand men, 600 of whom are sailors and 400 men-at-arms, including archers, men with shields and arbalists, who throw naphtha. . . . Some of the Chinese own large numbers of ships on which their factors are sent to foreign countries. There is no people in the world wealthier than the Chinese."[3]

Also unlike Columbus, Zheng He wasn't searching for the riches of Asia; he was carrying them. The cavernous hulls of the treasure ships were filled with delectable Chinese delicacies, especially silk and porcelain, which he exchanged for spices, incense, medicines, precious gems and pearls, carpets, and scented woods. In that sense, Zheng He's journeys encapsulated all of the major elements that made China a superpower—political, economic, technological, and civilizational. They were an extension of the Chinese self-belief in their own exceptionalism and long-held universalistic governing ideology.

The Ming pronouncement of Chinese hegemony was more than symbolic. Zheng He was not merely showing the flag; he backed it up with real, tangible power. The new dynasty was willing to intervene in local affairs in foreign lands to support rulers friendly to China and its interests. The biggest beneficiary of Ming meddling was Malacca. The newly emerging Southeast Asian state was quick to seek support from the newly forged Chinese dynasty to help it fend off envious rival kingdoms in Java (today's Indonesia) and Siam (Thailand). The Ming were equally quick to realize Malacca's geopolitical value. Located on the narrow strait between the Asian mainland and the (now Indonesian) island of Sumatra, Malacca sat astride a water link connecting China and India. Having a loyal servant there was key to maintaining Chinese influence in this vital region. No wonder, then, that Zheng He's fleets routinely visited Malacca, making clear to its disgruntled competitors that the Ming stood behind their vassal. In case anyone missed the point, Yongle personally composed an inscription on a tablet for Malacca, declaring that it desired "to be treated as a subject state of the Middle Kingdom in order to excel and be distinguished from the barbarian domains."[4]

In other instances, more than imperial declarations were necessary to assert Chinese authority. Modern Chinese historians like to portray the voyages of Zheng He as evidence that China was a peaceful superpower by contrasting them with the rapacious colonial conquests the Europeans would begin unleashing on unprepared societies a century later. But that's a bit of rewritten history. While China wasn't interested in outright dominion over foreign states, it was no accident that Zheng He brought soldiers along with silk on his treasure fleets. The official history of the Ming Dynasty states plainly that the Yongle emperor dispatched Zheng He because he "wanted to display his soldiers in strange lands in order to make manifest the wealth and power of the Middle Kingdom." The fleets "went in succession to the various foreign countries, proclaiming the edicts of the Son of Heaven and giving gifts to their rulers and chieftains. Those who did not submit were pacified by force."[5]

Zheng He's soldiers and weaponry were not only a show of force, but a force to be reckoned with, and the admiral put them to good use when he had to. On his very first outing, from 1405 to 1407, he fought and defeated the pirate leader Chen Zuyi, who had been harassing shipping from his base on the island of Sumatra. The Chinese records claim Zheng He burned or captured seventeen of the pirate's ships and slaughtered five thousand of his followers. During a later voyage, in 1415, to the kingdom of Semudera on Sumatra, Zheng He was attacked by a pretender to the throne named Sekander who was angered that he didn't receive imperial gifts. The admiral beat off the offensive, pursued Sekander into the jungles, captured him and his family, and—to make sure he would cause no further trouble for the ruler recognized by the Ming—brought him to China, where he was executed.

Nor would Zheng He brook slights to the great Ming. His most dramatic escapade took place on Ceylon (now Sri Lanka) during the third voyage, which sailed between 1409 and 1411. The admiral had stopped by the island on his first journey and received a hostile reception from a local king, Alakeshvara, who, according to the Ming records, "had been rude and disrespectful and intended to kill Zheng He." The treasure fleet departed for India, but the strong-willed Zheng He didn't forget the affront. Meanwhile, Alakeshvara's statelet started preying upon the shipping between South and Southeast Asia—a direct challenge to Chinese power in the region. Upon his return to Ceylon, Zheng He was drawn into a meeting with Alakeshvara's son, but the conference was a trick. If Zheng He did not offer gold and silver, fifty thousand concealed troops were to plunder the treasure fleet. Zheng He was too smart to fall for the ruse, but as he attempted to return to his fleet, he found himself and his party blocked by trees Alakeshvara had felled to impede his retreat. Our seafaring hero was trapped!

Or was he? Zheng He devised an ingenious plan. If the Ceylon king has already sent off his army to the coast after Zheng He's fleet, then the capital must be lightly defended—and vulnerable. "They are saying that we are only an invading army that is isolated and afraid and incapable of doing anything," the admiral contended. "But if we go forth and attack them, then contrary to their expectations we may gain our objective."[6] Zheng He then led two thousand men in an assault against the capital. Taking the town by surprise, the Chinese troops breached the earthen walls and took the king and his family prisoner. The foolhardy Alakeshvara, too, was brought back to China, but this time, the emperor apparently deemed the king too ignorant to be held responsible for his actions, and surprisingly pardoned him.

Still, the message was duly sent: don't mess with the Ming. Zheng He's bold exploit was later canonized in verse:

*Cleaning out in a single sweep those noxious pests, as if
    winnowing chaff from grain. . . .
These insignificant worms, deserving to die ten thousand times
    over, trembling in fear . . .
Did not even merit the punishment of Heaven.*

Thus the august emperor spared their lives,
And they humbly kowtowed, making crude sounds and
Praising the sage-like virtue of the imperial Ming ruler.[7]

Zheng He was obviously proud of his military achievements. In an inscription he left in 1431, he boasted that "when we arrived at the foreign countries, barbarian kings who resisted transformation (by Chinese civilization) and were not respectful we captured alive, and bandit soldiers who looted and plundered recklessly we exterminated." These interventions were beneficial for all. "Because of this the sea routes became pure and peaceful and the foreign peoples could rely upon them and pursue their occupations in safety."[8]

Yet the emperor, Yongle, did not characterize the armadas in terms of power politics. The treasure ships were carrying something

The Yongle emperor of the Ming Dynasty, who reigned in the early fifteenth century AD, was among China's most aggressive at expanding his country's diplomatic and economic clout across the known world.

National Palace Museum, Taipei, Taiwan / Pictures from History / Bridgeman Images

of far greater significance than mere silk or soldiers. The imperial design could never be so mundane, so coarse! No, their purpose was grander than the grandeur of their scale and scope: to shine the glory of Chinese civilization on the far corners of the world. What Zheng He carried most of all was the civilizing grace of the Son of Heaven. Yongle encapsulated this vision in an inscription he prepared for a stone tablet Zheng He was to ferry to the trading state of Cochin in southern India. "I promote the ways of the ancient Sagely Emperors and Perspicacious Kings, so as to accord with the will of Heaven and Earth," he wrote.

> I wish all of the distant lands and foreign regions to have their proper places. Those who respond to the influences and move towards culture are not singular. The country of Cochin is far away in the Southwest, on the shore of the vast ocean. . . . It has long inclined towards Chinese culture and been accepting of civilizing influences. When the Imperial orders arrived, the people there went down on their hands and knees and were greatly excited. They loyally came to allegiance and then, looking to Heaven, they bowed and all said: "How fortunate we are that the civilizing influences of the Chinese sages should reach us."[9]

Yes, the Son of Heaven brought civilization to the world. He brought peace. The Chinese were on the top of the world. Where they belonged. The world was in harmony.

=

Zheng He died in 1433, possibly on the oceans during his final voyage, which would have been a fitting end. And the great treasure fleets died with him. Never again would the Ming proclaim China's greatness to the lands beyond the beyond; never again would the treasure ships rule the waves. China's Age of Discovery came to a close.

The expeditions of Zheng He were an undeniable showpiece of China's economic, political, and technological supremacy in East Asia. But they were also an aberration. Rarely did the Chinese seek to reach out to the world in such a flamboyant fashion. Secure in the superiority of their civilization, they were content to let the world come to them. The Confucians believed that the benevolence of the Son of Heaven shone so brightly that foreigners would be drawn to him like iron to a magnet. With one tribute-bearing embassy after another lining up before the Ming court, their sense of exceptionalism seemed perfectly justified. The primacy of the Son of Heaven was assured, and in the eyes of the penny-pinching Confucian bureaucracy, the expense and trouble of Zheng He's flotillas were unnecessarily burdensome.

It is intriguing to ponder how the world might have been different if the Chinese had continued to explore it. But it wasn't to be. The armadas of Zheng He were the result of an unusual coalescence of factors in Chinese politics that were short-lived. Insecure in his own position after a contested succession, the Yongle emperor who sponsored the seaborne adventures was an imperial rarity: a Son of Heaven who felt the need to prove he really was superior to all others. With his death, so too died Ming inquisitiveness and showmanship. In fact, the Ming were in many respects more distrustful of outsiders and isolationist than arguably any other dynasty.

It's understandable. The Ming were a reaction against the humiliation of Mongol rule. After four centuries of barbarian incursions, foreigners and foreign influence were perceived as dangerous. The Ming emperors spent much of their dynasty's 276 years trying to keep the rest of the world out. In that never-ending conflict between Chinese universalism and xenophobia, the latter predominated in the Ming.

That began with the Ming's founder, Zhu Yuanzhang, known as the Hongwu emperor. Here we find another of the monumental figures in the Chinese history of the world who goes generally unnoticed in the West. He is one of the story's great rags-to-riches fables. Born to a poor peasant family in southern China, he was orphaned at age sixteen and found refuge in a Buddhist temple; he had to beg on the street for alms. Zhu was clearly proud of his humble origins. "In comparison with a ruler born and bred deep inside the palace, unfamiliar with the world, . . . how different it was for me," he once wrote.[10]

His temple was later burned down by the Mongols, who feared it was a hotbed of Chinese resistance to the Yuan Dynasty. The most powerful anti-Mongol movement did emerge out of the Buddhist establishment, the White Lotus Society, which believed that the Buddha of the Future would come to wipe away the wicked—to them, the Mongol barbarians. Zhu became involved with a related militant group, the Red Turbans. He rose in the ranks, and in 1356 led a Red Turban army that took the city of Nanjing, which would become the first Ming capital. Unlike other rebel commanders, all seeking to overthrow the hated Mongols and claim the Mandate of Heaven, Zhu had a knack for administration as well as generalship, and he wooed talented scholar-officials to manage the territories he conquered by the sword. Realizing he was better off on his own than with the ineptly led Red Turbans, he broke from them in 1366. Two years later, he tossed the Mongols out of Beijing and founded the Ming Dynasty. China was reunited and free of barbarians for the first time in 250 years.

Zhu and his scholar-officials liked to portray the Ming as a rebirth of the Han or Tang, those great—and undeniably Chinese—dynasties of the heroic past. Zhu did revive and strengthen certain traditional institutions of Confucian Chinese government. In 1370, he restored the civil service examinations and again made them the sole route into the elite state bureaucracy. In practice, however, Zhu's Ming was a departure from its predecessors in critical ways. Though the Son of Heaven always in principle possessed absolute authority, his freedom of action was constrained by ritual practice, Confucian ideology, and his coterie of learned advisors protective of their own privileges. Zhu brushed aside many of the usual niceties of Confucian government and ruled more as an autocrat. Court ministers, who had governed in conjunction with the emperors, found themselves sidelined or ignored by the tyrannical Zhu. Suspicious, self-righteous, and sensitive to slights, he purged government officials by the tens of thousands, including some of the empire's most distinguished scholars and generals, in a bloodbath perhaps unparalleled at that point in China's history. By one estimate, he executed one hundred thousand officials in his three-decade reign. Still, Zhu seemed to have perceived himself and his regime as largely traditional. Fancying himself something of a Confucian sage, he insisted his dictates on morality be read out loud in every village of the empire each month, in order to foster virtue among the masses and loyalty to the Son of Heaven.

Yet the Ming's attempt at a proper restoration of Chinese-Confucian government brought with it a Confucian conundrum. If Heaven granted the Mandate to rule based on *de*, or virtue, and the Chinese possessed superior *de*, then how exactly could the Mongol conquest of China be explained? It was a thorny question that many writers of the Yuan and early Ming period left unanswered. The official history of the Yuan just recorded the dynasty's events, without the usual commentary. The Mongol period simply didn't compute. The Ming solution to this ideological Rubik's Cube was to pick up where the Song Dynasty left off. The Yuan may have been a real dynasty, but it was a deviation from the long-standing norm, and the Ming were setting the course of the Chinese history of the world back on track. "Since ancient times the emperors had been ruling all-under-Heaven with the Middle Kingdom in the inner realm to control the barbarians and the barbarians in the outer world to serve the Middle Kingdom," Zhu broadcast to the people of north China during his rebellion against the Yuan in a 1367 proclamation. "It was unheard of that barbarians should claim the Middle Kingdom and rule all-under-Heaven." Heaven, appalled by the corruption and misrule of the Yuan, had withdrawn its blessing and handed the Mandate instead to a new virtuous sage. "I respectfully oblige the Heavenly request, not daring to indulge in my own comfort, ready to send forces north to expel the hordes of barbarians, save the people from the abyss of misery and restore the dignity of Han governance," the proclamation continued. Even more, Heaven recognized that only a true-blue Chinese was fit to rule over China. "Heaven shall appoint one from the Middle Kingdom to gratify the Chinese people. How could barbarians be their ruler?" Zhu announced.[11]

The Ming political movement, then, was not simply a change from one dynasty to another. It had a nationalist edge to it. Zhu kicked out the foreign barbarians and created an authentically Chinese dynasty led by authentic Chinese and founded on authentically Chinese institutions and political philosophy. Zhu and his armies had performed a cleansing exercise, rooting out the barbarians and their bestial ways. In a message to the Japanese government, the

Ming founder simply said that "the northern barbarians entered and occupied our China, propagated their barbarian customs, and made our central land stink."[12] But thanks to the Ming, the stench was gone; civilization was restored in China.

And so was China's place in the world. Now that a true Son of Heaven was on China's throne, how could the grace of Chinese civilization not shine upon the far corners of the earth? How could it be any other way? If the Son of Heaven was the indispensable link between the divine and humanity, and proper harmony again prevailed in the universe, then the emperor was again ascendant above all. Ideologically, the Ming picked up where the Song had left off, as if the horrific intrusion of the Yuan never happened. The Mongols may have been militarily superior; they may have gained political control over China by force. But like the Xiongnu or the Jurchens, they hardly presented a challenge to Chinese exceptionalism. The diehard Chinese faith in their own civilization remained fundamentally unshaken. And that ultimately was what Zheng He's imposing squadrons were all about. Maybe the rest of the world thought the Son of Heaven was extinguished by the Mongol hordes. Well, think again. China was as rich and powerful as it always had been. Better come kowtowing if you want to participate in its greatness.

That the Ming felt the need to show off in such a way is a sign, though, of how the Mongol experience shook traditional Chinese thinking on foreign affairs. There had been relatively few emperors over the many centuries of imperial government who aggressively advertised Chinese power. Emperor Wu taught the devious leaders of Dayuan a lesson they never forgot; Taizong of the Tang Dynasty would not rest until the Koguryo threat in Korea was eliminated. But for the most part, the Son of Heaven was content to let his grandeur speak for itself. As the Confucians believed, his virtue, *de*, was sufficient power to command the world. But the Ming takeaway from the Mongol catastrophe was that this was not entirely true. How else could the destruction of the Confucian Song be explained? *De* was all well and good, but it had to be paired with swords and soldiers in order to be truly effective. And while power without *de* was improper and would lead to failures—that, too, was proven by the Mongols, with their embarrassing defeats in Japan and Southeast Asia—power backed by *de* was perfectly justified, since such force was bathed in the warmth of Chinese civilization. In other words, moral power had to be backed by real power.

The Ming founder, however, believed such virtuous power should be used sparingly. He had a different vision of Chinese greatness than the Han's Wu or Tang's Taizong. Zhu was content to control what he perceived as the zone of Chinese civilization, the proper homeland for the Chinese people, and was generally disinterested in foreign military adventures. Expansionism, he believed, was ultimately dangerous to China. The Ming engaged in only brief and mostly unsuccessful efforts to reconquer far-flung territory once held by the Han and Tang Dynasties. Hongwu even listed fifteen countries that should never be the target of punitive military expeditions, including Korea, Japan, and Java. Of course, Hongwu claimed he had unified "all under Heaven"—as any good Son of Heaven should—but for him, building the empire was not a contest with the past.

That doesn't mean Zhu had no interest in foreign affairs. He very much enjoyed the tribute missions that appeared at his court, seeing them as a mark of his new dynasty's legitimacy. But the man who made his name expelling the Mongol barbarians from China was also terrified that they might return. That fear, combined with his usual paranoia and mania for control, turned Hongwu into one of China's premier xenophobes. If barbarians were going to do harm to the Chinese, it wasn't going to happen on his watch. He sought to separate the Chinese people from the outside world to a degree unseen in Chinese history at that time. Zhu restricted the movements of foreigners within the empire and tried to limit their contact with the Chinese. The fewer foreigners around, the less likely agents of predatory neighbors would be able to collect intelligence for future invasions. The coming of the Ming seems to have also fostered a surge in anti-foreign sentiment within China, especially against Muslims, who had held a privileged position under the hated Yuan. In Quanzhou, a major center for Islamic traders, angry Chinese burned down all seven of the port city's mosques.

Zhu went so far as to consider the active commerce China had with the rest of the world as a threat to the security of the dynasty. He generally distrusted private enterprise and sought to control the economy as he did all other aspects of Chinese society. His attitude toward trade was even more hostile. Chinese who demeaned them-selves by seeking profit by cavorting with foreigners were morally degenerate—or "vagabonds," and, he determined, "vagabonds are to be arrested."[13] Dealing with barbarians was best controlled by the state. The worst of all the mercantile barbarians were the "short pirates," as the Ming called the Japanese seafarers who preyed upon China's vulnerable coastline. Their misdeeds were not just a secu-rity problem, but also an affront to Hongwu's authority.

So the first Ming emperor took a startling and drastic decision: in 1371, he banned all foreign maritime trade. The regulations enacted left little room for interpretation. "Coastal people are prohibited from going to sea" and "are forbidden from contacting all foreign-ers." "Those who have trade dealings with 'barbarians' deserve the death penalty and their family members will be sent into exile."[14] In case that wasn't clear enough, ports were rendered useless with sunken stones and pine stakes. Hongwu ordered seventy-five for-tresses built and manned along the Zhejiang and Fujian coasts to en-force the ban. The only trade permitted was through official tribute missions and controlled by the court. And even that was severely re-stricted. In Chinese diplomacy, foreign states could not send embas-sies whenever they wished; the Chinese court determined when and how often barbarian rulers had to pay homage. Any envoy would have to present a "tally," awarded to tributary states, upon arriving in China to prove he was an officially appointed representative. Land on the coast without one, and the Ming considered you a pirate.

The prohibition on private maritime trade would stay in place for nearly two centuries. At times, it was enforced with a vengeance. One especially zealous sixteenth-century emperor dispatched two hundred thousand soldiers in pursuit of barbarian traders in coastal areas. In an especially draconian measure, the court in 1525 practi-cally closed down the entire China coast by prohibiting any vessel of two sails or more from even venturing offshore. As a saying at the time went, "Not a plank was allowed out to sea."[15] In 1549, ninety-seven merchants were beheaded in Zhejiang province for violating the stricture. Thousands more were killed in military op-erations to maintain the ban.

The policy, and the effort, expense, and brutality required to enforce it, seem to defy logic. China's trade had stimulated wealth, industry, and tax revenues, and bolstered the country's stature on the world stage. But under the Ming, trade became a vehicle for exerting political authority and a tool of foreign policy. When advisors recommended that the Yongle emperor (the one who sent Zheng He to sea) tax incoming foreign goods to raise revenue, he seemed offended. "It is not for profit that the government should tax foreign merchants," he responded. "They are attracted by our morality and righteousness, not by profit! How shameful for us to make profit out of them. . . . We have more dignity than profit!"[16]

Yet these strenuous efforts to isolate China from the world failed miserably. The Ming's ban on trade was ineffective. The lure of profit was so great—however much it insulted the emperor—and the demand for Chinese-made luxuries like porcelain so large that merchants, both Chinese and foreign, were willing to risk beheadings to trade. The Ming court issued the injunction thirty times—both an indication of how seriously it took the matter and a backhanded admission the policy wasn't working and the locals had to be reminded over and over again. At times it was hard to tell there was a ban on maritime trade at all. Choe Bu, a Korean official shipwrecked in China, found the port flourishing in the town of Suzhou in 1488. The ships were gathered "like clouds" waiting to load vast quantities of silks, gold, and jewels. "The people live luxuriously," he wrote. "Market quarters are scattered like stars."[17]

Ming administrators often acquiesced in the cheating. In 1493, Min Gui, a commander in southern China, griped to the court that too many foreign ships were landing unannounced on the coast and not abiding by the appropriate tribute schedule. In its response, a minister told Min to chill out. Yes, the barbarians had to be kept under wraps, but taking action would sour foreign relations and curtail profitable commerce.

The Ming eventually gave up on controlling trade. The court loosened the ban in the 1540s, then, in 1567, lifted it entirely. While the Ming rulers never lost their suspicion of trade, the notion that it made sense to micromanage it had fallen out of favor as more officials came to see its benefits. Freer trade would help squash piracy while enriching the empire's coastal regions. "Strengthening China's maritime defenses is inseparable from cherishing maritime traders," argued one Confucian scholar-official in Guangdong.[18]

Chinese trade quickly resumed its usual torrid pace. Between 1685 and 1723, 2,500 private ships sailed between China and Japan.[19] The Chinese seafarers bring "the most valuable commodities; and, at the same time, allow their own people to disperse themselves unto a great number of foreign parts, whither they carry their silks, porcelain, and other curious manufactures," one foreign trader noted at that time. "They trade into most parts of East India; . . . No wonder then that it [China] is so opulent and powerful."[20] China was simply too integrated, its economy too central, and its products too desirable and profitable to be shut off from the world.

=

That didn't stop the Ming from trying in even more strenuous ways. While struggling to fend foreigners off the coast, they invested even more sweat and silver along the northern border with the steppe. There, the detested nomads still threatened Chinese civilization. The early Ming rulers chased the onetime Mongol oppressors deep into the steppe to keep them as far away as possible from the new dynasty. In 1388, one vengeful Ming army destroyed Karakorum, once the capital of the globe-spanning Mongol empire. Such defeats were a blow to Mongol prestige, but not much else. The Ming discovered, as emperors had since the Han Dynasty's Emperor Gaozu 1,600 years earlier, that chasing the barbarians round the barren northern wastelands was expensive in lives and money, and not particularly effective. The Mongols, like the Xiongnu and the Turks before them, simply melted into the wilderness and returned to raid and fight another day.

Conciliation was not an option, either. The Ming emperors generally held to a hard line against their old foes, often restricting or outright banning trade with Mongol chiefs. That kept tensions along the frontier at a fever pitch throughout much of the Ming period. Deprived of the grain and goods they required to survive on the windswept steppe, the Mongols were forced to raid the Chinese borderlands, creating a never-ending cycle of violence and endless debates at court over how to protect the empire.

This inept border policy produced a crisis that could have brought down the dynasty in the 1440s. A Mongol leader named Esen expanded his control along the China frontier and into the old

Western Regions in today's Xinjiang, which worried the Ming. He also abused his tribute privileges by sending excessively large delegations to the Ming court, compelling the ever-generous emperor to dole out extensive and expensive gifts to their many participants. Irked, Ming officials curtailed how often Esen could send embassies and scaled back the presents given to the Mongol envoys. As along the coast, the Ming were using trade as a weapon of foreign policy and political control. Esen accused the Ming of unfair trade practices, and in 1449, launched an assault on China.

At the Ming court, a much-despised eunuch named Wang Zhen, who had through corruption and manipulation taken control of the government, determined to meet the threat and convinced the young emperor to lead the army personally. The haughty Wang, underestimating the barbarians, marched into the steppe with little planning or strategy and soon found himself surrounded by Esen's hardened horsemen. The Mongols decimated the Ming army, killing Wang and capturing the Son of Heaven. The road to Beijing was wide open.

Fortunately for the Ming, Esen delayed his descent on the capital, and by the time he arrived, local officials had installed the seized emperor's brother on the throne and fortified the city's defenses sufficiently enough to convince Esen to return home. The Ming's defeat, however, did allow the Mongols to claim the strategic Ordos region, within the grand loop of the Yellow River, leaving the Ming even more vulnerable in the future.

It was a close call. And though the immediate danger passed, the long-term fallout from the defeat lingered for the remainder of the dynasty. The Ming were placed permanently on the defensive against the steppe nomads. And there was no Emperor Wu around to stiffen the court's backbone. The heightened urgency intensified the incessant political wrangling at the palace over what to do about the Mongol foe. One camp argued for an aggressive approach, to mass an army and retake the vital Ordos region. Others noted the likely futility of reclaiming and then holding the exposed and barren territory. Though the hawks repeatedly gained the emperors' support, the Ming military was never able to mount a serious campaign. Nor were the emperors willing to adopt a more diplomatic policy, advocated by some scholar-officials, to encourage trade and tribute relations with the Mongols as a method of both satisfying their need for Chinese goods and controlling them. Such a strategy was rooted in that ageless view of the northern nomads as incorrigible beasts, who could and should be treated like animals. "Just like dogs, if they wag their tails, bones will be thrown to them," explained statesman Zhang Juzheng, "if they bark wildly, they will be beaten with sticks; after the beating, if they submit again, bones will be thrown to them again. . . . How can one argue with them about being crooked or straight or about the observation of law?"[21]

But any sort of accommodation with those felt-wearing barbarians was unacceptable appeasement to the Ming hard-liners. With the court deadlocked in factional strife, military commanders stumbled into the only option left to defend the border: building walls. At least with a wall standing in their way, the rampaging horsemen could not simply storm into China and ravage at will.

The result was the Great Wall of China. The country's most iconic symbol, largely a Ming creation, was not a specially designed and constructed fortification. It was in effect built by default, since Ming officials could never agree on a more coherent frontier policy.[22] The Ming didn't even refer to the structure as the "Great Wall," but the "nine border garrisons." There is some unfortunate irony here. The Great Wall became the ultimate physical manifestation of what the Western world has imagined China's posture toward outsiders to be—a greater tendency to shut the world out rather than engage with it. The Chinese were a people so hostile to foreigners that they erected a stone barrier across the entire length of the country to keep them out. And yet, the Great Wall was more or less an accident of history.

The first great wall-builder was an official named Yu Zijun posted to the Ordos frontier as grand coordinator in 1471. His argument to the court was that attacking the nomads was fruitless. Better to build walls to hamper their raids, giving frontier townships greater security to farm and thus improving the economy of the borderlands. His insistent memorials at first were dismissed as the court fixated on launching an offensive to drive the Mongols from the Ordos, but as those plans faltered, Yu's proposal won more support. The wall he erected in the early 1470s stretched for about 570 miles along the Ming's northwest frontier, in the provinces of Ningxia and Shaanxi. It had eight hundred towers, sentry posts, and other strong points, and required forty thousand men to construct.

However, the Ming didn't build the Great Wall as we know it today for another one hundred years—during the middle and late sixteenth century. By then, the Mongols had become an even greater threat. In the early 1540s, a new paramount leader, the Altan Khan, unified the clans in a confederation more powerful than any steppe empire since the fall of the Yuan. He made repeated requests for trade and tribute relations with the Ming, and the Ming unwisely rejected them. The Mongol raids that followed were inevitable.

Once again, with the court embroiled in bitter infighting over a Mongol strategy, walls became the default option. Unlike earlier structures, which were made mostly of pounded earth and eroded over time, the new Ming fortifications used more brick and stone, making them more formidable and permanent, but also more costly in both money and manpower. The official who championed the effort this time was Weng Wanda, who in the 1540s oversaw the construction of border walls west of Beijing, in today's Shaanxi and Shanxi provinces. These became the base of the most important segment of the defenses—more than five hundred miles of wall that was augmented over time. These barriers quickly proved their worth. When Altan Khan launched a full-scale attack on the Ming in 1549, he smashed into Weng's fortifications and couldn't get through.

Yet Altan's assault also exposed the walls' weakness. Even if the Mongols couldn't so easily surmount the walls, they could very easily get around them. All they had to do was shift their avenue of invasion to the east—which they did, crushing the Ming forces and descending on the suburbs of Beijing. Officials could climb the walls of the capital and see the marauding Mongols trashing the outskirts. The steppe army withdrew, but the problem was obvious.

Weng's suggestion: build more walls. What followed was the most extensive defensive building program in Chinese history. The Ming constructed walls until the end of the dynasty, with much of the effort focused to the east of Beijing, stretching nearly to the sea. The final result was the bastion that came to be known as the

Great Wall, which protected the entire frontier with the barbarians. Surely that would keep the good Han people safe, right?

===

It didn't. In fact, the Ming were still tinkering with the walls right up to the time when China was again overrun by steppe barbarians. They were the Manchus, and they formed one of China's most powerful dynasties, the Qing.

The end of the Ming was long in coming. By the start of the seventeenth century, the vitality of the dynasty had been sapped by corruption and mismanagement. Effective, decisive emperors were sadly lacking in the late Ming. One emperor refused to hold court or read official documents for twenty years after his ministers blocked his plan to elevate a favorite consort to the position of empress (since he already had one). Factions of Confucian officials and power-hungry eunuchs clashed relentlessly while the emperors dithered. Meanwhile, the bloated palace establishment became a burden on the finances and functioning of government. By the end of the dynasty, the state was supporting some one hundred thousand eunuchs and another one hundred thousand members of the royal family. Famines in the 1620s sparked peasant rebellions, which the Ming attempted to suppress ruthlessly, but not successfully. In 1644, one rebel leader, Li Zicheng, captured Beijing, and the last Ming emperor hanged himself on a hill overlooking the Forbidden City. Li founded a new dynasty, the Shun.

He proved even more inept than the fallen Ming. His undisciplined army ransacked the capital, and his officials were corrupt and vindictive. A respected Ming general, Wu Sangui, defending the northern border, was horrified by the chaos in the capital and withdrew his stout army from the frontier to chase the rebel Li out of Beijing, leaving the empire open to invasion. The Manchus jumped the Great Wall and were parked in Beijing by the end of 1644, with a new boy-emperor on the Chinese throne.

Much of the country, exhausted by the turmoil of the Ming's final death throes, accepted Manchu rule peacefully. But there was also fierce resistance to the barbarian intruders, just as there was to the Mongols. As was the case after the fall of the Song Dynasty, some Ming officials refused to serve the foreigners, and withdrew from government or committed suicide. Wang Fuzhi was one scholar who steadfastly rejected the Manchu regime and spent the rest of his life writing philosophical tracts, some bristling with anti-Manchu ire. The mixing of Chinese and Manchu, in his eyes, was nothing short of a subversion of the divine order of the world. "The Chinese are like the barbarians insofar as their general physical characteristics are similar and they are both subject to assemblies and divisions," he wrote.

> But the Chinese cannot be put in the same category as the barbarians. . . . If man does not draw lines of demarcation in order to set himself apart from other creatures, the order of Heaven is violated; if the Chinese do not draw lines of demarcation in order to set themselves apart from the barbarians, terrestrial order is violated.[23]

A major misstep by the Manchus stiffened resistance. Shortly after claiming Beijing, the Qing issued an edict that all Chinese men had to adopt the standard Manchu hairstyle—a shaven forehead with the remaining hair pulled back into a braid or queue. "The Emperor is like the father, and the people are like his sons," the edict read. "If they are not as one then it will be as if they had two hearts and would they then not be like the people of different countries?"[24] Large numbers of Chinese men were outraged. The traditional Chinese male hairstyle—kept long and tied into a bun on the top of the head—was a core part of their identity. The Chinese considered shaving the head a defacing of the body given by their parents and therefore a severe offense against the prized Confucian virtue of filial piety. There is little likelihood the Manchus stumbled unknowingly into this coiffure crisis: the edict must surely have been a purposeful insult, a way to make the Chinese feel the painful sting of subjugation to their new, foreign overlords. But it was a strategic misfire. Chinese men revolted across the empire, barricading themselves into fortresses and resisting the Manchus for years to come. Forever after the queue became a symbol of barbarian repression of the Han nation.

The Manchus responded to such recalcitrance with terror worthy of Kublai Khan. In 1645, when the trading metropolis of

Yangzhou refused to submit, the Manchus slaughtered almost the entire population—men, women, and children alike—to teach the Chinese a lesson. "Here and there on the ground lay babies, trampled by people or horses," one eyewitness wrote of the horrific scene. "Blood and gore soaked the fields, which were filled with the sound of sobbing. We passed gutters and ponds piled high with corpses; the blood had turned the water to a deep greenish-red color and filled the ponds to the brim." Of the author's many gut-turning memories, the most chilling was listening helplessly to the murder of his two brothers, while he hid on the top of a wooden canopy in an adjoining room of a house. "Scarcely had I regained my breath when I heard the sound of my younger brother wailing, coming from the other side of the wall. Then I heard the blows of the sword. After three blows there was silence. A few minutes later I heard my elder brother implore, 'I have silver in the cellar at home. Release me and I will go and fetch it for you.' There was one blow, then silence again."[25]

=====

The Manchus, however, were not your run-of-the-mill barbarians. Their leadership had been preparing to rule China for decades. At the core of the Manchu community were tribes living in what is now northeast China that claimed descent from the Jurchens (who turned the Song Dynasty into the Southern Song in the 1120s by overrunning northern China). Starting in the early seventeenth century, their leader, named Nurhaci, co-opted or compelled other tribes of steppe peoples into his confederation. Then he organized them into a system of "banners"—units of fighting men and their families that served military, economic, and other social functions. (There were eventually eight such banners, separated on ethnic lines.) Nurhaci's successors then layered on top of this tribal-feudal society a Chinese-style state crowned by an emperor and a royal court, complete with Chinese scholar-officials disenchanted with the corrupt Ming acting as administrators. The Manchu rulers translated ancient Chinese texts into their own language to better absorb Confucian political philosophy and set up a government with a secretariat and six ministries like a Chinese dynasty. When the Manchus took control of Beijing, they simply imported this ready-made, Chinese-influenced state system into China itself.

Though initially the Manchus were somewhat ambivalent about Confucian principles of governance, over time, the Qing became "more Chinese." Again, the case of the Manchus, as with the Jurchens, Mongols, and other invading barbarians, raises the question of who really did the conquering. This question is especially relevant with the Manchus. Unlike the Mongols, who never fully trusted the Chinese elite and their traditional institutions, the Qing embraced the Chinese and their ways much more wholeheartedly. The Mongols, for instance, didn't completely reinstate the civil examination system, preferring to control government appointments and lock out the Chinese as much as was practical. The Qing, by contrast, quickly reestablished the exams to woo the support of the influential literati. In 1679, the Manchu regime even held a special exam in which it offered a larger-than-usual number of degrees.

Whatever misgivings the Manchus had about adopting Confucian rule vanished with the ascent of the Kangxi emperor, considered even by Chinese historians as one of the greatest in imperial history. Though he technically took the throne in 1661 as a young boy after the early death of his father, he was kept under the thumb of an imperious regent until 1669, when the sixteen-year-old tossed him in prison and took control of the Qing court. Though Kangxi enjoyed a good hunt, like any self-respecting Manchu should, he also enthused over Chinese intellectual pursuits, often participating in debates with the literati. He sponsored a compilation of Tang Dynasty poetry, a standard dictionary of the Chinese language, and a major encyclopedia. In a gesture that would have pleased Confucius—who believed a burdensome state was a bad one—in 1713 he permanently froze the tax rate on land.

The Manchus, however, did not go entirely Chinese, either. Even as they basked in Chinese court pomp and Confucian scholarship, they strove to maintain their own Manchu identity as well. Manchu leaders continued to engage in hunts, archery, and other traditional steppe arts. The court also promoted the use of the Manchu language and barred Manchus from the practice of binding women's feet, which had become popular among the Chinese elite during the Ming period. More curiously, the Qing also prohibited Chinese from migrating into the Manchu homeland in northeast China, called Manchuria, to enshrine it as a bastion of Manchu cultural heritage.

In fact, the Qing emperors reveled in their multiculturalism. The Qianlong emperor (who ruled from 1735 to 1795), promoted Manchu archery, horsemanship, and language; commissioned histories of the Manchus that linked them to previous foreign dynasties in China, such as the Jurchen Jin; and appropriated the legend of Genghis Khan to legitimize Qing perceptions of itself as a world-encompassing empire. Meanwhile, he also patronized Tibetan Buddhism and, in his own quest for enlightenment, was initiated into a Buddhist sect. At an imperial retreat north of the Great Wall, he constructed a theme park with architecture from around the empire, including a mini-Tibetan palace and a Chinese-style temple. Yet Qianlong didn't forget Chinese culture, either. In the ultimate display of Confucian filial respect, he ended his sixty-year reign one day short of his grandfather Kangxi's. Once again China, as it had been in the days of Emperor Wu, Taizong of the Tang Dynasty, and even Kublai Khan, was a universal empire indeed.

=

The ambitious Manchus had prepared themselves not just to conquer China, but much else as well. In 1638, even before their troops entered Beijing, the Manchus had created a specific bureau, the Court of Colonial Affairs, to administer the non-Chinese parts of the empire. Its main duties were to manage relations with the other ethnic groups under the large Qing umbrella, like the Jurchens and Mongols. Kept separate from the scholar-official bureaucracy and staffed mostly by non-Chinese, it organized hunts, diplomatic exchanges, and other rituals to appeal to these other cultural groups. As the Qing expanded, so did the types of peoples handled by this special agency. And expand the Qing did. When their armies finished their vast conquests, the Qing enlarged the Chinese empire to an extent unmatched in its history—bigger than the Han or Tang, and twice the size of the Ming.

The Qing got drawn into Central Asia by the rise of a major Mongol power, the Zunghuaria empire. At first, the Qing court had relatively good relations with their Mongol neighbors, and its main preoccupation was simply keeping the peace in the steppe. But in the 1670s, one Mongol chieftain, Galdan, took control of a confederation of Mongol tribes, based roughly in what is now Kazakhstan and Kyrgyzstan, and then extended his writ east into the Mongolian heartland and south into the oasis towns of today's Xinjiang—those famous Silk Road market towns of Kashgar, Turpan, and Yarkand. He had dreams of reconstituting the old Mongol Empire, with himself as the Great Khan.

Nothing struck fear into a Chinese dynasty (even a Manchu one) more than talk of a Mongol revival. The two empires spiraled toward a conflict after Galdan's attacks on Mongol opponents north of China's border destabilized the frontier. The Mongol chief also abused his trading privileges by sending excessively large tribute missions to the Qing court. An annoyed Kangxi responded by placing stiff restrictions on Galdan's embassies, undermining the legitimacy of the Zunghar leader.

Eventually, Kangxi decided something had to be done. In 1690, he personally led the Qing's first campaign against the Zunghars. The two armies clashed at a place called Ulan Batong, but the results were inconclusive. Galdan's soldiers successfully used their camels as a defensive barricade. As the two sides talked peace, Galdan slipped away in the darkness and fled north.

The emperor had been compelled to return to the capital before the battle, and he was not happy with the outcome. Though Galdan sent a written oath of submission to the Qing—which Kangxi accepted—and pledged to stay far from the Chinese border, the emperor was furious he had escaped in the first place, and took out his anger on his generals, demoting the commander and whipping and imprisoning other officers.

Six years would lapse before Kangxi took another shot at Galdan. In the spring of 1696, Kangxi again marched with a large army in pursuit of his Mongol rival. "We were committed . . . by our sacrifices to the gods and the ancestors, by the tenacity of the troops and even their servants—to finish off Galdan," Kangxi wrote.[26] In all, four armies participated in the campaign, with a combined eighty thousand soldiers. The plan was for a main force to tramp toward Galdan's camp from Beijing, to either assault the Mongols head-on, or scare Galdan into fleeing. If the latter, another branch of the Qing army would be waiting for him. The timing had to be perfect. If Galdan got spooked by Kangxi's main force before the other wing was in place, he'd escape the emperor's clutches yet again. Travel through this wilderness of mud, snow, and sand, however, defied precision. Kangxi resorted to deception to hold Galdan in place as long as possible, sending envoys to the Mongol chieftain to discuss restoring normal relations. Kangxi pretended he had come in person to negotiate.

Galdan did flee, as Kangxi expected, and did fall into the Qing trap as planned, at a place called Jao Modo, in the middle of the Mongolian desert. It was a small valley with a river running through it. The Qing forces claimed the advantage by occupying the hills, allowing them to shoot their cannon directly into Galdan's camp. As the Qing troops advanced behind wooden barricades wearing padded-cotton armor for protection, the outnumbered Mongols broke and ran. Manchu cavalry slaughtered thousands. But Galdan, once again, managed to slip away with a party of about fifty loyalists.

Still not satisfied, Kangxi set out on a third mission to capture Galdan in 1697. This time, his ministers tried to dissuade him, arguing that the Mongol chief was no longer a threat worth pursuing. One general tried to distract Kangxi with a hunt, a favorite pastime. But the almost-obsessed Kangxi would not be deterred. "Let's cancel the hunt and rest the horses, and then go hunting Galdan. How about that?" he told his advisors.[27] In the end, he didn't have to. Galdan, abandoned by all but a handful of supporters, died under mysterious circumstances in April 1697.

Kangxi's Galdan itch was finally scratched. But the Zunghar Mongols remained as irritating as ever. A new leader emerged in Galdan's place, named Tsewang Rabdan. Qing efforts to eliminate the continued threat in the late 1710s plunged Chinese soldiers into the old "Western Regions." With the surrender of the ancient oasis town of Turpan, Chinese control extended farther west than it had in a full millennium. The ruins of Han and Tang fortifications were waiting for the Qing troops when they arrived. But the main battlefield in the Qing-Mongol contest was in the most unlikely of places—not the wild steppe of the icy north, but the wild mountains of icy Tibet. In 1717, Tsewang Rabdan's Zunghars swept into a politically divided Tibet and occupied the capital, Lhasa. There they made themselves instantaneously unpopular by ransacking monasteries and massacring monks.

The Qing could not accept this quietly. The Manchus had involved themselves in the affairs of the high-altitude Tibetan empire since its earliest years in China. The Dalai Lama, the spiritual (and often temporal) leader of the Tibetans, ventured to the young Qing court in Beijing back in 1654. As he departed, a Chinese official chased after him with a gold seal bestowing upon the Tibetan one of those honorary titles the Chinese emperors doled out to tributary leaders. In modern times, Chinese nationalists believe this is proof that the Dalai Lama and his government submitted to China, a claim the Tibetans stridently deny. Neither party thought much of it at the time. The Dalai Lama believed his friendly sojourn in Beijing had bolstered his stature as the ruler of Tibet; upon returning home, he donated the imperial seal to a Buddhist shrine. For their part, the Qing thought they had gained a powerful ally in the West.

But the Manchus did become heavily embroiled in Tibet's often tumultuous political affairs. With the Zunghars in Lhasa, the Qing worried their Mongol opponents would use control over the Dalai Lama, greatly respected by Mongol Buddhists, to forge yet another dangerous steppe alliance. In 1720, Kangxi sent a Qing army into Tibet to expel the Mongols; by then, Zunghar rule had descended into utter chaos, and the Qing entered the Tibetan capital with ease. That was a major turning point in Chinese and Tibetan history. During the Tang Dynasty, Tibet was a rival to Chinese power in inner Asia. Now Kangxi remade Tibet. The eastern part of the Tibetan realm was chopped off and absorbed into the Qing empire; the government in Lhasa was reorganized; and in 1727, Beijing appointed two officials, called *ambans*, to oversee Tibetan affairs. After more domestic political machinations, the Dalai Lama was left in charge of a rump nation, with the Qing looking over his shoulder.

The final chapter of the Manchu struggle with the Zunghars was written in the 1750s, and it was an especially ugly one. The Zunghar state in Central Asia was torn asunder by internecine warfare, with some leaders seeking protection and aid from the Qing. The emperor in Beijing, Qianlong, decided to take advantage to rid the empire of the Zunghar nuisance once and for all. But Qianlong became frustrated as his armies chased Mongol chieftains across the steppe, never able to nail the coffin shut. "The pursuit of the rebels is in the hands of timid, ignorant men," the emperor and backseat commander lamented.[28] By the winter of 1756–1757, Qianlong's temper boiled over. He ordered nothing short of genocide. A Final Solution. "Massacre these crazy Zunghars," he ordered in one edict. In another: "Show no mercy at all to these rebels. Only the old and weak should be saved."[29] Women and children were captured and distributed as servants to loyal Mongol tribes or Manchu soldiers. They might live on, but their Zunghar identity would be extinguished. Soon Qing detachments were hunting down and slaughtering Zunghars by the thousands.

The Zunghar people, perhaps some six hundred thousand of them, vanished from history—killed by the Qing, eliminated by disease, or parceled out as slaves. The area in which they had roamed was effectively depopulated. As one Chinese historian put it, "For several thousand *li* there was not one single Zungharian tent."[30] The region was later resettled with loyal Qing subjects. The Zunghars were the sole Mongol horde to persistently resist the might of the Qing Dynasty. They paid the ultimate price.

Qianlong was not yet done. He launched one last, great Qing campaign of conquest into the old Western Regions. There two Khojas, the Islamic noble rulers of the oasis city-states, rose up against the Qing. In 1758, they occupied the famed Silk Road market towns of Kashgar and Yarkand, building stout walls around the cities and denuding the countryside of crops to leave the approaching Qing armies nothing to eat. At the Battle of Blackwater Camp, just outside of Yarkand, the Khojas' army surrounded a greatly outnumbered Qing force and held them under siege there for three months. But an attack on Kashgar by a nomadic tribe compelled the Khojas to flee to a place called Badakhshan, where they were killed and their remains eventually turned over to the Qing and shipped to Beijing.

The Chinese had, as we've seen, made their way to the far west before, during the days of Emperor Wu in the Han Dynasty, and later in the first decades of the Tang Dynasty. Both of those attempts at conquest eventually faded as the remote region proved too difficult to hold. Not this time. The Qing stayed, and the region of Xinjiang, or "New Dominion," became part of the Chinese empire.

With the Qing armies came Chinese culture. The conquests of the Qing emperors were also civilizing missions, through which the Chinese brought to the barbarians what they continued to see as a superior culture. Chinese overlords infused their language, marriage practices, patrilineal family structures, agrarian land systems, tax policies, and other aspects common to Chinese society into the added territories. In this sense, the Qing conquests were not all that different from the colonial endeavors of the major European powers. As the Europeans' traders and soldiers took control over parts of Asia, Africa, the Americas, and the Middle East beginning in the late fifteenth century, turning them into colonies or protectorates, in their wake came administrators, missionaries, schoolteachers, and social activists, bringing their religion, political ideals, laws, books, and other cultural practices that they believed would "civilize" the savages in these "backward" societies. Modern Chinese like to distinguish between what they perceive as China's peaceful engagement with the world compared to the rapacious imperialism of the Europeans. However, Qing China's expansionism and the Chinese attitude toward the peoples they absorbed in inner Asia had similar characteristics to the colonial adventures of the West.

By 1760, the Qing had annexed an incredible amount of territory, comprising Mongolia, Tibet, and Xinjiang, much of it bequeathed to future governments—including the current Communist People's Republic. In a geographic sense, the Qing built the modern Chinese nation-state. The irony is that the national boundaries of today's China were actually delineated by those stinky, no-good, mutton-chomping barbarians.

=

By the time of the Qing, Chinese dominance in East Asia was largely unquestioned. Throughout nearly all of the Ming and Qing periods—some five centuries—China sat firmly at the center of a region-wide system of diplomacy and trade that it controlled. All the other major states in the region generally accepted (though sometimes grudgingly) Chinese hegemony. It was China's rules of statesmanship that defined relations between East Asian states. It was the humongous Chinese economy that drove regional trade. It was Chinese culture that formed the foundation of East Asia's civilization. Ambassadors from many Asian states routinely appeared before the Son of Heaven to perform the expected kowtows, accepting his suzerainty. Whatever shifts in emperors, policies, and attitudes occurred at the Chinese imperial court toward trade, territorial expansion, and foreign influence, the Chinese world order remained entrenched.

The only serious attempt to challenge the Chinese order in East Asia between the founding of the Ming in 1368 and the late nineteenth century came in the 1590s, from Japan. The Japanese emperors had only occasionally been comfortable with second place in Asia, and had sent formal tribute missions to the Chinese imperial court irregularly. Kowtowing to the Son of Heaven was not their bag. But the Japanese also gritted their teeth, bowed to reality, and acquiesced to China's supreme position. That was until 1592, when the Japanese general Toyotomi Hideyoshi shipped an army across the Sea of Japan and invaded Korea, intending to march up the peninsula into China itself.

He never made it. Despite throwing a half million Japanese troops into the fray over the next half decade, Hideyoshi's army was blocked by allied Korean and Ming Chinese forces, and the Imjin War ended in Hideyoshi's disgrace. After his death in 1598, the Japanese abandoned his quest for empire. Japan wouldn't attempt to contest the supremacy of imperial China for another three hundred years.

This war was a rarity. China's world order was not held together by force, or at least not directly. While Qing armies were marching and conquering in the north and west, in the east, they barely unsheathed a sword. Like any government, the Chinese dynasties did not deal with all other peoples exactly the same way. In the eyes of the Chinese, not all barbarians were created equal. Some were a security threat that had to be eliminated—Galdan, for instance. Some were hopelessly uncivilized and always would be. But others were tolerable, even somewhat respectable. They were "like us." Or they at least tried to be. They were cultural compatriots, sharing many elements of a common civilization. With these states, the emperors were not as quick to send out the generals. During the entire period from the founding of the Ming in 1368 and the end of the imperial age in 1911, the Chinese invaded another East Asia state only once—in the early fifteenth century, when the Ming tried to reconquer northern Vietnam. It ended with a Chinese army of one hundred thousand getting thrashed by resistance fighter Le Loi in 1427. Together with the Imjin War, that makes for two wars in East Asia over a period of five centuries.[31] Compare that to the almost incessant conflict between European states during that same stretch of time.

There is a case to be made that the sheer size and power of the Chinese empire was enough of an existential threat to its neighbors that they had little choice but to accept Chinese superiority. Better to do a bit of kowtowing than have a Ming or Qing army camped outside your capital's gates. After his hard-won victory, Le Loi, one of his nation's most revered heroes and founder of the Le Dynasty, immediately sought to become a vassal of Ming China, hoping to secure the peace and set aside resentful feelings. In response, a gracious Ming emperor confirmed his erstwhile enemy as his country's rightful leader. The peace held. The next time the Chinese sent troops rushing to Vietnam was in 1788, and they did so, ironically, to restore that very Le Dynasty, whose king had gotten booted from his throne by a peasant rebellion. The Chinese made it rather effortlessly to the Le's capital of Hanoi only to discover their task was hopeless. They were chased back home, harassed by the victorious rebels. The Chinese didn't try invading Vietnam again until 1979, when the emperors were long gone.

Terrified of China or not, there were real benefits to participating in the Chinese order, most of all economic. Becoming a tributary often came with preferential access to trade, especially during the Ming, whose emperors tied tribute and trade together much more tightly. The emperors of the Ming and Qing Dynasties still held to the rule that giving is better than receiving, and for the imperial courts, hosting embassies from foreign vassals was as expensive as ever. During the Ming, the court not only handed out lavish gifts of cash, silk, silver, and other goodies, but also purchased trade items brought by foreign embassies, often at highly inflated prices. Between 1403 and 1473, the Ming spent the equivalent of seven years of national income supporting this system of tribute and trade.[32]

The prestige of the Chinese dynasties was also so great that rulers throughout the region sought the Son of Heaven's approval to legitimate their stature at home. In 1767, after the Siamese pushed out Burmese invaders who had left the Southeast Asian kingdom in tatters, a provincial governor named Taksin requested recognition from the Qing as Siam's new ruler. After dispatching a delegation to investigate, the Chinese court decided Taksin was the best man for the job, and awarded him the (somewhat tentative) title of "lord of the country." Then, fifteen years later when Taksin was deposed, Rama I, the founding king of the Chakkri Dynasty, sought Qing recognition as well. Rama told the emperor that he was taught "to have care for our own sovereign land and to honor the Heavenly Dynasty" of China.[33] Such imperial favor could have more than symbolic meaning. In 1403, the sultan of the state of Malacca, on the Malay peninsula, sought Ming support to bolster his position against rivals Siam and Java by becoming a tributary of the Chinese emperor; in return, the Ming ensured a sufficiently imposing fleet appeared off the Malaccan coast to make their support known. The Siamese were furious, but also helpless. They knew better than to challenge Chinese supremacy, and they continued to acknowledge it. Siam sent seventy-eight tribute missions to China between 1371 and 1503.[34]

Yet accepting Chinese suzerainty had its downsides, too. Though the Chinese emperors more or less left their so-called vassals to govern their own affairs without much interference, there were moments when they could be irritatingly intrusive. In the early nineteenth century, when a king in Vietnam sought recognition of his newly minted dynasty, the Qing court in Beijing objected to the name the Vietnamese used to refer to their own realm—Nam Viet—since it was the same as a long-ago state once based in southern China that had dominated the region. After a few annoyed exchanges between the two courts, officials in the Forbidden City recommended swapping the two elements. Thus the name Vietnam was actually created by the Chinese. The Vietnamese accepted this compromise, but other demands from the Son of Heaven were not swallowed as easily by others. In 1408, the Ming court sent a eunuch to Korea to fetch young virgins for the imperial harem; the king in Seoul sent three hundred beauties, though was not happy about it. He was even more galled a year later, when a request came for more. It was humiliating, but the Koreans felt they had to comply.

China did not always have its way with its vassals, however. Though officially all other states were considered subordinate to China—the Son of Heaven had no equals—in reality, relations were more balanced than the official diplomatic rhetoric and imperial audience ceremonies suggested. In 1725, for instance, Vietnam snatched promising copper mines by claiming land about forty miles north of its mutually recognized border with the Chinese empire. The Qing emperor decided to compromise, adjusting the formal demarcation line between the two dynasties and leaving a majority of the disputed land in Vietnamese hands.

Still, whatever its pros and cons, imperial China's style of foreign relations has always been controversial in the West. To Western ears, the Chinese diplomatic system may sound embarrassingly condescending, whatever its purported benefits. We are accustomed to the (relatively new) concept of equal status between nation-states, regardless of differences in size and wealth. Accepting the superiority of a foreign ruler, even nominally or rhetorically, and even one as illustrious as the Son of Heaven, might appear an intolerable concession of national pride, or more importantly, sovereignty. Western distaste has focused on the act of the kowtow, that obsequious bow, which has been seen as a ritual of total submission. The mere fact that China demanded and expected such deference from foreign peoples is sickening in and of itself. Who did these Chinese think they were, anyway?

Others in the West dispute that there was anything particularly "Chinese" about Chinese foreign relations at all. Some modern scholars have characterized these tribute relations as no more than a ceremonial disguise for the more mundane politics of power and trade rather than some unique "Chinese system." The entire notion of a peaceful, well-run Chinese "order" in East Asia, with China comfortably orchestrating it all from the top, they consider little more than a myth created by Western observers attempting (and failing) to understand the more complicated realities of Chinese foreign policy.[35]

Here, however, we need to be cautious. It is all too easy to impose our Western notions of diplomacy and, more broadly, human relations onto the Chinese world of centuries past. What may appear unbearable to us in the West was not necessarily perceived the same way in Asia at the time. Hierarchical relationships, so distasteful to us today, were widely accepted in East Asian societies as simply the norm. Bowing was a commonplace custom; even the kowtow was (and is) a routine Chinese religious practice. We also have to prevent our imagination from running amok with fantasies of a despotic East. China's foreign relations were not characterized by trembling sycophants cowing before the all-domineering Chinese emperor. Even the notorious kowtow was not quite what it seems. This ritual was not performed at the feet of the emperor, as it is simple to assume, but usually outside the audience hall, and not in his immediate presence.[36]

Nor should we think of Chinese foreign affairs as a uniform, unchanging "system" operating like clockwork century after century. Needless to say, attempting to squish a society's foreign relations into a set formula is analytical folly. The Chinese emperors and their ministers did not trot out the same fixed menu of principles to confront every diplomatic or strategic issue they encountered. As we've seen, Chinese leaders used a wide variety of tools to achieve their foreign policy goals. And of course, no power, no matter how super, can have its way or impose its will in all circumstances. Relations between states in one part of the world—in trade, diplomatic exchanges, or political alliances—can take on similar characteristics, no matter which cultures might be involved.

At the same time, it is equally simplistic to deny there was a typically Chinese foreign policy. Clearly, the Chinese had their own worldview, rooted in their own history, political philosophy, and self-perception. In that view, China should stand atop a pedestal all its own, head and shoulders above the masses of other peoples. Ideologically, the Son of Heaven could have no peers on earth. That meant relations between China and the rest of the world had to be hierarchical, at least in form if not always in substance. They had diplomatic rules and rituals that they most certainly expected all comers to obey.

Surely, not every ambassador kowtowing at the Beijing court sincerely believed his own ruler or country inferior. It is also probably safe to assume that Chinese court officials were not always oblivious to the fact that their grandiose proclamations could sometimes be more rhetoric than real-life. Yet throughout there was a Chinese *ideal*, based on a self-image of exceptionalism that was grounded in ancient political ideology. In this ideal, China reigned supreme over "all under Heaven"; every other people or state was a subordinate vassal, which acknowledged and accepted China's superior position. The Chinese routinely strove to impose this ideal, to create a world around itself in which it was ascendant, both in figurative and factual terms. When reality did not meet the ideal—which it often did not—the Chinese bitterly resented it. But when China was powerful, as it was during much of the Ming and Qing period, they closed that intolerable gap between the ideal and the real.

There was more going on here than the projection of power. The benevolent Son of Heaven could never sully his righteousness with the crude concerns of mere mortals! Recall that the Son of Heaven was the critical connection between the divine and humankind; only he could bring order and harmony to the world. By attracting foreign rulers to become his tributaries, he was recruiting loyal assistants in this quest for good government and peace. From that standpoint, other rulers were not subservient slaves to the great lord, but honorable (albeit lesser) participants in this grander Chinese mission.[37] Two thousand years after Confucius thought he could save the barbarians, the Chinese still believed their civilization could transform the world. And for the most part, the states of East Asia played along. For them, the rules of the Chinese world were simply the way diplomacy and trade worked. The fact that so many diverse rulers over such an extended length of time cooperated with these norms gives credibility to the argument that the Chinese system had legitimacy among its participants. Part of the reason is that China and its eastern neighbors shared a common civilization. The major states of East Asia—Korea, Vietnam, and, to an extent, Japan—were all Sinicized, meaning they had readily adopted Chinese institutions, culture, and philosophical ideals. The diplomatic hierarchy within the region was determined not by size of population or purse, or military power, but by cultural achievement—which meant, of course, how closely their societies resembled China's.

These East Asian states were becoming "more Chinese" during the Ming and early Qing period as well. Neo-Confucianism, that fresh adaptation of the great sage's teachings from the Song Dynasty era, spread widely in East Asia, advancing Confucian values and ideas throughout the region. In Korea, the Chosun Dynasty, formed in 1392, enlisted Neo-Confucian scholar-officials who drafted its tenets into the state's legal codes, transforming inheritance practices, the role of women in society, family rituals, and other core aspects of Korean custom based on Confucian principles. Chinese-style civil service examinations became an indispensable feature of public life under the Chosun, too. Though not as influential in Japan, Neo-Confucianism was popular within the country's Buddhist community, while local Confucian scholars did receive some official sponsorship from the Tokugawa shogunate founded in the early seventeenth century. Japanese scholars consulted their Chinese counterparts and looked to Chinese models when developing laws for their own government. Confucianism was entrenched in Vietnam as well, taught as in China through civil service exams that produced the top echelon of the nation's policymakers. The spread of Confucianism continued to bind the states of East Asia to one another and provide a shared cultural foundation for their relations.

Far from seeing their ties to China as a national abomination, officials in tributary states often considered participation in a tribute mission a high honor. The diplomatic corps across East Asia was steeped in Chinese philosophy, literature, and history and sincerely respected Chinese civilization. Scholars around the region often referred to China as the "central efflorescence" or "domain of manifest civility."[38] The opportunity to visit the cultural heart and soul of Asia and experience what they had studied in books was seized with relish. Upon being named an envoy to the Qing, Ho Si-Dong, an eighteenth-century Vietnamese scholar-official, noted with pride that "now I was fortunate to . . . view the (moral) radiance of the Esteemed Kingdom (China). . . . This was truly a meeting of the minds."[39] An earlier Vietnamese statesman to China, in the fourteenth century, committed his excitement to verse:

> *I will sincerely report our fief's efforts when I visit the Celestial*
> *Court [of China]*
> *The benevolence we bathe in is as if from a golden goblet*
> *brimming to the rim*
> *Already the radiance seems so close as I set off to receive his*
> *[the Chinese emperor's] moral blessings*
> *In this distant wilderness we will joyfully maintain this enterprise*
> *for ages to come.*[40]

So respected, in fact, was the Chinese order in East Asia that its rules governed relations not only between China and other states, but between those states themselves. Korea, for instance, sent officials of lesser stature to Japan because it had lower status in the tributary order. The Koreans would have undercut their own high standing in East Asia if the court broke protocol and, for instance, sent a royal family member to negotiate with the Japanese. The two also had their own rules and patterns of "tribute" missions and trade between them based on the Chinese model.

Diplomacy and trade in East Asia, therefore, operated on a substantially different set of principles than in the West. In Asia, relations had a built-in superior-subordinate distinction. These were the rules of the game, simply the way states in East Asia communicated and resolved conflicts with one another. And these rules were created and enforced by China. From the Chinese standpoint, it should have always been that way.

As it turned out, though, not everyone agreed.

Eight

THE WESTERN OCEAN BARBARIANS

Often one can't keep from smiling when they [the Europeans] start off on a discussion. How can they presume to talk about "the great principles of China?"

–Kangxi, Qing Dynasty emperor

Into this Chinese world floated an entirely new breed of especially strange and unruly barbarians in wooden sailing ships. In 1517, they appeared off the coast of Guangdong near the famed trading haven of Guangzhou. The language they spoke was an unintelligible mystery, their eight vessels were puny by the standards of Zheng He's treasure junks, and their ultimate origins were a bit hazy. But like all other seaborne ruffians, they wanted to trade for the rich silks and other wonders of China. The Chinese came to call them *folangji*, or "Franks," a generic term used at the time to refer to Europeans. More specifically, they were the Portuguese, and they were the first Europeans to sail all the way from Europe to China.

The adventurous mariners from the kingdom of Portugal had burst into the Indian Ocean in 1498, when Vasco da Gama rounded the cape of Africa and found his way to the southwestern coast of India. It was an earth-rattling moment. Until then, Western Europe had been on the fringes of a world economy driven primarily by exchanges between China, India, and the Islamic world. Portugal, situated on the Atlantic Ocean, was on the fringe of that fringe. Now all that would change. The arrival of the Portuguese in Asia heralded the coming ascendancy of the "West"—Europe, and later, America.

The Portuguese incursion was an equally critical turning point in the Chinese history of the world. In fact, it would alter the course of China's strand of history more drastically than anything that came before it, with the possible exception of the original Qin unification in 221 BC. It was one of those rare moments in time when two narratives of world history that had been meandering along quite separately—the Chinese and the West's—suddenly came crashing into each other. They quickly became entangled, and would never again be unwound.

The Chinese, of course, couldn't have known any of this in 1517. To them, the Portuguese seemed just like any other trade-hungry barbarians who had ventured to China by boat, horse, and camel over countless centuries—whether Sogdian, Indian, Persian, Japanese, or fill in the blank. What the Chinese didn't know was that that wasn't true. The Portuguese brought with them from Europe very different notions of trade and diplomacy than the Chinese had encountered before. More than that, though, the Portuguese were carrying on their wooden caravels an entirely different civilization than others the Chinese had previously encountered. Unlike the usual barbarians, who tended to adopt at least in part Chinese cultural practices, or participate in the rules and norms of the Chinese world order, the Portuguese and their European comrades who followed them to Asia thought their own civilization to be superior. What was about to occur was a clash of peoples who each believed their civilization to be better than all others. The Chinese were simply unaccustomed to and unprepared for this sort of challenge from outsiders. As we've seen, the foreign barbarians could defeat China militarily, and even overrun the empire, but, in Chinese eyes, the Mongols, Xiongnu, and other foreign pests never upset the Chinese self-perception of their exceptionalism. The supposed conquerors often seemed more like the conquered. The Europeans, fully confident in the value of their own civilization, would present a threat to the Chinese world order the Middle Kingdom had never faced before. And it would change everything.

There were already signs of what was to come from the earliest days of the Portuguese presence in Asia. When Vasco da Gama and his successors sailed into the Indian Ocean, they entered a world of well-established, multicultural trading networks and practices that had existed for eons. In the past, new entrants had simply joined in the fray—including the Chinese. Zheng He, for example, wished to impress the world with Chinese power but didn't seek to dominate the region and its trade. Wherever the Portuguese made landfall in Asia, the Chinese had already been. In southern India, Vasco da Gama was told tales of light-skinned, bearded men who had visited the coast generations earlier—references to Zheng He's fleets, which had sunk their anchors off the coast almost a century earlier.

The Portuguese, though, were bred amid the mercantilist brutality of Europe, where separation between trade, war, and power was barely perceptible. They intended not to simply participate in the trade between East and West, but control it. And they used new, aggressive tactics and superior weaponry to impose their will. When they reached the flourishing entrepôt at Malacca in Southeast Asia—the same sultanate Zheng He had been sent to support—the Portuguese sought to conquer, which they did in 1511. The maritime states of South and East Asia had never seen anything quite like the Portuguese before.

Bottled up by the paranoid Ming, the Chinese were not quite aware of who they were dealing with and what they were up to, either. And of course, the Ming authorities could never have foreseen that the dramatic historical winds that carried the Portuguese to the south China coast could blow down the Chinese world order.

But we're getting ahead of our story. In the early sixteenth century, the Portuguese were about as much of a threat to the great Ming empire as gnats to an elephant. Both could be easily swatted away. And at first, the Portuguese did little to challenge the Chinese system of trade. They sought relations with China very much like the standard seaborne barbarians who had been floating to Guangzhou for centuries. The 1517 mission carried Tomé Pires, a former pharmacist appointed by the Portuguese king as the country's first official envoy to the Ming court. The Portuguese intended to become a "vassal" state of the Ming Son of Heaven and participate in tribute and trade like other barbarians, in order to gain access to lucrative Chinese goods. Their goal, in other words, was to join the Chinese world, not subvert it.

Things got off to a rocky start. The flotilla, under the command of Fernão Peres de Andrade, was denied access to Guangzhou by a local naval commander. The suspicious Ming were constricting foreign trade; Portugal was not a formal tributary state, and therefore was not recognized by the dynasty's officials as having the right to trade. After a month of waiting, Andrade threatened to sail on anyway, and the nervous local commander relented. Once at Guangzhou, Andrade unwittingly alarmed the town's fussy functionaries by firing his cannon in salute, a serious faux pas in Chinese protocol. The Ming authorities were no more amused by Portuguese boasting about deposing Malacca's king, a longtime loyal Chinese vassal.

Fortunately, the honest and diplomatic Andrade smoothed matters over, and soon the two parties were exchanging pleasantries. The Portuguese were dazzled by what they found in Guangzhou. Its incredible wealth far surpassed anything back in Portugal. One contemporary Portuguese account records their wonderment at a lavish ceremony to welcome a governor returning to the city. "The ramparts were covered in silken banners, while on the towers reared flagstaffs from which also hung silken flags, so huge that they could be used as sails," the account reads. "Such is the wealth of that country, such is its vast supply of silk, that they squander gold leaf and silk on these flags where we use cheap colors and coarse linen cloth."[1]

Andrade had arrived at an auspicious moment, when the emperor, Zhengde, was less hostile to foreigners and international exchanges than most of his Ming predecessors. Chinese officials in Guangzhou agreed to accept onshore the envoy Pires and his retinue, to await permission to visit the emperor. When Andrade departed in 1518, he left relations with China on a solid footing. "Andrade had arranged matters in the city of [Guangzhou] and the country of China so smoothly that, after he had left, commerce between Portuguese and Chinese was conducted in peace and safety, and men made great profits," one Portuguese scribe recorded.[2]

Not for long. Portuguese bellicosity quickly undid Andrade's good work. His brother, Simão de Andrade, arrived on the China coast from Malacca in 1519, but this Andrade was a significantly different personality—"pompous, arrogant and spendthrift" by one account.[3] He almost instantly alienated his already uppity hosts by building a fort on a Chinese island, forbidding other foreigners from trading ahead of him, and then abusing a Ming official who tried to assert control over the situation. By far the worst affront this Andrade committed was purchasing Chinese children, probably as servants. But the horrified Chinese thought the Portuguese roasted them for dinner. Such a claim even made its way into the official history of the Ming Dynasty. The Portuguese went "so far as to seize the children for food."[4] One Portuguese writer lamented that "within a few days their wretched behavior earned them the reputation not of friends and allies but of vile pirates and enemies."[5]

The reports of this atrocious behavior sent to Beijing doomed the already troubled Pires mission. The Portuguese ambassador had made his way to the capital, where he awaited an audience with the emperor. The climate was somewhat hostile. Chinese officials sent memorials to the court condemning the Portuguese for their ill treatment of the king of Malacca and advocating that the emperor reject the Pires embassy. Making matters worse, Pires handed to the court a letter from the Portuguese sovereign, King Manuel I, that the Chinese found impertinent. It was composed "in the manner he customarily adopted towards pagan princes," according to a Portuguese description.[6] The death of the emperor in 1521 signaled the final death knell of the mission. Pires was hustled out of Beijing the next day and sent back to Guangzhou. There he was forced to write to King Manuel of the emperor's demand that the Portuguese restore the sultan of Malacca to his rightful throne, and Pires was held hostage for compliance. He would never leave China. Sometimes held in harsh conditions and fettered, he died there in 1524.

The situation got uglier still when a new flotilla of Portuguese came to trade shortly after the emperor's death. When news of his demise trickled to Guangzhou, local officials ordered the Portuguese and all other foreign traders to depart. But the ornery Portuguese, already conducting business, refused. The Chinese assembled a sizable fleet and attacked the outnumbered Portuguese, sinking one of their vessels and taking prisoners. On two other occasions in the months that followed, Portuguese trading ships and Chinese war junks came to blows. Then, in 1522, another Portuguese squadron showed up off the Chinese coast with a commission to forge peaceful relations with the Ming. Unaware of the conflict that preceded them, they blithely sailed into a Chinese onslaught that sank two of their three ships. Those unfortunate Portuguese captured in these engagements endured a horrible end. "Twenty-three individuals were each hacked to pieces, losing their heads, legs and arms" one surviving eyewitness recounted. "Their genitals were stuffed in their mouths, and the trunk of each body was wrapped around the belly in two chunks."[7]

The Portuguese were pushed to the shadows of the China trade. Barred from official exchange, they spent the next thirty years engaged in the illegal, but still vibrant, trade that evaded Ming control. Yet eventually, they were brought in from the cold. The trade with Portugal proved too lucrative to ignore, and local Ming officials began to perceive the usefulness of these belligerent newcomers. In 1557, Ming mandarins in southern China allowed the Portuguese to settle in a trading colony on the peninsula of Macau, a short distance from Guangzhou. Within five years, a community of about nine hundred Portuguese had collected there, with two churches and some modest homes. As trade became more liberal in the later Ming, the colony flourished even more. To the Chinese, Macau became a truly foreign place, with strange architecture, stranger people, unfamiliar religious processions, and that clanging of church bells. Some local Chinese saw the settlement in Macau as a bad omen; others complained that it was no longer part of China. One European noted in the 1580s that it was "the natural tendency of the Chinese to fear and to bear ill will towards foreigners." They called the Portuguese "foreign devils."[8]

Odder than Macau itself, though, was that the colony and its trade existed at all. The settlement was clearly outside the usual rules of trade and diplomacy that governed the Chinese world. Portugal was not able to forge formal relations with the Ming court like other countries that traded with the empire. Macau survived because it profited local officials and merchants who possessed the authority and nerve to defy the central government. An official Ming history criticized one such independent-minded mandarin for "valuing the precious goods (of the Portuguese), pretending to forbid but secretly allowing the evil to continue to grow."[9] From its inception, relations with the West ran by different rules.

The Chinese, though, retained the upper hand. The Portuguese had some nifty military technology, most of all their highly effective cannon, which the Chinese duly noticed. But the handful of ships they were capable of deploying on the China coast could not possibly challenge Ming supremacy. (In fact, the expert seafarers of Portugal learned a thing or two about shipbuilding from the Chinese, including the practice of waterproofing wooden hulls with a coating of bitumen.) And just in case these folangji got out of line, a wall and gate were constructed across the narrow point of the Macau peninsula in 1573, and the Portuguese were forbidden to cross it. Significantly, little farmland was enclosed on the Macau side of the wall, which left the Portuguese dependent on the Chinese for food. The Ming could simply lock the gate and starve these barbarians into submission. Macau existed only at China's pleasure.

Other gnats from the far-off "Western Ocean" were swatted just as effortlessly. In 1570, the Spanish, led by Miguel López de Legazpi, sailed across the Pacific from Spain's empire in the New World and took control of Manila in what became the Philippines. Almost immediately—in 1573—the first shipment of Chinese goods was dispatched from Manila to Acapulco in New Spain (now Mexico). The Spanish, like the Portuguese, tried to forge formal trading relations with the Ming but, like the Portuguese, got nowhere. Nevertheless, Manila became a major hub of the China trade, with bulging Chinese junks arriving with prized porcelain and other products that then got shipped on to Mexico on Spanish galleons.

Next came the Dutch. The first Dutch vessel appeared off Macau in 1601. The Portuguese chased off the competition, but they were back soon enough—too soon, if you asked the Ming authorities. These hongmao, or "red hairs," as the Chinese called them, earned a reputation even worse than the folangji. In 1622, the Dutch occupied islands off the Fujian coast, started constructing a fort, and dispatched an ultimatum to the Ming authorities: if they didn't allow Chinese traders to conduct business with them, the Dutch would attack Chinese shipping and coastal towns. When they didn't receive a satisfactory response, the Dutch plundered hamlets and burned Chinese junks around the city of Xiamen. That was too much for the Chinese, who assembled a naval squadron in early 1624 and attacked the Dutch position, eventually forcing them to evacuate. Unable to gain a foothold on the Chinese coast, the Dutch instead settled on the island of Taiwan, where they erected a stout fortress called Casteel Zeelandia in 1639. Chinese junks sailed from Fujian to this Dutch outpost to trade. It wasn't the kind of trading relations the Dutch preferred, but it was all they had. These new barbarians, despite their persistence, were pushed to the margins of the Chinese world.

==

The misunderstandings and missteps between the Europeans and Chinese continued into the early years of the Qing Dynasty. Though not as hostile to foreigners as the isolationist Ming, the new Manchu regime didn't quite know what to make of these seaborne barbarians, either. The Dutch continued to work at forging formal trade relations with China, and finally seemed to achieve a breakthrough. The management of the Dutch East India Company decided to send an official mission to the Qing court in 1655. The eighteen-man delegation was led by two merchants with long experience in Asia, Pieter de Goyer and Jacob de Keyser. After negotiations with top officials in Guangzhou—focused to a good degree on the size and timing of what were effectively bribes—the delegates were permitted to travel to Beijing, hauling along their gifts for the emperor, which included cloth, coral, mirrors, and guns. In the capital, a new round of negotiations began over matters of protocol and the Dutch request for trading rights. A gap opened soon enough. The Qing still linked trade with tribute; the Dutch were willing to send an embassy now and then, but desired the right to trade regularly.

Finally, in September 1656, the Dutch were ushered into the imperial palace for their audience with the emperor. An account of this amazing and historic event—the first time Europeans participated

in a real tribute ceremony before the Son of Heaven in the flesh—
was left to us by one of the members of the Dutch delegation, traveler and writer Johannes Nieuhof. At dawn, as the party waited
in one of the palace's courtyards, Nieuhof's eyes were first drawn
to three black elephants, "gallantly adorned" and standing senti-
nel. Elaborately dressed dignitaries flooded into the palace around
them. "The recourse of people was here so great, as if the whole
city had been thronged together in this one place," he recounted.
Needless to say, the Dutch stood out from the pack, and attracted
attention. "All the grandees, . . . came round gazing and looking
upon us with great admiration, as if we had been some strange
[African] monsters," he wrote. They were taken through one court,
then another, to the pavilion with the emperor's throne, flanked on
each side by 112 soldiers wearing black hats with yellow feathers.
A host of other officials stood nearby, holding umbrellas and standards adorned with dragons. Before the steps leading to the throne
were six white horses, their bridles sparkling with pearls and rubies.
The officers of the court and other notables "wore all one sort of
habit, which was extraordinary rich; they had blue satin coats on,
curiously interwoven with golden dragons and serpents . . . ; they
had caps embroidered with gold, and decked with diamonds and
other precious stones, which signified their degrees and qualities."

Through all this fussing and pomp, the emperor—it was Shun-
zhi, the first Qing sovereign to reign from Beijing—"sat about thirty
paces from the ambassadors, his throne so glistened with gold and
precious stones, that the eyes of all that drew near dazzled." Unfortunately, though, Nieuhof could say little about the man himself.
"We endeavored what we could to get a sight of the emperor in his
throne as he sat in state, but the crowd of his courtiers about him
was such, that it eclipsed him from us in all his glory." Only one
member of the Dutch delegation caught a fleeting glimpse of the
Son of Heaven. "For as much as he could discern of him, he was
young, and of fair complexion, of middle stature, and well propor-
tioned, clothed and shining all in clinquant gold."

When the ceremony began, the eminent personages, in groups
one after another, approached the emperor and performed the
kowtow—or, as Nieuhof described, "bowed down their heads
nine times to the ground." Then it was the turn of the Dutch. "The

herald called to them aloud, 'Go and stand before the throne'; thereupon we made up to the throne; then the herald called again, 'Step into your place,' which accordingly was done; then he spoke again, 'Bow your head three times to the ground,' which we did; at last he called to us 'to rise up,' and we rose, and this happened three times one after another; last of all the herald cried aloud 'Return to your place,' whereupon we returned to our stand."[10]

And with that the Dutch became the first Europeans to become official vassals of the Son of Heaven, or so the Chinese court believed. "Holland" got scribbled into the official Qing records as a new tributary state. But neither side seemed entirely clear about who and what they were dealing with. The delegates kowtowing to the emperor were representing no more than the Dutch East India Company, not the Dutch government. For their part, the Dutch had only a hazy notion of the full meaning of their kowtowing. And they didn't much care. If it meant finally establishing trading rights with China, so be it.

They were disappointed. The Qing permitted the Dutch to trade formally with China, but only in conjunction with tribute missions—which the court mandated were only welcome every eight years. That restriction became an even bigger problem after a Chinese pirate, Koxinga, pushed the Dutch off of Taiwan in the early 1660s, ending their informal trading there. The Dutch tried to win over the Qing by cooperating with Chinese efforts to quash Koxinga, sending three substantial squadrons to participate in Qing offensives between 1662 and 1665. The Qing found their new allies impetuous, truculent, and, most importantly, potentially dangerous. The firepower of their vessels was perceived as a potential threat rather than a helpful aid against the common piratical foe. Still, in return for their assistance, the Qing granted the Dutch the right to trade every other year.

The Dutch managed to botch the arrangement anyway. Officials at the Asia headquarters of the Dutch East India Company at Batavia (now Jakarta, capital of Indonesia) had little understanding of how Qing diplomacy worked, and didn't much care to find out. They figured they'd send another embassy to the emperor when there was something important to discuss. The emperor, however, was not asking for a tribute mission every eight years; he was expecting one. Vassals had to follow the dictates of the Son of Heaven. So when the Europeans failed to dispatch another embassy on time, the court took it as a serious breach of diplomatic protocol. Eventually the Dutch realized their error and sent a second mission in the mid-1660s, but it was too late. Their inexcusable infraction, combined with other transgressions—most of all, the plundering of Buddhist temples at a cherished monastery by rampaging Dutch seamen—got their trading privileges revoked.

Soon thereafter, however, the Qing attitude toward trade changed drastically. In 1684, the Qing broke the link between trade and tribute. From that point on, any seaborne barbarian could come to Chinese ports to trade, whether formally from a vassal state or not. Tribute missions still came and went from Beijing, as part of the normal diplomatic order in East Asia. But to the Portuguese, Dutch, British, and French, that meant little. The Europeans had never really been part of the traditional system; by the late seventeenth century, they were effectively exempted from it.

The potential risks of all these new barbarians showing up at Guangzhou did not go unnoticed by the Chinese. Chen Mao, a general who had been engaged in maritime trade as a young man, protested in the early eighteenth century that precautions should be taken to ensure security, such as ordering the removal of cannons from visiting vessels. The proposal was accepted, but enforced with little enthusiasm. Trade with the Europeans was peaceful and profitable. A provincial governor told Beijing in 1724 that "the customs receipts are increased, people from afar are duly impressed, and there is nothing that can give rise to further trouble."[11]

The Ming and Qing tolerated these new barbarians because it was simply good business. European demand for Chinese goods was huge. From the early seventeenth to the late eighteenth centuries, the Dutch East India Company imported almost forty-three million pieces of porcelain from China, while other European trading companies brought at least thirty million more—everything from large platters and small dishes to wine jars, bottles, basins, candlesticks, and vases. The insatiable appetite for Chinese porcelain in Europe—where it was called "white gold"—sparked investment in new kilns at the main production center at Jingdezhen, and swelled the workforce there. By the late Ming, some two hundred private kilns were in operation in the town, on top of those owned by the imperial court, and thousands of smaller workshops popped up alongside these larger industrial operations. Often these kilns produced porcelain specially designed for the European consumer, based on designs recommended by European merchants.

To pay for all that dinnerware, silk, and other exports, the Europeans brought something the Chinese valued tremendously—silver. After the brutal triumphs of the Spanish conquistadors in the Americas from the early sixteenth century, the Europeans got their hands on immense quantities of the precious metal. The silver strike at Potosi, in what is now Bolivia, in 1545 was one of the great finds in history. Silver flowed liberally from the New World to the Old. And then it flowed into the China trade. In fact, the Chinese proved to be the chief beneficiaries of the wealth extracted from Spain's new American colonies. By one estimate, a staggering three-fourths of all the silver mined in the Americas between 1500 and 1800 ended up in China.[12] More silver came from mines in Japan, another avid consumer of Chinese goods. As a Portuguese merchant put it in 1621, "Silver wanders throughout all the world in its peregrinations before flocking to China, where it remains, as if at its natural center."[13] The Chinese economy was so advanced and its wares so desirable that it absorbed the riches of the world.

Meanwhile, the linkages between China and other countries continued to expand. In the 1780s, ships began arriving in Guangzhou from the northern Pacific coast of America, carrying cargoes of furs. Some of these vessels were from the newly independent United States. The very first US merchant ship landed in Guangzhou in 1784, and the trade grew rapidly. By 1800, trade with the United States swelled to as much as 20 percent of the Western total. Over the course of the eighteenth century, though, it was the British who shoved aside the Dutch, Portuguese, and French to dominate the China trade. And that was to a great degree the result of a single product: tea.

Over the millennia, as we've seen, China generated all sorts of inventions and products that shaped global society—whether silk, porcelain, or gunpowder. But none had a bigger impact on the Chinese history of the world than tea. Yes, those dried leaves might seem innocuous enough. But the tea business led to a series of economic and political events that so drastically altered China's position in the world that the effects are still being felt today.

Tea drinking most likely originated in China all the way back in the second millennium BC. At first it was probably stewed with a potpourri of other forest herbs and tree barks into a medicinal soup in the region of today's Yunnan province. The Chinese were enjoying tea as we do now—boiled into a soothing brew on its own—by the third century BC in the area of Sichuan. China was already exporting the leaves to Japan and Southeast Asia by the ninth century, but it was the mariner Zheng He who first shepherded large quantities of Chinese tea outside of East Asia in the bowels of his great "treasure ships" in the fifteenth century. Tea, though, didn't become a truly global phenomenon until the British got addicted to it three centuries later. The exotic brew first appeared in British coffeehouses in the mid-seventeenth century. One such establishment advertised tea as an "excellent, and by all physicians approved, China drink."[14] Yet the amount imported from China at this point was fairly small. Seriously pricy, tea was consumed only by the rich and famous merchants and dignitaries of London as they debated local politics and the affairs of the world.

That changed along with consumer tastes in Great Britain. By the late eighteenth century, tea had become the Brits' national beverage and seen as almost a staple necessity for every kitchen. Served in a distinctly un-Chinese form—drowned in milk and sugar— "afternoon tea" became a daily social event, as well as an easy way to get a shot of midday nourishment. The tradition highlights the global impact of Chinese production. Often, tea was served in the porcelain pots and cups that also came from China (or, increasingly, were copied by European manufacturers). Tea was one of the first products of long-distance trade to transcend elite luxury and become readily available to the average dinner table.

With this new market, tea became big business in China. Grown mostly in the hilly areas of southeast China and shipped out of Guangzhou, tea overtook porcelain and silk as China's most important global industry. Between 1720 and 1765, the amount of tea China exported increased about eight times. The British were buying most of it. The English East India Company, which held a royal monopoly on the kingdom's trade with China, imported a mere two hundred pounds of Chinese tea a year into Great Britain in the late seventeenth century; by the early nineteenth, it was shipping twenty-eight million. With this upsurge in sales, the tea industry sucked in larger and larger numbers of job seekers in China, often working for minimal wages, which kept prices low and consumer demand high. China was a low-cost, highly efficient exporter of tea, which allowed it to dominate the world market.

Both sides in this exchange got what they most desired. The British paid for all that tea with silver, which the Chinese needed to lubricate their domestic economy; the British received the main ingredient for their cherished afternoon repast. But the British weren't happy with the arrangement. The English tea-drinking habit was draining the empire of hard currency and shipping it off to China. The merchants of the English East India Company desperately searched for some product to exchange for tea instead, to better balance their account with China. They had some success with Indian cotton, until demand for it dried up in the early nineteenth century, and they tried hard to push British woolens, but they received poor prices from Chinese buyers. The Chinese simply weren't interested in what the British had to sell, and silver kept pouring out of English coffers and into China. The problem persisted until the English finally stumbled upon something the Chinese *did* want. What they found changed history.

=====

With the European merchants from the Western Ocean came another group of new barbarians: European missionaries. Just as Buddhism and Islam had filtered into China from the west through trade, so did Christianity.

The early missionaries, mostly of the Jesuit and Franciscan orders, collected in Macau after its founding in the late 1550s, where they tended to their foreign flock. But their target was China proper, where they salivated at the prospect of preaching the Gospels to the untold millions of heathen Chinese souls. In that, they initially were disappointed. The jittery Ming authorities were not keen on a bunch of strange barbarians running amok in the countryside teaching who knows what to the unwashed and all-too-often rebellious masses. But Christian hopes were renewed by the Jesuit Alessandro

Valignano, who was placed in charge of the society's activities east of Africa. While in Macau in the late 1570s, he determined that the missionaries appeared too unfamiliar to appeal to the Chinese. To win converts, the Jesuits—like so many barbarians before them, whether Turk, Mongol, or Manchu—would have to become converts themselves—to Chinese civilization. Breaking with common practice, Valignano permitted the Jesuit Fathers to learn Chinese language and customs. The first Jesuit to take advantage was Michele Ruggieri, who arrived in Macau in 1579 and immediately began studying Chinese. Then he went further. In 1582, he accompanied some Portuguese officials to Zhaoqing in Guangdong province and met the governor, who, suitably impressed, invited Ruggieri to return. There he and a colleague moved into a Buddhist temple, shaved their heads, and dressed in monks' robes. They "have become Chinese in order to win China for Christ," Ruggieri wrote.[15]

The man who did more to promote the Jesuit cause in China than any other joined Ruggieri in Zhaoqing in 1583—Matteo Ricci. The Italian possessed just the right mix of knowledge, skill, and flexibility to penetrate Chinese society as no Western Ocean barbarian yet had, perhaps since Marco Polo. Ricci began studying the Confucian classics and familiarized himself with the core ideas held by all Chinese elite. Taking a suggestion from a Chinese associate, Ricci realized that the way to the Chinese heart was through the Chinese head: nothing appealed to the book-loving literati more than scholarship. So Ricci determined to market his true faith within the Confucian context they could appreciate, while at the same time piquing their curiosity with dashes of new ideas and learning from the far West. That entailed ditching the disguise of a Buddhist monk and re-creating himself as a Confucian gentleman. Or as he put it, "It was better now to proceed confidently as though we were in fact men of China."[16] The shift in strategy required a new image. "We have grown our beards and hair down to our ears, and at the same time we have to wear a particular garment, which the literati use during visits"—a long silk robe, Ricci explained in a 1595 letter. "We no longer wear the clothes we wore before as monks."[17] Ricci, though, knew more than his attire needed a makeover. So did Christianity itself. Using his knowledge of Confucianism, he began explaining Christian concepts with the language of the doctrine the Chinese most cherished, and related Christian ideas to their own long-held Confucian principles. The Jesuit Fathers called their teaching the "Learning from Heaven" and the Christian God "the Lord of Heaven," to make them sound more familiar. In his own writing, Ricci referred to passages in China's literary classics that rooted Christian concepts in ancient Chinese precedents. "I make every effort to turn our way the leader of the literati sect, that is Confucius, by interpreting any ambiguities in his writing in our favor," Ricci wrote.[18] The idea was to engage the Chinese scholars on their own terms, to win them over to Christianity through rational explanation based on traditional Chinese education. One debate with a noted scholar and his disciples, Ricci noted, "left them surprised, since they saw me argue so well using doctrine and arguments taken from their own books."[19]

Ricci, however, did not go entirely native. A big part of his appeal was his exotic foreignness, and the Chinese called him "Li of the Far West." He played on their curiosity, packing his home with Western technical oddities, from maps to mechanical clocks to musical instruments, often using his visitors' interest in such scientific knowledge to lure them into discussions of faith. The mix worked wonders. In 1601, Ricci was able to set up shop right in Beijing, where he would remain for the rest of his life. He attracted a steady stream of scholars from around the country, who marveled at his European art, books, and gadgets, and got drawn into Ricci's discourses on the Learning of Heaven.

By the time of Ricci's death, in 1610, he was a fixture in the capital, and so were the Jesuits. His successors remained there and, even better, made their way into the service of the emperor. In 1628, an influential Christian convert submitted to the throne calculations made for a solar eclipse using the Jesuits' superior astronomical methods that were more accurate than the court's own. That led to the formation of a new office to revise the Chinese calendar using Western know-how, with two Jesuits appointed to serve in it. They proved up to the task—one, in fact, had studied with Galileo. This expertise helped the Jesuits survive the transition from the Ming to Qing dynasties in 1644. The first Qing emperor in Beijing was so enamored with the senior Jesuit, Adam Schall von Bell, that in 1650 he had land allocated in Beijing for a new church and donated an inscription in gold for the interior.

The ever-inquisitive Kangxi emperor was especially tickled by the missionaries and their scientific expertise. He enjoyed academic debates and learning, and the new ideas brought by the Westerners fed his voracious appetite for knowledge. And since the Jesuits strove to learn Chinese language and culture, he also trusted and respected them. Throughout his reign, he maintained a group of Jesuits at his court, whom he dispatched on an important diplomatic mission to Russia, assigned the task of mapping the empire, and engaged in other duties. He also enjoyed showing off the Western science and mathematics they taught him. "On inspection tours later I used these Western methods to show my officials how to make more accurate calculations when planning their river works," he once wrote. "I myself planted the measuring device in the ground, and got my sons and bodyguards to use their spears and stakes to mark the various distances. I held the calculating tray on my knee." Deeply impressed by a mechanical clock based on Western technology, Kangxi composed an ode about it in 1705.

> The skill originated in the West,
> But, by learning, we can achieve the artifice;
> Wheels turn and time turns round,
> Hands show the minutes as they change.
> Red-capped watchmen, there's no need to announce
>   dawn's coming,
> My golden clock has warned me of the time,
> By first light I am hard at work,
> And keep on asking, "Why are the memorials late?"

Kangxi was also generally tolerant of the Jesuits' religion, too. In 1692, he issued what is known as the Edict of Toleration, which offered official protection to the missionaries and their flock. The emperor, in effect, made it fully legal to be Christian.

Yet even the open-minded Kangxi had his misgivings about the missionaries and their activities in China. Who knows what they could be preaching; maybe they weren't men of religion at all, but agents of the European merchants. So he allowed missionaries to stay in the country only if they signed certificates pledging to remain in China for life and, more importantly, respect Chinese

The powerful Kangxi emperor of the Qing Dynasty engaged in intellectual discussions with Jesuit missionaries from the West, and though he appreciated their scientific skill, he still believed their knowledge paled in comparison with that of the Chinese.

The Astronomers, Beauvais Workshop, 1711 (tapestry), Belin de Fontenay, Jean-Baptiste (1653–1715) / Musee Leblanc-Duvernoy, Auxerre, France / Bridgeman Images

Confucianism and its practices—most of all, ancestor worship. Those who refused got deported.

Ultimately, for Kangxi, the Jesuits were still barbarians, and he could be somewhat dismissive of them and their talents. Whatever skills they might possess, the Westerners were still not superior to the Chinese. "After all, they know only a fraction of what I know, and none of the Westerners is really conversant with Chinese literature," the emperor wrote. "Often one can't keep from smiling when they start off on a discussion. How can they presume to talk about 'the great principles of China'?" Nor were their technological achievements as impressive as China's. "Even though some of the Western methods are different from our own, and may even be an improvement, there is little about them that is new," the emperor thought. "The principles of mathematics all derive from the *Book of Changes* [one of the ancient Chinese classics], and the Western methods are Chinese in origin."

Kangxi was even less impressed by aspects of Western culture. Respecting one's ancestors with a long period of mourning and other ceremonies was a measure of one's virtue in Chinese society, and the Westerners' comparative disregard for their deceased family Kangxi saw as a moral failing. "Even little animals mourn their dead mothers for many days; these Westerners who want to treat their dead with indifference are not even equal to animals. How could they be compared with Chinese?" Even their religion was something of a muddle. He recalled asking one of the missionaries "why God had not forgiven his son without making him die, but though he had tried to answer I had not understood him." He told another that "I would gladly witness some of the miracles they talked about, but none was forthcoming."

In the end, the great Kangxi didn't quite trust these strange, new foreigners. Sure, he certainly enjoyed his engagements with the Jesuits, and their fancy clocks and maps. And the silver they brought to China was just fine with him, too. But there was something about these Western Ocean barbarians that just wasn't right. What were their real intentions anyway? "The Westerners continued to cause me anxiety," he wrote. He recorded that he warned the governors of the coastal regions that "I fear that some time in the future China is going to get into difficulties with these various Western countries."[20]

And if the enlightened Kangxi felt that way, imagine what many other Chinese thought of the men from the West. The missionaries were a recurring target of anti-West sentiment. The Jesuits and their fellow proselytizers were, after all, spreading a strange foreign doctrine that could subvert good old-fashioned Chinese virtues. In the 1660s, a writer named Yang Guangxian argued that Christianity—whatever Ricci claimed—did not share the core values of Confucianism, and was therefore a danger to both Chinese traditional culture and the Qing Dynasty itself. The missionaries "really aim to inveigle the people of the Qing into rebelling against the Qing and following this heterodox sect, which would lead all-under-Heaven to abandon respect for rulers and fathers."[21] His attack gained enough support in the early Qing court that the Beijing Jesuits were temporarily imprisoned and nearly executed. That incident proved a minor setback.

But the crackdown ordered by Kangxi's successor, the Yong-zheng emperor, was much more severe. As heavy-handed and conservative as Kangxi was liberal, the new emperor claimed the throne in 1722 after a succession struggle with his brothers tainted his ascension with a whiff of illegitimacy. Yongzheng tried to wipe that away by being more autocratic and orthodox. Just over one year after he took power, he banned Christianity, expelled the missionaries from the provinces, and turned churches into public buildings or temples for other religions. Those Jesuit Fathers in Beijing were able to remain, but as mere functionaries of the court, fiddling with their calendar calculations. It was a sign of what was to come. The Qing would become more nervous about these Western Ocean barbarians, and more intent on controlling them.

As if to confirm their worst fears, Qing authorities were shocked to discover a well-organized community of Christian converts still very active in Fuan in Fujian province, in China's southeast, after the emperor's ban. Even more distressing, the missionaries who led it were sending lists of the converts' names to Dominican friars in Spanish Manila. The Qing tried to break up the community in 1746 by arresting five missionaries. That didn't dissuade their convert-supporters, who followed their leaders in the thousands as they were hauled off to prison. The Fuan episode seriously shook up the Qing. Here the authorities saw foreign priests spreading a foreign doctrine to create a fifth column within Chinese society that could be directed by communications with foreign powers—to what nefarious ends court officials could only imagine. Clearly these new barbarians were becoming a threat to national security. The emperor ordered the suppression of Christian communities throughout the empire. In 1749, Qing officials issued new rules for Macau that included a ban on converting Chinese to Christianity.

The distrust spread from church to commerce. The European crews who sailed to Guangzhou were persistently unruly—brawls between the different nationalities were all too common—and probes by the traders to conduct trade with ports elsewhere on the coast heightened suspicion of their intentions in Beijing. In the mid-1750s, the British attempted to open trade at the port of Ningbo (not far from modern Shanghai), which elicited a torrent of paranoia. Official reports panicked that the Brits might gather military intelligence if permitted to trade at Ningbo, or local "rascals" might cooperate with them and cause trouble. A 1757 imperial edict worried that if the Ningbo port was opened, "in the future foreign ships will gather like clouds, and (foreigners) will remain there for longer and longer times, so that it will become another Macau. This is of great importance for an important part of our coastal frontier and for the customs of our scholars and people."[22]

Enough was enough. Between 1757 and 1760, the Qing instituted a new, strict regime for foreign trade. All ports were closed to trade with the Europeans save one—Guangzhou. There foreigners were restricted to their warehouses (called "factories") along the Guangzhou waterfront and were not allowed in the walled Chinese city, or just about anywhere else. European merchants were not permitted to remain in Guangzhou permanently; if their ships departed, they had to be on them. They couldn't even send letters into China without official permission. A group of Chinese merchant houses, known as *hongs*, were awarded a partial monopoly on trade with the Europeans. These restrictions created what became known as the "Canton system"—Canton being the old name for Guangzhou. The Europeans detested the regulatory fetters and did their required complaining, but the Qing effectively told them, "too bad." Trading with China was a privilege granted by the caring and loving Son of Heaven to please the barbarians, and only those who played by Chinese rules enjoyed that privilege. "If you can not get a tolerable profit upon your goods, you must not in future bring any, as it is of very small consequence to this country," one Qing official informed them.[23]

Still, the two communities attempted to get along. William Hickey, a British attorney who visited Guangzhou in 1769, recalled attending two parties at the country estate of one of the hong merchants. The first was "a dinner, dressed and served a la mode Anglaise, the Chinamen on that occasion using, and awkwardly enough, knives and forks, and in every respect conforming to the European fashion," Hickey recorded in his memoirs. After the meal, a play was performed. "In one of the scenes an English naval officer, in full uniform and fierce cocked hat, was introduced, who strutted across the stage, saying 'Maskee can do! God damn!' whereon a loud and universal laugh ensued, the Chinese quite in an ecstasy, crying out 'Truly have muchee like Englishman.'" The next night, the tables were turned. "Everything was Chinese, all the European guests eating, or endeavoring to eat, with chop sticks," Hickey recalled. "At night brilliant fireworks (in which they also excel) were let off in a garden magnificently lighted by colored lamps."[24]

However, the Canton system left few opportunities for such frivolity, or for the Europeans and Chinese to get to know each other. The chasm between Chinese and Westerner led to recurring disputes. Hickey recounted how one escalated almost instantaneously into fisticuffs. A British longboat was sailing to Guangzhou when it was chased by a Qing patrol, which ordered it to turn back. "The style in which this order was given offended the British tars, and they refused to comply," Hickey wrote. "The Chinamen then absurdly attempted to enforce their order by violence, and were all plumped into the river, with a few not very gentle mementoes from the fists of John Bull. . . . This transaction set the whole city in a ferment, mandarins were seen in every direction, all trade and even the daily supply of provisions to the ships was stopped."[25]

These incidents added to the Europeans' grievances. The traders began to feel ill treated under Qing law. The problem came under a gruesome spotlight in 1784 after two Chinese in a boat were accidentally killed when a British ship, the *Lady Hughes*, discharged a cannon salute. The Qing forced the British to hand over the gunner by cutting off all trade, then executed him, even though all parties agreed the poor man did not intend to harm anyone. The incident reinforced an increasingly prevalent view among the Europeans that their relations with China had to drastically change.

For their part, the Qing grew more uneasy about the Europeans, too. Part of the problem was that the court had no real mechanism through which to form a coherent policy toward these new barbarians. Qing officials dealt with foreign affairs through the lens of tribute diplomacy, but these foreigners were never consistent participants in it. Chinese court records count only ten European "tribute" embassies to Beijing in the first 150 years of Qing rule.[26] That left the Qing handling relations with the Europeans in an ad hoc, unfocused way that left few channels of direct communication. The few Europeans living in Beijing—the Christian astronomers—were at best curiosities; at worst, part of those foreign-linked networks of potential spies. As the Europeans' global influence expanded, and their confidence with it, the Qing were ill prepared and ill informed about these new barbarians, their culture, their ambitions, and their power. But who cared? Trade with the Western Ocean men was lucrative, and the troubles they occasionally created seemed manageable and had an effect mainly on the fringes of the empire. Gorged with its conquests in Central Asia, ridiculously wealthy, and militarily unchallenged, the new barbarians in far-off Guangzhou seemed of little concern to the Qing court. They were still gnats on an elephant, at least in the eyes of the Beijing court, even in the late eighteenth century. For millennia, the outside world had changed for China; China didn't change for the world.

===

The contest between a tradition-bound China and an emerging European order began in earnest in 1793, when George Macartney arrived in China. The experienced British statesman had been dispatched by King George III to lead an embassy mission to the Qianlong emperor, hoping to tackle the vexing issues Great Britain had with the Qing empire. Like the other European states, the British had groused about the restrictions imposed on their commerce, but generally acquiesced to them. Now, the increasingly assertive British wanted Qing trade practices to become fairer and freer, and they were taking their case straight to the top. Macartney was tasked with negotiating, in effect, an end to the suffocating Canton system by convincing the Qing court to open more ports to their commerce; allow the British to establish a trading hub on the China coast along the lines of Portuguese Macau; and install a permanent minister in Beijing to handle British affairs directly with the Qing national leadership, rather than provincial officials in Guangzhou. The Europeans had convinced themselves that they failed to get a decent hearing on their complaints because they were talking to stubborn and ineffective local functionaries; surely if their message got directly to the Qing emperor, he'd see the justness of their case. From a Western perspective, this all seemed perfectly reasonable. The British were simply trying to expand their relationship with an important trading partner.

But looking at it through the eyes of the Qing, the British requests were downright radical. The Chinese dealt with other states through the prism of their hierarchical tribute diplomacy, which they regulated as they saw fit. Though the Europeans had never been fully integrated into this regional order, its rules still dominated how Chinese officials understood China's relations with the rest of the world. In that system, the Qing did not exchange full-time ambassadors like European governments, or allow foreign nations to open missions within Beijing. That's because the Chinese did not engage in state-to-state relations, in the way they were developing in Europe. The Chinese were accustomed to deciding what their relations with another state would be. The British were attempting to impose their own diplomatic practices and principles onto the traditional Chinese world order. In some instances, Macartney and his colleagues purposely tested the boundaries of Chinese diplomacy—they knew full well they were breaking protocol—but at others, they seem to have simply not understood how their actions would upset the Chinese, or only realized the consequences after they had stumbled into them. Whatever motivated Macartney, his mission didn't go well.

The British signaled their rebellious intentions upon their arrival. Western Ocean envoys had always stopped at Guangzhou and then traveled through the country to Beijing. Macartney flouted this usual practice. The mission insisted on sailing up the coast and entering China through Tianjin, close to Beijing. He also brought unusual gifts for the emperor, meant to show off British advanced technology—including a planetarium that required time-consuming assembly. The Chinese accommodated these deviations, wishing to make a good impression on Britain's first ambassador to the imperial court. The British were the more troublesome of the empire's Western trading partners, and the Qing hoped that a display of Chinese wealth, strength, and culture would transform these barbarians into orderly vassals, as Chinese civilization always had.

But Macartney's departures from the norm flummoxed the ceremony-obsessed Chinese bureaucrats. A frenzy of paperwork ensued, with memorials, missives, and instructions, some in eye-crossing detail, flying between the court in Beijing, provincial officials, and the unfortunate mandarins tasked with escorting the uppity embassy. But more than that, the emperor and his ministers were unsure how to deal with such a mission at all. Though they called it, as always, a tribute mission, and tried to squeeze the Macartney embassy into the rules of their usual diplomatic protocols, they also had so little experience with the men of the Western Ocean that they struggled to make sense of Macartney's decisions and devise the right approach to the British arrivals. "When dealing with barbarians one ought to strike the mean between being too lavish and too frugal," one letter from Beijing instructed officials receiving the English envoys. "This time, when the English tribute Envoy arrives, although the entertainments as a whole should not be more elaborate than those set by precedent, yet since the tribute Envoy will have sailed from afar across the sea, and it will be his first time of visiting our illustrious country he should not be classed with Burma or Annam [in Vietnam] and other places that come to pay tribute every year."[27] Imagine, for a moment, the bewilderment this order must have elicited from the poor Chinese bureaucrats left deciphering what "the mean" actually meant.

The most protracted disagreement between the two sides had to do with a critical piece of ritual—the kowtow. All barbarians, the Western Ocean brand included, had dutifully observed this practice in the past. But this time, Chinese officials had gotten a sense that the polite but prickly Macartney might not be as amenable. The court sent off a dispatch to Macartney's Chinese handlers for clarity on that important point, suggesting that they softly broach the matter with the British ambassador if necessary, while still en route to the capital. When they explained to Macartney that all envoys always performed the kowtow, the barbarian made clear that "though I had the most earnest desire to do everything that might be agreeable to the Emperor, my first duty must be to do what might be agreeable to my own King."[28] Aware that a potential disaster was looming, Macartney's minders became more desperate and insistent. Three days later, Macartney recalled, "they pressed me most earnestly to comply with it [the kowtow], said it was a mere trifle: kneeled down on the floor and practiced it of their own accord to show me the manner of it, and begged me to try whether I could perform it."[29]

At first, this resistance was kept hidden from the court, but eventually Macartney penned a letter formally informing the Qing that he would agree to kowtow only if a Chinese official of similar rank to his own would undertake the same obsequious prostrations before a portrait of King George, which he had conveniently brought with him. When Chinese officials continued to pressure him to relent, Macartney got to the heart of the matter: "I dwelt upon the propriety of something to distinguish between the homage of tributary Princes and the ceremony used on the part of a great independent Sovereign."[30]

The Chinese knew of no such distinction. There was the universal Son of Heaven, and his vassals, and that was all. Faced with this unique resistance to its rules—and even more, its entire political philosophy—the emperor became angry and vindictive. He canceled an opera and other entertainment originally planned for the envoy. "If they tend to be in the least haughty then they are not destined to receive our favor," the court instructed. "We should immediately cut down the ceremony of their reception in order to demonstrate our system."[31]

In the end, the Qing conceded. The compromise reached allowed Macartney to show his respect for Qianlong by getting down on one knee, as he would before his own king. The ceremony took place in September 1793, in a circular tent set up on the grounds of the imperial summer retreat north of Beijing, where the emperor was residing at the time. Macartney, clad in velvet and topped with a plumed hat, reverently delivered a letter to the Qianlong emperor from King George. What Qianlong witnessed from his throne, however, was a foreign barbarian's head nowhere near its proper place—pressed to the ground, over and over again.

The emperor could not have been pleased. In instructions to provincial officials along the route of Macartney's departure—he was taking the traditional exit through Guangzhou—the court again warned about being too hospitable to these barbarians. Earlier in Macartney's visit, local officials "were exceedingly liberal and generous in their treatment to the point of overflow, without regard

The Qianlong emperor of the Qing Dynasty presides over an audience with Lord Macartney, the first official ambassador to China from England, in 1793. The mission ended in acrimony when Macartney, as shown in this contemporaneous sketch, insisted on kneeling before the Son of Heaven instead of performing the usual kowtow.

WD 961 Emperor receiving the Embassy; Macartney's first meeting with Qianlong, from an "Album of 278 Drawings of Landscapes, Coastlines, Costumes and Everyday Life Made During Lord Macartney's Embassy to the Emperor of China," c. 1792–94 (pencil, pen & ink, wash and w/c on paper), Alexander, William (1767–1816) / British Library, London, UK / © British Library Board. All Rights Reserved / Bridgeman Images

for ritual protocols, thus increasing the embassy's arrogance and recklessness." On his way out, officials should not make the same mistake and spoil the barbarians again. Macartney was to be taken care of and supplied with necessities, but no more. "If they [foreigners] are reverent, obedient, humble and respectful, then we increase our grace," the directive continued. "If they do not understand aspects of the rite, then We guide them by means of ritual practices."[32]

The Qing willingness to compromise only went so far. Macartney kept attempting to discuss matters of trade and other business with Qing officials, but they consistently dodged the conversations. The British envoy did not know that tribute missions were for paying homage, not negotiating policy. Macartney received the Qing's response to the British requests in two letters from Qianlong addressed to King George. Obviously irritated, he rejected all of them. The reason was simple: the demands strayed from usual Chinese diplomatic practice. The British proposal to post a permanent ambassador at the Qing court "is contrary to all usage of my dynasty and cannot possibly be entertained," the emperor wrote. "How can our dynasty alter its whole procedure and system of etiquette, established for more than a century, in order to meet your individual views?" The Qing court apparently had no idea that exchanging ambassadors was common in European statecraft. "Supposing I sent an Ambassador to reside in your country, how could you possibly make for him the requisite arrangements?" the emperor asked rhetorically.

The letters went on to make clear that the British traded with China only at the emperor's pleasure. From the standpoint of the empire, this commerce was of little consequence. "We possess all things. I set no value on objects strange or ingenious, and have no use for your country's manufactures," the emperor bluntly told the British king. Even so, the Son of Heaven was generous and realized that not all states were as fortunate as his own, so, out of the kindness of his magnanimous heart, he had graciously shared his empire's bounty with the barbarian peoples of the world. "As the tea, silk and porcelain which the Celestial Empire produces, are absolute necessities to European nations and to yourselves, we have permitted, as a signal mark of favor, that foreign *hongs* should be established at Canton, so that your wants might be supplied and your country thus participate in our beneficence," the emperor continued. "Your England is not the only nation trading at Canton. If other nations, following your bad example, wrongfully importune my ear with further impossible requests, how will it be possible for me to treat them with easy indulgence?" Yet the emperor understood that such civilized ways were perhaps unfamiliar to those so far away. "Nevertheless, I do not forget the lonely remoteness of your island, cut off from the world by intervening wastes of sea, nor do I overlook your excusable ignorance of the usages of our Celestial Empire."[33]

The message was as it had been since time immemorial: two thousand years since the Han Dynasty, the Chinese emperor was still at the apex of the world, smiling down upon his barbarian vassals. The Qing tried to forget the whole, unpleasant affair. In the dynasty's official records, no mention was made of anything unusual happening during the Macartney mission. The Chinese history of the world continued, unfazed, undaunted—and unaware.

Nine

SUPERPOWER, INTERRUPTED

Among all the conservative nations on the globe there is probably not a single one which has been kept intact.... It will not be long until we become Turks and Negroes.

–Kang Youwei, Confucian scholar

Lin Zexu was a man on a mission. He arrived in Guangzhou in 1839 as a special commissioner appointed by the emperor, tasked with confronting a crisis unleashed by those irksome Western Ocean barbarians. In a passionate letter to Great Britain's Queen Victoria, the scholar-official pled with her to aid his fight with all the moral compunction and rational argument of the Confucian gentleman. "In coveting profit to an extreme, they [the English traders] have no regard for injuring others," he wrote. "Let us ask, where is your conscience?"[1]

It was a good question. The crisis Lin was determined to quell was an opium epidemic, brought on by the barbarian traders—most of all, the British. Opium was the solution the English East India Company found to balance its trade with China. The drug was already known throughout Asia for centuries as a tonic for stomach pain. It becomes addictive when smoked—back then, usually mixed with tobacco, another import from the West. Lots of it grew in British-controlled Bengal (in today's India), and in 1773, the East India Company granted itself a monopoly over the industry and began promoting its export. At that time, about sixty tons of opium was being shipped to China each year; by the mid-1830s, the amount had surged twenty-five times. More importantly, from the British point of view, it became the one commodity that they could rely on to find a market in China. By the late 1820s, the opium exported into China exceeded the value of the tea the British brought back to England. Opium had solved Great Britain's China trade problem.

But at tremendous cost to Chinese society. This trade was illegal—the Qing had long before banned dealing in opium—and then, as the epidemic spread, the court specifically barred its import, too. But as had often been the case with Chinese maritime trade, what was illegal in imperial edicts flourished on the remote coast anyway. Smugglers met ships coming from India offshore to surreptitiously slip the drug into the country. Opium seeped deeper and deeper into China's cities and villages.

Calamity ensued. By the mid-nineteenth century, a staggering 10 percent of the empire's population may have been addicted. The increasing imports of the drug were also devastating for the Qing economy. For centuries, China had been the world's major recipient of silver; now, due to the scale of opium imports, the precious metal began flowing out. That constrained the supply of currency in an economy dependent on the precious metal, contributing to a severe and punishing economic downturn in the first half of the nineteenth century.

Something had to be done, and Lin Zexu intended to do it. The incorruptible Lin had already proved his mettle by curtailing the opium trade as a provincial governor-general in central China, and he became one of the leading voices in the Qing administration urging action on the wider crisis. His formula was a mixture of harshness and benevolence. Those caught selling opium were jailed or executed; addicts were first nursed in special hospitals to wean them off the drug. Opium and the pipes to smoke it were rounded up and publicly burned, the ashes dumped in a river. The opium scourge, he came to believe, was a mortal threat to the empire. "If left in a lax state, then after a few decades, there will be no soldier in this Central Empire to fight against invaders, nor money to bear the military expenses," he told the emperor in late 1838. "If the evil be suffered to grow at this critical moment, there may be no more chance for remedy."[2]

It was this strategy he brought with him to Guangzhou, the entry point for most opium streaming into the country. After lengthy consultations with the emperor in Beijing, Lin made his way south to take up his new assignment. During the journey, he passed near the home of the greatly respected scholar and reformer Bao Shichen, whom Lin invited onto his boat. Could the statesman share any wisdom to aid Lin in his important task? "To clear a muddy stream you must purify the source," the elderly man advised. Lin knew what it meant: to succeed, he must cut off the opium at its very source.[3]

That meant going after the foreign traders. On March 18, a mere eight days after reaching Guangzhou, Lin sent off a strongly worded letter to the barbarian merchants. Reiterating what the emperor had told Macartney, he reminded them that the great Qing allowed foreigners to trade only out of sensitivity to their needs; the Chinese themselves were in want of nothing. Yet despite this generosity, the Western Ocean traders amassed immense profits from a product that so damaged the lives of others. Lin told them flatly that the days of opium were over. In the future, anyone caught dealing in opium—even foreigners—would face the death penalty. "I now call upon you to hand over for destruction all the opium you have on your ships and sign an undertaking that you will never bring opium here again," he commanded.[4] He gave them three days to accept his ultimatum. To pound home that he meant business, the next day he confined the foreigners to their waterfront factories until they turned over their opium.

For Lin, the new get-tough approach just made sense. The barbarians were breaking the law and he was simply enforcing it. Even more, he failed to see how his moral arguments could not sway even the most uncivilized of barbarians. The "poison," as he called opium, was undermining the fundamental Confucian values of Chinese society by dissolving the bonds of those sacred relationships— father to son, husband to wife, and ruler to subject.

Lin Zexu was appointed by the Qing emperor to end the foreign trade in opium, but his actions instead led to the disastrous First Opium War between China and England in the mid-nineteenth century. He is pictured here in an 1843 Chinese drawing.

Pictures from History / Bridgeman Images

But the barbarians were unmoved, even indignant. To the British the dispute over opium added to those long-standing grievances about restricted trade that had annoyed the Europeans for decades. The pressure to pry open the China market had built further as the economy of Great Britain roared. With ever more efficient methods of industrialized, mass production, British factories churned out more and more manufactured goods, which required new markets and customers. An ideology of economic liberalism captured the minds of Europe's elite: free trade was good for everyone, including those Chinese; they were just too backward to realize it. Lin's threats to execute foreign nationals convinced the Western Ocean men that Qing law was barbaric and they had to be protected from it. Frustration with China's bureaucratic hassles, overbearing restrictions, and meddlesome officials was simmering even before Lin arrived in Guangzhou. Lin was causing it to boil over. What Lin didn't appreciate was that he was not just taking on a bunch of unscrupulous barbarian merchants and drug smugglers. He was running headfirst into Europe's new confidence in its power, culture, and national spirit.

So the British did not comply with Lin's demand. Nearly a week passed and the commissioner had received no firm response. So Lin decided further inducement was necessary. In the past, Chinese authorities had been able to bring the foreigners to heel by halting their trade. Lin tried again. On March 24, he ordered all loading and unloading of ships to cease. Artisans working for foreign merchants were to end their service. If the merchants tried to evade these new regulations, Lin would get permission from Beijing "to put a stop to their trade for ever," he told them.[5] He also cut off the factory compound by stationing armed guards around it and bricking up some of the entranceways. Lin didn't even allow fresh food into the factories. If they did not obey, Lin intended to starve the barbarians into submission.

Two days later, the British superintendent, Charles Elliot, panicked. He had sailed to Guangzhou from Macau intending to bring Lin to his senses; instead, he got bottled up with the rest of the foreigners inside the factories. With terrifying visions that Lin would slaughter the traders en masse—to the British, it was the Chinese who were barbarians—Elliot capitulated. He ordered the traders to hand their opium over to Lin in the name of the Crown, and promised them the British government would compensate them. Lin's haul was staggering: nearly one thousand tons of opium, so massive that it took weeks for all of it to arrive. Lin prepared a site near the mouth of the Pearl River where he planned to destroy the "poison" in pits of lime and water before draining it off into the waterway. On June 1, Lin performed a sacrifice, "advising the [Sea] Spirit to tell the creatures of the water to move away for a time, to avoid being contaminated," he recorded.[6] Then the dirty work began, under close guard so no one could pilfer the opium. "The foreigners passing by in boats on their way up to Guangzhou and down to Macau all get a distant view of the proceedings, but do not dare show any disrespect," Lin informed the emperor in mid-June as the process was underway, "and indeed I should judge from their attitudes that they have the decency to feel heartily ashamed."[7] Clearly, these barbarians had learned their lesson. In another message to the emperor three weeks later, Lin recounted a lecture he gave to a delegation of American merchants. Though they had never dealt in opium, merely abstaining from the illegal trade, Lin told them, was insufficient; they had a responsibility to convince the others not to break Chinese law. "The foreigners listened attentively and respectfully, with heads bowed in sincere obedience. Their attitude certainly suggested whole-hearted acceptance of your Rule."[8] For Lin, this whole opium business was finished.

Lin, however, did not have a clear idea who he was dealing with. Though he had been in Guangzhou for months, handling the Europeans at close range, he learned little about them. Lin is often portrayed as highly inquisitive about the Western Ocean barbarians, questioning foreign visitors and having their books translated into Chinese. But in the end, he digested little of what he supposedly heard and read. Just as the writers of the Zhou Dynasty period, more than two thousand years earlier, took scant notice of the cultures of the Rong, Di, and Man—beyond their strange, uncouth customs—Lin considered the Western Ocean men curiosities. The Qing court took even less interest. Three hundred years had passed since the Europeans first appeared off the coast, and the Chinese had never bothered to learn much about them.

Their ignorance was all too obvious in a letter Lin wrote to the emperor in early September 1839. Did these Western barbarians, the Son of Heaven had asked Lin, buy young girls by the thousands, as he had heard? Maybe to be sacrificed in some dark sorcery? Lin had his doubts. The barbarians' home countries didn't have many people, so they valued every life they could get and, believe it or not, preferred girls over boys! Insane, yes, but it meant they probably wouldn't just massacre a bunch of youngsters, Lin told the emperor. But Lin still had his suspicions. He had seen a couple of young boys on a foreign vessel, who had tattoos on their bodies and didn't at all look like the Europeans. One of them told an aide of Lin's that they were the sons of sailors. But Lin suspected they had been kidnapped and carried off to sea.[9]

Two days after responding to the emperor, Lin toured Macau, where he marveled at the residents' odd, three-storied homes and peculiar fashion—the men in floppy hats and jackets, the women in low-cut dresses baring their chests. "They do really look like devils," he wrote in his diary of the Portuguese men, with their short, curly hair and small tufts of beard. "They also have devil-slaves, called black devils, who come from the country of the Moors. . . . They are blacker than lacquer, and were this color from the time of their birth."[10] Amazing indeed.

Lin had no idea what these barbarians were up to on the other side of the Pearl River delta. The same day he began his return journey from Macau to Guangzhou, Elliot had fired upon some Chinese war junks near the island of Hong Kong. Amid another dispute, Lin had barred the British from receiving supplies until they handed over the suspected murderer of a Chinese man, and after frustrated attempts to access food, Elliot got into the scuffle with the junks.

When Lin eventually found out, he was not too perturbed. It took him two weeks to bother the emperor with this bit of news, and his report painted the minor naval skirmish as a grand Qing triumph, with numerous casualties inflicted on the British. (The claims were false.) Lin was as confident as ever that he had these barbarians well in hand. "A vast display of imperial might has shaken all the foreign tribes," Lin wrote in a poem, "and if they now confess their guilt we shall not be too hard upon them."[11]

=

Even the arrival of a large fleet of British warships laden with cannon off the coast near Macau in June 1840 didn't shake Lin's usual cockiness. He had been hearing rumors of such a force heading his way, but dismissed them, and he was not much more bothered once the gossip proved all too true. It took Lin several days to dispatch a memo to the emperor about the squadron's appearance. Not to worry, he assured the Qing court: this was just a big opium smuggling operation, albeit one more heavily armed than the norm. "This is all they are doing, and as Your Majesty rightly observed, there is really nothing they can do," he wrote.[12] The warships then departed as suddenly as they had appeared, off into the open sea.

Lin failed to recognize the threat. What he did not know is that Elliot, at the height of the opium confrontation the previous year, had dashed off a scathing report to London, arguing that China needed to be taught a lesson. The Qing "must be made to understand its obligations to the rest of the world," he chided.[13] The British government agreed, and the fleet off Macau had been ordered to do just that. After leaving Macau, it sailed north to the area around Hangzhou and, in early July 1840, bombarded the town on the island of Zhoushan. The whole "battle" lasted less than ten minutes. And no wonder. Upon occupying the island, the British discovered one of the cannons defending the place was cast in 1601. Then they continued north, leaving ships here and there to blockade the Yangzi River and other ports, with the main body settling off the coast near Tianjin, where Macartney had made his way to the capital, to deliver a letter to the Qing emperor from Lord Palmerston, the British foreign secretary. It explained that the British force was sent to China "to demand from The Emperor satisfaction and redress for injuries inflicted by Chinese Authorities upon British subjects resident in China, and for insults offered by the same Authorities to the British Crown." The appropriate "redress" included compensation for the destroyed opium and "one or more sufficiently large and properly situated Islands on the Coast of China" to be ceded to Great Britain as a safe base for its citizens and commerce.[14] Elliot was instructed by Palmerston to, in effect, dismantle the entire Canton system of trade with China by opening new ports to British merchants, ending the monopoly of the *hong* business houses and ensuring the right to try British citizens in China under British, not Qing, law—something known as "extraterritoriality."

The confrontation spelled the end of Lin Zexu. Shortly after receiving Palmerston's letter, the Daoguang emperor shot off one of his own to Lin, accusing the formerly beloved official of sending the throne misleading reports and failing in his main task of quelling the opium trade. "So far from doing any good, you have merely produced a number of fresh complications," the emperor scolded.[15] In an attempted defense, Lin only dug himself a deeper hole. He informed the emperor that the British were at the end of their resources, that since they wrap themselves in rugs in the cold, they couldn't tolerate the coming winter. And it wasn't his confiscation of opium that provoked the English. They had been displeased with their trade in China long before. But now, he advised, "if we do not overcome them by force of arms there will be no end to our troubles. Moreover there is every probability that if the English are not dealt with, other foreigners will soon begin to copy and even outdo them."[16] In that, the intelligent but obstinate Lin was finally prescient.

==

Lin, at least, was spared the unenviable task of contending with the rebellious Western Ocean barbarians. The emperor sacked him and passed his responsibilities to another official, Qishan. He didn't fare any better. Negotiations between Qishan and Elliot began in Guangzhou in December, but the Qing haughtily rejected most of Palmerston's demands. That got the cannon roaring again. In early January 1841, Elliot attacked and took the two key forts on each shore at the mouth of the Pearl River—one of them in a mere twenty-five minutes. For good measure, he also annihilated almost the entire Chinese fleet defending the waterway. Everywhere the story was the same—ill-trained troops fled in panic before the British guns, or were slaughtered in packs, their outdated armaments no match for the advanced English cannon. British losses, meanwhile, were minimal. That should have woken the Qing to how dangerously unprepared they were to combat the British and their superior technology and tactics. Qishan was wide awake. The cannon at the Guangzhou defenses were "quite inadequate in number," he wrote in a report. "Many of the guns are obsolete in type and are not in working order." The Qing troops, meanwhile, were "in some cases of very poor quality." When soldiers threatened to disband unless they received extra pay, the commanding admiral pawned his clothes to raise the money.[17]

The Chinese had been aware of the excellence of European weaponry since the first arrival of the Portuguese, more than three centuries earlier, but, their self-confidence as high as ever, they had done little to update their arsenal or upgrade their defenses. That stark reality was still lost on the court in Beijing. Even the handful of concessions Qishan had made to Elliot—including some financial compensation and permission for a Macau-like settlement on Hong

Kong Island—were unacceptable to the belligerent Daoguang. In obvious ill temper, the emperor wrote Qishan that he considered "the demands of the rebellious foreigners totally excessive. . . . It's time to dispatch a punitive mission to suppress them. . . . There will be no wavering at all."[18] But what Daoguang did not understand is that the British were not supplicants seeking the favor of the Son of Heaven. Their ships did not arrive packed with tribute, but gunpowder (ironically, a product of Chinese inventive genius).

With negotiation at an end, the British assault turned relentless. In March 1841, they finished off the defenses along the river to Guangzhou and bombarded the city. All the while, the emperor kept up his barrage of irate directives. "Hurry to find a way to cut off the foreigners' retreat and ruthlessly exterminate them, to impress upon them how mighty we are," he ordered one general.[19] "We only know one word: 'Attack!'" read another missive.[20] Daoguang was unable to even imagine that these seaborne barbarians on a few boats could possibly pose a threat to the great Qing. To be fair, the court was often kept in the dark by its officials in the field, who, fearing for their jobs or even their heads, repeatedly hid the truth of Chinese military weakness and the extent of the army's desperation. The barbarians "fled in terror, no longer daring to advance," Daoguang was told in mid-March as the English surrounded Guangzhou.[21] Throughout the conflict, devastating defeats were miraculously transformed into crushing Qing victories in dispatches from commanding generals to the throne; setbacks, when courageously reported, were blamed on mysterious traitors and collaborators. The generals conjured up fifth columns everywhere; villagers, they imagined, were greedy turncoats, lured by barbarian cash to subvert the Manchus as they risked life and limb to defend the nation.

There were occasional moments of heroism. In May 1841, thousands of hardy peasants, angered by British looting and desecration of tombs and armed with no more than spears, swords, and shields, ganged up on foreign soldiers in the rice paddies outside of Guangzhou, killing five. This minor skirmish was subsequently enlarged into the epic "Sanyuanli People's Anti-British Struggle." Named after a nearby village, the scuffle was mythologized into a popular uprising by patriotic peasants against the foreign aggressor. In the Chinese retelling hundreds of British soldiers were slaughtered; others begged for mercy. As one poem describes the contest,

Wielding hoes and rakes as weapons,
Teams of multi-colored banners
Line the mountains and valleys all around.
The foreigners blanch as soon as they see us. . . .
They want to flee, but have no wings,
How easy it is to destroy these villains.[22]

The British were not nearly as frightened as the poets dreamed. Realizing Guangzhou was in the eyes of the Qing court still a peripheral outpost, British commanders sailed north, intending to make their point closer to the heartland. In late 1841 and 1842, the British snatched a series of port cities up the coast one after another, then cruised up the Yangzi and severed the Grand Canal. Occasionally the Qing forces put up a valiant resistance, but the outcome was the same nonetheless: the Qing could not contend with British military superiority. An attempt to reclaim the town of Ningbo in early 1842 failed in a tangle of inept planning, meager provisions, and undisciplined troops. "Our soldiers fled precipitously," one Chinese staff officer recorded. "But the streets and lanes were so narrow and soggy that they could not get away, and our losses were very heavy."[23] Shanghai fell in June 1842 almost without a fight. "The guns that were being fired were those of the foreigners!" one district warden scribbled in his diary. "I knew now that the worst was at hand. I hid my wife, and blocked up the gate and doors. . . . Suddenly, fire rose from the Prefecture, and at the same time the foreign soldiers arrived in force, both by land and from their ships." He reproached himself for not performing his patriotic duty and fighting the English, but, he rationalized, why sacrifice his life in a lost cause? "As all the officials fled long ago, even if I were to seek death at the hands of the enemy, there would be no one to report upon it," he wrote.[24] At Zhenjiang, on the Yangzi, the battle that raged for the walled city "was watched by thousands of spectators who had crowded on to the hill" above the town, recorded a local poet escaping the carnage. "'The people in the city must be wondering why no help comes to them from outside,' they murmured to each other with a sigh."[25] Late the next month, he noted rumors swirling that tens of thousands of Chinese troops were on their way to completely destroy their fleet, "so not a fragment of sail or oar remains. In that way our disgrace will be wiped out and the Middle Kingdom will breathe again." The diarist had his doubts, saying that it was "the kind of story that was bound to get about."[26]

His skepticism proved warranted. Within days, the Opium War, as it is ignominiously known, was over. The hard-line Daoguang was still demanding his generals annihilate the barbarians even as the English cannonaded their way up the Yangzi. In fact, two years into the war, the emperor had little notion of who, exactly, he was fighting or what they wanted. Where, he asked his courtiers in May 1842, was England located anyway, and why were Indian troops fighting with them?[27] But in late July, with the fall of Zhenjiang and the English fleet closing on Nanjing, the former Ming capital, even Daoguang began to see reality and allowed his commanders to negotiate. Talks got off to an inauspicious start. When Zhang Xi, the envoy sent to parlay with the English, unaware of the contents of Palmerston's letter, heard their demands, he spit on the desk in front of him. If he had the authority, he told them, "I should, first of all, arrest you, cut your bodies into ten thousand pieces, grind your bones, and spread your ashes as revenge for the victims—the soldiers and the people—in order to quench the anger of the whole empire," he told the (probably astonished) British.[28] The commanding generals at Nanjing did not take the British requests seriously, either; the original list got filed away by an officious secretary who deemed them "very problematic."[29] They sent off the envoy Zhang Xi with the authority to offer mere token concessions on trade regulation, and only when the British promised to shell Nanjing the next morning did the dumbfounded Qing generals finally take a close look at the British demands. After that, at the point of a cannon, they quickly agreed to terms. On August 29, the two sides signed the Treaty of Nanjing that ended the war.

The British generally got whatever they wanted. The Qing ceded the island of Hong Kong (which became a British colony for the next 150 years), opened five ports to British trade and residence (including Shanghai), ended the *hong* merchant monopoly, and agreed to pay $21 million in reparations over four years, a sum that greatly taxed the dynasty's finances. Perhaps most importantly, the English imposed the European style of government relations on the Qing, something Macartney had tried a half century earlier. No longer would the British Empire be treated as a tributary state. Not only did the treaty award Queen Victoria the same status as the Qing emperor—whom the document called "Our Good Brother"—a clause also placed "the Subordinates of both Countries on a footing of perfect equality."[30] China was being dragged, with a gun pointed at the imperial head, into a new world of foreign affairs, in which the Son of Heaven was not above all, and China was treated as a nation-state, no different than any other. The Western Ocean men were never part of the traditional Chinese diplomatic order; now they were dismantling it.

=====

Today, Lin Zexu is a national hero, the fearless patriot who stood up to the Western Ocean barbarians to protect the homeland and the Han people. A statue of him stands in the town of Dongguan near the pits where he destroyed the British opium in 1839, now preserved on the grounds of a museum dedicated to honoring the struggle against the English. But much like other nationalist champions, such as the fiery Song Dynasty general Yue Fei, he wasn't appreciated at the time. Blamed by the emperor for starting the Opium War, he was eventually banished to the barrens of Xinjiang. There, Lin was able to reflect on the conflict from a safe distance. The conflict had finally woken him to a terrifying conclusion: maybe the great Qing was not so great after all, and maybe, just maybe, the Chinese had something to learn from these new barbarians. "The rebels' ships on the open sea came and went as they pleased," he wrote in a letter to a friend in 1842. "If we tried to put up a defense everywhere, not only would we toil and expend ourselves without limit, but also how could we recruit and transport so many troops, militia, artillery, and ammunition, and come to their support quickly?" Lin realized the need for more advanced gunships and cannon if the Qing was to defend the empire. Yet he also knew the Qing court was not ready to hear the truth. "But at this time I must strictly observe the advice to seal my lips as one corks the mouth of a bottle."[31]

In the aftermath of the disastrous Opium War, the Qing court remained somewhat oblivious to what exactly had happened, and its consequences. The empire's devastating loss to a mere handful of foreigners did not shake China's usual confidence in the superiority of its own institutions. The immediate reaction of senior Qing officials was to think of the Western Ocean barbarians as just another version of the barbarians China had been managing for two thousand years, since the days of the Xiongnu. As history taught, from time to time foreigners just had to be placated. But they were still inferior. In a memorial in 1844, one of the negotiators of the Treaty of Nanjing told the emperor that "there are times when it is possible to have them follow our directions but not let them understand the reasons." This envoy recognized that the Europeans were not like previous foreigners; their form of government was different, and so were their expectations about relations with the Qing. Nevertheless, "with this type of people outside the bounds of civilization, who are blind and unawakened in styles of address and forms of ceremony, if we adhered to the proper forms . . . and let them be weighed according to the status of superior and inferior, even though our tongues were dry and our throats parched (from urging them to follow our way), still they could not avoid closing their ears and acting as if deaf. . . . Truly it would be of no advantage in the essential business of subduing and conciliating them."[32] Chinese writers held almost identical views about the Xiongnu: here, again, China was confronted by a bunch of barbarians so utterly hopeless that they could never see the civilizing beauty of Chinese culture, so they would just have to be tamed.

There were other voices aside from Lin's warning of danger ahead, however. Historian Wei Yuan scolded his own government for its ignorance of these foreigners. How could they fight the enemy if they didn't know the enemy? "Regarding these countries, with which we have had trade relations for two hundred years, we indeed know neither their locations nor their interrelations of friendship or enmity. Can it even yet be said that we are paying attention to frontier affairs?" he wrote. Wei tried to fill the void by conducting extensive research on the Western countries, as well as

Qing military and maritime history, in an attempt to form a method of confronting the new threat. But he was a prisoner of his Confucian training, which trapped him in standard thinking on foreign affairs. Though like Lin, he advocated that "it is proper for us to learn their superior techniques in order to control them," he also trotted out the old adage "to use barbarians against barbarians."[33] The Qing, he thought, could do what Chinese dynasties always had with barbarians: divide and rule.

That wasn't going to work. The European barbarians may have had their differences, but when it came to prying open the Chinese economy, they were of one mind. Banding together, they wrung more concessions from the Qing. In a supplemental agreement with the British in 1843 and new treaties signed with the United States and France in 1844, the Qing coughed up extraterritoriality rights to the Westerners—which allowed their citizens to be governed by their own, rather than Qing, law while in China—and "most favored nation" status, in which the court promised to grant them any further concessions made to other European countries. Together with the Treaty of Nanjing, these agreements were the first of what the Chinese call "unequal treaties," as embarrassing to their prestige as the pay-for-peace settlements inked by the old Han Dynasty with the Xiongnu (see chapter 3).

The Qing, eager for peace, gave away these rights without realizing the long-term consequences. These treaties ate away at Qing sovereignty, by stripping it of the power to enforce its own laws and control its relations with other countries. And even that wasn't enough to satiate the Europeans. By the mid-1850s, the British had again become frustrated with their trade with China. Business was not expanding as quickly as they had hoped after the Treaty of Nanjing. Their balance of trade also tilted against them once again, and industrialists in England clamored for better access to the Chinese market. They grumbled that the Qing weren't living up to their side of the bargain.

A warmongering British consul found a pretext to start shooting in late 1856, when Qing police boarded a ship called the *Arrow*, suspected of hauling opium. The consul claimed they also took down the Union Jack and insulted the British sovereign; that proved not to be true. But no matter. The British navy began shelling Guangzhou, and the Second Opium War began.

This time, the French also joined in the fray. In 1858, a joint European squadron sailed up the coast and occupied Tianjin, about one hundred miles from the capital. That quickly resulted in a treaty that opened new ports to foreign commerce along the coast and the Yangzi, thus unlocking the Chinese interior to international business, and also forced the Qing to accept European-style permanent diplomatic missions in Beijing. The Qing court, however, still denying military reality, refused to implement the terms and restarted hostilities. The English stormed into Beijing, the emperor fled north of the Great Wall, and the invaders took their revenge on the Summer Palace, which they looted and burned. The emperor's younger brother, Prince Gong, was left behind to clean up the mess, and he signed a convention committing the court to abide by the original treaty, and tossed in British control of Kowloon, across the harbor from Hong Kong, for good measure. It was yet another addition to the growing list of humiliations the Chinese suffered at the hands of the Western Ocean barbarians.

====

The occupation of Beijing, however, finally stirred the Qing elite from their dangerous delusions. In 1861, after the death of the emperor, the able Prince Gong and other reform-minded officials outmuscled rival factions and claimed the regency that ruled in the name of the new child sovereign. They began to reshape Qing policy in a concerted effort to match the power of the Europeans. More than that, the Qing finally began to realize that they weren't dealing with their ancestors' barbarians, but a group of foreigners with very different goals, intentions, and methods. "The present case is somewhat different from the (barbarian invasions) of former dynasties," the prince wrote in an 1861 edict. "If we overlook the way they have harmed us and do not make any preparations against them, then we shall be bequeathing a source of grief to our sons and grandsons."[34]

What began is known as the "self-strengthening" movement—a process of reform aimed at making Qing China more like the West. Prince Gong formed the Zongli Yamen, akin to a Chinese Department of State, to deal with foreign affairs in a more European form, and Beijing began assigning ambassadors to European capitals for the first time. A bureau to import and translate tracts on

Western science and politics was introduced. Students were sent to the United States and Europe to learn more about their advanced technical skills and social and cultural life.

Change, too, came to the economy. China had not merely fallen behind in certain technologies, but in industry more generally. Back in the days of the Song Dynasty, Chinese manufacturing in steel, porcelain, and other goods was far more advanced than anything in Europe. But since then, Europe had undergone the great Industrial Revolution, with the emergence of modern factories. China had not developed this type of industry, and so had to play catch-up. Textile mills, steel works, and arms factories based on European technologies popped up around the country. A shipyard to build vessels to compete with those of the British and French was opened in Fujian. Though Chinese-owned, these factories often operated with imported machinery and were run with the help of foreign engineers and managers. China was in a mad rush to join the European world.

At no point in the two-thousand-year history of imperial China had the Chinese felt the need to borrow so actively, rapidly, and consciously from barbarians. And inevitably, the reforms met stiff resistance. Confucian education taught that the foundation of good government is virtue; fixing the problems of the empire, therefore, required moral cultivation, not foreign ideas and machines. How could those barbarians, devoid of civilization, have anything to offer the Chinese anyway? Woren, a court secretary and leader of the opposition to reform, argued that the Qing should not "seek trifling arts and respect barbarians." Borrowing foreign ways and doctrines, he warned in 1867, would weaken, not strengthen, the empire by whittling away at superior Chinese traditions. "Your slave has learned that the way to establish a nation is to lay emphasis on propriety and righteousness," he contended. "The fundamental effort lies in the minds of people, not in techniques. . . . From ancient down to modern times, your slave has never heard of anyone who could use mathematics to raise the nation from a state of decline or to strengthen it in time of weakness."[35]

The reform movement, however, was, at its core, quite conservative already. The advocates of change did not question the ultimate superiority of Chinese civilization or the imperial system it created.

The idea was to cherry-pick a few technologies and update scientific knowledge to strengthen the empire's military and economic capabilities so it could defend itself against the Western powers. Perhaps a tweak here and there to government institutions was necessary, too. But there was no serious thought about an overhaul of the Qing government or Chinese society, nor the core ideology that underpinned them. "It is my opinion that today we should . . . take the foreign nations as our examples," explained Feng Guifen, a respected scholar-official and reform champion, in 1861. "They live at the same time and in the same world with us; they have attained prosperity and power by their own efforts. . . . If we let Chinese ethics and Confucian teachings serve as the foundation, and let them be supplemented by the methods used by the various nations for the attainment of prosperity and power, would it not be the best of all solutions?"[36]

What flummoxed the Chinese in the second half of the nineteenth century was the dawning reality that men of the West were not at all like the other foreigners who had flocked to China over the previous millennia, whether Xiongnu or Mongol, Persian or Sogdian or Indian. It was nothing new in the Chinese historical experience to lose to outsiders on the battlefield. As we've seen, the Chinese dynasties had been defeated by many invaders and predators over the centuries. Other foreigners, especially traders, came to exchange goods and didn't bother much with anything else. They were happy to play by Chinese rules of trade and diplomacy, to buy silk and porcelain, and make money. But the Westerners were different. Sure, they possessed an edge in military technology and tactics, like the Mongols, Jurchens, and so many others had in the past. Their cannon and warships were not the main challenge the West presented to China. The threat was an entirely new one, something the Chinese had never faced before.

It was civilizational. In the eyes of the Chinese, the Mongols, Xiongnu, Khitan, Jurchens, and other tribesmen might have been able to trample Chinese defenses, but not Chinese culture. Chinese civilization still reigned supreme. In fact, rather than imposing their own culture onto China—which they could have done by force of arms—these barbarians chose to adopt aspects of Chinese civilization, a mark of its true virtue. But these Western barbarians seemed disinterested in the ways of China. Worse, they derided China as backward; its society archaic; its social norms barbaric! Sure, there was the occasional Matteo Ricci, who tried to ingratiate themselves by learning Chinese language, literature, and philosophy. But generally, the Westerners perceived their own civilization as superior. They expected China to adopt Western religion, philosophical ideals, methods of government, diplomacy, and economic organization. Even the great Ricci, after all, adorned himself in the trappings of Chinese life only to promote his own faith. Rather than becoming "more Chinese" like other barbarians, the men of the West wanted the Chinese to become "more Western." Oh, the arrogance! Everywhere these new barbarians settled in China, they didn't adopt the lifestyle of the Chinese; they altered their surroundings to make China more like Europe. In Hong Kong, Shanghai, and the other ports open to foreigners, they re-created home halfway around the globe. Up went their churches, their homes, their shops, their banks. The buildings erected along the waterfront in Shanghai—called the Bund—could easily have been airlifted from London; the concession area of the city handed to the French became a marvel of Paris townhouses. Just as the Qing had feared, Macaus were sprouting like weeds across the empire—bastions of un-Chineseness, with foreigners in their oddball outfits, ringing their church bells and speaking incomprehensible languages.

The Westerners expected China to change for them. They had no intention of changing for China. And with their military advantages, the people of the West didn't have to. Instead, they were imposing their own ideas onto China.

=====

The rising power of the West in East Asia did much more than influence the politics and economy of China. It remade the entire Chinese world as well. As we've seen, for the previous five hundred years, China's supremacy in the region was almost unchallenged, with Beijing's special form of diplomacy acting as the "rules of the game" of international relations. The West, though, had little respect for or understanding of this Chinese world order, and with their guns and goods, they also brought an entire new mode of international diplomatic relations and economic exchange, based on their experience both in Europe and, increasingly, around the world they were colonizing. Simply, the West rewrote the rules for East Asia and pried it away from Chinese influence.

Steadily, but surely, the Western Ocean men picked apart the Chinese world by absorbing its participants into their expanding colonial empires. In Vietnam, for instance, the highly Sinicized vassal state had come under the thumb of the French. First Vietnam's king was compelled to cede the country's south to the French; then they came marching north for what was left. As the Vietnamese dynasty became more desperate, it sent a mission to the Qing court, pleading for the protection it was owed as a tributary in good standing. In an attempt to uphold its responsibilities (and its entire diplomatic system), the Qing declared war on France in 1884. The outcome, however, was sadly predictable. Though Qing ground forces had some success against the undermanned French in northern Vietnam, the Chinese navy again got trounced at sea. The French fleet not only smashed eleven of China's newest warships in a single short engagement, it went on to flatten the Qing's main naval yard in Fujian as well. The inevitable treaty, signed in 1885, ceded to France suzerainty over Vietnam.

It soon dawned on the remaining nations of East Asia that China was no longer master of the region. The kingdom of Siam (now Thailand), a reliable tributary of the Chinese court, sent a mission to kowtow to the Qing in 1853. It ended up being their last. Each subsequent time the Thais were scheduled to send an embassy, some sort of chaos impeded it. One mission was attacked by bandits, the gifts it carried for the emperor pilfered. The following mission was canceled; chaos unleashed by rebels made safe passage impossible. The next time, in 1860, "it was learnt that the city of Guangzhou was at war with England, and that the Governor-General himself was not residing there," a Thai official wrote in a letter to a Chinese counterpart. "If Siam were to send envoys, no one would receive them. Then (in 1862) . . . it was learnt that England and France were penetrating as far as Beijing and that Beijing was in the midst of a great war."37 Eventually, the Thais gave up. Trade with China was redirected into the seaborne shipping controlled by the British and French. In 1882, the Thai kingdom declared it was no longer a vassal of China.

Nothing proved more destructive to the traditional Chinese world than the ascent of Japan. The Japanese had always had something of a love-hate relationship with China—on the one hand, admiring Chinese institutions and culture; on the other, chafing at the idea of being a second-class citizen in the East Asian hierarchy. The Tokugawa shogunate, founded in the early seventeenth century, had avoided sending tribute missions to Beijing. But in the 1800s, Japan found itself in a similar pickle to China: isolated and wary of Western influence, the shogunate had fallen frightfully behind the Europeans in technology and economic might. And, also like China, the Japanese had their own uncomfortable awakening to that stark reality. In the 1850s the Americans, frustrated, as in China, by Japan's heavy restrictions on international commerce, floated a naval squadron to Tokyo (then called Edo), which scared the Japanese into prying open the country wider to trade.

As in China, the experience was a shocking one. But in response, Japan committed itself much more wholeheartedly to change than the vacillating, tradition-bound Qing. In 1868, a group of reform-minded officials overthrew the Tokugawa shogun and (at least officially) returned authority to the emperor. This seminal event, known as the Meiji Restoration, was a "restoration" only in name. In reality, it was a bold break with the past to modernize Japan. Perhaps China would allow itself to become a pathetic plaything of Western imperialism; the Japanese intended to be the predator, not the prey. The entire governing system got a major shakedown. The feudal aristocracy that prevailed before the Meiji Restoration was renovated into a Western-style centralized state with a professional civil service. Adopting foreign technology like an eager convert, the new state rapidly developed a modern industrial sector and armed forces equipped with high-tech weaponry. Just as the Japanese had once studiously mimicked Chinese legal codes, now officials immersed themselves in Western international law. In less than two decades, Japan had transformed itself into a regional power capable of contending with the Western Ocean men—and victimizing their former Chinese overlords.

With its newfound swagger, Japan quickly joined the Europeans in feasting upon a weakened China. In 1870, shortly after Japan's reforms began, the new Meiji government requested a treaty of friendship with the Qing. The ensuing pact, signed the next year, was the first Western-style diplomatic treaty concluded by the Qing with a non-Western country. In it, the Qing recognized Japan as a sovereign state on the basis of equality with China, and the two courts exchanged permanent ambassadors—both firsts in the long history of relations between them. That, however, was not enough for the increasingly confident Japanese. In 1874, the Meiji sent troops to occupy the kingdom of the Ryukyus, an island chain south of Japan and a long-standing tributary of China. Five years later, Japan converted it into a regular prefecture. The helpless Qing sat by and did nothing. Li Hongzhang, one of the Qing's most senior reformists, had to concede that the historical order of tribute and trade had become an "empty name."[38]

Next Japan went after the most loyal of China's tributaries—Korea. As the Japanese tried to expand their influence in the ailing Chosun Dynasty, they tipped off a contest with the Qing, who were desperate to hold on to one of the empire's last reliable allies and relics of its former regional dominance. To that end, the Qing adopted tactics from Western diplomacy that it had never used before to promote its commercial and political interests in East Asia, such as placing an "advisor" at the Chosun court and implanting its own armed force on the peninsula. The Qing also arranged treaties between the Western powers and the Chosun, in an attempt to bolster international support for its position there. The inevitable war between China and Japan erupted in 1894.

It wasn't much of a contest. Japanese forces decimated a newly equipped Qing army near Pyongyang, while Japan's navy annihilated a newly built Qing fleet at the mouth of the Yalu River. The Japanese army then marched into Qing territory, where it claimed Port Arthur in the northeast, and then a significant port in Shandong further south.

The rapid defeats exposed the shallowness of Chinese "self-strengthening" reforms. So much silver had been expended on new factories, armaments, and ships, but it all seemed a waste. What went wrong? There was no shortage of targets for finger-pointing. The industrialization effort was half-hearted. Rather than a capitalist revolution, the state designed and managed most of the programs. Corruption siphoned off critical funds. Most famously, the powerful Empress Dowager snatched silver meant to requisition new warships to rebuild the burned-down imperial Summer Palace.

The renovations, ironically, included a marble boat that, of course, could never float. But overall, the reforms did not go far and deep enough. The advanced technology of the West could not be grafted onto the spiritless institutions of the Qing Dynasty. Not only had China fallen behind, it had fallen into decay.

The Treaty of Shimonoseki that ended the war between China and Japan, signed in 1895, was the most humiliating the Qing had yet to swallow. In it, Korea was declared no longer a tributary of the Qing, which, in essence, turned the kingdom into a Japanese protectorate. Then the Qing ceded the island of Taiwan to Japan. But the most damning provisions handed over core chunks of the Qing empire to Japanese control—most of all, the Liaodong peninsula, the southern part of the Manchu homeland in the empire's northeast.

Oh, how low China had fallen! Defeated not by some fierce barbaric northern tribesmen, as had happened before, or even the Western Ocean men, with their high-tech guns and ships, but by another East Asian nation, one that had been a vassal of the Son of Heaven and a member of the Sinicized world. In the millennia-long Chinese history of the world, nothing quite like it had happened before. China's humiliation was complete.

The defeat left China adrift. With the loss to Japan, the "unequal treaties," the sense of hopelessness, the great empire of China was brought to the brink of colonization. The universal Son of Heaven had become a pawn of foreign barbarians, barely able to control his own domain, let alone assert his divinely sanctioned authority on the rest of the world.

The elite of China were facing an unprecedented crisis. Yes, China had been subjugated by barbarians before. Yes, its dynasties had collapsed into civil strife. But never before had all the pillars of Chinese power crumbled as they did in the late nineteenth century. Industrialized Europe overtook China in wealth, innovation, and global clout; its own trade was controlled by the English and other barbarian seafarers. China's neighbors were looking to the West, not China, to learn how to govern, grow rich, and become modern. The Japanese and other Asians were learning Western languages, reading Western books, and absorbing Western ideals, about government, ethics, law, business, and diplomacy. The Chinese world order was evaporating. The Son of Heaven was unable to govern his own empire. How could he civilize the world?

The gravity of China's predicament was not lost on some Chinese scholars. They looked around the world—one increasingly dominated by the Western powers—and saw what was coming. The same foreigners plaguing the Chinese, grabbing its territory, invading its cities, infiltrating its economy, and corrupting its society were doing the same throughout the world. Everywhere, traditional empires and proud ancient civilizations were becoming slaves of the Westerners. India, that other grand Asian civilization, the birthplace of beloved Buddhism, had succumbed to the British. The Ottoman Empire based in Istanbul, once the terror of Europe and the Middle East, was on the verge of dismantlement, too. Africa was being chopped up into a kaleidoscope of European colonies. The Russians had consumed the once glittering states of Central Asia. The British, French, and Dutch had gobbled up the former vassal states in Southeast Asia. Why wouldn't China be next? "China is in imminent peril," wrote Confucian scholar Kang Youwei in 1895, in the wake of the catastrophic defeat to Japan. "How much more so will it be when there are ten nations who are sharpening their teeth and watering at the mouth, desiring to share the surplus?" The territories of the grand, old empires of the world "have been either reduced or annexed, and among all the conservative nations on the globe there is probably not a single one which has been kept intact. Our enfeebled China has been lying in the midst of a group of strong powers and soundly sleeping on the top of a pile of kindling. . . . It will not be long until we become Turks and Negroes."[39]

Oh, could China face a worse fate! The Son of Heaven a puppet of barbarians! The empire no better than a colonized Africa! The leaders of China began a painful search for answers. What had gone wrong, and how could it be fixed? In 1895, during the peace negotiations to end the war with Japan, Chinese statesman and modernizer Li Hongzhang was asked by his Japanese counterpart why Chinese reform had failed. "Affairs in my country have been so confined by tradition that I could not accomplish what I desired," Li responded despondently.[40]

That lament was about to tear China apart.

Ten

MAKING CHINA GREAT AGAIN

There is not a single one of the Chinese people's sentiments, customs, or political and legal institutions which can be favorably compared with those of the barbarians. . . . Even if we beg to be on an equal footing with the barbarians, we still cannot achieve it, so how can we convert them to be Chinese?

–reformer Tan Sitong

In June 1898, the young Qing emperor, Guangxu, held a long conference with a noted Confucian scholar. Usually, this wouldn't be worth mentioning. Emperors had been seeking the counsel of Confucians since the earliest days of the dynasties. But this particular scholar, Kang Youwei, was no standard-issue Confucian, and the discussion he had with the Son of Heaven was unlike any held in the previous two thousand years.

Kang had gotten the attention of the emperor by sending the court repeated memorials with his recommendations for a national renewal—mainly, a bolder program of government reform. Now Kang made his pitch in person. "Unless we change the old institutions entirely and make them new again, we cannot make ourselves strong," Kang said, according to a later account of the audience.

The emperor agreed, then Kang continued: "It is not because in recent years we have not talked about reform, but because it was only a slight reform, not a complete one; we change the first thing and do not change the second." Again, the emperor agreed, and Kang pressed his case. "The prerequisites of reform are that all the laws and the political and social systems be changed and decided anew, before it can be called a reform."

The two talked for five hours. They discussed the impediments to reform: the entrenched, ultraconservative ministers who blocked change. Kang blamed the outdated civil service examination system, which, he believed, swamped the best and brightest in useless, arcane trivia. Qing scholars "do not read the books written since the Qin and the Han [dynasties]," leaving them ignorant of current affairs. "None of them can adapt himself to circumstances," Kang said. The only way to rush reform was to avoid the Confucian-trained bureaucracy—the emperor, with unlimited authority, had to take charge of the reform effort personally.[1]

Guangxu was ready and able. Bubbling with youthful energy, and frustrated by resistance from within his own palace, the emperor was eager for an opportunity to resurrect the Qing's dissipating fortunes—and his own. After their talk, Guangxu named Kang secretary of the Zongli Yamen—the Qing version of a ministry of foreign affairs—and granted the scholar the power to initiate reforms.

The drastic decision was a sign of just how desperate the Qing had become. The treaty that ended the war with Japan three years earlier had tipped off a scramble among the foreign powers for new concessions. Though pressure from the Russians and others prodded Japan into withdrawing from the Liaodong peninsula, which had been ceded to it in the treaty's terms, St. Petersburg then demanded a lease on the ports there, Dalian and Port Arthur, for itself. Not to be outdone, the British extracted a port in Shandong, as well as the New Territories, a parcel of Qing territory that it added to its Hong Kong colony. The Germans in 1897 used the murder of two missionaries as a pretext to seize a long-coveted port in Shandong, too. The Qing leased the Kaiser's government control of the area, which the Germans turned into the city of Qingdao. From these chunks of coastline, the foreigners created "spheres of influence" deep into the interior, in which they expected preferential access to markets, mines, and other business opportunities. With the Westerners and Japan biting into the Qing—or as the Chinese colorfully described it, "carving the melon"—the empire's integrity, even the survival of China's independence, was threatened for the first time since the Mongol invasion six centuries earlier.

Kang's solution was far more radical than the Qing's previous reformers had ever imagined. The Qing plan had been to import Western guns and factories, but more or less leave the imperial system intact. Kang and his cohorts believed that was impossible. If China was to save itself, change had to reach into the heart of Chinese government and society. "Our present trouble lies in our clinging to old institutions," Kang wrote in early 1898. "Our present institutions are but unworthy vestiges of the Han, Tang, Yuan and Ming dynasties; . . . Under the present circumstances reforms are imperative and old institutions must be abolished."[2] Confucian education had indoctrinated the Chinese elite to seek answers to current problems in the country's traditions and distant history. But Kang and his disciples believed just the opposite—it was tradition that was holding China back and leaving it weak and vulnerable. "Those who insist that there is no need for reform still say, 'Let us follow the ancients, follow the ancients,'" Liang Qichao, Kang's most influential student, wrote in 1896. "They coldly sit and watch everything being laid waste by following tradition, and there is no concern in their hearts."[3]

In place of the old, Kang and his followers advocated a wide range of alternative—and sometimes bizarre—ideas. They were influenced by a rush of new philosophical discourse flooding in from the West—from Hobbes to Adam Smith, Darwin to Rousseau. The Westerners were not only forcing China open to foreign trade and diplomacy, but to modern ideas about politics, human rights, economics, race, and law. None of this was particularly popular among Qing conservatives, of which there were still many. Kang himself was widely derided as a heretic who was not a true Confucian. Within Kang's writings, Confucius was no longer an ultra-reactionary fuddy-duddy enraptured by an idealized antiquity, but a progressive prophet and proponent of many of the modern ideas about politics and society that were driving the advance of Europe and America. Tan Sitong, another Kang follower, believed that "when Confucius first set forth his teachings, he discarded the ancient learning, reformed existing institutions, rejected monarchism, advocated republicanism, and transformed inequality into equality." The perception that Confucius was anything else was a smokescreen, blown by subsequent scholars who distorted his message to deceive and control the Chinese people. Now those detrimental deformities had to be cleansed. Even the traditional Confucian relationships between husband and wife, father and son, and ruler and minister, which had long been the bedrock of Chinese civilization, had to go. Tan wrote that those bonds were "like hell."[4] Kang wished this refurbished Confucius to become the focus of a Christian-style religion, with state-sponsored churches where worshippers would recite the Confucian classics.

Endorsed, they believed, by this reformist Confucius, Kang and his team were no less radical in their politics. They latched on to democracy as the solution to China's woes. Kang at first favored a constitutional monarchy. Constraining the authority of the emperor by law (rather than Confucian moral exhortation) would, he argued, strengthen the Qing, because "the sovereign and the people are welded together into one body politic."[5]

Even before his conversation with the Guangxu emperor, Kang had shaken up the ceremony-bound Qing political scene. In 1895, Kang was in Beijing for the national civil service examinations when the news broke of the treaty to end the war with Japan. Its terms were so humiliating that Kang was compelled to act. He organized his fellow degree candidates into a protest movement, calling upon them to submit memorials demanding the court reject the treaty. More than 1,200 of them signed one petition alone. "The traffic was blocked in the streets as the scholars went back and forth in groups (to submit their petitions), and they surrounded the carriages of the high officials," Kang later recalled.[6] To follow it up, Kang started a "study society," which in effect became a pro-reform lobby outside of the mainstream of Qing government—another unusual form of civic action in China. Thus Kang is often credited with launching modern mass participation in politics in China.

So in 1898, when Kang had the emperor's attention, he tried to make the best of his opportunity. With the aid of Liang, Tan, and other reformers, who joined him in the capital, Kang unleashed a steady stream of reform proposals. The education system would be modernized, with schools at all levels teaching a Western curriculum. Civil service examinations would test knowledge of current affairs. The central government was to be reorganized along Western lines, with ministries, a cabinet, and an independent judiciary.

This was too much for the conservatives. In September 1898, the aged Empress Dowager Cixi reestablished her control of the court. Guangxu was banished to internal exile, on an island in an imperial park in Beijing. Kang escaped and fled to Hong Kong, and Liang made his way safely to Japan. Tan Sitong was not as fortunate. He was publicly executed.

The period known as the Hundred Days Reform was snuffed out. The Qing, once again, chose tradition over change. But Kang's ideas were not forgotten. Kang and his cadres were simply ahead of their time. Rather than an odd aberration to the Chinese history of the world, the episode was a harbinger of what was to come. At the heart of Kang's plans was a concept that was so extreme, so destabilizing, to the Chinese self-image that the country was not yet ready to accept it: Chinese civilization was, in fact, not superior. For thousands of years, confidence in their own culture had remained unshaken. The rise and fall of countless dynasties, the invasions of Turks, Jurchens, and Mongols, green-eyed beauties, Buddhist monks—nothing shook the conviction that Chinese civilization *was* civilization. That cardinal tenet had sustained the entire imperial system, the Chinese view of themselves and the world around them, their relations with other peoples—the Chinese history of the world itself. Now, however, the Chinese ran smack into an alternative civilization that owed nothing to China's own, believed itself to be superior, and had the guns, money, and power to back its claim. The experience rattled the Chinese elite to their very bones; for the first time, they began to harbor serious doubts about the value of their historic traditions and place in the world. "Your idea of despising our enemies arises because you think that they are still barbarians," Tan Sitong once wrote in a letter to a friend. "This is a common mistake of the scholars and officials of the whole empire and they must get rid of it. . . . Now there is not a single one of the Chinese people's sentiments, customs, or political and legal institutions which can be favorably compared with those of the barbarians. Is there any bit of Western culture which was influenced by China? Even if we beg to be on an equal footing with the barbarians, we still cannot achieve it, so how can we convert them to be Chinese?"[7]

=

Copying the West was not popular with everyone in China. The Chinese reaction to the political, social, and economic changes wrought by the Western intrusion took a variety of forms amid the uncertainty and disorder of the slow, agonizing decline of Qing authority. As should be predictable in a society with, at best, ambivalent attitudes toward outsiders, some Chinese simply wanted to kick the new barbarians out of the empire. Maybe that would get things back to normal.

The most dramatic outburst of this anti-foreign sentiment was a movement called the Righteous and Harmonious Fists, known to history as the Boxers. What began as a society of mystical martial artists in eastern China exploded in 1900 into a popular rebellion aimed at expelling the Western barbarians and rescuing the Qing. The Boxer Rebellion sparked a major international crisis, resolved by the creation of the world's first multilateral military expedition. When it was over, whatever bit of fight the Qing had left to resist European power was gone.

The whole notion that a Chinese nativist movement rose up in support of a foreign Manchu dynasty shows just how alarming and distressing the penetration of the West into China was for many ordinary Chinese. Even more, the fact that the Boxers first emerged in a section of the country—northern Shandong province—that was comparatively unscathed by foreign interference also tells us how widely the social and economic changes unleashed by the West were spreading in China—as was the discontent and anger they spawned. Known for cotton growing and weaving, the households of northern Shandong were hit hard by a burgeoning influx of imported cloth and yarn. For a community already suffering from flood, drought, and a decline of traffic on the nearby Grand Canal, the further erosion of economic fortune was too much to bear for many households, making the region ripe for revolt. Outrages by heavy-handed German authorities in Qingdao didn't help. In response to protests against railway construction projects, the Germans had shot villagers and burned a respected library. Justifiably, the local communities were riled up and eager for vengeance.

But the real source of local ire was intensified proselytizing by Christian missionaries, most of all an especially aggressive German Catholic order called the Society of the Divine Word. It was bad enough these weird outsiders were spouting ideas many villagers saw as thoroughly un-Chinese; worse still was how the foreign missionaries used their influence and privileges handed them in "unequal treaties" to protect and advance the interests of Christian converts. (A fair number of those who converted were criminals trying to escape punishment or evade the law.) Nor did the missionaries endear themselves with their condescending attitude toward China's traditional culture. The Society of the Divine Word made that clear in its own literature. "The crudities of Chinese life," it said approvingly of one of its senior bishops, "revolted him." He made "disparaging observations about the Chinese people in general."[8]

All this coagulated into a virulent xenophobia that infected the Boxer movement. The Boxers have their roots in martial arts societies common to many villages that usually did not have political motivations. Their anti-Christian ideology seems to have first emerged in a Shandong town called Liyuantun, where in the mid-1890s members of one of those local societies came to the defense of non-Christians in a long-running dispute over the construction of a church. The rising ire toward Christians in the area was captured in a placard posted in a nearby district in 1898: "The patriots of all the provinces, seeing that the men of the West transgress all limits in their behavior, have decided to assemble . . . and to kill the Westerners and burn their houses. Those whose hearts are not in accord with us are scoundrels."[9] But the Boxers who actually set off the rebellion seem to have formed elsewhere in northern Shandong, where they mixed the usual martial arts training with spiritual rituals in which members believed themselves to be possessed by gods, a state that made them invulnerable to modern weaponry. The men who led these boxing clubs were usually of little social stature—one was a Buddhist monk, another a landless farm laborer who sold peanuts on the side to earn extra cash. At first, the assaults on Christians in the area were limited mainly to extorting them for money, robbing their homes, and defacing churches. But the movement took a turn toward greater violence after an incident in the Shandong county of Pingyuan in late 1899. Boxers again collected to support non-Christians in another village fracas, but this time, the incident culminated in a pitched battle between the martial artists and Qing troops near a local temple. The Boxers got the worst of it, but the challenge to the Christians enthralled residents of other villages, and the rebellion spread like a human wildfire, rolling across the north China plain under the banner, "Support the Qing, destroy the foreign." The Boxers killed missionaries and their converts, torched churches, and tore up other symbols of Western influence, such as railways and telegraph lines. Bursting out of the countryside, the Boxers rushed into Tianjin and Beijing. There they plastered wall posters to spread their antiforeign message. One read:

> When at last all the foreign Devils
> Are expelled to the very last man,
> The Great Qing, united, together,
> Will bring peace to this our land.[10]

The Qing court then made the disastrous decision to ally with the Boxers. They saw the movement as perhaps the dynasty's last and best chance to rid itself of the dangerous Western barbarians. The conservative Empress Dowager encouraged provincial officials to support the Boxers. (Few of them actually did, which limited the Boxer movement to east-central China.) In the capital, Qing troops besieged the foreign legations, which defended themselves behind a makeshift barricade of sandbags and whatever else they could find. The German and Japanese envoys were killed.

In response to panicked cries for help from their harried diplomats in Beijing, Great Britain, France, Germany, Russia, Japan, the United States, Italy, and Austria-Hungary forged a joint armed force of nineteen thousand to march to their relief. The Boxers, as it turned out, were heroic but not impervious to bullets, and the Qing's regular soldiers performed as they had become accustomed, which means poorly. As the foreign invaders reached Beijing, the court was again compelled to flee—the Empress Dowager ignominiously disguised as a Buddhist nun. This time, they didn't stop until they arrived in Xi'an in China's west, the new version of the old Han Dynasty capital of Chang'an. The siege of the legations was lifted, and the foreign troops occupied the Forbidden City itself, the symbolic heart of the imperial system, in August 1900. After staging a military parade in its stately courtyard, the officers enjoyed tea "handed out by real blue-button mandarins," according to one account.[11]

====

Today, the Boxers are heralded as patriotic nationalists who sacrificed themselves for China. At the time, they heralded the final, painful gasp of a dying dynasty. The Qing court survived, almost by default—the Europeans could think of no better way to govern the massive empire than by reinstating the Empress Dowager, who returned to the Forbidden City, this time in a more regal procession. The Western powers were content to keep the Qing on life support while they sucked China dry. But the Boxer Rebellion brought the Qing to a point of no return. In the conflict's settlement, the foreign victors demanded an indemnity nearly twice the size of the empire's total national budget, a financial anvil that crushed the Qing's hopes of rebuilding its strength. In another significant infringement of Qing sovereignty, the foreign invaders retained the right to maintain their troops in the country to defend their citizens resident there. Even the empress herself recognized how dire the situation had become. "The dynasty has been brought to the precipice," she wrote.[12]

The elite of China knew that the Qing had to go if the country was to be saved. The questions was, What should take the dynasty's place? Such a question hadn't been asked since the unification of the Qin 2,100 years earlier. Through all the ups and downs of those many centuries, and the social and economic changes they brought, the political class of China had remained committed to restoring the imperial system whenever it fell apart. The institutions of the dynasties were considered sacrosanct, handed down from the ancestors. They had survived because they worked. After all, China had been a superpower for most of its history, an unmatched paragon of civilization for the rest of the world to emulate and admire, an economic powerhouse with barely a rival, a fountain of philosophy and literature with wide appeal, a throne to which "all under Heaven" bowed in respect and deference.

But at the beginning of the twentieth century, with China helplessly prostrate before the world's imperialists, that enduring confidence in this ancient system had been badly shaken. Its inability to contend with the challenges of the times—both internal and external—was glaringly obvious to all. And while the Qing ineptly floundered about in search of solutions, unable to restore its vitality, those Westerners were clearly doing something right. They had all the wealth and power; China was losing both. They were innovative and energetic; a lethargic China seemed stuck in a different era. But what was the West's secret? What did the West have that China did not?

The man who tried to answer these questions more intensely than any other was Liang Qichao, Kang Youwei's partner in reform. Liang is known to history as a politician and activist, but where he really made his mark was as a journalist. His writings, from exile in Japan, were smuggled into China, where they reached a huge audience of young literati—perhaps as many as two hundred thousand. His musings on politics, philosophy, and society laid the intellectual groundwork for a generation of reformers who sought to revitalize a failing China.[13]

Liang's work was a quest for the special sauce behind the West's success, those nuggets of pearly wisdom that could help China become strong, energetic—and most of all, *modern*. He was a rarity among Chinese intellectuals; hardly ever in China's history did its scholars bother examining civilizations other than their own. The thinking dating back to Confucius and Mencius had not fundamentally changed: those foreigners had nothing worth learning about. At the turn of the twentieth century, however, it became impossible for some educated Chinese to think they had all the answers. Liang was at the forefront of this dramatic shift in the Chinese image of their own role in the world. From sage and teacher, the source of civilization itself, China was becoming the student.

In 1903, as part of his exploration into the ways of the West, Liang traveled through the United States for five months. What he found did not always please him. Liang was disturbed by the gap

Philosopher, reformer, and journalist Liang Qichao had tremendous influence on political thought in China during the early twentieth century.

Pictures from History / Bridgeman Images

between rich and poor in New York City, and the squalor of its tenement wards. But overall, he was deeply impressed. Everywhere he looked, these Americans were in a hurry, to get somewhere, to do something; cities were a buzz of energetic efficiency. The United States was a country with purpose, its people paragons of civic responsibility, the whole place a vision of modernity. By comparison, the Chinese seemed so . . . backward . . . dissolute . . . *barbaric*!

In Liang's eyes, the Chinese could do little right. Liang was "amazed" that university libraries did not have staff to handle the books, but allowed the students to take and return them on their own. "In this can be seen the general level of public morality," he commented. "Even a small thing like this is something Orientals could not come close to learning to do in a hundred years." At an

American shop, "one of [the staff] does the same amount of work that it takes three of us to do. It is not that the Chinese are not diligent, they are simply not intelligent." The Chinese couldn't sit politely through a speech, or keep public spaces clean, or even walk properly. "When Westerners walk their steps are always hurried; one look and you know that the city is full of people with business to do, as though they cannot get everything done," Liang described. "The Chinese on the other hand walk leisurely and elegantly, full of pomp and ritual—they are truly ridiculous."

Where had the Chinese gone so wrong? He ticked off the reasons. "1. Our character is that of clansmen rather than citizens. . . . 2. We have a village mentality and not a national mentality. . . . 3. We can accept only despotism and cannot enjoy freedom."[14] The defining difference between China and the Western powers, Liang concluded, was that China had never become a true "nation." All those centuries of centralized dynasties had never forged the Chinese into one people, with loyalties toward the country. Instead, the Chinese favored their families or localities. They didn't know how to be true citizens of a modern nation, with responsibilities toward the community around them. What was missing? Liang determined the Chinese required "rights." The secret ingredient behind the wealth and power of the West was that common people participated in the process of governing. That made them feel a part of the greater nation, with duties toward their fellow citizens. The state became stronger, the sum of the collective energy of a people mobilized to pursue their common, national interests.

This was crazy stuff. Confucianism had always taught that government was the purview of the most educated, who had a responsibility to enter public service and care for the people. For its entire history, the imperial system and its Confucian ideology was designed to consume the individual in the larger interests of an imposed "harmony" within the family and greater society. Influenced by Western thinkers, Liang now believed the dynamism of the individual had to be unleashed and harnessed to the service of the greater mission of preserving China.

That entailed adopting the political systems of the West: a constitution, representative assemblies, and open elections. Liang wanted democracy. He saw an American-style republic as an ideal though for China he favored something more like a constitutional monarchy, at least at first.

But Liang also thought that China was ill prepared for such an enlightened form of government. The people, unaccustomed to the duties of self-rule, simply weren't ready for it. "If we were to adopt a democratic system of government now, it would be nothing less than committing national suicide," he wrote.[15] First, there had to be a reformation, to transform the Chinese into a "new people" to form the foundation of Liang's modernized Chinese nation. "We must not depend on a temporary wise emperor or minister to allay the disorder, nor expect a sudden rise of one or two heroes from the rural countryside to lead our struggle for success," Liang wrote. "It is necessary to have our people's virtue, people's wisdom, and people's power of the whole number of four hundred million all become equal to that of the foreigners." To do that did not mean simply copying foreign ways, but also awakening to the common bonds and culture that could bring the Chinese people together. "From morals and laws down to customs, habits, literature and fine arts, all share a kind of independent spirit which has been handed down from grandfather to father and inherited by their descendants," he wrote. "Thus, the group is formed and the nation develops. This is really the fundamental source of nationalism. Our people have been established as a nation on the Asiatic continent for several thousand years, and we must have some characteristics which are grand, eminent, and perfect, and distinctly different from those of other races."

Thus, Liang argued that China had been a "nation" for millennia. Now that national spirit had to be marshaled for the cause of reconstruction and renewal. Liang and many of his fellow reformers were heavily influenced by social Darwinism—the notion that peoples, like species, were in a constant struggle for survival, and only the fittest would thrive. Chinese nationalism had to fight it out with other nationalisms or perish. "The reason for European development and world progress has been the stimulation and growth of extensive nationalist feeling everywhere," Liang wrote. "What does nationalism mean? It is that in all places people of the same race, the same language, the same religion, and the same customs regard each other as brothers and work for independence and self-government, and organize a more perfect government to work for the public welfare and to oppose the infringement of other races." In order to "save China from great calamity and rescue our people, the only thing for us to do is to adopt the policy of promoting our own nationalism."[16] Simply, Liang wished China to morph from a traditional empire to a modern nation-state. Liang was imagining the incredible: a China without a universal, all-powerful Son of Heaven; a China where the emperor, if he existed at all, would have to share the stage of government with the common masses. The West was making the Chinese think the unthinkable.

=====

What exactly would this new, Western-style, China nation-state look like? In the days of the Song and Ming Dynasties, literati believed there was a "China proper"—the area that was home to the Han Chinese people, with historic and rightful boundaries enclosing a Chinese cultural zone and lands traditionally in Chinese hands, with the Great Wall separating the civilized from the uncivilized worlds. With the Qing conquest, not just of the Ming's domain but also the surrounding regions west and north—Xinjiang and the Mongol steppe—and its control over Tibet, the Manchus had developed a different definition of "China," one reborn as a multicultural empire of various ethnicities, cultures, and regions previously considered outside the true-blue Han world. As Emperor Qianlong put it in a 1755 edict, "There exists a view of China, according to which non-Han people cannot become China's subjects and their land cannot be integrated into the territory of China. This does not represent our dynasty's understanding of China."[17]

Such a view was distinct from how the Chinese defined the world going all the way back to the Han Dynasty. There existed an "inner" and "outer" world, a separation between civilization (in other words, China) and the barbaric lands beyond (in other words, chaos). Though Chinese governing ideology considered the Son of Heaven a universal sovereign, and at times the imperial court believed it was the center of a larger, geographic order—such as the Tang Dynasty's Emperor Taizong, who claimed he was the qaghan of the Turks as well as the emperor of the Chinese—the lines between "inner" and "outer" were at best blurred. But by the mid-nineteenth century, Chinese literati began to accept the Qing view of an expanded, polyglot "China" as their own. That's why scholar Gong Zizhen wrote that "the great Qing state is China"— adding, for good measure, that it had been so since the days of the mythical sage-kings of antiquity.[18] As China was morphing from a dynastic empire into a European-style state, the borders of the expansive Qing domain became the legitimate borders of "China," the country, with all of its assorted Turkish Uighurs, Tibetans, Mongols, and other barbarians enclosed within them. In the minds of the Chinese, "China" was becoming the China of today's maps.

There was, however, an ethnic minority the Chinese did not welcome into their new "China"—the one that created it. As the empire tottered, the Chinese elite became more convinced that the Manchus had to go if China was to recover its former glory. Only the "real" Han Chinese could and should build a new, modern China able to fight off the West. Emerging Chinese nationalism took on a decidedly anti-Manchu tenor, in the process reaffirming the idea of the "Chinese" as a select ethnic group, with a shared lineage, language, culture, and history. The Han Chinese people, the thinking asserted, had to unite together to expel the barbarian rulers and take back control of their own country—and destiny. If that did not happen, they were doomed to sink to the bottom of a race-based global hierarchy instead of leading it, as they rightfully should.

Many of the early twentieth-century reformers and revolutionaries were highly influenced by the racial diatribes of Wang Fuzhi. Until then, the seventeenth-century Confucian scholar was little known. Underlying much of his prose was a die-hard commitment to preserving Chinese civilization from the impure corruptions of barbarians. That, in itself, was not necessarily new: Chinese had long lamented that foreign invaders would make their lands "stink." But Wang characterized the Chinese-barbarian confrontation in strikingly tribal terms. The Chinese, like any specific group, had to defend their land and culture from dangerous outside forces. "Even the ants have rulers who preside over the territory of their nests, and when red ants or flying white ants penetrate their gates, the ruler organizes all his own kind into troops to bite and kill the intruders, drive them far away from the anthill, and prevent foreign interference," he wrote in an especially influential passage. If only, Wang dreamed, the Chinese had just such a ruler to force out the invading pests—the Qing Manchus. "I look forward eagerly to the advent of an enlightened ruler, who will restore sovereignty to the country, accomplish its mission, and stabilize its frontiers, and thereby guard the central territory and drive off the barbarians forever."[19]

The modern reformers shared his dream. "When the Manchus came, they killed our ancestors, violated our women, occupied the territory of Han race, made their vile, contemptible race into a noble class, . . . this was indeed despicable, and still they craved to be parasites!" the manifesto of one anti-Qing revolutionary society proclaimed. "They only look after the foreigners, and give us up to the foreigners to act as third class slaves. . . . Therefore our revolution first must revenge our ancestors and secondly must be planned quickly in order to avoid the extinction of our descendants."[20]

The Chinese had always believed themselves a superior civilization; now they began to perceive themselves as a superior race. The white race may have gotten the upper hand for the moment, the thinking went, but the Han Chinese, with their thousands of years of civilization, were surely more advanced than those black, red, and brown peoples—and, of course, the steppe Manchus. In a highly influential 1903 tract called *The Revolutionary Army*, young writer Zou Rong asserted that "the Han race is the most outstanding race in East Asian history." But, he lamented, "the Han race, although made up of so many, have become merely the slaves of another race." He went on: "The reason for this is that the people have no ethnocentric or national ideas; thus, they can do things humiliating to our ancestors, the men becoming robbers and the women prostitutes."[21] Such sentiment sometimes turned vicious. "Kill! Kill! Kill!" radical writer Chen Tianhua proclaimed in a 1903 pamphlet called *Alarm Bell*. "Advance en masse: kill the foreign devils, . . . If the Manchus help the foreigners kill us, then first kill all the Manchus."[22]

China's long distrust of foreigners was being brewed with hatred of the Manchus, bitterness toward the humiliations inflicted by the Western powers, and emerging Western theories about natural selection into a potent stew of Han nationalism—which was about to boil over.

=

As the twentieth century dawned—the twenty-second in China's imperial history—the empire was seething with ideas, movements, and political and economic forces it had never confronted before. Even the conservative Qing finally accepted that the past could no longer be the future. In 1901, Empress Dowager Cixi, who had crushed the Kang reform effort three years earlier, initiated a program that copied many of his plans. In an edict issued while still in her Xi'an exile, the empress said the goal was to "blend together the best of what is Chinese and what is foreign."[23] In the resulting program, called the "New Policies," European-style ministries of finance, foreign affairs, commerce, justice, and others were formed, as was a supreme court to top an independent judiciary. A committee to examine adopting a constitutional government was set up, with Liang Qichao, brought back from exile in Japan, as a consultant. The creation of elected assemblies at the municipal and provincial levels began in 1908. Easily the most radical step taken came in 1905, with the abolition of the once-cherished civil service examination system. In its place, the Qing fostered a network of modern schools with a Western curriculum. Suddenly cast aside was the traditional, Confucian-trained scholar who had been the mainstay of Chinese administration for a millennium. A "New Army" was to be created, equipped with modern weapons and staffed with officers from Western-style schools. Finally, the Qing were catching up to the West—and joining the modern world.

Too late. As was the case with other decrepit empires of the age, like the Ottomans in Istanbul, the reforms meant to strengthen the existing government only bolstered the forces behind its demise. The educated elite of China, rather than supporting traditional forms of government, were racing to embrace major political change. And the heavy-footed Qing could not keep up.

In seeking modern education, Chinese students flocked to foreign universities in unprecedented numbers in the first decade of the twentieth century, most of all to Japan. There they imbibed mind-bending ideas that radicalized their thinking on Chinese reform. The Japanese had latched onto the concept of "pan-Asianism"—the notion that the "yellow race," sharing, to a great degree, a common (Chinese) culture, had to stand together against the white Europeans invading the region. The Chinese students also learned new political concepts the Japanese had absorbed from the West. In fact, the words in Chinese for *democracy*, *republic*, *revolution*, and *constitution* were inherited from the Japanese language. When these students returned home, they brought these concepts with them. For much of its history China had shared its philosophy, literature, and governing institutions with the world; now the flow was thrown in reverse, with outside ideas traversing through those centuries-old connections of language and culture into China. The Chinese had become disciples of their disciples.

These students hastened the end of the Qing by spreading these fresh ideas throughout society. But it was the members of the traditional political elite—the gentry, merchants, and exam graduates—who brought down the empire. They, too, had become enraptured by Western political systems, most of all, the idea of a constitution. The powerful nations victimizing China at that time had constitutions. Japan had adopted one as part of the Meiji reforms. So there must be a connection between constitutions and national strength. These elite flooded into the elected assemblies formed by the Qing's New Policies, and pressed the court to convert itself into a constitutional monarchy.

The Qing, of course, responded far too slowly. They pushed off the promulgation of a constitution and the formation of a permanent national legislature. The educated of China wanted their rights, and they weren't getting them quickly enough. "The people possess inalienable rights," radical writer Zou Rong wrote, sounding very Jeffersonian. "Life, liberty, and all the other benefits are natural rights. No one shall infringe upon freedom of speech, freedom of thought, or freedom of the press."[24] The Manchus, unwilling to acknowledge the escalating hostility toward their dynasty and themselves, sealed their fate. In 1911, a new cabinet was introduced, supposedly to quiet the thunderclaps for reform; but it was stacked with Manchu royals, and thus a stinging slap to the Han people. The carved melon had become ripe for revolt.

It is an all too common turn of phrase to say something "sparked" a revolution, or that a tense situation was a "powder keg." In the case of Qing China in October 1911, that was literally the case. One member of a small cell of revolutionaries in Wuchang, the capital of Hubei province (and now part of the city of Wuhan), dropped cigarette ashes into the gunpowder he was stuffing into rifle shells, setting it off and revealing the existence of an anti-Qing plot. Fearing exposure, revolutionaries within the local New Army garrison mutinied. The next day, the local assembly supported the mutineers and declared the province had seceded from the Qing Dynasty. Over the next several weeks, province after province followed suit. The Qing court watched almost helplessly as its empire dissolved. Hatred of the Manchus exploded with near-genocidal ferocity. In the town of Xi'an, some ten thousand Manchu men, women, and children were executed. The last Qing emperor, Xuantong, agreed to abdicate in 1912—or more precisely, his regents decided for him, since he was a mere six years old. After more than 250 years, the Qing went out with a whimper.

By then, dynasties had been coming and going for 2,100 years. Each time one ruling house lost the Mandate of Heaven, there were always princes, nobles, and rebels ready to rebuild the imperial system under a fresh Mandate. Even barbarian invaders retained the core of the Chinese imperial system. That does not mean all the dynasties were the same. They weren't. But since the First Emperor unified China in 221 BC, the ruling elite had remained committed to the basic elements of the imperial government—a Son of Heaven, sitting atop a centralized bureaucracy and immersed in the rituals of the ancients. There had never been much doubt that such a governing model was the best for China. So each time one dynasty fell, another took its place. It was the single most remarkable feature of Chinese political history.

This time was different. In 1911, large swaths of the gentry and literati—the folks who decided how China was governed—did not want to reestablish the old imperial system. After the Western encroachments and lost wars, the traditional institutions had proven incapable of their first order of business—defending the country—and with their minds awash in new ideas about constitutions, democracy, race, and nationalism, the nation-state they wished to build had no place for a Son of Heaven, at least not in the traditional sense. No more would the emperors hold the power over life and death.

But if not another dynasty, then what? Something foreign, of course. Democracy had no historical roots in China. Its political class did not look back fondly on the Greek and Roman republics. That was another history of the world. China's had known nothing but near-absolute monarchies; their ideal state was topped by a sage-king. But China wanted to be "modern," and quickly; to do that it needed a twentieth-century government, not leftovers from ancient kingdoms. In December 1911, representatives of the seceded provinces met in Nanjing to form a new national government—the Republic of China.

The man placed in charge of this nascent democracy was a doctor and professional activist, Sun Yat-sen. He is widely honored as the "Father of the Nation" by political movements on varied sides of the Chinese political spectrum, which agree on little else. Sun was born in 1866 near Hong Kong, but spent much of his life outside of China. At thirteen, his family sent him off to live with a brother in Hawaii. He attended medical school in Hong Kong— among the first Chinese students to graduate—and spent time in Japan, where he embraced the spirit of the Meiji reforms.

Sun earned his stature, though, as China's most relentless professional revolutionary—though at first, not a particularly successful one. He was involved in organizing several small uprisings against the Qing—all of which were summarily squelched—and an alliance he forged of revolutionary societies in 1905 effectively dissolved within a few years. When the real revolution broke out in 1911, he was in Denver, fundraising for his cause. He and his supporters had almost no role in toppling the Qing.

Once the dynasty was gone, however, Sun took center stage. When the new government was founded, Sun stood out as the revolution's only legitimate leader and was named the first president of the Republic of China. On top of his tireless record of anti-Qing struggle, the cosmopolitan Sun also was the only Chinese politician with both extensive international contacts and a relatively coherent vision for China's future. His ideas coalesced into the "Three

Principles of the People"—nationalism, democracy, and livelihood. Though often vague, Sun's philosophy was an appealing cornucopia of exciting foreign and familiar Chinese concepts born out of the intellectual ferment of the times. Sun believed China's new government needed to be representative to bind the people to the state and marshal their energy and spirit to rebuild Chinese strength. But to bring the country together, Sun also favored strong national leadership with a powerful executive. His aim was not the personal liberty of the American revolution, but the "liberty of the nation"—to free China of its imperialist oppressors. Achieving such a deft political balance entailed making "the distinction between sovereignty and ability."[25] Though the state should possess sufficient powers to control China's fractious society and guide its quest for renewal, ultimate sovereignty rested with the people, who could choose and recall their leaders. His ideal government had five branches—three borrowed from the United States (executive, legislative, and judicial) plus two more adopted from China's traditional system (an independent civil service and a censorate to police it). "A state with such a government," Sun proclaimed, channeling Lincoln, "will indeed be of the people, by the people, and for the people."[26] On China's economy, Sun preferred a mix of state initiative and private enterprise to industrialize and toss off the yoke of foreign domination. The goal of these political and economic reforms was the redemption of the Han nation. "With common customs and habits, we are completely of one race," he explained. "Compared to the other peoples of the world we have the greatest population and our civilization is four thousand years old; we should therefore be advancing in the front rank with the nations of Europe and America. But the Chinese people have only family and clan solidarity; they do not have national spirit. . . . Other men are the carving knife and serving dish; we are the fish and the meat. . . . If we do not earnestly espouse nationalism and weld together our four hundred million people into a strong nation, there is danger of China's being lost and our people being destroyed."[27]

Sun, though, could not hold on to his position. Within weeks, he had surrendered the republic's presidency to a vastly different figure, Yuan Shikai. The former Qing dignitary controlled the Chinese military, and that meant he controlled China. Sun instead formed his own political party, the Kuomintang, or Nationalists, and became a voice of opposition. In return for stepping aside, Sun extracted a pledge from Yuan to uphold the republic's democratic political principles.

Pluralism, however, was not Yuan's idea of good government. After national elections in late 1912—which the Nationalists won handily—a top official of the party was shot dead on a Shanghai train platform, on Yuan's orders, it was widely presumed. In 1913, Sun's supporters staged another revolt—this one no more effective than his others. Yuan then snuffed out China's first, promising experiment with representative government by banning the Kuomintang and dissolving the newly elected legislature in early 1914. In its place, he promulgated a new dynasty in late 1915, with himself as emperor.

That went too far. Facing resistance from provincial governments, intellectuals, and even his own army officers, Yuan backtracked and abolished his monarchy after only three months. When he died in 1916, the country fractured into dozens of squabbling fiefdoms. Technically, the Republic survived; in practice, a central government existed in name only. Rather than a resurrection, the revolution hurtled the country into one of the most horrific and violent periods in its horrifically violent history. It was the déjà vu version of the Warring States era.

The reform-minded of China were despondent. The hapless Qing was no more, but China was still a melon, bleeding under the carving knife, broken into pieces. What had gone wrong? With disappointment came radicalism. China's problems ran deep—so deep that even the fall of the dynasties had failed to resolve them. No more should the Chinese aspire to infuse the best of the West with China's own values. To an assertive crop of young thinkers, Chinese civilization itself was holding China back. Tradition was a dungeon, where the youth of China were condemned to rot amid the stench of mildewed Confucian books; their fathers were the oppressive guards. Women were locked down there, too, cloistered in a prison of kitchens and bedrooms, slaves to lust. The fetters must be smashed! Sons had to be freed from their fathers, women from their husbands! Only as individuals, empowered to act on their own will, not archaic ritual, could the Chinese save themselves and their nation. The Confucian family, what the scholars had long thought elevated the Chinese over barbarians, had to die. "The family is the origin of all evil," one writer blasted in 1907. "The destruction of the family will . . . lead to the creation of public-minded people in place of selfish people."[28] That convoluted classical language that the literati still preferred—that had to be replaced, too, with the vernacular, to spread knowledge and the spirit of change. "Those who use a dead classical style will translate their own ideas into allusions of several thousand years ago and convert their own feelings into literary expressions of centuries past," explained Hu Shi, one of the most important thinkers of the time. "If China wants to have a living literature, we must use the plain speech."[29] Even Chinese history had to be reexamined with a modern, critical eye.

Everything must go! "All our traditional ethics law, scholarship, rites and customs are survivals of feudalism," writer Chen Duxiu proclaimed in 1915. "Revering only the history of the twenty-four dynasties and making no plans for progress and improvement, our people will be turned out of this twentieth-century world, and be lodged in the dark ditches, fit only for slavery. . . . I would much rather see the past culture of our nation disappear than see our race die out now because of its unfitness for living in the modern world."[30]

Chinese civilization no longer defined civilization. What was Chinese was rotten, backward, and useless; what was foreign was fresh, exhilarating, and useful. The West was the font of modernity, the birthplace of the civilization of the future, the place to find better ideas on just about everything. But inspiration could be found anywhere. The brave anticolonial struggle in India caught attention, too. "It is crucial for China to learn from Gandhi," journalist Zou Taofen wrote. He thought Kemal Atatürk, who lifted modern Turkey from the ruins of the Ottoman Empire, worthy of emulation, as well. "Seeing how Turkey was able to pull itself out of a dangerous crisis, we have to do whatever it takes to enable China to also win its future back," he proffered.[31] Imagine. The Chinese learning from Hindus and Turks. What would Confucius think?

The pinnacle of this movement for a new culture came in 1919. Amid the horrors of World War I, the Chinese had found reason for optimism. President Woodrow Wilson, upon bringing the United

States into the conflict, propounded his Fourteen Points, which promised self-determination for the world's colonial peoples—a message that inspired the Chinese. "Throughout the world, like the voice of a prophet, has gone the word of Woodrow Wilson strengthening the weak and giving courage to the struggling," read a 1919 pamphlet from the Shanghai Student Union. "And the Chinese have listened and they too have heard."[32]

Yet these hopes were soon dashed. The peace settlement betrayed Wilson's lofty principles. The news that the victorious allies awarded Germany's Qingdao concessions to Japan rather than to the Chinese republic was a vicious slap in China's face. On May 4, 1919, three thousand irate students marched past the Forbidden City in Beijing to protest. They chanted anti-Japan slogans, of course; but they also attacked their own government, too weak to defend the nation. And the civilization that had laid China so low, too. "Destroy the old curiosity shop of Confucius!" they yelled.[33]

This symbolic protest left such a deep imprint on modern Chinese history that the entire quest for drastic political and cultural reform became known as the May Fourth Movement. It was a national turning point. "We had no political theory to guide us at that time, only our strong patriotic enthusiasm," recalled one sixteen-year-old participant. "Our political awareness awakened a new spirit in us during our struggle."[34]

=

The student who wrote those words, Deng Yingchao, later married one of the most commanding figures of twentieth-century China, Zhou Enlai, who would serve as the premier of Communist China for twenty-seven years. Deng herself got heavily involved in party politics. The philosophy of Marx and Lenin joined nationalism, democracy, and capitalism among those that filtered into China and altered the nation's history.

Marx's vision of a new society built upon the ruins of the corrupt old did not get much attention in China until the 1917 revolution in Russia. But then its appeal to the young, idealistic, and frustrated of China was obvious: a small but committed coterie of revolutionaries could overthrow an outdated and incompetent political order and bring a backward empire into the modern world.

The student protests that erupted in China on May 4, 1919—here pictured in central Beijing—were sparked by anger over their country's poor treatment in the treaty ending World War I, but they came to symbolize growing political activism and demands for radical change among Chinese youth.

Pictures from History / Bridgeman Images

Why couldn't the same happen in China? "In the course of such a world mass movement," professor Li Dazhao wrote of Russia's revolution, "all those dregs of history that can impede the progress of the new movement—such as emperors, nobles, warlords, bureaucrats, militarism, capitalism—will certainly be destroyed as though struck by a thunderbolt."[35] Study societies formed at Chinese universities to read translated works of Marx and Lenin.

With this latest foreign doctrine came another foreign power, the Soviet Union. In 1919, Moscow renounced the "unequal treaties" that the now defunct tsars had coerced the now defunct Qing to sign, buffing the Soviets' image among young Chinese nationalists. It also formed the Comintern to promote the gospel of Communist revolution around the world, and it quickly infiltrated its tentacles into China. Comintern agents encouraged the formation of Communist societies in major cities across China, and then, in 1921, the Chinese Communist Party itself, founded by Chen Duxiu and Li Dazhao in the French concession area of Shanghai.

Soviet influence penetrated even deeper than that. Comintern missionaries also found their way to Guangzhou, where Sun Yat-sen was attempting to rebuild the ruined Republic. With Soviet advice and aid, Sun refashioned the Kuomintang into a leaner, meaner political machine with a modern army to reconquer the nation from the warlords. As a condition for its assistance, Moscow demanded Sun forge an alliance with the fledgling Communists. Sun was no Marxist, but he found enough common ground with the Communists to agree.

After Sun died of cancer in 1925, control of the Kuomintang passed to an extremely different character, Chiang Kai-shek. He had risen up in the party through its expanding military arm, and was the first commandant of its officer-training academy. The desire for emperors may have waned, but not for a united China, so in 1926, Chiang marched north out of Guangzhou at the head of a 100,000-man army to corral the warlords and reunify the country. The campaign was like those other horribly bloody wars of unification waged by the Qin or Sui, with which China had all too much experience. Two years later, Chiang had conquered or co-opted most of the warlords, but at the staggering cost of three hundred thousand dead.

China was one once again, but the question of what government it should have remained unanswered. The power-hungry Chiang had little interest in Sun's democratic principles, and he transformed the republic into a one-party dictatorship. Such a regime had no room for partners. Chiang had never trusted the Communists, and in 1927, he unleashed a blood-soaked purge of his supposed allies, nearly annihilating the entire movement. A rump of survivors eventually found refuge in the remote hills of Shaanxi province in the northwest.

Chiang had hopes of industrializing and rebuilding the nation with a heavy-handed state. He also clawed back some Chinese sovereignty by reversing parts of the old "unequal treaties," still very much in effect even though the dynasty that signed them was not. His government, for instance, regained control of the country's customs, lost after the First Opium War. But his opportunity was rudely cut short. China was not done playing the melon to foreign knives. In 1932, Japan chopped off Manchuria into a puppet state called Manchukuo, officially ruled by the last Qing emperor but in reality a Japanese colony. Then, in 1937, the Japanese pushed into northern China. While the West was preoccupied with the evils of Hitler, the first shots of the war with fascism were actually fired in China. And Japan's legions were as brutal as the later German blitzkriegs. Angered by the fierce resistance they met at the historic city of Nanjing, the Japanese unleashed an organized campaign of terror and murder. The infamous Rape of Nanjing left as many as three hundred thousand Chinese dead.

Almost a century after British warships pointed their cannon at the same town, China's humiliations continued.

===

With Japan's surrender in 1945 and the close of World War II, things were looking up for China. As one of the victorious allies, the country's international stature was on the rise. Chiang had attended the Cairo Conference in 1943 with Roosevelt and Churchill, and his republic was slated to gain a coveted permanent seat on the Security Council of the new United Nations, among the world's other great powers. But as it happened, the end of one conflict simply started another: the final confrontation between Nationalists and Communists for ultimate control of China. In their isolated bastion, the Communists had been resuscitated by a new larger-than-life personality, Mao Zedong. He had transformed the party of the urban proletariat into a rural mass movement (not all that distinct from a Chinese peasant rebellion), complete with a Red Army that had honed its skills ambushing the invading Japanese. Chiang had overwhelming superiority in men and material—much of it generously supplied by the United States, first to help the Nationalists fight Japan, then to combat godless Communism. But what advantage Chiang possessed in resources he frittered away in corruption and ineptitude that alienated the Chinese populace and, eventually, the Americans too, who withdrew their support as the civil war raged. On the battlefield, Chiang's poorly led and unmotivated troops wilted before Mao's smaller but more disciplined army. Clearly, Chiang did not possess Heaven's Mandate. In 1949, he and his Kuomintang fled the Chinese mainland for the island of Taiwan, home to the Republic of China to this day. Mao ascended the Gate of Heavenly Peace in Beijing on October 1 and proclaimed the People's Republic of China. "The Chinese have always been a great, courageous and industrious nation; it is only in modern times that they have fallen behind," he told a Communist Party plenum a few days earlier. "Ours will no longer be a nation subject to insult and humiliation. We have stood up."[36]

Just like Kang Youwei, Liang Qichao, Sun Yat-sen, and so many others, Mao had his own plan to make China great again—and his, too, was based on Western thinking. The Communist program he unleashed brought more drastic change than China had ever witnessed in such a condensed period of time, perhaps since the Qin unification twenty-two centuries earlier. For its entire existence, China's domestic economy was primarily private, with a passive state. Confucians liked it that way. Not Mao. He was well versed in Confucius's precepts, as were all educated Chinese, even after the dynasties' demise, but when it came to nation building, he preferred Stalin over the sage. Private property was abolished, industries nationalized, farms collectivized. Many Chinese capitalists joined the Kuomintang's panicked exodus to Taiwan or sought a safe haven in British-controlled Hong Kong. Foreign imperialists scurried off, too, abandoning their Shanghai townhouses. Meanwhile, Mao flexed his military muscles. The People's Republic went Qing, reconquering parts of the old Manchu empire that had strayed off during the decades of war. In 1950, the Red Army invaded Tibet, and a year later, Beijing arm-twisted Tibetan negotiators to submit to annexation—or, as the Communists put it in the agreement, "return to the big family of the Motherland."[37] Then Mao fought the world-beating Americans to a standstill on the Korean peninsula, where a half century earlier the Chinese were embarrassed by Japan. China was standing up indeed.

Anything seemed possible. In 1958, Mao launched the Great Leap Forward. Its purported goal was nothing short of magically transforming China from a poor, mainly agrarian society to a communist industrial wonderland in a mere handful of years. Farmers, press-ganged into communes, had to not only reach new heights of grain output but also produce their own tools. Everybody started making steel in backyard furnaces—even children. Anything to meet national targets! "The older students worked day and night to build steel furnaces on the old sports ground," recalled one young schoolgirl. "Students, once so attentive, came to class only to fall asleep. Awakened, they spoke excitedly of their great revolutionary production tasks."[38] To free women for the workforce, communal child-care centers and mess halls were established to lift the burden of such household drudgery. Surely China could surpass the Western powers on revolutionary zeal alone.

It couldn't. The homemade steel was useless; the effort to make it distracted farmers from their fields. Agricultural production plunged. But Communist cadres, too fearful of angering their superiors, falsely reported bumper harvests. Senior bureaucrats, believing the falsified data, extracted more and more grain from the countryside to feed the cities, denuding the rural areas of food. By 1960, the economy was in free fall. The famine that resulted from Mao's chaos may have killed thirty million people, one of the great man-made catastrophes in human history.

In 1966, Mao followed up that fiasco with another, the Cultural Revolution. Its goal was to speed the creation of a new society by reviving revolutionary spirit among the public and rooting out the final vestiges of the old Chinese world. More cynically, it was a maneuver by Mao to reassert his stature within the party, diminished by the Great Leap Forward. The Cultural Revolution was the ugly crescendo of China's attack on its own civilization. Troops of radicalized students known as the Red Guards hunted for the "four olds"—old ideas, old customs, old culture, and old habits—a task that entailed beating up their professors and destroying temples. Even the venerated shrine to Confucius in the philosopher's hometown of Qufu in Shandong province was ransacked, its famed statue of the Supreme Sage paraded through the streets and burned. Anyone suspected of being a "capitalist roader" or harboring secret reactionary thinking was banished to impoverished villages or gulag-style work camps to be "reeducated." Then Mao turned on his own protagonists, the Red Guards. Claiming they had gone too far, he exiled them, too, to the barren countryside.

Nor was Communist China able to regain the country's proper place on the world stage. Mao tried to export his brand of agrarian revolution; it proved far less popular overseas than the emperors' Confucianism. In the wake of its victory in World War II, the United States had reshaped the old Chinese world order in East Asia, forging a network of alliances with China's former vassals—including the detestable Japanese—to surround and contain the country. The British still held on to Hong Kong, the Portuguese to Macau. The Americans even protected the Communists' archenemies, the Nationalists, snugly encamped on Taiwan. And though Mao was able to finally wrestle away the United Nations Security Council seat from those Nationalists in 1971, the United States still didn't officially recognize his regime. Even within the Communist world, China was not welcome. A schism with the Soviet Union turned the Russians from allies to adversaries.

By the time Mao died in 1976, China was not much closer to becoming a modern, powerful nation than it had been a century earlier, when the rusty wheels of the Qing machinery first creaked toward self-strengthening reform. In many respects, China was worse off. Increasingly isolated on the world stage, mired in desperate poverty, and technically backward, China was just another third world country.

What, oh what, could make China great again?

Eleven

SUPERPOWER, RESTORED

China has stood up. It will never again tolerate being bullied by any nation.

–Xi Jinping, president of China

In February 1979, Deng Xiaoping found himself in an unlikely setting for a career Communist—a Texas rodeo. The longtime revolutionary luminary would probably have been much more comfortable marching with peasant soldiers or maneuvering in Beijing's cloistered halls of power. But unlike most other party brass, the personable and open-minded Deng knew how to play to the crowd, whoever might be in it. Donning a ten-gallon cowboy hat, Deng earned himself a hearty whoop from these otherwise red-blooded, anti-Red spectators. "Deng Xiaoping not only went west, but went Western," one television reporter quipped approvingly.[1]

The rodeo was just one stop on a nationwide campaign for American hearts and minds. Deng sat atop a replica of the rover that explored the moon at the Houston Space Center. In Atlanta, Deng toured a Ford car factory—his guide, no less a figure than Henry Ford II—and then dined at the Georgia governor's mansion, on a menu of "spinach soufflé, thinly sliced veal and vanilla mousse—all foods especially selected for eaters unskilled in the use of a knife and fork," *Time* magazine thoughtfully noted.[2] Earlier, in Washington, Deng attended a gala at the Kennedy Center to watch performances by John Denver, the Harlem Globetrotters, and the National Children's Choir, which sang in Chinese. Deng was delighted.

So was President Jimmy Carter. In a meeting at the White House, Carter pressed Deng on Beijing's restriction of emigration, which Washington saw as a human rights violation. Deng joked that populous China could "send you 10 million immigrants right away." Afterwards, a beaming Carter called Deng's visit "one of the most historic events in our nation's history."[3]

Not everyone was so charmed. Deng was still a godless Communist, after all. Washington had only normalized diplomatic relations with the People's Republic a month earlier, after thirty years of icy hostility. The Texas governor welcomed Deng only grudgingly. "We will turn out in a normal show of Texas hospitality," he said in advance of Deng's arrival. "Whether we agree with him politically, philosophically or whether we like chop suey or not, is beside the point."[4] But Deng did more than chomp barbecue and tell a few jokes to win over China's former enemy. Like Chinese leaders had done for centuries to tame the barbarians, he dangled the riches of China before America's profit-seeking eyes. The Communist was sure to mention how his nation required billions of dollars of investment to rebuild the economy and talked of importing lots of grain and allowing American oil companies to develop his country's energy resources. "Friendly cooperation between our two peoples is bound to exert a positive and far-reaching influence on the way the world situation evolves," Deng said at a Washington ceremony.[5]

It most certainly did. The partnership that Deng forged with the United States altered the Chinese history of the world—or actually, the *entire* history of the world. It would restore China to the strand of history it had followed for millennia before it was rudely interrupted by the West: China always had been a superpower, and would be a superpower again.

That's what Deng's trip to the United States in 1979 was really about. The crafty Communist was wise enough to realize he could not fix the Chinese history of the world without an accommodation with the West. For 150 years, China had struggled to come to terms with a civilization that thought itself superior and refused to conform to Chinese rules, norms, and culture. Some Chinese, such as Liang Qichao and Sun Yat-sen, had hoped copying from the West could strengthen China to the point where it could again chart its own course in the world, only to face recurring disappointment. Others, from Commissioner Lin Zexu to the mystical Boxers, chose confrontation, a route that led only to lost wars and humiliations. Those were still very raw in the Chinese psyche. Even as Deng enjoyed Texas barbecue, Washington was still supporting the Communists' mortal enemies—the Nationalists ensconced on Taiwan and the Japanese fascists, now American allies, who had reconstructed their war-torn islands into a rising economic powerhouse. Deng was duly reminded of his government's fraught relationship with the United States during his tour. While in Houston, hundreds of angry, pro-Taiwan protesters gathered to greet him.

But Deng was willing to let bygones be bygones, at least for the moment. He understood that the old Chinese world order had collapsed, and in its place the West had crafted a new world order in its own image. China's former vassal states were now tied to the United States through defense treaties and bonds of commerce so strong they formed a cordon tight enough to strangle China itself. The West had forged new global institutions and installed international laws and practices to manage the global economy and guide relations between Western-style nation-states. The tribute envoys journeyed no more; the fleets of Zheng He, a hazy, distant memory. China could no longer afford to resist. For now, at least, China would have to do some kowtowing of its own, to the reality around it. If China couldn't beat the West, it had to join the West.

Even Mao had an inkling of that uncomfortable truth. The ice between the United States and China was cracked seven years earlier, when Mao hosted then president Richard Nixon at a summit in Beijing. After Mao's dramatic break with the Soviet Union, the United States and China shared a common interest in containing Moscow. Deng, though, desired more than a thaw. He had grand plans for China, to finally fulfill the promise of the Chinese revolution that began with such hope seven decades earlier. But that would not be possible in isolation. If China were to rise again, it would have to do so within the world around it, and would need American cooperation. The Ford factory, the high technology of the space center—that's what China desired. And the United States— the richest, most advanced, most powerful nation on earth, the new Rome (or Tang)—was the place to get it.

It was pragmatic thinking, something the idealistic revolution had distinctly lacked. But it was Deng's hallmark. Unlike the ideo- logue Mao, content in constant revolutionary upheaval, Deng had proven himself an adept administrator and practical policymaker. "It does not matter if it is a yellow cat or a black cat," he once fa- mously said, "as long as it catches mice."[6] It was Deng who helped pick up the impoverished pieces left by the Great Leap Forward.

That level-headedness won him plaudits from many, but not from Mao, who devised the Cultural Revolution to purge the independent-minded within the party. Deng was stripped of his ti- tles and banished to labor at a tractor factory.

But by the early 1970s, the Communists needed Deng's steady hand more than ever. The Cultural Revolution had plunged the country into turmoil; the economy was paralyzed, the govern- ment in tatters. Deng had cleaned up Mao's messes before; he was called upon to do so again. Returned to the party's senior echelon, Deng slowly but surely—as was his method—built a coalition for change. What Deng had on his mind was more than merely re- storing order to a nation broken by disorder. Destitution ruled the countryside. Industry was archaic. The world was passing China by—again. Something had to be done. How much more could the poor, brutalized people of China take? When would their frustra- tion boil over and turn against the Communists, as they had the Qing? China was, again, desperate. It was time for a dramatic new direction. A new revolution.

His comrades in the party were primed for change. Mao died in 1976; his radical allies, known as the Gang of Four (which in- cluded his widow), were imprisoned. The country was weary of the nonstop instability and uncertainty of the Mao years. Deng sensed the shift in mood. Only six weeks before the Texas rodeo, on De- cember 13, 1978, Deng stood before the party's top cadres at a con- ference and called for a stark shift of course. The country, he told them, needed ingenuity, not conformity; results, not revolution. "The primary task is to emancipate our minds," Deng told the cadres. Some misguided senior party bosses had "set up ideological taboos or 'forbidden zones' and preached blind faith," and as a result "no one was allowed to go beyond the limits they prescribed; anyone who did was tracked down." Under such conditions, "people were naturally reluctant to use their brains." The solution, Deng proffered, was to "seek truth from facts"—not to be wedded to theories or books, or simply blow with the prevailing winds of party politics. "The more Party members and other people there are who use their heads and think things through, the more our cause will benefit," Deng said.

Then he became even more radical—or by Communist standards, reactionary. Class struggle, the core of Mao's revolution, should be set to one side; developing the nation had to take center stage. "Revolution takes place on the basis of the need for material benefit," he said. "It would be idealism to emphasize the spirit of sacrifice to the neglect of material benefit." And that meant unleashing the entrepreneurial energies of the Chinese masses, then submerged by state control and overbearing ideology. "To make revolution and build socialism we need large numbers of pathbreakers who dare to think, explore new ways and generate new ideas," he told his audience. "Otherwise, we won't be able to rid our country of poverty and backwardness or to catch up with—still less surpass—the advanced countries."[7] Nine days later, the party adopted a remarkable document. The time for revolutionary mass movements had come to a close. Now was the right moment "to shift the emphasis of our Party's work and the attention of the people of the whole country to socialist modernization." It was a decision that "reflects the demands of history."[8]

What followed was a torrent of new proposals, experiments, and creative policy tinkering. Rarely did Deng personally initiate the reforms. He was a Communist, not an economist. But he knew a good idea when he heard one, and his "yellow cat, black cat" sensibility made him amenable to all sorts of suggestions. Along the way, Deng's reforms dissolved much of the program erected by Mao. The Chinese leadership had tried out one foreign doctrine—Marxism-Leninism—and found it wanting. Now they were embracing another: capitalism. Deng and his comrades could never admit that, at least not officially. They were still card-carrying members of the Chinese Communist Party. Reactionary "capitalist roaders" remained enemies of the revolution. Deng preferred to call the new economic system he was creating "socialism with Chinese characteristics." But as has so often been the case throughout Chinese history, the gap between formal promulgations and the reality on the ground was wide. Deng and his team, in effect, chose the market over Mao. "Just imagine the additional wealth that could be created if all the people in China's hundreds of thousands of enterprises and millions of production teams put their minds to work," Deng told the party in his December speech.[9]

The people of China were eager for such freedom. Even as Deng was telling his comrades to "seek truth from facts," farmers in the province of Anhui, an especially impoverished area, were already doing just that. The "facts," as they figured it, were that the oppressive system of collectivization was a failure and left them hungry and destitute; the "truth" those facts revealed was that the Maoist communes had to go. Without waiting for official sanction, they began dismantling them and portioning out the land to individual households. They expected retribution. But it never came. The farmers didn't know it at first, but they had a protector in the province's party secretary, Wan Li. Desperate to improve sagging agricultural production, Wan allowed the insurgency to spread. To the farmers, he was a hero. But to conservatives, Wan was an enemy of socialism, guilty of undoing Mao's legacy. It was Deng, of course, who cast the deciding vote. In 1983, he promoted Wan Li to vice-premier and put him in charge of agricultural policy. The Anhui rebellion against Maoist excess went national. Returning the farms to the farmers was too drastic a step for a Communist regime; private ownership of farmland was still a no-no. But allocating the rights to till specific plots to households was ideologically acceptable. In effect, the family farm was reborn.

So was private enterprise. Mao had more or less eradicated any economic activity not directly controlled by the state; now Deng's reformers encouraged ordinary people to form small businesses, shops, and other services. Chinese cities were soon awash with barbers, repair shops, food stalls, and other handy services once again.

The managers of the large state firms that dominated industry were handed greater autonomy over their finances and operations. No more would the economy be micromanaged by meddlesome planners and bureaucrats.

For China's place in the world, however, the most critical reform was reopening the country to trade and international business. Foreigners were generally unwelcome in Mao's China, especially the capitalist-imperialist kind. China could not rise again with barbarian predators feasting on the Chinese melon. But what was satisfying to nationalist ire was disastrous for economic progress. The Chinese economy rotted with outdated technology and a paucity of capital. Deng was fully aware of the problem. "One important reason for China's backwardness after the industrial revolution in Western countries was its closed-door policy," Deng told a visiting delegation from Japan. "The experience of the past thirty or so years had demonstrated that a closed-door policy would hinder construction and inhibit development."[10] The phrase "opening up" joined "seek truth from facts" as one of the mantras of the reform movement.

But the question was how. How could China invite in foreign imperialists without submitting to the pillage and pilfering of the past? The answer emerged early in 1979 when two party secretaries from Guangzhou—long the country's window to the world—suggested demarcating chunks of China as specified "zones," in which foreign business would be allowed to operate. To entice them, regulations would be looser in the zones than the rest of the economy. But by barring them from any activity outside the zones, China could draw in the money and expertise it required while preventing the barbarians from stampeding across the economy. The idea harks back to the old Canton system through which the Qing had both benefited from and controlled foreign trade. It also reminded some conservatives of the foreign "concessions" granted in the infamous "unequal treaties."

Deng, though, instantly approved. Three months later, the central government sanctioned four initial "special economic zones," all conveniently placed to absorb investment from China's richer neighbors: in Shenzhen (across the border from posh British Hong Kong), Xiamen (across the strait from wealthy Taiwan), Zhuhai

US President Jimmy Carter and China's paramount leader Deng Xiaoping forged a partnership in a 1979 summit in Washington that underpinned the success of Beijing's capitalist reforms and the country's
economic rejuvenation.

Universal History Archive/UIG / Bridgeman Images

(next to Macau), and Shantou (also on the Guangdong coast).
China was open for business once again.

But would anybody come? On the face of it, China had little to
offer the world. The empire that had once been the beating heart of
the global economy, the source of the silk and porcelain the world
craved, and home to the eye-popping wealth that dumbfounded
Marco Polo was long gone. The China of Deng Xiaoping had been
disconnected from the world for decades. Its populace was destitute; its factories, outdated. Economic might was always a core
pillar of China's superpower stature. Without it, Chinese civilization could never return to the top of the global pyramid, where it
obviously belonged.

Yet ironically, there was hope in China's poverty, thanks to
major shifts in technology and production taking place around
the world. With faster, cheaper, and more reliable communications

and transport—brought about by massive container ships, fax machines, the personal computer, and other innovations—companies in one part of the globe could much more easily produce their wares in another to take advantage of beneficial local conditions, such as lower manufacturing costs than they could enjoy at home. The trend became known as "offshoring," and many of China's neighbors, most notably South Korea, Singapore, and the island of Taiwan, were already growing rich off it. As factories opened in those places to supply the American market, they created new jobs, boosted incomes and investment, and sparked mouth-watering rates of economic growth.

Here China had an undeniable advantage: The world's manufacturers were on the lookout for cheap hands to sew blue jeans, put together television sets, and stuff stuffed animals; and no country had more of them than China. Even better, from the capitalists' perspective, poor Chinese farmers were willing to man assembly lines for wages that were mere pennies compared to those of workers in the United States or Europe.

All those hands, however, would remain idle without an accommodation with the United States. Unless the world's largest economy was open to exports from China, factories would have no reason to locate there. Here's where Deng's rodeo antics in the United States paid off. Deng needed Washington's help to ensure the success of his new revolution; Jimmy Carter was eager to cooperate. His decision in 1979 to grant China "most-favored nation" status—the right to export to the American market on the best terms offered by Washington—gave the green light to companies to come to China from all over the world, build factories, hire Chinese workers, and ship their goods to rich American consumers. Deng wanted to reconstruct Chinese economic power; the United States made that possible.

And the factories did come, sprouting within the new "special economic zones," like brick and metal rice shoots. Villagers migrated to these enclaves like Israelites to the promised land. And they were, indeed, something of a new Canaan. Sure, the jobs in the new factory towns weren't milk and honey. The hours were long, the conditions often harsh, the pay was meager—a few dollars a day, if you were lucky. But the income was a fortune for the impoverished Chinese farm boys or, in many cases, farm girls, a golden ticket out of poverty for families still scraping a hardscrabble existence from the earth. The Chinese, as they had since the days of Emperor Wu, proved especially adept at mass production of the stuff the world's shoppers wanted. What China churned out may not have been the luxurious porcelain coveted by kings; it was sneakers and plastic toys. The technology and designs, the investment capital, and the machinery were from outside of China. So were many of the managers. But the world wanted the stuff, in ever-increasing volumes, which created more and more jobs in China. With surprising speed, the Chinese got richer.

The consequences of China's reforms were not fully apparent in the 1980s. The shift of a few clothing factories to the Chinese coast didn't appear to be a development of earth-rattling magnitude. China remained a miserably poor place. The West seemed as ascendant as ever. But Deng Xiaoping's reopening of China was among the most momentous events of modern times. It was one of those pivotal hinges in human history, when the future course of our lives is altered forever. The stage was set for China to resurrect its traditional, central role in the world, along the way reestablishing the ancient trade connections between the Middle Kingdom and the other great civilizations, this time on a grander, more global scale than ever before. And through it all, the Chinese history of the world became ever more entangled with the West's. The world would never be the same.

===

Deng's reforms had an equally transformative effect on China itself. As state control over society loosened, new pressures emerged. The opening up and domestic change rekindled the by then century-old debate about what the new China should look like. For some, the burgeoning partnership with the West made its ideals more attractive than ever. Clearly, those Westerners knew what they were doing, and the Chinese had still not learned enough from them to rebuild their nation. The Chinese continued to doubt the value of their own civilization. That meant opening China's door to the world even more widely was critical and indispensable. Outspoken scholar Fang Lizhi favored "complete Westernization." "We need to acknowledge that, when looked at in its entirety, our culture lags far behind that of the world's most advanced societies," he said in 1986. "Attempting to set our inviolable 'essence' off limits before it is even challenged makes no sense. . . . Open China up and face the challenge of more advanced societies head on, in every aspect. . . . What is good will stand up, and what is not good will be swept away."[11] Such talk was not limited to radical literati. In 1984, Hu Yaobang, general secretary of the Communist Party and a core Deng ally, went so far as to advocate that the Chinese ditch their habit of dining out of common dishes with chopsticks and eat instead like Western people, believing it more civilized. "We should prepare more knives and forks, buy more plates and sit around the table to eat Chinese food in the Western style, that is, each from his own plate," Hu said. "By doing so we can avoid contagious diseases."[12]

The conservatives, however, were not amused. Learning from the barbarians was as controversial among the Chinese as ever. All of this liberal chatter about foreign things was too dangerous. Students and intellectuals were even talking about democracy, a Western import less welcome than forks. Deng's early reforms were marked by a tolerance for freedom of expression rarely seen in the Communist period. At first, Deng permitted it. He urged the people to emancipate their minds, and he was getting what he asked for. But he did have opponents to worry about—the old Maoists who were down but not out, and were not fully on the reform bandwagon. Nor did Deng himself intend on allowing Communist Party control to slip. So he tried to walk a line, to support enough free thinking to fuel his economic reforms while limiting threats to the regime. In 1983, Deng endorsed a campaign against "spiritual pollution"—unhealthy thoughts and habits streaming in from the West that were seen as corrupting Chinese Communist morality. Too-short miniskirts, face cream, dancing, knowledge of foreign technical skills, all came under attack as signs of imperialist decadence; science fiction stories with too much sex and not enough socialism were condemned; so, too, were farmers who earned more money than others. The movement soon spiraled into the most concerted assault on outside ideas since the Cultural Revolution. Fearing it could undermine his reforms, Deng squashed the campaign within a few weeks. Still, balancing the desire for economic openness with a commitment to political closure began to split the Communists. In 1987, Hu Yaobang was forced to resign as the party's general secretary amid accusations he was too soft on dissent.

But minds, once emancipated, were not so readily reenslaved. The dream of democracy, floated by Liang Qichao, Kang Youwei, and Sun Yat-sen, had never died away, even after decades of Communist suppression. The spirit of the reform period emboldened calls for change. In need of foreign know-how, students, officials, and academics were traveling overseas to the United States, Europe, and other democracies in larger numbers, where they inhaled the fresh air of free speech and ogled at two-car garages. Foreign books from Kant to Kafka were translated and widely read at home. In this environment, the disgrace of the liberal-minded Hu Yaobang acted not as a warning, but a source of frustration. For many, especially young students, the promise of reform was being stymied, once again, by out-of-touch hardliners. Hu's sudden death in April 1989 turned into a lightning rod for this discontent. What began as a few students honoring his memory with wreaths on Tiananmen Square outside of the Forbidden City quickly morphed into pro-democracy protests of a scale unprecedented in the Communist period. Just as the young and idealistic of China called for change in the same place during the May Fourth Movement of 1919, so a new generation of hopefuls did so again. Within days, more than one hundred thousand protesters were on the square. In mid-May, some students went on a hunger strike, spurring even greater sympathy. Millions of people came out onto the streets of Beijing and cities across the country. It was the most serious political crisis the Communists had faced since the founding of the People's Republic, on that very same square, four decades earlier.

For weeks, the leadership dithered and debated how to react. There were voices among the senior party bosses who advocated for compromise; political change and economic reform had to go hand in hand. But as the protests swelled, the liberals got pushed aside. The response, when it came on June 4, 1989, was conclusive. Tanks crushed the student movement, killing perhaps thousands of people. The brief period of intellectual ferment was over. Five days later, Deng addressed the military officers who had led the suppression. "Their goal was to establish a bourgeois republic entirely dependent on the West," he said of the protesters.[13] China might join the West, but it would not go Western.

The reaction of Deng's new partners abroad was a torrent of outraged denunciation. China, still too weak, would have to swallow indignity and interference from these hypocritical Western powers, who spoke of human rights but started the Opium War. "When it comes to the international situation, three sentences can summarize it," Deng advised his fellow cadres in the wake of the massacre. "First, we should observe calmly. Second, we should secure our position. Third, we should cope with affairs calmly. We need to be calm, calm, and calm; we should focus on our own job and do it well."[14] China would bide its time.

=

More than two decades later, in 2012, when a new Chinese leader, Xi Jinping, took control of the Communist Party, China was a vastly transformed nation. The free-market reforms that had once been experiments, confined to special "zones," were taken national by Deng's successors and sparked one of the greatest economic booms in the history of human civilization. As the Communist planners receded, the entrepreneurial energies of the Chinese people rushed into the void, as Deng had hoped. In place of the destitute communes, dilapidated apartment blocks, and antiquated factories rose five-star hotels, Louis Vuitton shops, and robot-stuffed car plants. Once again, traders tramped to China from the far corners of "all under Heaven." Trains and planes replaced the camels and sailing ships of yesteryear, but they still traveled long distances in search of what was made in China, hoping like Sogdian caravan masters and Portuguese adventurers to grasp their share of the Chinese bounty. When Deng told the party to "seek truth from facts" in 1978, China's entire national output totaled a mere $150 billion, a measly 6 percent of America's. By 2010, China's economy was more than forty times larger, reaching $6.1 trillion, and ranking as the world's second-largest, lagging only the United States. China had probably never experienced such rapid advancement in its long history. Hardly any nation ever had.

The bigger China's economy grew, the more immersed the country became in the world created by the West. The Communist government joined all the foundational institutions of the US-dominated global economic system: the International Monetary Fund, the World Bank, and the World Trade Organization. Increasingly wealthy Chinese wore Nike sneakers, sipped Starbucks lattes, and chatted over Apple phones. McDonald's opened its first burger joint in China in 1990; General Motors, the venerable American automaker, rolled its first car off a Chinese assembly line in 1998, a Buick *Xin Shi Ji*, or Century. Maybe China was going Western after all.

Yet the Chinese history of the world tells us that China will take a different path. The Chinese have never been comfortable living under other peoples' rules or cultures. Their civilization was at the center of everything; they set the terms of their engagement with the rest of the world, not the other way around. Chinese ideas, products, and institutions flowed outward; the world came to China seeking its wealth, its books, its philosophy, and its wonders. The Chinese self-perception of exceptionalism, that their civilization was superior and thus deserved to be on top of a world hierarchy, had not faltered for nearly all of its lengthy history. Only when China was weakened did the Chinese grudgingly accept the dictates and norms of others. The Han Dynasty, too feeble to fight, had to endure the indignity of acknowledging parity with the beastly Xiongnu in a bipolar Asia; the Song similarly swallowed dynastic pride with the Khitans and Jurchens. After the Mongol invasion of the thirteenth century, the Chinese were closely integrated into the greater global empire of the Great Khans, but never came to terms with it. During these periods, as Jia Yi, that foresighted Han Dynasty statesman, put it more than 2,100 years ago, the world was "upside down." Each time, the Chinese watched and waited for their moment to set the world right-side up, and as soon as they regained their usual strength, they began reasserting their own world order, where China again reigned supreme. The Son of Heaven was made ascendant, his virtue shining upon all in the four directions. The tributaries came to kowtow. The riches of Chinese civilization shared. As it always had been. As it always should be.

This recurring cycle of the Chinese history of the world is repeating itself right now. China participated in the Western global system only because it had no other choice. While the Qing emperors and Maoist revolutionaries had resisted that stark reality, Deng Xiaoping had accepted it as the sole route to restoring Chinese power. He was willing to keep China's head down and focus on rebuilding national might, until the Chinese possessed the power to rise on the world stage again, as they had so many other times in their history of the world.

In recent years, with the arrival of Xi Jinping, the Chinese believe that moment has finally arrived. The indignities inflicted by the Western powers must be avenged, the Chinese world order reassembled. Xi calls his vision for China's future the "Chinese Dream"—an amorphous concept that boils down to another imperial restoration, not all that different than the Ming's after the Mongol horrors, or the Tang's after the divisions and intrusions of the Period of Disunion. Once again, we are witnessing a resurrection of the Chinese empire and its usual role at the center of the globe. In the twenty-first century, new chapters are being written to the Chinese history of the world that connect to older ones, before the interruption of the West. Yes, China was again laid low by the barbarians. But this latest age of humiliation was a mere handful of pages in China's multivolume epic. And, as it so often had been in the past, the Chinese history of the world is being placed back on track. Now the world has to be set right-side up. The Son of Heaven made ascendant.

Of course, China no longer has a Son of Heaven, at least officially. The government is a Communist dictatorship of the proletariat, not a Confucian-tinged monarchy. But if we look past the semantics, the jargon of formal promulgations, and the labels on ministry office doors, what we find is a Chinese governing system not all that removed from the dynasties of earlier chapters. China is a top-down autocracy, with authority emanating from the capital through an intensive bureaucracy, as it had been since the Qin unification in 221 BC. And it is increasingly infusing itself with borrowings from the old imperial courts as well. In a clear reversal of its previous vilification of Confucian doctrine and other "olds," the Communist Party in the twenty-first century has latched on to traditional Chinese culture and governing principles. Xi routinely drapes himself in the robes of Confucian ideology, like a good Son of Heaven should. His speeches are regularly filled with references to Confucian sayings and moral precepts. "Chinese civilization has formed a unique value system over several millennia," Xi once said. "The brilliant traditional Chinese culture is the essence of the nation. . . . Today, we advocate and carry forward the core societal values through absorbing the rich nourishment of Chinese culture, so as to invigorate its vitality and broaden its influence."[15] Rather than a sharp break with the past, the destroyer of a corrupt and failed feudal society, the Communist regime is more and more characterizing itself as a successor to the dynasties—just like the Ming had portrayed itself as a restoration of the Tang, and the Tang of the Han. This places the Communists in the natural progression of the Chinese history of the world. "Chinese Communists have always been the faithful successors and promoters of China's excellent traditional culture," Xi said (disingenuously) in a 2014 speech. "We all pay attention to absorbing its active nutrients, from Confucius to Sun Yat-sen."[16]

Xi himself appears a reincarnation of the empire-building emperors of old. Though Xi is a product of the Communist regime, his father a comrade of Mao, his career a steady climb up the cadre ladder, he is today a shadowy, imperious figure, cloistered in the modern equivalent of palaces and an object of public veneration, his every utterance treated as near-divine wisdom. Like Emperor Wu of the Han Dynasty, he is confronting global challenges by strengthening his state and his own position at home and abroad. Similar to Emperor Taizong of the Tang Dynasty, he is capitalizing on the successes of his predecessors to stress the more expansive and universalistic aspects of China's worldview. But perhaps most of all, Xi is spiritual kin of the Ming Dynasty founder, the Hongwu emperor. Both introduced more personalized rule to the collegial model that prevailed before them. Through much of the imperial age, and especially during the Song Dynasty, the emperor in theory held absolute authority but in day-to-day governance ruled in conjunction with his senior Confucian councilors and statesmen. The Communist Party after Mao's death had also adopted something of a government-by-committee, with top cadres managing affairs as a collective. (Even the great Deng denied himself key titles and acted more like a first among equals.) But Xi and Hongwu grasped greater power in their own hands, ruling more like autocrats than traditional emperors. Xi, much like the Ming founder, has a penchant for moral exhortation, and an expectation that the Chinese masses would study and follow their sagely guidance. And most importantly for the Chinese history of the world, Xi and Hongwu are two of China's fiercest nationalists, equating their imperial restorations with a triumph of the Chinese over the barbarians. Hongwu painted his new dynasty as a revival of Chinese rule after a century of discrimination under the Mongols; Xi characterizes himself as the champion of the Chinese nation after a century of humiliations by the Western Ocean barbarians and their allies. The narrative of Chinese history that Xi's propaganda machine drills into the minds of his modern subjects is a tale of national renewal that could easily have been scrawled in a Hongwu edict. "Since the Opium War of the 1840s the Chinese people have long cherished a dream of realizing a great national rejuvenation," Xi told professors and students at Peking University in 2014. "China used to be a world economic power. However, it missed its chance in the wake of the Industrial Revolution and the consequent dramatic changes, and thus was left behind and suffered humiliation under foreign invasion. . . . We must not let this tragic history repeat itself. . . . China has stood up. It will never again tolerate being bullied by any nation."[17]

This "us versus them" story has all the trappings of the traditional Chinese worldview. As we've seen, the Chinese have experienced periods of both great openness to foreigners and foreign ways, and eras of tremendous arrogance and distrust of outsiders. The Deng reform period can be equated with the Tang Dynasty, when foreigners, their trade, ideas, and customs were generally welcome at a moment when the Chinese believed such an influx was contributing to their greatness. Now, under Xi, the pendulum is swinging once again, to a more Ming-esque xenophobia. The "opening up" of Deng has been replaced by a nationalistic quest to promote Chinese business and culture over the foreign. The Ming built the Great Wall to keep out the raiding barbarians; Xi fortified the Great Firewall to block unwanted foreign influences on the Internet. To the current Chinese leadership, their home is the realm of order and harmony; the lands beyond are the "wild domain" of barbarism and immorality that could corrupt the Han people. Ban

Gu's distinction between the "inner" and "outer" worlds—between civilization and chaos—remains alive and kicking, two thousand years later.

And also much like past dynasties, most of all the Song, Xi and his colleagues are rabid about reclaiming what they consider the rightful territory of the Han people. Remember how the imperial literati agonized in verse over the "loss" of chunks of the supposed homeland to the Khitan Liao or Jurchen Jin, and the lamentations of the Han folk "left behind" beneath barbarian rule; how the hero-general Yue Fei longed to reconquer the zhongguo from the barbarians, and slake his nationalist thirst with their blood. So today, Chinese leaders are appropriately apoplectic about pieces of real estate they believe should be part of China. Persistent denials that Tibet ought to be part of China—including from some Tibetans themselves—are met with official outrage. Beijing regards the exiled Dalai Lama, the Tibetans' political and spiritual leader, as a dangerous separatist. As China's power has grown, it has been able to recover Chinese property stolen by the Western barbarians. In 1997, the British returned Hong Kong, extracted from the Qing Dynasty after the Opium War, to Chinese rule. "The return of Hong Kong to the motherland after going through more than one century of vicissitudes indicates that from now on, Hong Kong compatriots have become true masters of this Chinese land," China's president at the time, Jiang Zemin, proclaimed on the day of the handover.[18] Two years later, the Portuguese gave Macau back to China, too, more than four hundred years after first settling there. But from Xi's perspective, the task is hardly complete. Most sensitive of all is the status of Taiwan, where the government formed by the Nationalists after their flight to the island in 1949 is as entrenched as ever. Beijing refuses to recognize that government and lashes out at anyone who dares call Taiwan an independent country. More recently, China has pressed claims to much of the South China Sea, a vital waterway for global commerce located to its southeast. China's neighbors dispute this position, and the United States and other major powers don't recognize it, either. But Beijing has fortified the area with military installations on man-made islands to assert Chinese sovereignty, and responds with hysterical fury to any challenge. After an international tribunal ruled against Beijing's claims in 2016, the state media compared the verdict to yet another humiliation at the hands of the West, akin to the "unequal treaties" and Opium War. "We do not claim an inch of land that does not belong to us, but we won't give up any patch that is ours," insisted one Communist Party mouthpiece.[19]

More broadly, Xi's imperial restoration is also reviving the traditional Chinese system of foreign relations. The hope in the West has been that China would become so integrated in the current world system crafted by the Western powers that it would commit to that system, that once the strands of Chinese and Western world histories became entangled, that they would knot, never to separate again. The Chinese, though, have other ambitions. For its entire history, the Chinese have preferred things their way, and when they were too weak to insist others follow their rules of diplomacy and foreign affairs, as during the Mongol conquest, or when threatened by Xiongnu or Khitan, they didn't like it all that much. To Xi, chafing under a global order designed by the West is not all that different than being consumed in the Mongol world empire. The Chinese will set their own rules, based on their perception of themselves and their appointed role in the world, as they always have. "We are resolved to go our own way," Xi said in 2014. "We have a big stage to display our advantages on [and] a long and rich history to draw benefit from. . . . We should modestly learn from the best of other civilizations, but never forget our own origin. We must not blindly copy the development models of other countries, nor accept their dictation."[20]

Increasingly, Xi's new Chinese Dream appears to be déjà vu. In today's China, political scientists and other thinkers are reviving the usual Chinese self-image as a superior civilization, destined to hold a superior position in the global pecking order.[21] One Shanghai professor argues that since China is a great civilization, it deserves to have more say in world affairs than other countries. The "criteria of today should be civilization, and civilization should transform barbarism," as he put it, sounding much like a Han Dynasty literatus. "We must have confidence in order to change barbaric countries."[22] The geographic scope of this outlook theoretically has no bounds. The glory of Chinese civilization was to extend over "all under Heaven"—the entire civilized world. In the old days, limitations of technology and transport realistically limited the extent of China's reach. Now, in an age of jumbo jets and instant-messaging apps, the Chinese world order can literally go global.

Xi has embraced this rejuvenated, expansive vision of China's position within "all under Heaven." The Chinese emperors never accepted other peoples as equals, and Xi sees no good reason to start doing so today. His favored diplomatic program—called the Belt and Road Initiative—is designed to re-create the China-centric trade links of the overland Silk Road and the old maritime routes once sailed by the mariner Zheng He by building ports, roads, and other infrastructure across the Eurasian landmass and beyond. And much like Zheng He's treasure fleets, Belt and Road is meant to be a grand pronouncement of the revival of Chinese power in the world and to entice foreigners to come running to Beijing to pay their respects to the new Son of Heaven. On two occasions, in 2017 and 2019, Xi called a summit of all the nations participating in the program, and each time, dozens of world leaders or their envoys answered the summons, much like the tribute missions of the imperial age. Just as the Han, Tang, and Ming reveled in exotic embassies as a mark of their global stature, so, too, today's Communists perceive these foreign embassies streaming into the capital as evidence of China's restored centrality in world affairs. Those who come and agree to China's terms enjoy the rewards of Beijing's gracious generosity. In today's case, Beijing is offering their tributaries railways and power grids in place of the gold and silk gifted by the emperors.

Of course, the Chinese Communists deny any desire to re-create the imperial world order. They routinely insist that China is a model of peaceful development with no interest in dominating others, in contrast to the European and American imperialists. China "will never follow in the footsteps of the big powers which seek hegemony once they grow strong," Xi said in 2014.[23] Relations between China and its neighbors in East Asia, he has said, would be based upon "friendship, sincerity, reciprocity and inclusiveness."[24]

Whatever their protests to the contrary, today's Chinese don't seem to think the dynasties' trade and tribute diplomacy was such a bad idea. In 2018, US Secretary of Defense James Mattis proffered that, for China's current leadership, "the Ming Dynasty appears to be their model, albeit in a more muscular manner, demanding other nations become tribute states, kowtowing to Beijing."[25] The Chinese were outraged—well, sort of. One response, a commentary in the *Global Times*, a newspaper run by the Communist Party, blasted Mattis's suggestion as "childish and simplistic." But, the writer went on, Mattis's comments also "seem to have misunderstood China's tributary system and condescendingly overrated the advantages of the U.S.' foreign relations." Rather than a nefarious method of suppression, the tribute model was a form of "peaceful engagement," the article declared. "What took center stage in China's attracting regional countries to the system was not economic and military prowess, but trade and civilizational pull."[26]

The reality on the ground is that Xi's government often deals with other countries as the emperors did their tributaries. Those who abide by Chinese rules and show the proper deference—like those countries appearing at Xi's Belt and Road forums—are permitted to savor China's riches and benevolence. However, those wayward states that defy the Chinese and disregard their edicts are denied the magnanimity of China. In 2016, South Korea agreed to install an American missile defense system that Beijing considered a threat to its own security. When the government in Seoul rebuffed Beijing's demands to reverse its decision, the Chinese treated the Koreans as disobedient vassals: Chinese officials encouraged boycotts of Korea-branded products and stores in China, denied entry to popular Korean pop music stars, pulled Korean programs off Chinese television, and canceled tour groups traveling to Korea. Sales of Korean cars and cosmetics plunged. That's what happens when you offend the emperor!

=====

It is telling, though, what happened to that missile defense system. It's still deployed. In late 2017, the government of China ended its feud, without achieving its aim. That is just one indication of the difficulties facing Xi in his quest for a new Chinese world order: he does not yet possess the power to impose it. To be sure, even at their height, the emperors didn't always have their way in relations with other states. In recent years, though, Xi has gotten embroiled in a series of often nasty disagreements with many of his neighbors, including Indonesia, India, the Philippines, and the "Sinicized" Japan and Vietnam. Far from quaking before a re-charged China, the other countries of East Asia have stayed wary of Beijing's encroachments and, in many cases, committed to their alliances with the West. Though the burgeoning riches of the Chinese economy have reconnected the old ties of business and trade, that has not proven sufficient to rebuild China's diplomatic and strategic order. The China of today may wish desperately to restore its former superpower status. And it may well be on its way. But China isn't quite there yet, either.

China is certainly a rising power, yet it has not re-erected all the pillars of its former greatness. As we've seen, the foundation of Chinese power comprised many parts, the most critical of which were neither political nor military. Technologically, China had been a world leader, and much of its global clout rested upon the high-value goods it shipped to the world. But today's China is still catching up with the West in innovation, and probably will be for years—perhaps decades—to come. Xi is feverishly trying to fill in the gap more rapidly with state-backed programs to develop cutting-edge telecommunications systems, eco-friendly cars, and smart robots, with the hope that these wares will become the silk, porcelain, and tea of China's future. If unsuccessful—and the verdict is out—China will remain as dependent on the West for its technology as it has been since the Opium War.

The pillar that had been most important of all to sustaining China as a superpower—the civilizational—is also the least recon-structed. Through all the thick and thin of China's epic saga—the tumbling dynasties, bad emperors, invasions, rebellions, military catastrophes—the glittering attraction of Chinese culture was the constant, the mainstay that held together the Chinese world order in East Asia. But with the arrival of the Western powers, and the vi-cious assaults Chinese Communists and reformers unleashed upon their own traditions, the allure of China as a civilization contracted. No longer does the educated elite of Asia look upon China's civi-lization with awe and wonderment and copy its rituals and insti-tutions. China's neighbors still use some Chinese characters, but their governments, education systems, and pop culture are based on Western models and influences. The Japanese, Koreans, Taiwanese,

Filipinos, even the Vietnamese now gaze toward the United States for support, ideas, and university degrees. Their diplomacy and trade are guided by the rules of the West, not China. As Chinese economic clout has grown, it has helped to boost the appeal of Chinese culture to some extent. Studying Chinese language is becoming more popular around the world today. But reversing the trend of Westernization will not be easy. While societies in Asia are more and more adhering to Western-influenced open democracy as their political system of choice, Xi's imperial restoration is taking China in the opposite direction. The West remains a fierce civilizational challenge to China, as it has been for more than two centuries.

Here, too, Xi is working hard to advance Chinese civilization once again. He talks often of enhancing China's "soft power"— the cultural appeal that could again cement other peoples to the Middle Kingdom. Xi is promoting Chinese language and culture through institutes backed by Beijing's government and cleverly named after the sage Confucius, who for long had served as China's unofficial international ambassador for Chinese civilization. Hundreds of these Confucius Institutes have been founded at universities worldwide. "The strengthening of our cultural soft power is decisive for China to . . . realize the Chinese Dream of rejuvenation of the Chinese nation," Xi told top party cadres in 2013. "We should popularize our cultural spirit across countries as well as across time and space, with contemporary values and the eternal charm of Chinese culture."[27]

Will China again be the center of a world order, its civilization a brilliant light, its wealth—in money, ideas, and literature—flowing outward to enrich the world? Those chapters of the Chinese history of the world have yet to be written. We can't predict for certain what will be in them. But history has a habit of repeating itself, and in no case is that truer than with China. Again and again, China seemed on the precipice—its armies crushed, its cohesion smashed, its riches swindled. Barbarians ruled. Chaos reigned. And yet, again and again, the Chinese put the pieces back together. The nation rose. The Son of Heaven, ascendant and resplendent. Its world placed in order. Can history be denied? The new chapters added to the Chinese history of the world could well resemble the old. "The empire, long divided, must unite; long united, must divide."

ACKNOWLEDGMENTS

There are as many people who helped with this book as there are Chinese dynasties. I must first thank my editor at PublicAffairs, John Mahaney, for his strong support for this project, without which it probably would never have happened. I also must thank my literary agent, Michelle Tessler, who has stuck with me through some failures and disappointments but hasn't lost faith in me or my writing.

The research for this book would also have been impossible without the kind cooperation of the Beijing Center, which allowed me access to their rare and wonderful library of books on China. For that, I have to thank the center's director of academics, faculty, and research, Simon G. M. Koo, administrator Emily Xiong, chief librarian Heather Mowbray, professor Francis Hannafey, assistant Sherry Song, and the entire library staff.

Fortunately, many of the important Chinese sources used in this book have been translated by hardworking Sinologists, in full or in part. For material only in Chinese, I must thank Jane Ho for her invaluable help in translation. Her contributions give this project an added degree of analysis and heft.

This book also benefited from the insights of Jim McGregor, Tim Fox, and Eunice Yoon, who kindly donated their time to read the manuscript ahead of publication, and whose recommendations improved the book.

I have been fortunate in researching this book to have received generous guidance from academics with far greater expertise in aspects of Chinese history than my own: Sarah Allan at Dartmouth

College; Mary Beard at Cambridge University; Peter Frankopan at Oxford University; Paul Goldin at my alma mater, University of Pennsylvania; Valerie Hansen at Yale University; James Hevia at the University of Chicago; David Kang of the University of Southern California; Sabina Knight at Smith College; David Pankenier at Lehigh University; Yuri Pines at Hebrew University of Jerusalem; Roderich Ptak of Ludwig Maximilian University of Munich; Prudence Rice of Southern Illinois University; Walter Scheidel at Stanford University; and Michael Seth of James Madison University.

BIBLIOGRAPHY

Chinese Classic or Historical Texts

Analects. Usually attributed to Confucius, but compiled after his death. I mainly used two translations: James Legge's well-known version from 1861 can be found at the Chinese Text Project, https://ctext.org/analects. I also used D. C. Lau's, published by Penguin of New York in 1979.

Book of Lord Shang. Traditionally attributed to Shang Yang but likely written at a later date. I used a translation by Yuri Pines entitled *The Book of Lord Shang: Apologetics of State Power in Early China*. New York: Columbia University Press, 2019. Kindle edition.

Chunqiu Zuo Zhuan, or the *Zuo Commentary on the Spring and Autumn Annals*. The University of Virginia has kindly placed a translation by James Legge originally published in 1872 online at www2.iath.virginia.edu:8080 /exist/cocoon/xwomen/texts/chunqiu/tpage/tocc/bilingual.

Hanshu, or *The History of the Former Han Dynasty*. Written mostly by Ban Gu in the first century AD. One of the versions I used was translated by Homer Dubs and published by Waverly Press, Baltimore, in 1944. It has been placed online by the University of Virginia at http://www2.iath.virginia .edu:8080/exist/cocoon/xwomen/texts/hanshu/tpage/tocc/bilingual. I also had some parts translated specifically for this project by Jane Ho. She used a Chinese version, which is at https://zh.wikisource.org/wiki/%E6%BC%A2%E6 %9B%B8/%E5%8D%B7094%E4%B8%8B.

Hou Hanshu, or *The History of the Later Han Dynasty*. I used outtakes on the Han Dynasty's contacts with Rome, which can be found at the "East Asian History Sourcebook," kindly placed online by Fordham University at https:// sourcebooks.fordham.edu/eastasia/romchin1.asp.

Mencius. Though often attributed to Mencius himself, this text was probably written after his death. I used the translation by James Legge at the Chinese Text Project, http://ctext.org/mengzi.

Ming Shilu. The parts of this text used in this book were translated by Jane Ho. The text is online at the Chinese Social Science Net, a website affiliated with the Chinese Academy of Social Sciences, http://db.cssn.cn/sjxz/xsjdk/zgjd /sb/jsbml/mtzsl/201311/t20131120_843671.shtml.

Shangshu, or *Classic of History.* Translated by James Legge, at Chinese Text Project, http://ctext.org/shang-shu/canon-of-shun.

Shijing, or *Classic of Poetry.* The translation is by James Legge from 1895, at https://ctext.org/book-of-poetry.

Suishu, or *The Book of Sui.* The parts I used of this history were translated for this book by Jane Ho. The original text can be found at https://ctext.org /wiki.pl?if=gb&chapter=584840&remap=gb.

Taiping Guangji. I used a partial translation under the title *Tales from Tang Dynasty China* edited by Alexei Kamran Ditter, Jessey Choo, and Sarah M. Allen and published by Hachette in 2017.

Other Historical Texts

Bacon, Sir Francis. *The Works of Francis Bacon.* Vol. 1. Philadelphia: Parry & McMillan, 1857.

Fan Chengda. *Riding the River Home.* Translated by James M. Hargett. Hong Kong: Chinese University Press, 2008.

Faxian. *A Record of Buddhistic Kingdoms.* Translated by James Legge. Hansebooks, 2017. Kindle edition.

Hickey, William. *Memoirs.* Edited by Alfred Spencer. London: Hurst & Blackett, 1919. This edition is online at https://archive.org/stream/memoirsof william015028mbp/memoirsofwilliam015028mbp_djvu.txt.

Ibn Battuta, Abu Abd Allah Muhammad al-Lawati. *Travels in Asia and Africa 1325–1354.* Translated and edited by H. A. R. Gibb. London: George Routledge & Sons, 1929. The full text can be found here: https://archive .org/stream/in.ernet.dli.2015.62870/2015.62870.Ibn-Battuta-Travels-In-Asia -And-Africa_djvu.txt.

Luo Guanzhong. *The Romance of the Three Kingdoms.* Translated by Moss Roberts under the title *Three Kingdoms: A Historical Novel.* Berkeley: University of California Press, 2004.

Ma Huan. *Yingya Shenglan*, or *The Overall Survey of the Ocean's Shores.* Translated and edited by Feng Chengjun. Bangkok: White Lotus, 1997. This work was originally published in 1433.

Nieuhof, Johannes. *An Embassy from the East-India Company of the United Provinces, to the Grand Tartar Cham, Emperor of China.* London: John Mackock, 1669.

Ouyang Xiu. *Wudai shiji, or the Historical Records of the Five Dynasties.* Translated by Richard Davis. New York: Columbia University Press, 2004.

Pliny the Elder. *The Natural History*. Translated by John Bostock and H. T. Riley. Taylor and Francis, 1855. You can find the full text here: http://www.perseus.tufts.edu/hopper/text?doc=Perseus%3Atext%3A1999.02.0137%3Abook%3D1%3Achapter%3Ddedication.

Polo, Marco. *The Description of the World*. Translated by Sharon Kinoshita. Indianapolis: Hackett, 2016. Kindle edition.

Seneca, Lucius Annadsus. *Moral Essays*. Translated by John W. Basore. The Loeb Classical Library. London: W. Heinemann, 1928–1935. You can find the text here: http://www.stoics.com/seneca_essays_book_3.html.

Sima Guang. *Zizhi Tongdian*. (Chinese only.) The piece of this text I used was translated for this work by Jane Ho. The original text is here: http://www.cngdwx.com/yiwenshangxi/zizhitongjianbaihuawen/22628.html.

Sima Qian. *Shiji*. I used several translations. Most of the quotations are from Burton Watson's translation, *Records of the Grand Historian*. Hong Kong: Columbia University Press, 1993. A partial translation by Herbert Allen Giles can by found at the Chinese Text Project, http://ctext.org/shijie. Another is *The Grand Scribe's Records*. Edited by William H. Nienhauser. Bloomington: Indiana University Press, 1994.

Tacitus, Cornelius. *Annals*. From the *Complete Works of Tacitus*. Edited by Alfred John Church, William Jackson Brodribb, and Sara Bryant. New York: Random House, 1942. You can find the text here: http://www.perseus.tufts.edu/hopper/text?doc=Perseus%3Atext%3A1999.02.0078%3Abook%3D2%3Achapter%3D33.

Anthologies of Translated Texts and Documents

de Bary, Wm. Theodore, and Irene Bloom, eds. *Sources of Chinese Tradition: Volume 1, from Earliest Times to 1600*. 2nd ed. New York: Columbia University Press, 1999.

de Bary, Wm. Theodore, and Richard Lumano, eds. *Sources of Chinese Tradition: Volume 2, from 1600 Through the Twentieth Century*. 2nd ed. New York: Columbia University Press, 2000.

Ebrey, Patricia Buckley. *Chinese Civilization: A Sourcebook*. New York: Free Press, 1993. Kindle edition.

Lawrence, Alan, ed. *China Since 1919—Revolution and Reform: A Sourcebook*. New York: Routledge, 2004.

Swartz, Wendy, Robert Ford Campany, Yang Lu, and Jessey J. C. Choo, eds. *Early Medieval China: A Sourcebook*. New York: Columbia University Press, 2014. Kindle edition.

Teng Ssu-yu and John King Fairbank. *China's Response to the West: A Documentary Survey 1839–1923*. Cambridge: Harvard University Press, 1979.

Watson, Burton. *Chinese Rhyme Prose: Poems in the Fu Form from the Han and Six Dynasties Periods*. New York: Columbia University Press, 1971.

Watson, Burton, ed. and trans. *The Columbia Book of Chinese Poetry: From Early Times to the Thirteenth Century*. New York: Columbia University Press, 1984.

Willis, Clive, ed. *China and Macau*. New York: Routledge, 2017. Kindle edition.

Other Sources

Abu-Lughod, Janet L. *Before European Hegemony: The World System AD 1250–1350*. New York: Oxford, 1991.

Adshead, S. A. M. *T'ang China: The Rise of the East in World History*. New York: Palgrave Macmillan, 2004.

Alcock, Susan E., John Bodel, and Richard J. A. Talbert, eds. *Highways, Byways, and Road Systems in the Pre-Modern World*. Malden, MA: Wiley-Blackwell, 2012.

Allan, Sarah. "Erlitou and the Formation of Chinese Civilization: Toward a New Paradigm." *Journal of Asian Studies* 66, no. 2 (May 2007): 461–496.

Allan, Sarah. *The Heir and the Sage: Dynastic Legends in Early China*. Revised ed. Albany: State University of New York Press, 2016. Kindle edition.

Baum, Richard. *Burying Mao: Chinese Politics in the Age of Deng Xiaoping*. Princeton, NJ: Princeton University Press, 1994.

Beckwith, Christopher I. *Empires of the Silk Road: A History of Central Eurasia from the Bronze Age to the Present*. Princeton, NJ: Princeton University Press, 2009. Kindle edition.

Beckwith, Christopher I. *The Tibetan Empire in Central Asia: A History of the Struggle for Great Power Among Tibetans, Turks, Arabs and Chinese During the Early Middle Ages*. Princeton, NJ: Princeton University Press, 1987.

Bettinger, Robert L., et al. "The Transition to Agriculture at Dadiwan, People's Republic of China." *Current Anthropology* 51, no. 5 (October 2010).

Birrell, Anne. *Chinese Mythology: An Introduction*. Baltimore: Johns Hopkins University Press, 1999.

Blaszczyk, Regina Lee. "Porcelain for Everyone: The Chinaware Aesthetic in the Early Modern Era." Paper presented at GEHN Conference—Les Treilles, March 20–25, 2006.

Brindley, Erica Fox. *Ancient China and the Yue: Perceptions and Identities on the Southern Frontier, 400 BCE–50 CE*. Cambridge: Cambridge University Press, 2015. Kindle edition.

Brook, Timothy. *The Troubled Empire: China in the Yuan and Ming Dynasties*. Cambridge: Belknap, 2010. Kindle edition.

Campbell, Frederick B. *Archaeology of the Chinese Bronze Age: From Erlitou to Anyang*. Los Angeles: Cotsen Institute of Archeology Press, 2014.

Chen Dingding and Wang Jianwei. "Lying Low No More? China's New Thinking on the Tao Guang Yang Hui Strategy." *China: An International Journal* 9, no. 2 (September 2011): 195–216.

Cranmer-Byng, J. L. "Lord Macartney's Embassy to Peking in 1793." *Journal of Oriental Studies* 4, nos. 1, 2 (1957–1958): 117–187.

Dardess, John. "Ming T'ai-Tsu on the Yuan: An Autocrat's Assessment of the Mongol Dynasty." *Bulletin of Sung and Yüan Studies* 14 (1978): 6–11.

Davis, Richard L, *Wind Against the Mountain: The Crisis of Politics and Culture in Thirteenth-Century China*. Cambridge, MA: Harvard University Press, 1996.

Dawson, Raymond. *The First Emperor*. Oxford: Oxford University Press, 2007. Kindle edition.

di Cosmo, Nicola. *Ancient China and Its Enemies: The Rise of Nomadic Power in East Asia History*. Cambridge: Cambridge University Press, 2002. Kindle edition.

Dikotter, Frank. *The Discourse of Race in Modern China*. Revised ed. New York: Oxford University Press, 2015. Kindle edition.

Dreyer, David L. *Zheng He: China and the Oceans in the Early Ming Dynasty 1405–1433*. New York: Pearson Education, 2007.

Ebrey, Patricia Buckley. *Emperor Huizong*. Cambridge: Cambridge University Press, 2014. Kindle edition.

Elman, Benjamin A. *A Cultural History of Civil Examinations in Late Imperial China*. Berkeley: University of California Press, 2000.

Esherick, Joseph W. *The Origins of the Boxer Uprising*. Berkeley: University of California Press, 1987. Kindle edition.

Fairbank, John King, ed. *The Chinese World Order: Traditional China's Foreign Relations*. Cambridge, MA: Harvard University Press, 1968.

Fan Lizhu. "The Cult of the Silkworm Mother as a Core of Local Community Religion in a North China Village: Field Study in Zhiwuying, Boading, Hebei." *China Quarterly*, no. 174 (June 2003): 359–372.

Fogel, Joshua A. "Race and Class in Chinese Historiography: Divergent Interpretations of Zhang Bing-Lin and Anti-Manchuism in the 1911 Revolution." *Modern China* 3, no. 3 (July 1977): 346–375.

Frankopan, Peter. *The Silk Roads: A New History of the World*. New York: Bloomsbury, 2015. Kindle edition.

French, Howard W. *Everything Under the Heavens: How the Past Helps Shape China's Push for Global Power*. New York: Alfred A. Knopf, 2017. Kindle edition.

Gold, Thomas B. "'Just in Time!': China Battles Spiritual Pollution on the Eve of 1984." *Asian Survey* 24, no. 9 (September 1984): 947–974.

Goldin, Paul R. "Steppe Nomads as a Philosophical Problem in Classical China." In *Mapping Mongolia: Situating Mongolia in the World from*

Geologic Times to the Present, edited by Paula W. Sabloff. Philadelphia: University of Pennsylvania Museum of Archeology and Anthropology, 2011.

Gong Yuxian, et al. "Biomolecular Evidence of Silk from 8,500 Years Ago." *PLoS* 11, no. 12 (2016), https://www.ncbi.nlm.nih.gov/pmc/articles/PMC5152897/.

Good, Irene. "On the Question of Silk in Pre-Han Eurasia." *Antiquity* 69, no. 266 (1995): 959–968.

Graff, David A. *Medieval Chinese Warfare: 300–900*. London: Routledge, 2002. Kindle edition.

Graff, David A., and Robin Higham, eds. *A Military History of China.* Updated ed. Lexington: University Press of Kentucky, 2012. Kindle edition.

Hansen, Valerie. *The Silk Road: A New History*. Oxford: Oxford University Press, 2012. Kindle edition.

Hartwell, Robert. "A Revolution in the Chinese Iron and Coal Industries During the Northern Sung, 960–1126 A.D." *Journal of Asian Studies* 21, no. 2 (February 1962): 153–162.

Heiss, Mary Lou, and Robert J. Heiss. *The Story of Tea: A Cultural History and Drinking Guide*. Berkeley: Ten Speed Press, 2007.

Hevia, James L. *Cherishing Men from Afar: Qing Guest Ritual and the Macartney Embassy of 1793*. Durham, NC: Duke University Press, 1995. Kindle edition.

Hevia, James L. "'The Ultimate Gesture of Deference and Debasement': Kowtowing in China." Supplement, *Past & Present* 203, no. S4 (2009): 212–234.

Holcombe, Charles. *The Genesis of East Asia: 221 BC–AD 907*. Honolulu: University of Hawaii Press, 2001.

Hsia, R. Po-chia. *Matteo Ricci and the Catholic Mission to China, 1583–1610*. Indianapolis: Hackett, 2016. Kindle edition.

Jay, Jennifer W. *A Change of Dynasties: Loyalism in Thirteenth-Century China*. Bellingham, WA: East Asian Studies Press, 1991.

Kang, David C. *East Asia Before the West: Five Centuries of Trade and Tribute*. New York: Columbia University Press, 2010. Kindle edition.

Keay, John. *China: A History*. London: HarperPress, 2009. Kindle edition.

Kerr, Rose, and Nigel Wood. *Science and Civilization in China: Volume 5, Part 12: Ceramics Technology*. Cambridge: Cambridge University Press, 2004.

Knight, Sabina. *Chinese Literature: A Very Short Introduction*. New York: Oxford University Press, 2012. Kindle edition.

Kuhn, Dieter. *The Age of Confucian Rule: The Song Transformation of China*. Cambridge: Belknap Press, 2009.

Kuhn, Dieter. *Science and Civilization in China: Volume 5, Part 9: Textile Technology*. Cambridge: Cambridge University Press, 1988.

Langlois, John D., Jr. *China Under Mongol Rule*. Princeton, NJ: Princeton University Press, 1981.

Leggett, William F. *The Story of Silk*. New York: Lifetime Editions, 1949.

Levathes, Louise. *When China Ruled the Seas: The Treasure Fleet of the Dragon Throne, 1405–1433*. Originally published by Oxford University Press, 1997. This Kindle version released by Open Road Distribution, 2014.

Lewis, Mark Edward. *China Between Empires: The Northern and Southern Dynasties*. Cambridge, MA: Belknap Press, 2009. Kindle edition.

Lewis, Mark Edward. *China's Cosmopolitan Empire: The Tang Dynasty*. Cambridge, MA: Belknap Press, 2009. Kindle edition.

Lewis, Mark Edward. *The Early Chinese Empires: Qin and Han*. Cambridge, MA: Belknap Press, 2007. Kindle edition.

Li Feng. *Early China: A Social and Cultural History*. Cambridge: Cambridge University Press, 2013. Kindle edition.

Li Kangyang. *The Ming Maritime Trade Policy in Transition (1368–1567)*. Wiesbaden: Harrassowitz Verlag, 2010.

Link, Perry. "The Limits of Cultural Reform in Deng Xiaoping's China." *Modern China* 13, no. 2 (April 1987): 115–176.

Liu, James T. C. "Yueh Fei (1103–41) and China's Heritage of Loyalty." *Journal of Asian Studies* 31, no. 2 (February 1972): 291–297.

Loewe, Michael. "Spices and Silk: Aspects of World Trade in the First Seven Centuries of the Christian Era." *Journal of the Royal Asiatic Society of Great Britain and Ireland* 2 (1971): 166–179.

Loewe, Michael, and Edward L. Shaughnessy, eds. *Cambridge History of Ancient China: From the Origins of Civilization to 221 BC*. Cambridge: Cambridge University Press, 1999.

Lorge, Peter. "Song Gaozong's Letters to Yue Fei." *Journal of Song-Yuan Studies* 30 (2000): 169–173.

Lovell, Julia. *The Opium War: Drugs, Dreams and the Making of China*. London: Picador, 2011. Kindle edition.

Lowry, Priscilla. *Silk: From the Myths and Legends to the Middle Ages*. 2nd ed. Auckland: St. John's Press, 2015. Kindle edition.

Maddison, Angus. *The World Economy: A Millennial Perspective*. Paris: Organization for Economic Cooperation and Development, 2001.

Mair, Victor M. *The Columbia History of Chinese Literature*. New York: Columbia University Press, 2001. Kindle edition.

Matten, Marc Andre. "The Worship of General Yue Fei and His Problematic Creation as a National Hero in Twentieth Century China." *Frontiers of History in China* 6, no. 1 (March 2011): 74–94.

May, Timothy. *The Mongol Conquests in World History*. London: Beaktion, 2012. Kindle edition.

McDermott, Joseph P., ed. *State and Court Ritual in China*. Cambridge: Cambridge University Press, 1999.

McLaughlin, Kevin. "Just Fooling: Paper, Money, Poe." *Differences: A Journal of Feminist Cultural Studies* 11, no. 1 (1999): 38–67.

McLaughlin, Raoul. *The Roman Empire and the Silk Routes: The Ancient World Economy and the Empires of Parthia, Central Asia and Han China*. Barnsley, UK: Pen and Sword History, 2016. Kindle edition.

Medley, Margaret. *The Chinese Potter: A Practical History of Chinese Ceramics*. 3rd ed. London: Phaidon Press, 1989.

Menegon, Eugenio. "Yongzheng's Conundrum: The Emperor on Christianity, Religions, and Heterodoxy." In Barbara Hoster, Dirk Kuhlmann, and Zbigniew Wesolowsk, eds., *Rooted in Hope* zu Seinem 65. Geburtstag. Routledge—Monumenta Serica Institute, 2017, vol. 1, 311–335.

Mote, Frederick W. "Confucian Eremitism in the Yuan Period." In *The Confucian Persuasion*, edited by Arthur F. Wright. Stanford, CA: Stanford University Press, 1960.

Mote, Frederick W., and Denis Twitchett, eds. *The Cambridge History of China*. Vol. 7, *The Ming Dynasty (1368–1644)*. Cambridge: Cambridge University Press, 2004.

Muhlhahn, Klaus. *Making China Modern: From the Great Qing to Xi Jinping*. Cambridge, MA: Harvard University Press, 2019. Kindle edition.

Muthesius, Anna Maria. "The Impact of the Mediterranean Silk Trade on Western Europe Before 1200 A.D." Textile Society of America Symposium Proceedings, 1990, 613.

Nathan, Andrew J. *Chinese Democracy*. New York: Alfred A. Knopf, 1985. Kindle edition.

Normile, Dennis. "Massive Flood May Have Led to China's Earliest Empire." *Science*, August 4, 2016, https://www.sciencemag.org/news/2016/08/massive-flood-may-have-led-chinas-earliest-empire.

Ostler, Nicholas. *Empires of the Word: A Language History of the World*. New York: HarperCollins, 2005.

Pai Hyung II. "Culture Contact and Culture Change: The Korean Peninsula and Its Relations with the Han Dynasty Commandery of Lelang." *World Archaeology* 23, no. 3 (February 1992): 306–319.

Perdue, Peter C. *China Marches West: The Qing Conquest of Central Eurasia*. Cambridge, MA: Belknap, 2005.

Perdue, Peter C. "The Tenacious Tributary System." *Journal of Contemporary China* 24, no. 96 (2015): 1002–1014.

Petriello, David Richard. *A Military History of China: From the First Recorded Battle to the Twenty-First Century*. Yardley, PA: Westholme, 2018. Kindle edition.

Pines, Yuri. "Beasts or Humans: Pre-Imperial Origins of the Sino-Barbarian Dichotomy." In *Mongols, Turks and Others: Eurasian Nomads and the Sedentary World*, edited by Reuven Amitai and Michal Biran. Leiden: Brill, 2005.

Pines, Yuri. *The Everlasting Empire: The Political Culture of Ancient China and Its Imperial Legacy*. Princeton, NJ: Princeton University Press, 2013. Kindle edition.

Pines, Yuri, Lothar von Falkenhausen, Gideon Shelach, and Robin D. S. Yates, eds. *Birth of an Empire: The State of Qin Revisited*. Berkeley: University of California Press, 2014.

Platt, Stephen R. *Imperial Twilight: The Opium War and the End of China's Last Golden Age*. New York: Alfred A. Knopf, 2018. Kindle edition.

Po, Ronald C. "Tea, Porcelain, and Silk: Chinese Exports to the West in the Early Modern Period." In *Oxford Research Encyclopedia of Asian History*, edited by David Ludden. Oxford: Oxford University Press, 2018, http://oxfordre.com/asianhistory/view/10.1093/acrefore/9780190277727.001.0001/acrefore-9780190277727-e-156.

Rahusen-de Bruyn Kops, Henriette. "Not Such an 'Unpromising Beginning': The First Dutch Trade Embassy to China, 1655–1657." *Modern Asian Studies* 36, no. 3 (July 2002): 535–578.

Ropp, Paul. *China in World History*. Oxford: Oxford University Press, 2010. Kindle edition.

Rossabi, Morris. *A History of China*. Chichester, UK: Wiley-Blackwell, 2014. Kindle edition.

Rowe, William T. *China's Last Dynasty: The Great Qing*. Cambridge, MA: Belknap Press, 2009. Kindle edition.

Schafer, Edward H. *The Golden Peaches of Samarkand: A Study of Tang Exotics*. Kindle edition from Pickle Partners, 2016. Originally published 1963 by University of California Press.

Schuman, Michael. *Confucius and the World He Created*. New York: Basic Books, 2015.

Schuman, Michael. *The Miracle: The Epic Story of Asia's Quest for Wealth*. New York: HarperBusiness, 2009.

Sen, Tarsen. *Buddhism, Diplomacy and Trade: The Realignment of India-China Relations 800–1400*. Lanham, MD: Rowman & Littlefield, 2016. Kindle edition.

Sen, Tarsen. "Maritime Interactions Between China and India: Coastal India and the Ascendancy of Chinese Maritime Power in the Indian Ocean." *Journal of Central Eurasian Studies* 2 (May 2011): 41–82.

Silbey, David. *The Boxer Rebellion and the Great Game in China*. New York: Hill and Wang, 2012. Kindle edition.

Sinor, Denis, ed. *The Cambridge History of Early Inner Asia*. Cambridge: Cambridge University Press, 1990.

Smith, Richard J. *The Qing Dynasty and Traditional Chinese Culture*. Lanham, MD: Rowman & Littlefield, 2015. Kindle edition.

Spence, Jonathan D. *Emperor of China: Self-Portrait of K'ang-hsi*. New York: Vintage, 1988. Kindle edition.

Spence, Jonathan D. *God's Chinese Son: The Taiping Heavenly Kingdom of Hong Xiuquan*. New York: W. W. Norton, 1996. Kindle edition.

Stargardt, Janice. "Indian Ocean Trade in the Ninth and Tenth Centuries: Demand, Distance, and Profit." *South Asia Studies* 30, no. 1 (2014): 35–55.

Sylwan, Vivi. *Investigation of Silk from Edsen-Gol and Lop-Nor*. Bangkok: SDI Publications, 2001.

Tackett, Nicholas. *The Origins of the Chinese Nation: Song China and the Forging of an East Asian World Order*. Cambridge: Cambridge University Press, 2017. Kindle edition.

Tatlow, Didi Kirsten. "China's Cosmological Communism: A Challenge to Liberal Democracy." Mercator Institute for China Studies, July 18, 2018.

Temple, Robert. *The Genius of China: 3,000 Years of Science, Discovery, and Invention*. London: Prion, 1998.

Thorley, J. "The Silk Trade Between China and the Roman Empire at Its Height, 'Circa' A.D. 90–130." *Greece & Rome* 18, no. 1 (April 1971): 71–80.

Townsend, James. "Chinese Nationalism." *Australian Journal of Chinese Affairs*, no. 27 (January 1992): 97–130.

Tsien Tsuen-Hsu. *Science and Civilization in China*. Vol. 5, Part 1, *Paper and Printing*. Cambridge: Cambridge University Press, 1985.

Twitchett, Denis, and Michael Loewe, eds. *The Cambridge History of China*. Vol. 1, *The Ch'in and Han Empires, 221 BC–AD 220*. Cambridge: Cambridge University Press, 1994.

Vainker, Shelagh. *Chinese Pottery and Porcelain*. 2nd ed. London: British Museum Press, 2005.

van Schaik, Sam. *Tibet: A History*. New Haven: Yale University Press, 2011. Kindle edition.

Vogel, Ezra F. *Deng Xiaoping and the Transformation of China*. Cambridge, MA: Belknap, 2011. Kindle edition.

Volker, T. *Porcelain and the Dutch East India Company*. Leiden: E. J. Brill, 1971.

von Glahn, Richard. *An Economic History of China: From Antiquity to the Nineteenth Century*. Cambridge: Cambridge University Press, 2016. Kindle edition.

Waida, Manabu. "Sacred Kingship in Early Japan: A Historical Introduction." *History of Religions* 15, no. 4 (May 1976): 319–342.

Waldron, Arthur. *The Great Wall of China: From History to Myth*. Cambridge: Cambridge University Press, 1990. Kindle edition.

Waley, Arthur. *The Opium War Through Chinese Eyes*. Stanford: Stanford University Press, 1968.

Wang Yuan-kang. "Explaining the Tribute System: Power, Confucianism, and War in Medieval East Asia." *Journal of East Asian Studies* 13 (2013): 207–232.

Wang Zhenping. *Tang China in Multi-Polar Asia: A History of Diplomacy and War*. Honolulu: University of Hawaii Press, 2013. Kindle edition.

Waterson, James. *Defending Heaven: China's Mongol Wars 1209–1370*. London: Frontline, 2013. Kindle edition.

Westad, Odd Arne. *Restless Empire: China and the World Since 1750.* New York: Basic, 2012. Kindle edition.

Whiting, Maryin C. *Chinese Imperial Military History 8000 BC–1912 AD.* New York: Writers Club Press, 2002.

Wills, John E., Jr., et al. *China and Maritime Europe 1500–1800: Trade, Settlement, Diplomacy, and Missions.* Cambridge: Cambridge University Press, 2011. Kindle edition.

Xi Chen. *Social Protest and Contentious Authoritarianism in China.* Cambridge: Cambridge University Press, 2012.

Xi Jinping. *The Governance of China.* Beijing: Foreign Languages Press, 2014. Kindle edition.

Xiong, Victor Cunrui. *Emperor Yang of the Sui Dynasty: His Life, Times, and Legacy.* Albany: State University of New York Press, 2006.

Yan Xuitong. *Ancient Chinese Thought, Modern Chinese Power.* Edited by Daniel A. Bell and Sun Zhe. Translated by Edmund Ryden. Princeton, NJ: Princeton University Press, 2011. Kindle edition.

Yang Xiaoyan, et al. "Early Millet Use in Northern China." *Proceedings of the National Academy of Sciences of the United States of America* 109, no. 1 (March 6, 2012): 3726–3730.

Yu Taishan. "A History of the Relationship Between the Western and Eastern Han, Wei, Jin, Northern and Southern Dynasties and the Western Regions." *Sino-Platonic Papers*, no. 131 (March 2004).

Yu Ying-shih. *Trade and Expansion in Han China: A Study in the Structure of Sino-Barbarian Economic Relations.* Berkeley: University of California Press, 1967.

Zhang Feng. *Chinese Hegemony: Grand Strategy and International Institutions in East Asian History.* Stanford: Stanford University Press, 2013.

Zhang Feng. "Confucian Foreign Policy Traditions in Chinese History." *Chinese Journal of International Politics* (2015): 197–218.

Zhang Zhongpei, et al. *The Formation of Chinese Civilization: An Archeological Perspective.* New Haven, CT: Yale University Press, 2001.

Zhao Gang. "Reinventing China: Imperial Qing Ideology and the Rise of Modern Chinese National Identity in the Early Twentieth Century." *Modern China* 32, no. 1 (January 2006): 3–30.

Zheng Yangwen. *China and the Sea: How the Maritime World Shaped Modern China.* Leiden: Brill, 2012.

NOTES

Chapter One: World History, Chinese Style

1. Luo, part 1, 5.
2. Spence, *Emperor of China*, first page of chapter "Ruling."

Chapter Two: Born Super

1. Sima Qian, *Shiji*, "Annals of the Xia" (Giles translation).
2. Sima Qian, *Shiji*, "Annals of the Xia" (Giles translation).
3. Li, *Early China*, 50.
4. Sima Qian, *Shiji*, "Annals of Yin" (Giles translation).
5. *Shangshu*, "The Speech of Tang," at the Chinese Text Project.
6. *Shangshu*, "The Announcement of Tang."
7. You can find translations of samples of oracle bone messages in Ebrey, *Chinese Civilization*, entry no. 1.
8. Sima Qian, *Shiji*, "Annals of Yin" (Giles translation).
9. *Shangshu*, "Great Proclamation I."
10. *Shangshu*, "Speech at Mu."
11. *Shijing*, "Da Ming."
12. Sima Qian, *Shiji* (Nienhauser translation), vol. 1, 63.
13. *Shangshu*, "Successful Completion of the War."
14. *Shangshu*, "Great Announcement," but in this case I used a translation from Loewe and Shaughnessy, *Cambridge History of Ancient China*, 314.
15. Holcombe, 13.
16. The description of these circles can be found in the chapter "Tribute of Yu," in the *Shangshu*.
17. Pines, "Beasts or Humans," 69.
18. Pines, "Beasts or Humans," 65.

19. Pines, "Beasts or Humans," 66.

20. Pines, "Beasts or Humans," 64.

21. Pines, "Beasts or Humans," 74–75.

22. *Analects*, 9:14.

23. *Mencius*, Ten Wen Gong A:4.

24. Pines, "Beasts or Humans," 78.

25. Fairbank, *Chinese World Order*, 26. (I tweaked the translation for clarity.)

Chapter Three: Superpower, Created

1. *Chunqiu Zuo Zhuan*, Xiang, part 7.

2. The data is from Li, *Early China*, 187.

3. Sima Qian, *Shiji* (Watson translation), vol. *Qin Dynasty*, 41–42.

4. Translation in de Bary, vol. 1, 229.

5. Dawson, viii.

6. Pines, *Birth of an Empire*, 233.

7. *Book of Lord Shang*, 18:2.

8. *Book of Lord Shang*, 2:12.

9. *Book of Lord Shang*, 17:4.

10. *Book of Lord Shang*, 17:2.

11. Sima Qian, *Shiji* (Watson translation), vol. *Qin Dynasty*, 42.

12. Pines, *Everlasting Empire*, 22.

13. See Alcock, chapter 2.

14. Sima Qian, *Shiji* (Watson translation), vol. *Qin Dynasty*, 79.

15. Dawson, 83.

16. de Bary, vol. 1, 372.

17. Sima Qian, *Shiji* (Watson translation), vol. *Han Dynasty I*, 226.

18. The figures are from Li, *Early China*, 285.

19. Pines, *Everlasting Empire*, 18.

20. *Mencius*, Wan Zhang A:30.

21. Pines, *Everlasting Empire*, 44.

22. Pines, *Everlasting Empire*, 51.

23. Pines, *Everlasting Empire*, 33.

24. Pines, "Messianic Emperor," 267–268.

25. Goldin, 232.

26. Nicola di Cosmo's masterful study, *Ancient China and Its Enemies*, offers a detailed analysis of Han-Xiongnu relations and was a major source of analysis for my own research.

27. Fairbank, *Chinese World Order*, 28.

28. Fairbank, *Chinese World Order*, 28–29.

29. The translation of this remarkable exchange is in di Cosmo, chapter 5, note 101.

30. Waldron, 41.

31. *Hanshu*, chapter VII (Dubs translation).

32. The comparisons are from Li, *Early China*, 282.

33. Goldin, 229.

34. Goldin, 229.

35. Goldin, 233.

36. See di Cosmo, chapter 7, for an explanation of why.

37. *Hanshu*, chapter 94B, translated for this book by Jane Ho.

38. Sima Qian, *Shiji* (Watson translation), vol. Han Dynasty II, 233.

39. Sima Qian, *Shiji* (Watson translation), vol. Han Dynasty II, 234–236.

40. Sima Qian, *Shiji* (Watson translation), vol. Han Dynasty II, 236.

41. Twitchett and Loewe, 408.

42. Sima Qian, *Shiji* (Watson translation), vol. Han Dynasty II, 39.

43. Yu, "A History of the Relationship," 2.

44. Sinor, 133.

45. Sima Qian, *Shiji* (Watson translation), vol. Han Dynasty II, 258.

46. Twitchett and Loewe, 413.

47. *Analects*, 16:1.

48. *Mencius*, 2:3.

49. Twitchett and Loewe, 421.

50. *Hou Hanshu*, from East Asian Sourcebook.

51. *Hanshu*; this translation from the East Asian Sourcebook.

52. *Hou Hanshu*, East Asian Sourcebook. I slightly altered the original translation for clarity.

53. *Hou Hanshu*, in East Asian Sourcebook.

Chapter Four: Superpower, Secured

1. This translation of Ban Gu's "Ode on Two Capitals" is by Jane Ho for this book.

2. Graff, *Medieval Chinese Warfare*, 47.

3. Graff, *Medieval Chinese Warfare*, 48.

4. Waltz, 24.

5. Lewis, *China Between Empires*, 162.

6. Brindley, 135. Brindley goes into much detail on views of the Yue; see especially chapter 5.

7. Holcombe, 22.

8. Holcombe, 54.

9. I am deeply indebted for the analysis of this chapter to Charles Holcombe and his excellent book *The Genesis of East Asia*.

10. Holcombe, 168.

11. Wang, *Tang China*, 16.

12. Wang, *Tang China*, 28.

13. Wang, *Tang China*, 29.

14. Graff, *Medieval Chinese Warfare*, 168.

15. Lewis, *China Between Empires*, 150.

16. Wang, *Tang China*, 41.

17. Wang, *Tang China*, 44.

18. Wang, *Tang China*, 72.

19. Fairbank, *Chinese World Order*, 43. I adjusted the translation for clarity.

20. *Suishu*, chapter 81, translated for this book by Jane Ho.

21. Fairbank, *Chinese World Order*, 44. I altered the translation for clarity.

22. de Bary, vol. 1, 565–566.

23. Beckwith, 127.

24. Sima Guang, chapter 216, translated for this book by Jane Ho.

25. Holcombe, 180–181.

26. Holcombe, 181.

27. Holcombe, 52.

28. Waida, 330.

29. Excerpts from the constitution are from W. G. Aston's "Nihongi: Chronicles of Japan from the Earliest Times to A.D. 697," in *The Transactions and Proceedings of the Japan Society of London*, Supplement 1, vol. 2 (London: Kegan Paul, Trench, Trubner and Co., Ltd., 1896), 128–33. The text is reproduced here as it appears in *Japan: Selected Readings*, compiled by Hyman Kublin (Houghton Mifflin Company), 31. You can find them here: http://afe.easia.columbia.edu/ps/japan/shotoku.pdf.

30. Holcombe, 205.

31. This figure is in Holcombe, 72.

32. Shafer, section "Foreign Settlements in Tang."

33. Holcombe, 51.

Chapter Five: Barbarians at the Wall

1. *Taiping Guangji*, 127–128.

2. de Bary, vol. 1, 583–584.

3. Ouyang Xiu, 273.

4. Tackett, 173.

5. Tackett, 207.

6. Tackett, 168.

7. Tackett, 62. I altered the original to replace the term "shidafu" with "literati" for clarity for the reader.

8. This section relies heavily on the analysis of Tackett in his book *Origins of the Chinese Nation*, especially the introduction and chapter 4.

9. Tackett, 199.

10. Tackett, 169.

11. Tackett, 180.

12. Ebrey, *Emperor Huizong*, 372. Ebrey goes into great detail in chapter 13 about the debates over an alliance with Jin and the negotiations that followed.

13. Ebrey, *Emperor Huizong*, 412.

14. Ebrey, *Emperor Huizong*, 428.

15. Ebrey, *Emperor Huizong*, 481.

16. Kuhn, *Age of Confucian Rule*, 69.

17. Lorge, 171–172.

18. This quote is from a document on Yue Fei posted online by Columbia University, which can be found here: http://afe.easia.columbia.edu/ps/china/full_river_yuefei.pdf.

19. Ebrey, *Chinese Civilization*, entry no. 39.

20. This poem, "At King E's Tomb," was translated by Ding Zuxin and Burton Raffel. You can find the poem here: www.en84.com/dianji/shi/201208/00010850.html

21. Watson, *Columbia Book of Chinese Poetry*, 318.

22. Tackett, 197.

23. Tackett, 145.

24. Tackett, 206.

25. Kuhn, *Age of Confucian Rule*, 79.

26. Tackett, 192.

27. Ebrey, *Chinese Civilization*, entry no. 39.

28. Kuhn, *Age of Confucian Rule*, 97.

29. Waterson, in chapter 8.

30. Waterson, in chapter 7.

31. Waterson, in chapter 8.

32. Kuhn, *Age of Confucian Rule*, 98.

33. *Analects*, 8:13.

34. Mote, "Confucian Eremitism," 227.

35. Mote, "Confucian Eremitism," 234.

36. Mote, "Confucian Eremitism," 236–237.

37. de Bary, vol. 1, 795.

Chapter Six: Made in China

1. Polo, 94 and 99.

2. Polo, 124.

3. Polo, 129.

4. Polo, 130.

5. Polo, 132.

6. Polo, 133.

7. Polo, 136.

8. Polo, 141.

9. Maddison, 263.

10. Faxian, chapter 1.

11. Hansen, 37. Hansen shares all sorts of fascinating information about the old documents discovered at Dunhuang and what they tell us about the Silk Road, especially the introduction and chapter 6.

12. Faxian, chapter 40.

13. Polo, 124.

14. Polo, 134.

15. Polo, 91.

16. Pliny, Book 6, chapter 20.

17. *Shijing*, "Qi Yue."

18. Seneca, Book 3, "On Benefits," VII. ix. 2-x. 1.

19. Pliny, Book 6, chapter 20.

20. Tacitus, Book 2, chapter 33.

21. Pliny, Book 12, chapter 41.

22. These comparisons are from Frankopan, 18.

23. For example, this view is expressed by Hansen; see chapter 1.

24. Tsien, 40. I altered the spelling of the name from the original to match the rest of the book.

25. Both of these translated passages on paper are from McLaughlin, "Just Fooling," 39.

26. Kuhn, *Age of Confucian Rule*, 237.

27. Kuhn, *Age of Confucian Rule*, 235.

28. Polo, 87.

29. Bacon, 431.

30. Temple, 150.

31. Needham, 121.

32. Tsien, 201.

33. Tackett, 14.

34. The estimates are from Hartwell, 155.

35. The comparison is from Lewis, *Early Chinese Empires*, 82.

36. The poem is by Sima Xiangru and is called "Fu on Shanglin Park." A translation is in Watson, *Chinese Rhyme Prose*, 41–42.

37. Schafer, section "Jewels."

38. Schafer, section "Sanderswood."

39. Schafer, section "Foreign Settlements in Tang."

40. Lewis, *China's Cosmopolitan Empire*, 117–118.

41. Schafer, section "Foreign Settlements in Tang."

42. Fan, 58.

43. Fan, 147.

44. Watson, *Columbia Book of Chinese Poetry*, 321–322.

Chapter Seven: Pax Sinica

1. Ma Huan, 155 and 159.

2. The translation is from Dreyer, 195.

3. Ibn Battuta, 234–236.

4. Levathes, in chapter 6.

5. From the *Mingshi*, translated in Dreyer, 187–188.

6. Dreyer, 68.

7. From Levathes, in chapter 6.

8. The translation of the edict is from Dreyer, 192.

9. Sen, "Maritime Interactions," 63.

10. de Bary, vol. 1, 781.

11. *Ming Shilu*, chapter 26, proclamation dated November 15, 1367. Translated for this book by Jane Ho.

12. Dardess, 7.

13. Li, *Ming Maritime Trade*, 10.

14. Li, *Ming Maritime Trade*, 3.

15. Brook, 223.

16. Li, *Ming Maritime Trade*, 7.

17. Frankopan, chapter "The Road of Silver."

18. Kang, 112.

19. Figure is from Kang, 120.

20. Kang, 132.

21. Fairbank, *Chinese World Order*, 31.

22. For a fascinating and exhaustive study of why the Great Wall got built, see Waldron's *The Great Wall of China*, especially Part II.

23. de Bary, vol. 2, 34–35.

24. Rowe, 22.

25. Ebrey, *Chinese Civilization*, entry no. 59.

26. Spence, *Emperor of China*, chapter 1.

27. Spence, *Emperor of China*, chapter 1.

28. Perdue, *China Marches West*, 280.

29. Perdue, *China Marches West*, 283.

30. Perdue, *China Marches West*, 285.

31. I'm borrowing the analysis of political scientist David Kang in his book *East Asia Before the West*, on which I rely heavily for this section. His theory is based on certain definitions of what makes for an interstate "war." And there is hardly consensus on this issue. Some historians believe the notion of a peaceful Asia to be a misreading of historical events.

32. This amazing statistic is from Kang, 115.

33. Kang, 67.

34. Statistic is from Kang, 68.

35. For a neat and well-argued summary of this position, see Perdue, "The Tenacious Tributary System."

36. Hevia, "The Ultimate Gesture of Deference," has a full explanation of the kowtow practices.

37. Hevia, *Cherishing Men from Afar*, explains this idea, especially in chapter 5.

38. Kang, 34.

39. Kang, 59.

40. Kang, 61.

Chapter Eight: The Western Ocean Barbarians

1. Willis, Part 1, section b.

2. Willis, Part 1, section c. The original translation uses the old name "Canton" for the name of the Chinese city, which I updated to "Guangzhou."

3. Willis, Part 1, section c.

4. Willis, introduction.

5. Willis, Part 1, section c.

6. Willis, Part 1, section e.

7. Willis, Part I, section d.

8. Willis, Part 3, section b.

9. Wills, 45.

10. Nieuhof, 125–127. I adapted the spelling and punctuation from the original to modern usage.

11. Wills, 199.

12. This figure is from Ropp, 91.

13. von Glahn, in section "The Silver Economy and the Seventeenth-Century Crisis."

14. Po, section "Entering the European Market."

15. Wills, 84.

16. Wills, 88.

17. Hsia, 79.

18. Wills, 91.

19. Hsia, 80.

20. All of the above quotes from Kangxi are from Spence, *Emperor of China*, chapter "Thinking."

21. de Bary, vol. 2, 151.

22. Wills, 229.

23. Wills, 231.

24. Hickey, vol. 1, 223–224.

25. Hickey, vol. 1, 215.

26. Figure is from Wills, 251.

27. Cranmer-Byng, 132.

28. Cranmer-Byng, 148.

29. Hevia, *Cherishing Men from Afar*, 99.

30. Cranmer-Byng, 160.

31. Cranmer-Byng, 159.

32. Hevia, *Cherishing Men from Afar*, 185.

33. The translation of this letter is originally from E. Backhouse and J. O. Bland, *Annals and Memoirs of the Court of Peking* (Boston: Houghton Mifflin, 1914), 322–331. But I used this copy, at https://sourcebooks.fordham.edu/mod/1793qianlong.asp.

Chapter Nine: Superpower, Interrupted

1. Teng and Fairbank, *China's Response to the West*, 25.

2. Platt, 353.

3. Platt, 365.

4. Waley, 34.

5. Waley, 36.

6. Waley, 46.

7. Waley, 49. I altered the place names in this quote for modern spellings.

8. Waley, 51.

9. Waley, 66–67.

10. Waley, 68–69.

11. Waley, 74.

12. Waley, 103.

13. Platt, 379.

14. A copy of the letter can be found here: https://en.wikisource.org/wiki/Lord_Palmerston_to_the_Minister_of_the_Emperor_of_China.

15. Waley, 117.

16. Waley, 120.

17. Waley, 134.

18. Lovell, 136.

19. Lovell, 145.

20. Lovell, 147.

21. Lovell, 144.

22. Lovell, 159.

23. Waley, 171.

24. Waley, 189–190.

25. Waley, 207.

26. Waley, 217.

27. Lovell, 232.

28. Lovell, 252.

29. Lovell, 253.

30. The Asia Pacific Center at the University of California at Los Angeles has kindly placed a copy of the Treaty of Nanjing online, here: http://www .international.ucla.edu/asia/article/18421.

31. Teng and Fairbank, *China's Response to the West*, 28.

32. Teng and Fairbank, *China's Response to the West*, 38–40.

33. Teng and Fairbank, *China's Response to the West*, 34.

34. Teng and Fairbank, *China's Response to the West*, 48.

35. Teng and Fairbank, *China's Response to the West*, 76.

36. de Bary, vol. 2, 237.

37. Westad, 80. I changed the name of the city from the older name of Canton used in the original source to Guangzhou used today.

38. Rowe, 226.

39. Teng and Fairbank, *China's Response to the West*, 152.

40. Teng and Fairbank, *China's Response to the West*, 126.

Chapter Ten: Making China Great Again

1. Teng and Fairbank, *China's Response to the West*, 177–179. This is a highly condensed version of the transcript of the discussion, with only segments of Kang's full argument to the emperor. I also altered spellings to match modern usage.

2. de Bary, vol. 2, 269–270.

3. Teng and Fairbank, *China's Response to the West*, 154–155.

4. de Bary, vol. 2, 282–284.

5. Nathan, chapter 3.

6. Nathan, chapter 3.

7. Teng and Fairbank, *China's Response to the West*, 160.

8. Esherick, 81.

9. Esherick, 158–159.

10. Esherick, 300.

11. Silbey, chapter 8.

12. Muhlhahn, 186.

13. For a nicely written summary of Liang's thought and importance to China, see Nathan, *Chinese Democracy*, chapter 3.

14. Ebrey, *Chinese Civilization*, entry no. 73.

15. Ebrey, *Chinese Civilization*, entry no. 73.

16. Teng and Fairbank, *China's Response to the West*, 221–222.

17. Zhao, 4.

18. Zhao, 20.

19. de Bary, vol. 2, 35.

20. Fogel, 346.

21. Rowe, 268.

22. Rowe, 267.

23. Rowe, 256.

24. Rowe, 269.

25. de Bary, vol. 2, 323.

26. de Bary, vol. 2, 326.

27. de Bary, vol. 2, 321.

28. de Bary, vol. 2, 395.

29. de Bary, vol. 2, 362.

30. Teng and Fairbank, *China's Response to the West*, 242.

31. Both of these quotes from Zou are from Muhlhahn, chapter 4.

32. Muhlhahn, chapter 4.

33. Schuman, *Confucius and the World He Created*, 89.

34. Ebrey, *Chinese Civilization*, entry no. 77.

35. de Bary, vol. 2, 406.

36. This quote is from the opening address by Mao Zedong at the First Plenary Session of the Chinese People's Political Consultative Conference, September 21, 1949. You can find the full text here: https://china.usc.edu/Mao-declares-founding-of-peoples-republic-of-china-chinese-people-have-stood-up.

37. van Schaik, 218.

38. Lawrence, 169.

Chapter Eleven: Superpower, Restored

1. From an ABC News broadcast, February 2, 1979. You can watch it here: https://www.youtube.com/watch?v=DNKhvixdV4o.

2. "Teng's Great Leap Outward," *Time*, February 5, 1979, http://content.time.com/time/subscriber/article/0,33009,946203,00.html.

3. Don Oberdorfer, "During Week in U.S., Teng Proves His Mastery of Political Positioning," *Washington Post*, February 4, 1979; and "Teng, on Capitol Hill, Says Peking Must Keep Taiwan Options Open," *The New York Times*, January 31, 1979.

4. Fox Butterfield, "Teng Speaks of Plans for Imports in Billions," *New York Times*, February 4, 1979.

5. A transcript of Deng's comments can be found here: https://china.usc.edu/jimmy-carter-and-deng-xiaoping-exchange-comments-and-toasts-white-house-jan-29-1979#Deng_Toast.

6. Schuman, *The Miracle*, 125.

7. A text of Deng's speech can be found here: http://en.people.cn/dengxp/vol2/text/b1260.html.

8. de Bary, vol. 2, 489.

9. Deng's speech, December 13, 1978.

10. Lawrence, 232.

11. Lawrence, 235.

12. John F. Burns, "Peking Has Seen the Future and It Lacks Chopsticks," *New York Times*, December 24, 1984, https://www.nytimes.com/1984/12/24 /world/peking-has-seen-the-future-and-it-lacks-chopsticks.html.

13. Lawrence, 244.

14. Chen, 197.

15. Xi's speech, March 4, 2014.

16. Tatlow.

17. Xi's speech from May 4, 2014, is reprinted in Xi, *Governance of China*.

18. Speech by Jiang, July 1, 1997. You can read it on the website of China's Ministry of Foreign Affairs: https://www.fmprc.gov.cn/mfa_eng/wjdt_665385 /zyjh_665391/t24924.shtml.

19. Tom Phillips, "China Attacks International Court After South China Sea Ruling," *The Guardian*, July 13, 2016.

20. Xi's speech of May 4, 2014.

21. Didi Kirsten Tatlow explores this idea in a paper from the Mercator Institute for China Studies, which you can find here: https://www.merics.org /en/china-monitor/cosmological-communism.

22. Tatlow.

23. Xi's speech of May 4, 2014.

24. Xi's speech of October 24, 2013, reprinted in Xi, *Governance of China*.

25. Mattis speech on June 15, 2018. You can read it here: https://dod .defense.gov/News/Transcripts/Transcript-View/Article/1551954/remarks-by -secretary-mattis-at-the-us-naval-war-college-commencement-newport-rh/.

26. Su Tan, "China's 'Tributary System' an Ignorant Catchphrase," *Global Times*, June 27, 2018, http://www.globaltimes.cn/content/1108659.shtml.

27. Xi's speech of December 30, 2013, reprinted in Xi, *Governance of China*.

INDEX

Eunice Yoon

MICHAEL SCHUMAN is an author and journalist with more than two decades of experience in Asia. He is currently a contributor to the *Atlantic* and a columnist for *Bloomberg Opinion*. His two previous books are *Confucius and the World He Created*, published by Basic Books in 2015, and *The Miracle: The Epic Story of Asia's Quest for Wealth*, released by HarperBusiness in 2009. Previously, Schuman was a foreign correspondent for the *Wall Street Journal* and *Time* magazine. His work has also appeared in the *New York Times*, *Businessweek*, *Forbes*, and the *Financial Times*.

PublicAffairs is a publishing house founded in 1997. It is a tribute to the standards, values, and flair of three persons who have served as mentors to countless reporters, writers, editors, and book people of all kinds, including me.

I. F. STONE, proprietor of *I. F. Stone's Weekly*, combined a commitment to the First Amendment with entrepreneurial zeal and reporting skill and became one of the great independent journalists in American history. At the age of eighty, Izzy published *The Trial of Socrates*, which was a national bestseller. He wrote the book after he taught himself ancient Greek.

BENJAMIN C. BRADLEE was for nearly thirty years the charismatic editorial leader of *The Washington Post*. It was Ben who gave the *Post* the range and courage to pursue such historic issues as Watergate. He supported his reporters with a tenacity that made them fearless and it is no accident that so many became authors of influential, best-selling books.

ROBERT L. BERNSTEIN, the chief executive of Random House for more than a quarter century, guided one of the nation's premier publishing houses. Bob was personally responsible for many books of political dissent and argument that challenged tyranny around the globe. He is also the founder and longtime chair of Human Rights Watch, one of the most respected human rights organizations in the world.

· · ·

For fifty years, the banner of Public Affairs Press was carried by its owner Morris B. Schnapper, who published Gandhi, Nasser, Toynbee, Truman, and about 1,500 other authors. In 1983, Schnapper was described by *The Washington Post* as "a redoubtable gadfly." His legacy will endure in the books to come.

Peter Osnos, *Founder*